MARRIAGE VOWS AND RACIAL CHOICES

MARRIAGE VOWS AND RACIAL CHOICES

Jessica Vasquez-Tokos

Russell Sage Foundation
New York

The Russell Sage Foundation

The Russell Sage Foundation, one of the oldest of America's general purpose foundations, was established in 1907 by Mrs. Margaret Olivia Sage for "the improvement of social and living conditions in the United States." The foundation seeks to fulfill this mandate by fostering the development and dissemination of knowledge about the country's political, social, and economic problems. While the foundation endeavors to assure the accuracy and objectivity of each book it publishes, the conclusions and interpretations in Russell Sage Foundation publications are those of the authors and not of the foundation, its trustees, or its staff. Publication by Russell Sage, therefore, does not imply foundation endorsement.

Library of Congress Cataloging-in-Publication Data

Names: Vasquez-Tokos, Jessica, author.
Title: Marriage vows and racial choices / Jessica Vasquez-Tokos.
Description: New York : Russell Sage Foundation, [2017] | Includes
 bibliographical references and index.
Identifiers: LCCN 2016036700 (print) | LCCN 2016049929 (ebook) |
 ISBN 9780871548689 (pbk : alk. paper) | ISBN 9781610448635 (ebook)
Subjects: LCSH: Interracial marriage—United States. | Hispanic Americans. |
 Mate selection—United States.
Classification: LCC HQ1031 .V27 2017 (print) | LCC HQ1031 (ebook) |
 DDC 306.84/60973—dc23
LC record available at https://lccn.loc.gov/2016036700

Copyright © 2017 by Russell Sage Foundation. All rights reserved. Printed in the United States of America. No part of this publication may be reproduced, stored in a retrieval system, or transmitted in any form or by any means, electronic, mechanical, photocopying, recording, or otherwise, without the prior written permission of the publisher.

Reproduction by the United States Government in whole or in part is permitted for any purpose.

The paper used in this publication meets the minimum requirements of American National Standard for Information Sciences—Permanence of Paper for Printed Library Materials. ANSI Z39.48-1992.

Text design by Suzanne Nichols.

RUSSELL SAGE FOUNDATION
112 East 64th Street, New York, New York 10065
10 9 8 7 6 5 4 3 2 1

Contents |

List of Tables |

About the Author |

JESSICA VASQUEZ-TOKOS is associate professor of sociology at the University of Oregon.

Acknowledgments |

I EXTEND HEARTFELT APPRECIATION to the organizations and people who supported this intellectual endeavor. I began this project while on the faculty at the University of Kansas, where I received General Research Fund Awards to conduct this research. Thank you to Joane Nagel, Joey Sprague, Shirley Hill, and Kelly Chang for feedback at the design stage of the project. I am much obliged to Bob Antonio and Mary Zimmerman for their faith in me and my work. An American Sociological Association/National Science Foundation Fund for the Advancement of the Discipline Award kickstarted the data collection by providing funding for fieldwork in two locations. I am grateful for the funding to conduct the research and for the assistance of Vanessa Tyson, Louba Benassaya, Yajaira Padilla, and Georgina Padilla during my time in Los Angeles.

Spending a year as a visiting scholar at the Russell Sage Foundation in New York City was crucial to the writing and intellectual development of this book. My fellow visiting scholars, including Naomi Gerstel, Natalia Sarkisian, Jennifer Lee, Paul DiMaggio, and Dan Clawson, provided insightful feedback on my work-in-progress that strengthened this book's arguments. Russell Sage program directors, board members, and affiliates who contributed to the ultimate shape of this book include: Aixa N. Cintrón-Vélez, Kay Deaux, Nancy Foner, Richard Alba, and Mary Waters. Special thanks to Robert C. Smith, who commented on multiple full drafts of the manuscript and whose feedback always advances my thinking. I extend gratitude to Suzanne Nichols, director of publications at Russell Sage, who encouraged me to "write the book I need to write" while simultaneously demanding high-quality scholarship.

A Ford Foundation Postdoctoral Fellowship granted me time to devote to writing the book manuscript. The University of Southern California Sociology Department hosted me during the Ford Fellowship. There I had the privilege to be under the tutelage of Pierrette Hondagneu-Sotelo, a scholar whom I admire and whose book was the very first to inspire me in graduate school. Upon transitioning to a faculty position at the University of Oregon, I became acquainted with a new set of supportive colleagues. I especially thank members of the sociology faculty writing group, whose ideas, commitment, and enthusiasm inspire me: Eileen Otis, Jiannbin Shiao, Aaron Gullickson, Jill Harrison, C. J. Pascoe, Patty Gwartney, Matt Norton, and Kemi Balogun. I gratefully acknowledge Kari Norgaard for our writing times at the teahouse—the friendship, supportive "thinking through" conversation, and creation that happens there sustains me. Tanya Golash-Boza and Ayu Saraswati, though this book was written after our paths diverged from Milton's, I owe you thanks for introducing me to collective writing efforts.

This book reflects contributions from numerous scholar-friends. Chris Wetzel was extraordinary in his thorough and incisive reading of every page of this book. I am inexpressibly indebted to his engagement with my ideas and prose. He is a top-notch writing partner, and I look forward to continuing our writing collaborations for as long as I can write. Edward Murguia, thank you for your mentorship; your input at early stages of this project improved the outcome. Christina Bejarano and Megha Ramaswamy, I am grateful for your friendship and for our conversations in which we plan and craft our books, from setting goals to wrestling issues to tracking progress. Since meeting in graduate school at a conference, I have appreciated the care and thoughtfulness with which Tomás Jiménez approaches my work; his supportive yet critical feedback is a perfect combination. Jennifer Randles, fellow family scholar and friend, thank you for helpful conversations along the way. I appreciate Priscilla Yamin, who read a portion of the manuscript and shared her expertise on marriage. While writing is often a solitary venture, it need not always be so.

Audiences at the annual meetings of the American Sociological Association, the Pacific Sociological Association, the Eastern Sociological Society, and the Critical Mixed Race Studies Conference provided helpful responses. Professional presentations have been productive forums in which to present preliminary findings and receive constructive questions and comments. Thank you to the audience members of invited talks given at the University of Oregon, Stanford University, the University of Southern California, Vassar College, City University of New York–Lehman College, City University of New York–Graduate Center, Russell Sage Foundation, University of Kansas Latino and Latin American Studies Colloquium and Close Relationships Interest Group Speaker Series, Young Women's Christian Association in collaboration with Hartnell College, the University of Cincinnati, and the University of Arizona.

I extend a debt of gratitude to the 109 respondents whose life histories are the basis for this book. The generosity with which they invited me into their homes and shared their personal stories is astounding. My respondents make me admire the resiliency of the human spirit: from confronting discrimination to escaping intimate partner violence, to struggling for representation, to rebounding from difficult partnerships and finding a more rewarding mate. My interviewees demonstrate that, short of changing the world, we can change our lives.

Friends and family have also cheered me on. Dorothy Mullison Smith, David Vasquez, Earl Smith, MaryLu Vasquez, Jason Vasquez, and Isabella Vasquez have inquired about my progress, expressed interest in the research, and patted me on the back as this project has developed. I am happy to have you all in my corner. Carrie Clough, Kimberly Clarke Arce, Rebecca Miner, Kanika Saniford, Linda Flory, and Aviva Cushner: you all give love and support so freely that I can only feel nourished. Speaking of love. It is so fitting that I met my husband, Derrick Ian Tokos, and his daughters, Sam and Lauren, when I was cogitating about love, desires, needs, and family formation. Derrick: I adore you. It is an honor and joy to live life together with you. Sam and Lauren: You are wonderful. I am so happy and proud that you are my family! And now we lovingly welcome Juliana into our family—you are a jewel and we already treasure you.

I learned much in the writing of this book, one lesson being the value of sharpening your desires and needs over time while remaining open to love. While academics talk about research and teaching as mutually reinforcing endeavors—one invigorating the other—it turns out that research and life can have a similarly reciprocal beneficial relationship.

Preface |

THIS BOOK PURSUES QUESTIONS about the role of marriage and family dynamics in racial-ethnic identity that arose from my first book, *Mexican Americans Across Generations*. That book explored the transmission and transformation of racial-ethnic identity across three-generation families. All of my Mexican American respondents in that book were middle-class by the third, if not second, generation. Much of the literature at that point in time predicted that Mexican immigrants and their descendants were likely to be integrated into an already marginalized subgroup; that racial-ethnic identity would be reinforced in an underclass; and that racial-ethnic identity would wane for those who gained upward mobility. In contrast to the prevailing image of Latinos in the United States when I was researching that book in the early 2000s—as synonymous with lower-class status, if not gang membership—I delved into the world of middle-class Mexican Americans: those who had risen from their forebearers' poverty and now owned homes and were earning college or graduate degrees. One message of the book is that assimilation (the loosening of ethnic ties in favor of mainstream culture) does not inevitably accompany middle-class achievement. Instead, an assimilation trajectory—what I describe as "thinned attachment"—is one possible outcome alongside another: "cultural maintenance," an ethnic identity trajectory geared toward retention.

One puzzle presented by that book inspired the research for this book: Precisely how do marriage and family dynamics fit into the picture of racial identity? In analyzing the second-generation (U.S.-born) Mexican American respondents in *Mexican Americans Across Generations*, I noted the emergence of a clear trend: those who intermarried with non-Hispanic whites were in the thinned attachment category, whereas those who intramarried with other Mexican Americans or Latinos were in the cultural maintenance camp. Although this was a distinct pattern, it raised the conundrum: Which came first, the chicken or the egg? (technically known as reciprocal causality). I was less interested in measuring the inputs and outputs characteristic of quantitative methods than in the rich sequence of life. I was fascinated by the life experiences, reactions, and thought processes that people leverage to arrive at major life decisions. Being an interviewer and interested in hearing people's stories and getting a peek into their internal worlds, I wanted to know about the process of *meaning-making* that people go through as they choose romantic partners. Do people intentionally seek to marry within or outside of their racial-ethnic group—and if so, why? What benefits do people think there will be to partnering with someone from the same or a different group? What are the effects of these different types of marital partnerships on racial-ethnic identity and practices? Do people attain what they sought in the first place? Moreover, how might other social features besides race-ethnicity, such as gender and class status, construct desires and play into outcomes?

I acknowledge that while my principal analytical lens is race-ethnicity, it might have little bearing on why people marry whom they do. As a good interviewer should, I let the interviewees tell me what was important to them and what drove their life-changing decisions. With mountains of interview transcripts in front of me (109 to be exact), it was my job to sift through the data, find the patterns, and answer the questions that demanded their own book. The pages that follow contain my best efforts to piece together the puzzle of why people seek whom they do for lifetime partners and the ramifications of these choices for themselves, for the next generation, and for race relations more generally.

Chapter 1 | Introduction: Considering Family Formation

THE FAMILY OF Xochitl Velasco, a thirty-nine-year-old Mexican American from Kansas, impressed upon her that she could move up or down the racial hierarchy through romantic partnership:[1]

> When [my cousins] brought white boyfriends home, it was kind of looked at like, "Congratulations!" Oh, she brought home this really nice-looking young man named Tad or Donny, Timothy or Chad or Dillon. . . . The white men were considered . . . moving up, successful. . . . [It] would never be appreciated to bring an African American man . . . [or] woman home as a boyfriend/ girlfriend. . . . African American men . . . [you] just don't bring them home unless you want trouble with your dad. White men were looked upon like, "Great!" And the Mexican men were looked . . . on as . . . status quo and not doing anything really great.

Ninety percent of Americans marry in the course of their lifetime—one of the highest marriage rates among Western countries—and each decision to marry is made within systems of racial, gender, and class inequality.[2] Even the most intimate relationships are not the outcome of entirely unrestrained personal choice. Despite the prevalence of marriage, people rarely consider how they make their marital decisions and their ramifications. After peering under the lid of formalized unions and asking people why they courted and married the people they did, I have found that families are subject to drives and constraints, desires and opportunities, and even local histories.

Notice how Xochitl's family hierarchized racial groups and attached meanings to each racial category, conveying the message that racial choices in romance can raise or lower one's own status by intimate association. Telling adjectives revealed her assessment of how society and her family assigned relative worth to heterosexual dating choices: whites are

1

"nice-looking" and "successful" (a double entendre referring to his achievements as well as her success in attracting him), Mexican Americans are "status quo," and African Americans are never "appreciated" and are cause for family "trouble." Given this background, it may be a surprise that Xochitl married another Latino, for reasons that included a desire for cultural commonality (as explored in chapter 5).

This opening vignette illustrates Latinos' awareness of the racial hierarchy—in addition to other axes of stratification such as gender, class, nation, and generation—as they make romantic choices. As personal as romantic choices feel, these individual decisions are steered by structural social forces such as racial politics, cultural mores, family conventions, and local demographics. In particular, my premise is that "the concept of race continues to play a fundamental role in structuring and representing the social world" as I turn the lens toward the private world in this book, asking how race shapes intimate decisions around romance and family formation.[3]

While marriage is about love, it involves much more than emotion. The contemporary Western ideal of "mythic love" that characterizes much discourse around romantic pairings does not fully account for the impact of residential segregation, persistent endogamy (same-race or coethnic couplings), racial-ethnic stereotypes, gender, and immigration on romantic tastes.[4] Love is only one ingredient in a present-day marriage; where people live, how they think about racial groups, and their expectations around gender all contribute to who they think are suitable partners. Moreover, the power of families—people's experiences within families and reactions to them—is an important consideration. If romantic preferences are not solely based on individual predilection, what do these socially produced desires that are held as eminently personal express? Scholarship of the late twentieth and early twenty-first-centuries has endorsed notions of individualistic romance as it traces the move from economically and politically motivated marriages to romance-based marriages, yet the chapters that follow uncover social processes that lead to both racial intermarriage and intramarriage.[5]

I argue that *negotiated desire* is the process by which people become attuned to what they want in a spouse and decide how to seek out a potential mate in a local context. The word "negotiate" has multiple meanings that are relevant to my usage here: "(1) to deal or bargain with another or others, as in the preparation of a treaty or contract; (2) to arrange for or bring about by discussion and settlement of terms; (3) to move through, around, or over in a satisfactory manner, as in to negotiate a difficult dance step without tripping or to negotiate sharp curves." The first dictionary definition highlights the interactional nature of romantic relationships as well as the voluntary, contractual quality of relationships. I expand on this first definition by noting that people must also deal with *themselves* mentally and emotionally as they determine their priorities in their love search. The second definition underscores the deliberative process that precedes a relationship: thoughtfulness and decision-making are required. The third definition emphasizes that the goal of negotiated endeavors—from a business deal to a romance—is to navigate a course of action "in a satisfactory manner." This final piece of a three-part definition reminds us that a goal of relationships is gratification—and that absent the fulfillment of needs and desires a breakup is probable. Finally, the signaling of "movement" in this last definition taps into the dynamism of relationships, forecasting that relationships change over time and require care and attention if they are to last.

I use "negotiated desire" to refer to three aspects of dating and marriage: (1) the *personal* aspects, that is, the internal mental and emotional process of deducing what one needs and wants in a spouse based on lessons learned from prior life experience; (2) the *interactional* aspects, given that each party in a romantic relationship must assess their own position and requirements relative to the offerings of the other; and (3) the *structural* aspects that come into play when the set of attractive qualities sought are not available in the local environment and a balance must be struck between desires that are held on to and desires that are dispensed with. This third aspect of dating and marriage is relevant to the "opportunity versus preference" debate (discussed later in the chapter). The term "negotiated desire" is not meant to suggest capitulation, or surrendering core beliefs, needs, or wishes. Instead, negotiated desire balances the necessity of dealing with one's self and another person with a context that offers a delimited set of romantic options in order to achieve a satisfying love life.

A keystone of negotiated desire is what I call *intersectional concerns;* grounded in race, class, gender, nation, and generation, these interconnecting concerns undergird marital decisions. I balance the reality of structure— namely, the opportunities for people to meet—with the cultural preferences that stem from their earlier confrontations with inequality. These preferences are not always overtly known or calculated; instead, they bubble up from prior experiences, such as natal family life and dating encounters, as people sharpen their desires over time. Sociologists have long studied assortative mating, or "the nonrandom matching of individuals into relationships," usually with an interest in matching across socioeconomic status and racial-ethnic and religious boundaries.[6] I pull back the curtain on romance to better understand the development of desire and family formation. Romantic preferences are not innate. Desire is negotiated through experience and then played out with others in the local dating scene.

As Xochitl explained in the opening vignette, the color line at the top end of the racial-ethnic hierarchy (between whites and Latinos) is more flexible than the color line at the bottom end of the hierarchy (between Latinos and blacks), with consequences for intermarriage and intramarriage. As Latinos and whites intermarry, Latinos come into closer proximity with whiteness, whites may shift their consciousness around race, and together they coproduce biculturalism. Latinos who intramarry within their same racial category do so for multiple reasons: because they seek cultural familiarity, because they want to find a refuge from the stereotypes coming from out-groups, or because their local space offers a greater number of possible Latino mates than any other racial group. Latinos who intermarry with non-Latino minorities do so because of the solidarity they find with another similarly marginalized racial category; whites are excluded from these relationships because these couples view whites as racially foreign and unknowable given their distinctly different social locations.

Families are not spontaneously generated; instead, family formation follows social patterns. Residential segregation, which isolates populations by race and class, thereby limiting interracial contact and possibilities for romantic liaisons, is strongly related to endogamy.[7] Owing to the "sheer force of propinquity," ethnic neighborhoods foster endogamy, whereas intermarried couples are more often located outside of ethnic neighborhoods.[8] Spatial isolation reduces the chances of meeting and becoming intimate with out-group members.[9] Marriages have historically been a way to consolidate political power, increase landownership, mark the transition to adulthood, amass wealth, and transfer wealth (or economic disadvantage) intergenerationally.[10] Even with the rise of other adult living arrangements, such as cohabitation and single-person households, the institution of marriage remains sacrosanct in American culture.[11] Even poor unmarried women are hopeful about marriage, avoiding it with unfavorable prospects because they "revere" the institution and its promise.[12]

This book's findings challenge the notion that Latino couples and families in the United States are formed exclusively according to personal desire and choice, untouched by societal influence. The findings show that race, ethnicity, gender, class, nation, and generation shape the formation of these families. By situating the personal topic of marriage and family within the wider social landscape of race relations, gender politics, class inequality, and migration, this book demonstrates that even our intimate relations are inflected with power dynamics that shape personal choice. By linking macro-level social structures, meso-level social institutions, and individual micro-level actions, the book elucidates the ways in which people's opportunities—even their lives—are affected by their social position. By connecting the societal to the individual, we can see the influence on even the most intimate relations of social structures and institutions that transcend individual lives. Yet even as macro- and meso-level forces organize our opportunity structures (where we live and work and who we have a chance to meet), individuals have decision-making power that endows their dating and marriage choices with meaning. People in the modern age marry for love, but love is not blind. Historical and social processes that put people in contact with potential mates culminate in the selection of a romantic partner for love and marriage who satisfies complex needs that arise from prior life experience.

THE CENTRAL QUESTIONS OF THE BOOK

Family demography illuminates marriage trends—who marries whom—but leaves unanswered the questions of why patterns are the way they are, how individuals make sense of their choices, and what impact these decisions have on culture, racial consciousness (understandings of race), and race relations. This book delves into the terrain that undergirds marital trends and examines both intermarried and intramarried Latinos and their spouses. I tackle three broad research questions. First, why do some Latino men and women and their spouses marry *within* their racial-ethnic group rather than *across* racial-ethnic lines? Second, what are the consequences of Latino intramarriage and intermarriage, for both partners, in terms of racial-ethnic identity, culture, and racial consciousness? Finally, given that the marriage choices of one generation have consequences for the next, how do children claim racial-ethnic identities and engage racial strategies in comparison with their parents? I answer these questions through analysis of data gained from interviews with self-identified heterosexual Latino respondents, their spouses, and their children (a total of 109 interviews).

As detailed in the preface, this book was motivated by the unanswered questions that arose from my earlier research for *Mexican Americans Across Generations* (2011). In that book on three-generation Mexican American families, I identify ethnic in- and out-marriage as crucial to whether families have a robust or diminished ethnic identity. Exogamy is associated with what I call "thinned attachment," an assimilationist trajectory, whereas endogamy is associated with "cultural maintenance," or ethnic solidarity. Yet it was unclear from my prior research whether people marry in or out of their ethnic group expressly because of their desire to either stay within the group or to depart from it. While these associations stood out, I was led to this project by curiosity about which came first—marriage or cultural detachment, attachment, or switching? Armed with life history data, I can now answer the questions of "which came first": *both* did. People craft their romantic desires based on past pleasing and displeasing experiences with their own and other racial groups, *and* they marry for other reasons that have unforeseen racial and cultural consequences.

Interviewing is especially well suited for learning how people make meaning and discovering how and why they make decisions. Life history interviews provided me with access to process: the sequence of events and meanings that are salient as people make life choices. A major contribution of this book is that it uncovers mechanisms at play in decision-making around romance and family formation. Survey data on marital pairings show us trends but cannot provide insight into *how* those trends came to be. This book documents the process of decision-making, meaning-making, and imaginative forecasting that is at work—often invisibly—to produce the marriages and families we see all around us. This study does not aim at generalizability or discovery of universal rules of partnership, but rather seeks to unearth the often unarticulated mental and emotional processes that lead people to choose one life path over another.

In *Marriage Vows and Racial Choices,* I question why Latinos and their partners choose to marry racially similar or dissimilar people and explore the ramifications of these choices on racial identity, cultural practices, and racial consciousness in families. We know the statistics of who marries whom, but we lack adequate understanding of *why* these marriages are made and why that matters. Rather than relying on a demographic argument that leaves marriage pairings up to the local marriage market (who is an available option in the region), I ask how experiences in one's childhood, adolescence, and young adulthood—including experiences based in race, class, region, and national origin—shape romantic desires in long-term relationships. I demonstrate that earlier experiences—such as racist encounters, rewarding friendships, media imagery, satisfying romances, or romantic failures—direct and sharpen these desires. By theorizing *preferences* and paying attention to *opportunities,* I look beyond the individual to discover how personal experiences and social location factor into ideas about who is an appropriate mate.

This book also looks at the ways in which intimate family life can either allow for happy continuity or prompt change with respect to culture, identity, and race relations. I understand marriage to act as a bidirectional conduit for cultural transmission, adding nuance to newer conceptions of race relations.[13] The numerous possibilities here include Latino affiliation with whiteness, whites' affiliation with Latino culture, cross-cultural teaching, social distancing strategies, and creative cross-racial nonwhite linkages. Investigating the marital trends of Latinos, the reasons behind those choices, and the ramifications of those pairings for the couple and the next generation illuminates the role played by marriage and child-rearing in race relations in American society.

Although this book's central questions concern the foundations for and consequences of Latino exogamy and endogamy, it touches on the question of whether the racial hierarchy is reconfigured through intermarriage and intramarriage. This query concerning the impact of family formation on race relations and the racial order in the United States is important in light of the enduring inquiry into how immigration reconstitutes domestic interracial relations.[14] Moving beyond historical and legal accounts of black-white intermarriage, one contribution of this book is its fresh look at how marital unions either reinforce or reconstitute the American racial hierarchy.[15] The answer is: they do both. Two broad processes that are in tension with one another are occurring simultaneously for different segments of the Latino (and, more broadly, the U.S.) population.

First, racialized processes, such as residential segregation, that facilitate racial intramarriage by structuring opportunity and creating preference suggest a durable and self-perpetuating racial hierarchy. However, even as racial endogamy consolidates racial boundaries, people within intramarriages can enact diverse racial strategies that may resist the constraints of their social location (see chapter 7). Racial endogamy, then, does not simply solidify individuals' placement within racial, class, and gender structures.

Second, out-marriage is driven by intersectional concerns that rest on race, class, and gender inequality and hopes to improve one's lot. Racial exogamy, by definition, brings racial out-groups into new racial territory, flexing racial boundaries. As intermarriage increases, a greater proportion of the population have family connections with multiple racial groups and boundaries between groups are blurred.[16] Yet intermarriage does not equate to a large-scale reconfigured racial hierarchy because the incidence of intermarriage remains slim in comparison to intramarriage, despite increases over time and generations.[17] Among Latino-white intermarriages, we see the creation of varying brands of biculturalism and changed racial consciousness among whites, signaling porousness in that racial boundary. Among Latino–non-Latino minority pairs, we witness a shared marginalization — couples forging a creative solidarity in their mutual nonwhite experience. While cross-racial minority bonds and shared compassions meld the interests of the middle and lower ranks of the racial hierarchy, persisting antiblack prejudice among those who have *not* intermarried with blacks strengthens the boundary against blacks. In sum, while opportunity creates preference for those who marry within their racial group, preference also creates opportunity to marry either outside or inside the racial group. Racial boundaries are somewhat flexed in intermarriage, and yet boundaries are not fate in intramarriage. While some racial boundaries are more durable than others, love and partnerships slowly, unevenly, and with some resistance change social relations.

CONTRIBUTIONS OF THIS STUDY

This book makes five contributions to what we know about family formation, racial-ethnic relations, and the Latino population. First, I contend
that it is imperative that we look at both sides of marital partnerships
(not just the minority perspective) in order to understand race relations
and racialization processes at the individual level. General findings on
group outcomes do not simply "reduce down" to the individual level;
instead, attention to dyadic relationships reveals the bidirectional nature
of cultural change and racial consciousness. Studying families from various angles sheds light on how people seek to satisfy their complex needs
through partnership choices.

Second, I argue that negotiated desire is a precursor to relationships.
Negotiated desire highlights how people utilize their pasts to create an
appealing vision of their future and how they recognize both intersections
and discrepancies with prospective partners. In the interplay between personal experience and local context, negotiated desire also illuminates how
structure interacts with individual lives to shape desire. Marriage is an *intersectional critical juncture* in the life course, a point at which deep-seated concerns around race, gender, and class play out, directing life decisions. For
example, the Latina women in this study who experienced gender oppression as a girl at the hand of a domineering father reacted by excluding either
all Latinos or an entire national-origin subgroup from their dating pool. As
another example, respondents who grew up poor were especially sensitive
to how marriage would affect their socioeconomic standing and therefore
wanted to marry their economic equivalent or higher.

Third, Latino marriage patterns, in slow and incomplete ways, reconfigure the racial hierarchy. The racial and cultural rationales for endogamy do
not simply maintain the racial hierarchy, for pan-ethnic relations and racial
strategies expand definitions of Latino identity. Marriage relationships that
cross racial lines challenge the standing racial order as whites become more
conscious of race and racism and experience an expanded cultural life and
Latinos in these pairings circulate in multiple racial networks. Further, marriages between Latinos and non-Latino racial minorities that are founded
upon a nonwhite perspective clarify the experience of racial subjugation
and serve as a source of solace, solidarity, and social critique.

Fourth, in this book I apply racial formation theory, which originated to
explain dynamics within nation-states, to the private domain.[18] Heeding a
call to link "multiple levels of analysis" (micro, meso, and macro), this book
stitches together these disparate societal levels, none of which operates in
isolation, to show their impact on each other.[19] For example, this book demonstrates how the opportunity to meet people (macro level), which is often

mediated by social institutions (meso level) such as education or religion, fosters desire (micro level). By attending to multiple levels of analysis at once, we see how social structure and collectivities connect with individual action. This book shows that race is foundational not only in state-building but in building personal relationships as well. By adding a personal dimension to racial formation, we see how societal-level processes filter down to the individual, how racial politics affects even intimacy.

Fifth, this book shows that parents' experiences and teachings shape but do not overdetermine their children's outlooks and trajectories.

These contributions to discussions about family formation, racial-ethnic relations, and the Latino population rest on and highlight the insight that race is *"performative,"* that racial and ethnic boundaries are "constituted by day-to-day affirmations, reinforcements, and enactments."[20] In all of their decisions—from daily routine decisions to those with more significant and long-term implications—people *perform race* (as well as gender, class, nationality, and generation) in ways that both etch racial boundaries through intimacy and reconfigure those boundaries.

THEORIZING LATINO FAMILY FORMATION IN THE UNITED STATES

The Intermarriage and Assimilation Literature

Intermarriage between Mexican women and Anglo men regularly occurred in the second half of the nineteenth century in the Southwest. No miscegenation laws barred Mexican and Anglo unions, yet racial endogamy was prevalent, especially as the status of Mexicans deteriorated.[21] In the mid-nineteenth century, as now, demographic shifts and intermarriage in traditional immigration gateways like southern California contributed to the "Mexicanization of many Anglos."[22] But despite this centuries-long history of interracial relations, the study of intermarriage as "the visible tip of a denser mass of interethnic contacts" did not erupt until scholars set out to explain the integration of arrivals from southern and eastern Europe at the turn of the twentieth century and their white ethnic descendants.[23]

Assimilation literature, while imperfect, nevertheless offers a theoretical starting point for the study of intergroup relations. A lead theorist of assimilation in the mid-1960s, Milton Gordon, posited that entrance into "the social cliques, clubs, and institutions of the core society at the primary group level" (structural assimilation) leads to intermarriage. Once people from varying backgrounds socialize together, they are likely "to love and to marry each other, blithely oblivious to previous ethnic extraction."[24] While Gordon called structural assimilation "the keystone of the arch of assimilation," he pictured intermarriage (marital assimilation) as unlocking a path-dependent course to a host of other types of assimilation predicated on boundary erosion.[25] Upon intermarriage, he forecasted, the minority group identity would be subsumed by the larger host society (identificational assimilation) and the offspring of intermarriage would be "indistinguishable" from "core society," prejudice and discrimination having been erased as social problems because mixed children would belong to an "in-group" of already merged primary groups.[26] Despite these early predictions of straight-line assimilation theory, continuing discrimination against later-generation native-born minorities has challenged the claim that intermarriage is a cure-all for racial antipathy.[27]

"Anglo-conformity" — what has been described as " 'pressure-cooker' Americanization" — stands as the most prevalent assimilation theory historically.[28] Two alternatives are the "melting pot" and "cultural pluralism" theories. Gordon referred to the melting pot as "a totally new blend, culturally and biologically, in which the stocks and folkways . . . were . . . indiscriminately mixed in the political pot of the emerging nation and melted together by the fires of American influence and interaction into a distinctly different new type."[29] This vision, while appealing for its idealism, omits the reality that the United States is a racially stratified society in which some "stocks and folkways" are more highly valued than others. As one scholar put it, "continuing racism invalidated the melting pot."[30] Rather than permit groups to "melt," U.S. laws have excluded particular racial and national-origin groups from immigration into the country or "repatriated" or deported them after they arrived on U.S. soil.[31] One variant of melting pot theory, the "triple melting pot," forecasts that major religious groupings (namely Protestants, Catholics, and Jews) will each constitute a "melting pot in itself," with adherents marrying within their religious group but irrespective of nationality or ethnicity.[32] This theory presages divisions that make melting across multiple boundaries appear unlikely in practice. Cultural pluralism, on the other hand, "posits the right of ethnic groups in a democratic society to maintain their communal identity and their own subcultural values."[33] While the presence of subcultures is evidence in this direction, subcultures tend to be relegated to lower-status positions and viewed as inferior to mainstream culture. Moreover, the cultural preservation inherent in cultural pluralism is contradictory to notions of cultural change, an outgrowth of subcultures interacting and intermixing.[34] By eliding subcultural contact and exchange, cultural pluralism overlooks the dynamism of cultures, implying that some cultures are immutable. Even in the contemporary era, which formally embraces multiculturalism and is characterized by a decrease in prejudice, "ascriptive or exclusivist norms" continue to define rigid expectations for American identity, such as whiteness and English proficiency.[35]

Even though intermarriage is considered a barometer of assimilation, we know little about how the heterosexual marriage of a Latino and a non-Latino reinforces or shifts identity for each spouse and for their children.[36] This standard framework of immigration and assimilation does not account for the experience of Latinos who have a long history in the United States, and it views Latinos as those who (should) change and prescriptively become more like mainstream whites. Another shortcoming of assimilation literature is that its laser-focus on Latinos obscures the role of non-Latinos in race relations: it is not simply Latinos married to non-Latinos who are affected by their marriage partner. How do Latinos affect those with whom they have close relations, be they Latino, non-Hispanic white, or non-Latino minority?[37] Bidirectional change is possible in such marital partnerships and parenting, but for the most part this creative space has been left empirically uninterrogated until now.

"New" assimilation theory contends that the mainstream will change as it eventually includes previously excluded populations. Even the title of Richard Alba and Victor Nee's classic *Remaking the American Mainstream* foreshadows their main argument that "assimilation, as a form of ethnic change, may occur through changes taking place in groups on both sides of the boundary."[38] Thus, both the mainstream and minority immigrant groups are changed through interracial contact, neither one inured to change. This conceptualization of the "plasticity of the mainstream" is a correction to outmoded understandings of assimilation as a one-way process that requires the shedding of natal heritage and wholesale adoption of host country ways.[39] It is also a formulation of multidirectional transformation that opens the door for this study, which charts the processes of union formation and the cultural and cognitive changes that result from shared lives. With families as the "taproot of ethnic identity," intermarriage drives the creation of the "composite culture" that results from the "incremental inclusion of ethnic and racial groups that formerly were excluded."[40] Intermarriage is a vehicle through which "boundary blurring" occurs, when "racial/ethnic difference becomes more continuous and less sharply differentiated."[41] Integration is usually studied as a multigenerational process, yet it can occur intragenerationally as well, and intermarriage is a key site from which to view shifts within a single generation.[42]

The lessons learned from this lineage of research on intergroup relations, intermarriage, and assimilation are many. First, intermarriage indicates that some people hailing from putatively different groups do not perceive any cultural gulf between them as wide enough to be a barrier to a long-term union.[43] This lowering of antipathy and increased acceptance not only signals but also produces decreased social distance between groups. Historically, as scholars forecasted the eventual amalgamation of

European stock, racial difference became a scapegoat for failed relationships, and people drew conclusions "couched in 'race' terms," thus "cali-
brating the [unsuitability] of various groups."[44] We will see this later in the
book as respondents justified their prior romantic failures and reworked
their desires in light of "cultural compatibility"—a "code word" for race.[45]
Second, as we shall also see in later chapters, antiblack prejudice has long
been exercised as a way to shield one's relative racial privilege, a strategy
that calcifies a racial boundary.[46] Third, race relations should be viewed
as both intergenerational and intragenerational processes, each shedding
light on racial dynamics. Finally, flaws in the prior literature set the stage
for the goals of this book. The intermarriage literature has been marred
by its exclusive focus on minority group change and its shortsightedness
concerning multidirectional cultural change. Instead of presuming that the
minority group will or must change—as older theory would do—this book
empirically examines *who* changes, *to what end* they change, and *the process*
by which these shifts occur.

Attention did not turn to the case of Latinos until late in the twentieth
century and early in the twenty-first century; this research was driven
by concern over changing national demographics, the "browning" of the
nation, and the fate of Latinos in the United States.[47] In 1970, Latinos comprised only 5 percent of the nation's population, but by 2010 their proportion of the population had more than tripled, to 16 percent.[48] The reality
that Latinos outnumber blacks as the largest minority group (in 2013,
according to U.S. census estimates, Hispanics were 17 percent of the U.S.
population and blacks were 13 percent) fuels the question of how Latino
family-building is affecting race relations and the racial hierarchy.

Scholarship on Latinos tends to be framed by issues of immigration and
assimilation. Assimilation is the process of incorporation into a host country in which the minority group adopts the norms, practices, and lifestyles
of the majority group, the idea being that its members will eventually reach
parity on various outcome measures (such as language, culture, education,
and socioeconomic status). Intermarriage is one component of assimilation. A problem with the notion that intermarriage produces a "breaking of
ties" with the minority's racial community is its asymmetry: nonwhites are
expected to break ties with their community of origin whereas whites are
not.[49] This is an expression of white supremacy that expects whiteness to
be valued and nonwhiteness to be forfeited. Current thinking about intermarriage is underdeveloped in two critical areas. First, intermarriage
may not amount to broken ties with a racial community. The possibility
that intermarriage may work counter to assimilation theory's prediction
of Latinos' social whitening and instead generate racial progressivism
and awareness of race and racism *among whites* is an important empirical

question.[50] A second shortcoming of intermarriage literature is the assumption that cultural and identity shifts exclusively work on Latinos, sidelining the possibility that non-Latinos become "affiliative ethnics" who adopt the beliefs and practices of the minority group.[51]

Two theories that stand apart from assimilation literature have been used to explain intermarriage: status exchange and status homogamy.[52] Status exchange theory posits that lower-status racial-ethnic groups trade resources such as wealth, education, youth, or beauty for a mate with a higher racial-ethnic status—colloquially known as "marrying up."[53] The calculus is that those who marry "downward" across racial lines "must be compensated by marrying up on some other dimension."[54]

In contrast to status exchange, which is predicated on inequality, status homogamy contends that similarity on important nonracial dimensions drives intermarriage. Status homogamy argues that educational homogamy (mates possessing similar educational backgrounds) or class homogamy facilitates marriage, including intermarriage. Groups that restrict membership to others like themselves ("ascriptive groups"), such as college sororities, act as marriage brokers that foster ethnic-racial and class endogamy.[55] Proponents of this perspective claim that similar levels of class and educational status characterize the dominant marriage pattern, regardless of the race of either spouse.[56] In this study, there is evidence of both status exchange and class homogamy, different strategies that reach the same intermarried end. Not intended to adjudicate among these theories, this book adds an analysis of power relations that helps us better understand how and why people from different social locations make marital decisions.

Endogamy: The Understudied Norm

Endogamy is the overwhelming norm: 87 percent of people in the United States marry within their own racial-ethnic category.[57] In 2010, a mere 4.3 percent of married couples contained one Hispanic and one non-Hispanic; most of these couples were concentrated in the West.[58] Race and ethnicity persists as the most powerful division in the marriage market.[59] Yet since people generally assume racial-ethnic intramarriage to be the unquestioned standard, it remains an uninvestigated topic.[60] This book examines the patterns that lead to in-marriage and explores variants of intramarriage such as cross-national marriage (for example, a Mexican-descent person married to a Peruvian-descent person), mixed-generation marriage (for example, an immigrant married to a third-generation person), and intragenerational marriage (spouses with the same generational status). This book reveals the diversity of racial intramarriage that is too often glossed over in the manufacturing of Latino similarity, which obscures important dimensions of Latino heterogeneity.[61]

Families in which there has been intermarriage attract attention because crossing racial boundaries is seen as unusual, if not transgressive. History reveals that black-white interracial sex was considered illicit, and interracial romances were regulated and discouraged by antimiscegenation laws, legal restrictions, and mob violence.[62] A chief concern behind prohibitions against interracial romance was protecting white femininity as virtuous and untainted. Yet when it came to white masculinity, the rules changed and white American men who married the native ranchero (Mexican American) elite did so "in the context of Euro-American manifest destiny," which facilitated the dispossession of Mexicans' land and white capital accumulation.[63] Because of the racial-ethnic, class, gender, and national inequalities present in many intermarriages, interracial boundary-crossing holds special appeal for scholars and laypeople alike.

Intermarriage studies, by definition, are unconcerned with intramarriage, leaving a gap in knowledge concerning racial endogamy. This literature assumes that once a racial minority intermarries with a majority-group member (a white), marriage with whites will continue in future generations.[64] Intermarriage studies equate intermarriage with assimilation over generations, overlooking the possibility of future in-marriage and obscuring *intragroup variation*.[65] Endogamy, or within-group marriage, deserves theoretical treatment as the flip side of intermarriage that gets the lion's share of scholastic attention. Endogamy has been eschewed as uninteresting because it is the (uninterrogated) norm. While demographics play a role in intramarriage, so too do preferences that perpetuate homogamous friendship networks and residential segregation. From a macro-level perspective, "group boundaries [are] set by the lack of interaction and spatial isolation."[66] This makes enduring residential segregation a problem that further entrenches racial-ethnic divisions and affects people's perceptions of their "in-group." As Mary Waters notes, "Humans have an in-group preference. The desire to feel good about themselves leads individuals to also want to feel good about their group."[67] In taking into account structural-level segregation patterns and micro-level desire for self-efficacy, this perspective sheds light on how both structure and personal wishes roll up into a preference for endogamous partnerships.

People sort on race-ethnicity, social class, and education level as they sift through options and decide on a mate, with most couples sharing equivalent statuses on these dimensions.[68] Demographics (the supply of people available in an area) and social pressures are primary reasons why people partner within their same racial-ethnic group.[69] Even though legal restrictions banning racial intermarriage (miscegenation) were overturned in 1967

(*Loving v. Virginia*) by the Supreme Court as unconstitutional, racial endogamy remains standard.[70] Notions of homogamy as "normal" are complicit
in reproducing same-race couplings. Erica Chito Childs notes that "just as
race is a social construction . . . the idea of couples being interracial (different from the norm of same-race couples) [is] also a social construction."[71]
With interracial couples attracting much attention based on the belief that
they are "unnatural," endogamous couples are an unmined source of
information about how and when race matters.[72] Far from presenting an
uninteresting dominant pattern, endogamous partnerships house fascinating cross-national, intergenerational, and intragenerational dynamics.

Of Love and Marriage

Marriage is a social contract. Long before passionate or companionate marriage, "mythic love," or the "love match" took center stage in Americans' conception of marriage, marriages were a chief way to forge political alliances,
acquire landholdings, amass wealth, and build a family economy.[73] Marriage
houses social bonds and economics as well as intimacy and children.

For all the "talk of love," marriage remains a political institution, one that
people locked out of narrow definitions of marriage mobilize to access.[74]
People hope to consolidate their economic well-being as well as find meaning in their lives through marriage as partners, parents, or both.[75] At the
same time, the state regulates people through marriage, throughout history
enforcing boundaries of race, sexuality, family size, and even gender ideals
through restriction, punishment, and reward.[76]

While love has not historically been a precursor to marriage, love is an
important predicate to contemporary U.S. marriages that are not arranged
by family or religious institutions but rest on individual choice.[77] I consider love to be entangled with a host of desires and other practicalities.
Love is braided throughout the narratives of the couples in this study, and
yet my focus is on understanding the precursors to love and marriage. My
aim is not to make love scientific but rather to gain understanding of the
constellation of factors that make love and lifetime commitments possible
and desirable, an end that is the culmination of complex sets of needs and
desires. Love certainly existed among the couples interviewed, and the
life history angle of the interviews illuminates how and why people fall
in love . . . and sometimes fall out of love . . . and then fall in love again
with another person.

By interrogating the rationales and desires that come before marriage
and being alert to the process—encompassing natal family systems, prior
experiences (including prior romances and breakups), and local contexts—
this book unveils how love and marriage come to be. In taking a social

scientific approach to love, I hope not to divest love of its richness but to shed light on some of its mystery and recognize how love and partnership can satisfy needs. While love is entered into by individuals, explanations for partnerships extend beyond the biological desire for sex, procreation, and companionship; this book uncovers the patterns behind partnerships, patterns that are socially produced rather than driven only by human agency. We choose whom we love, but we choose for reasons that are beyond our control: the families in which we lived as children; the socialization experiences that teach us about ourselves and others in ways that always implicate race, gender, and class relations; and the local community in which we live.

Mate Selection: Opportunities and Preferences

The opportunity to meet, mingle, and marry is partially dependent on group size, segregation, and contact. Demographers inform us that minority group size is inversely related to out-marriage rates with whites: the smaller the minority group population, the greater the chance they will marry outside the group, and vice versa. Owing in part to spatial separation, Hispanic coethnic dating and marriage rates remain high, especially in areas with a large supply of coethnics offering both native and foreign-born mates.[78] Thus, while intermarriage has nationally been on the rise, regions with sizable Hispanic populations have contributed to the "retreat from intermarriage." Areas boasting high numbers of Hispanics have high endogamy rates because coethnics are readily available to date and marry.[79] The same logic goes for residential patterns: the greater the degree of segregation, the greater the degree of endogamy.[80]

Residential segregation fosters opportunity for intramarriage. Because most Latino immigrants reside in coethnic immigrant neighborhoods that limit opportunities to date out-group members, most marry coethnics from the same country of origin.[81] As residential integration occurs over generations, Latino interethnic and interracial marriage increases over generations in the United States.[82] Mobility out of minority metropolitan areas requires financial means and is associated with intermarriage due to expanded networks.[83] Relatedly, those with more education and income also are more likely to out-marry.[84]

Demographics do not tell us about love and affinity. Patterns of love, desire, and compatibility present a gap in demographic literature: "All work that relies on 'marriage markets' has them operating as if a cool calculus produces sexual partnerships. Love, attraction, solidarities, and personal choice find little place in these approaches."[85] Demographic accounts identify structural reasons for marriage trends, but they do not answer my questions about the meanings that people attach to personal choices, what they hope to achieve in their decisions, and the multigenerational consequences of their choices.

While demographics shape *opportunities* for marriage, *preferences* are accumulations of sentiment that also direct desires. We know that "marriage patterns result from both preference and opportunity."[86] Marriage markets constitute opportunity, and yet preferences are the proverbial black box that needs to be filled in. The scant research on preferences tells us that race is a more important sorting criterion than education or religion and a forbidding line to cross.[87] Yet unanswered questions remain concerning how personal experience, intergroup contact, imagery, and structure inform preferences. Opportunities and preferences may not even be discrete entities but be better conceptualized as part of "feedback loops," rendering causes and consequences difficult to disentangle.[88] So are opportunities and preferences even separate entities? Or does opportunity shape preferences? Or do preferences lead to the intentional creation of opportunity? There is room for opportunity *and* preference, structure *and* culture in the equation that leads to marriage outcomes.[89] By problematizing the opportunities versus preferences debate and arguing that both matter, I provide a fuller picture of the multiple forces that bear on union formation. Through the use of life history interview data, I depict people's choices that are the fascinating and untold background to statistics on interracial and intraracial marriage and paint a rich picture of race relations and family formation.

Intersectionality: Race, Gender, Class, and Region

Intersectionality is the idea that we all occupy positions of privilege and oppression that *intersect* in our particular social location. Everyone occupies either a dominant or subordinate position on multiple axes of difference, the classic examples being gender, class status, and race-ethnicity. Everyone occupies varying levels of privilege and oppression on numerous dimensions, and these combinations of factors have multiplicative impacts on a person's relative advantage or disadvantage. For example, a white woman is privileged by her race but oppressed by her gender. As Patricia Hill Collins, a founder of intersectionality theory, has argued: "Placing . . . excluded groups in the center of analysis opens up possibilities for a both/and conceptual stance, one in which all groups possess varying amounts of penalty and privilege in one historically created system."[90] Two points are significant in this statement: First, excluded groups should be brought from the margin to the center to unearth ways of knowing that are suppressed when dominant groups control knowledge production. The periphery (nondominant groups) has "long been relegated to the analytical dustbin of cultural invisibility."[91] An intersectional perspective promises to reorient focus to the margins and acquire knowledge from these subordinated locations. Second, Collins claims that this analytic realignment holds "possibilities for a both/and conceptual stance," meaning that people may be "simultaneously oppressor and oppressed."[92] By teasing out varying levels of privilege and oppression according to different axes of difference, intersectionality yields deeper understanding of social processes that vary according to characteristics such as race-ethnicity, gender, and class.

Although race is a central concern in this book, by utilizing an intersectional approach I aim to understand from respondents' perspectives to what extent gender, class, or other issues were at stake in their marital decisions. An intersectional perspective to family formation makes my analysis attentive to the ways in which race-ethnicity, gender (as well as gender ideologies such as feminism or traditionalism), class, region, nation, and generation shape opportunities, constraints, desires, and actions. Prior scholarship has focused on how these axes of difference produce disparate outcomes, such as educational aspirations and achievement, expressions of class status, parenting strategies, and the production of gendered subjects.[93] An intersectional perspective maintaining that social features such as race-ethnicity, gender, and class are experienced simultaneously and lead to different outcomes has not been adequately applied to family formation. In my effort to honor the complexity and nuance that are the stuff of social life, I utilize intersectionality as the framework permitting access to multiple axes of difference that interlock to create various social positions. As the black feminist poet Audre Lorde opined, "There is no such thing as a single-issue struggle because we do not live single-issue lives."[94]

Not an axis of *oppression* in the same way as race, gender, and class, region is an axis of *difference* that bears on Latino family formation. Local demographics, politics, and the racial history embedded in a place all affect subjectivity and intimate relationships.[95] Regional racial histories matter because they shape the present: race is not "a misconception left over from the past, and suitable now for the dustbin of history."[96] Statewide and local political sentiment, race relations, and law enforcement all play into the cognitive frameworks and lived experience of both Latinos and non-Latinos and provide an indispensable backdrop for understanding contemporary marriage patterns and family dynamics in specific locales.[97]

While this book attends to multiple theoretical frameworks, intersectionality theory is especially well suited to be an overarching framework because it acknowledges multiple axes of oppressions without hierarchizing them. By the use of intersectionality, I avoid "the practice of 'Oppression Olympics' . . . where some forms of oppression are assumed to be worse than other forms"; such an analysis "pits groups against one another and diverts attention away from . . . structures, ideologies, and intersecting inequalities."[98] By skirting this hierarchical thinking that deems some forms of oppression more significant than others, I can instead see how oppressions "multiply" and work in tandem to produce specific experiences and reactions.[99] By examining the nexuses at intersections of identities, I break down bulk categories into constituent parts to explore the nuances that exist within broad categories but often are obscured beneath umbrella terms. Since one aim of this book is to unearth people's rationales for their crucial life choices, it is important not to presuppose answers but to allow them to percolate from people's life stories. Intersectionality allows interviewers to listen with open ears and hear the ways in which power differentials collide to produce particular patterned experiences. Since intersectionality informs us that race, class, gender, and other axes of difference are conditioned by each other, it is a reasonable starting point from which to investigate how advantage or disadvantage compounds to render logics for life choices.

Socialization and Decision-Making

Sociology has relied on socialization theory to explain how people are trained by institutions like family, religion, education, and peer groups to behave in culturally appropriate ways. Yet socialization theory over-emphasizes conformity and does not sufficiently theorize noncompliance or individual agency: "[socialization theory] lacks a theory of the individual as an *actor* involved in a process of actively constructing his or her life."[100] This book enters this gap by asking people about the choices they have made that have "actively construct[ed]" their lives. By centering on individuals' decision-making yet honoring their particular opportunity structures that both facilitate and hamper action, this book acknowledges general trends as well as individual variation. I heed Kathleen Gerson's advice in service of offering a deeper understanding of why people make the personal life choices they do: "We can ignore neither the subtle ways that childhood experiences influence later life choices nor the structural constraints on [people's] options. . . . A complete theory of . . . behavior must include how [people] themselves, as actors who respond to the social conditions they inherit, construct their lives out of the available raw materials."[101] By linking structure, personal experience, and agency, this book sheds light on the rationales that spur romantic decision-making, which, in turn, produces particular types of families.

How can we connect personal experience to crucial decisions like marriage in a way that allows for agency? Peter Berger and Hansfried Kellner consider marriage an exercise in "nomos-building."[102] Deriving from Greek, nomos refers to the social codes, habits, and customs that frame and order lived experience. Berger and Kellner contend that marriage is a protection against anomie—the breakdown or absence of social norms and values. A curative to a lack of social or moral standards, marriage as nomos-building "creates for the individual the sort of order in which he [sic] can experience his [sic] life as making sense."[103] Marriage is a significant relationship wherein people "construct, maintain, and modify" reality.[104] Linking to socialization theory, personal experience matters in that it endows present and future choices with meaning. If we consider marriage a "world-building relationship," marriage is a route to self-(re)definition.[105] This occurs through a process of "validation" whereby "truly significant others . . . [by] their continued presence will sustain . . . that nomos by which he [sic] can *feel at home in the world*."[106] This double entendre alludes to the powerful impact that home life can have on one's feeling about one's place in the world. "Home" in this sense signals the primacy of family life. Through the construction of a validating microculture, marital partners serve a "sustaining function" that orders and makes meaningful everyday life.[107]

Marriage "is a *dramatic* act in which two strangers come together and redefine themselves."[108] Marriage offers an opportunity for self-redefinition. If people are content, they may seek replication of their current nomos, norms, and culture in a partner. If, on the other hand, they are dissatisfied with their life patterns, or nomos, they can redirect their lives through marriage.

Electing to marry is a major life decision that leads to a consideration of the decision-making literature. This book answers two questions: What values do people bring to bear on the decision to marry? And how do people's life histories and present situations orient them toward one decision and not another? As people make choices they may conduct a rationale-choice-style cost-benefit analysis by weighing pros and cons.[109] Alternatively, actors may let emotions and values guide them through decisions as they "feel" their way to a decision. Decisions are often made without complete information, and people must rely on partial knowledge and assumptions.[110] Each of two theoretical perspectives on choice and decision-making—subjective/cognitive and objective/behaviorist—lends insight into how people select one action over another. Both perspectives postulate that actors may either take or refrain from action; that actors will activate a course of action that is most likely to produce outcomes in line with their values and well-being; and that since consequences are uncertain, choices represent "guesses" in the hopes of generating an intended result.[111] The subjective approach assumes that behavior is "purposive and goal-directed"—that people act in accordance with the degree to which they believe that a particular action or inaction will produce a specific outcome.[112] The behaviorist approach focuses on the effects of rewards and punishment: people base their decisions on their accumulated knowledge that certain actions are probabilistically associated with certain benefits or costs. The two perspectives are complementary in that they explain decision-making phenomena in different circumstances: subjectivists explicate decisions made under novel, nonroutine conditions (like whom to marry), whereas behaviorists elucidate decisions made in day-to-day, routine circumstances.[113] Although people use both decision-making logics as they navigate their lives, the subjectivist approach is compelling relative to marriage decisions because it highlights humans as goal-seekers.[114]

A "difficult and precarious" venture, marriage does not come with a guarantee of success.[115] Marital happiness and durability hinge on a mutually agreeable and confirming "little world."[116] If the nomos-building project is not shared but instead reveals disjuncture or discontinuity, this mismatch in social realities is likely to result in termination of the relationship. The search for satisfying partnerships that reflect back and share agreeable versions of reality ("validation") is crucial because of the primacy of a spouse in confirming or disconfirming one's nomos, sense of self, and worldview.

The Historical Contexts of California and Kansas: Facts and Imaginaries

I conducted interviews for *Marriage Vows and Racial Choices* in California and Kansas, and it is important to highlight that these two states are distinct in both factual and imaginary ways. California shares 140 miles of the nearly 2,000-mile international land border with Mexico.[117] It is home to the largest absolute number of Hispanics in the United States (14 million of a total of 50 million Hispanic residents as of the 2010 census) and serves as a traditional gateway for immigration from Latin America to the United States.[118] Notably, this southern border was crossed freely on a regular basis by "sojourner" or "circular" migrants, and such crossings were an everyday or seasonal part of transnational lives until 1924, when the U.S. Border Patrol was formed.[119] That the U.S. Department of Labor worked with Immigration and Naturalization Services (INS) to regulate entry into the nation highlights that the relationship between the United States and Mexico is principally based on economics and labor relations.[120] The United States systematically recruited Mexican labor during times of U.S. need, such as the worker shortages in World War I and World War II, and expelled this same labor power during economic downturns such as the Great Depression (Operation Deportation) and the post–Korean War recession (Operation Wetback).[121]

Mexican and other Latin American immigrants satisfy the demand in the United States for labor, a "structural" need that is built into the U.S. economy and, in conjunction with (expected) unauthorized labor flows, translates into a vulnerable, deportable, and disposable labor force.[122] Mexico, as the largest supplier of immigrant labor, "has provided U.S. capitalism with the only 'foreign' migrant labor reserve so sufficiently flexible that it can neither be fully replaced nor be completely excluded under any circumstances."[123]

The national trends of labor recruitment and expulsion most drastically affected the workforce and population in California and affected Kansas to a lesser extent. California's agribusiness, which turns on the cultivation of produce such as oranges, lemons, strawberries, lettuce, broccoli, garlic, and avocados, has a long history of dependence on low-wage migrant labor.[124] Mexicans "regularly passed through [Kansas] since the mid-19th century as cowboys on cattle drives from Texas or as wagoners on the Santa Fe Trail," and Latino migrant labor has filled a labor need in meatpacking, the cultivation of beets, and railroad construction since the early 1900s.[125] In the 1920s, railroad construction was a dynamic sector for employment of Mexican men, who "did the lion's share of heavy physical labor involved in laying rail lines," the U.S. Department of Labor reporting that "Mexicans constituted 85 percent of railroad track workers . . . and 75 percent of beet, fruit, and vegetable laborers."[126] Mexican workers were attracted to Kansas's employment opportunities in railroads and sugar beets from the outbreak of the Mexican Revolution in 1910 until 1930. After experiencing "interrupted" migration, labor flows to Kansas were renewed in the 1980s when the meatpacking industry boomed.[127]

California has a long history of labor in-immigration bringing Latinos to the region and, in turn, generating racial intermarriage. Since at least the 1800s, intermarriage between Mexican Americans and whites was a tactic for whites to consolidate political and landholding power. In the 1849 California State Constitutional Convention, Mexicans were granted the same citizenship rights as "free white persons."[128] The state constitution formally disenfranchised Indian and black populations, but the Anglo population considered Mexicans legally part of the white race owing to their mixed-blood ancestry. In the nineteenth century, marriages were arranged between daughters of the "Californio" elite (the historical term for the Mexicans of Alta California prior to the 1848 land secession to the United States) and wealthy Anglos to consolidate land, wealth, political power, and racial privilege. Californio women were "arguably trafficked between the old and emerging ruling classes," women and marriage serving as tools in "the larger colonizing processes."[129] Intermarriage between newcomer rich, white men and local Mexican women was a way for white men to acquire land without incurring financial debt, and it conferred some prestige to Mexican women, who were marrying into the dominant racial group and thereby gaining privilege.[130] The high-class status of the lower-status racial group made interracial marriage acceptable since financial status was "exchanged" for racial status.[131] These pairings served to pacify the newly colonized people, since the colonizers became family, thereby averting mutiny in a society where whites were outnumbered.[132]

By comparison, there is scant literature on intermarriage in Kansas. Instead, what we know about Latinos in Kansas, or the Midwest more generally, concerns migrant labor in meat-processing plants, newcomers' adaptation in rural locales, and intraracial relations.[133] In the Kansas context, the subject of marriage patterns is untouched. Standing theory suggests that when people face shortages of spouses with similar racial or national origins, their willingness to enter mixed marriages increases—a historical precedent taken up in this book.[134]

Not only are California and Kansas disparate in concrete ways such as demographics, histories, and race relations, but they also occupy different positions in the national imaginary. In his scholarship on national identity, Benedict Anderson conceives of the nation as an "imagined community."[135] The national body is *imagined* because members of the nation will never meet all of their fellow members, yet the image of community is powerfully installed in members' minds. Imagination plays a role here as people mentally produce an image of the nation without traveling all of its territory or meeting all of its residents. Fueled by both factual and fictive information about its many regions and populations, people impose meanings on portions of the nation. For example, California is envisioned as part of the "Wild West," as the "new frontier," and as a gateway for immigration from other nations to its south. Alternatively, Kansas is generally pictured as the "heartland," owing to its geographical location in the center of the nation, and as America's "breadbasket," a reference to its status as a top wheat-producing state.[136]

Agriculturally robust, Kansas does some cultural work to broadcast its position in the nation's "breadbasket." One testament to how native Kansans view their place in the nation is the cornucopia of produce, grains, and breads on the billboard signs dotting Interstate 70 and reading: "1 KANSAS FARMER FEEDS 128 PEOPLE PLUS YOU!" This sign highlights the agricultural nature of Kansas and proudly links the state's chief industry to the nourishing of the nation, including the interstate travelers who view the billboard. Popular cultural products, such as the book and movie *The Wizard of Oz*, cast Kansas as an agricultural and somewhat idyllic place (aside from the tornadoes) populated by a young rural white girl and her fictional dreamscape. These factual and fictive forces combine to portray Kansas as an inland agricultural space that is home to not many people beyond white people.

Alternatively, California's place in the national imaginary turns on its status as a border state, a bellwether of migration issues for the rest of the nation, and a place of technological innovation.[137] Pictured as a place of paradise and migration, California is where dreams are both dashed and realized.[138] Long an immigrant-receiving state, even predating the demarcation of the border, California has been built off of migrant labor while it simultaneously houses the dreams of migrant and native Californians alike. As the "golden state"—a term that can variously be applied to its gold rush history, its golden hills in summer, the landmark Golden Gate Bridge, or even Beverly Hills as the home of the Golden Globe Awards for excellence in film and television—California is a place where dreams might turn to gold. By setting these two disparate locales next to each other in this book, we can learn how region, as a mode of difference, influences notions around race and even the intimate sphere of family formation.

RESEARCH METHODS

In researching this book, I interviewed 109 people, representing forty-nine couples or multigenerational families.[139] Fifty-eight study participants were women, and fifty-one were men. Forty-nine participants (from twenty-four families) were from California, and sixty participants (from twenty-five families) were located in Kansas. The vast majority of respondents were U.S.-born (ninety-five people), and fourteen were foreign-born. Seventy participants (64 percent) identified as Latino/a only, twenty (19 percent) as mixed-race, fifteen (14 percent) as white only, three as Asian only, one as Native American only, and none as black only.

Recognizing the importance of color in navigating racial worlds, I created a skin color measure and coded respondents according to a five-point scale, regardless of race, from 1 (racially white appearance) to 5 (racially black appearance). To create this scale I selected one Latino celebrity from the Spanish-language *People* magazine website to correspond to each skin-color code.[140] Thirty percent (thirty-three) of all respondents were skin-color code 1; 27 percent (twenty-nine) were 2; 30 percent (thirty-three) were 3; 12 percent (thirteen) were 4; and 1 percent (one) was 5, or phenotypically black.

Considering the entire sample of adults and children, most respondents were married (eighty-four people, or 77 percent). Since the 1960s, marriage rates have declined: half of American adults (51 percent) were married in 2011 compared with 72 percent in 1960.[141] Marriage is being replaced by cohabitation, single-person households, and other adult living arrangements. Further, a "marriage gap" has emerged: marriage is now the norm for college-educated adults with solid incomes, but less likely to occur among the less economically advantaged, who consider economic security a precondition for marriage. In a reflection of the marriage decline, the American public is broadening its definition of family, rejecting marriage as the only path to family formation.[142]

Despite its prevalence, no cohabiting couples volunteered for participation in the study. When I loosened participation requirements, divorced people volunteered. With their inclusion, my sample, while slanted in the direction of economically stable, heterosexually married families, at least partially reflects the messy reality of unified, divorced, and remarried families. Five respondents were divorced, and twenty (mostly youth) were single or had never married. Although I used the language of "lifetime partners" in my recruitment materials with the intention of including homosexual couples, no same-sex couples consented to interviews. The age range for respondents was fourteen to seventy-six. Twenty-seven percent of respondents were between the ages of fourteen and twenty-nine, the majority (60 percent) were between thirty and fifty-nine, and 14 percent were over sixty years old.

As measured by education, occupation, and household income, a range of class strata were represented (see appendix B). Despite a wide range, the respondent pool was skewed toward the middle class, limiting the generalizability of the findings. A fraction of respondents had less than a high school education (2 percent). Many dependent children were currently in high school (13 percent), and 50 percent of all respondents had a high school degree or GED, some college experience, or were currently a college student. Twenty-one percent had attained a college degree, and 25 percent held a graduate degree. The middle-class standing of the majority of the respondent pool was reflected in their occupations. Nine percent of respondents held blue-collar jobs such as machinists, 19 percent were in service or sales jobs such as retail or the police, 45 percent held white-collar or professional jobs like teachers, architects, or lawyers, 18 percent were students, and 6 percent were unemployed (a figure that included homemakers). Retirees were coded as holding their most recent job, 3 percent of respondents being retired with undisclosed prior employment. In 2010, when the interviews were conducted, the median household income for the United States was $51,000. (In California median income was $59,540, and in Kansas it was $49,687.) The vast majority of my respondents earned a household income well above the national and statewide averages. Only 11 percent of respondents earned a household income below $50,000. Earnings were middle- and top-heavy: 38 percent earned between $50,001 and $100,000, 28 percent reported income of $100,001 to $150,000, and 16 percent earned above $150,000 in annual household income. These income figures for my sample are a reminder that processes around race and family formation may work differently at different class levels, an area of future research.

Table 1.1   Sample, by Marital Type

Intermarriage: Latino-White	Intermarriage: Latino–Non-Latino Racial Minority	Intramarriage: Latino-Latino	Total
n = 41 (27 adults, 3 adult children, 11 dependent children)	n = 12 (12 adults)	n = 56 (44 adults, 4 adult children, 8 dependent children)	N = 109 (83 adults, 7 adult children, 19 dependent children)
16 families (3 California, 13 Kansas)	6 families (3 California, 3 Kansas)	27 families (18 California, 9 Kansas)	49 families (24 California, 25 Kansas)
10 Latina women, 6 Latino men 5 white women, 9 white men	5 Latina women, 1 Latino man 1 non-Latino minority woman, 5 non-Latino minority men		

Source: Author's calculations.

Approximately half of the forty-nine families were intermarried couples and their mixed-race children (fifty-three respondents), and half were intra-married couples and their mono-racial children (fifty-six respondents) (see table 1.1). While most Latinos partner with other Latinos and those who out-marry tend to do so with whites, I included Latino intermarriages with Asians, blacks, and Native Americans in order to capture the variety of pairings that occur. In the table, respondents are defined as adults, "adult children" of adult interviewees (who were sometimes married, in which case I inquired about their marriages), or "dependent children" who were living at home or in college.

Table 1.2 shows the breakdown of intramarried couples and their chil-dren according to the more specific marital types that are the organizing principles for the empirical chapters. Cross-national marriages included individuals with different national origins (for example, Mexico and Bolivia) but excluded those who were international but of the same national origin (for example, Mexican national and Mexican American). Mixed-generation intramarriages included couples who were Mexican-origin but varied in terms of generation-since-immigration (for example, Mexican immigrant and third-plus-generation Mexican American). Intragenerational intra-marriages involved couples who shared not only a national-origin heri-tage (ethnic group) but also a generational status (for example, both were second-generation Mexican Americans).

Table 1.2   Intramarried Families, Including Children

Cross-National Intramarriage	Mixed-Generation Intramarriage	Intra-Generation Intramarriage	Total
n = 9 (9 adults, including 1 adult child)	n = 22 (18 adults, including 2 adult children; 4 dependent children)	n = 28 (20 adults, 4 adult children[b], 4 dependent children)	N = 59[a] (44 adults, 7 adult children, 8 dependent children)
6 families (3 California, 3 Kansas)	11 families (7 California, 4 Kansas)	11 families (8 California, 3 Kansas)	28 families (18 California, 10 Kansas)

Source: Author's calculations.
[a]This total number of fifty-nine is different from the fifty-six Latino-Latino intramarried in table 1.1 because three adult children are captured under the "intermarried with whites" category in table 1.1, whereas they are included here as children of intramarried couples.
[b]None of the adult children fit this marital combination (one single or never married, two divorced from a white person, one intermarried with a white person). Adult children were interviewed with respect to being children of their parents in this category as well as their own dating and marital lives.

My sample of intramarried couples and their children totals fifty-nine respondents representing twenty-eight families. Two-thirds of the intra-married families were from California (eighteen families) and one-third were from Kansas (ten families); this skew reflected the greater number of Latinos in the Southwest, which translates into a bigger marriage market. Recalling table 1.1, the greater number of intramarried Latino couples in California complements the greater number of Latino-white intermarriages in Kansas, which similarly attests to the power of population demographics in shaping dating pools. There were nine adults in the cross-national cat-egory, twenty-two (eighteen adults and four dependent children) in the mixed-generation group, and twenty-eight (twenty adults and four depen-dent children) in the intragenerational in-marriage category.

With field sites in California and Kansas, a comparative approach allows for analysis of systematic differences between a state that borders Mexico and has traditionally been a receiving state for immigrants and an inland state with less of a legacy of transmigration. By comparing the marital dynamics of a racially diverse state where whites are a minority with a majority-white state with minimal diversity, we can more fully grasp the effects of region, racial composition, and local racial hierarchies on marriage patterns. Studying couples residing in states with disparate immigration his-tories and Hispanic populations (as percentages of state populations) yields information about the lived experience of race in these different contexts. In comparison to 16.9 percent of the U.S. population being of Hispanic origin (of any race), California's population is 38.2 percent Hispanic, whereas Kansas's population is 11.0 percent Hispanic. These two states' share of non-Hispanic whites varies accordingly: California's population is 39.4 percent non-Hispanic white, whereas Kansas's population is 77.5 percent non-Hispanic white. California's Hispanic population is over triple that of Kansas, and its non-Hispanic white population is about half that of Kansas. California's racial diversity goes beyond Hispanics and non-Hispanic whites, with 13.9 percent Asian, 6.6 percent black, 1.7 percent American Indian, and 3.6 percent "two or more races," whereas Kansas is less diverse, with 2.6 percent Asian, 6.2 percent black, 1.2 percent American Indian, and 2.7 percent "two or more races."[143] Comparing a state with a long history of circular and permanent migration to fill U.S. labor needs with one that does not top the list of migration-receiving states and remains predominantly white provides insight into how migration histories, population demographics, and race relations play out in the intimate sphere of romance and partnership. Including an analysis of region sheds light on how place helps constitute racial meanings, the racial makeup of romantic possibilities, and performances of race and culture.[144]

A NOTE ON TERMINOLOGY

I refer to Latinos as a race, not an ethnic group, because respondents' narratives reveal that they are strictly categorized by others. Since racial categories are externally imposed, not electively asserted, and Latino respondents experienced their heritage to be more "mandatory" than "optional," race is an appropriate descriptor. The race theorists Michael Omi and Howard Winant define race as an "axis of conflict that refers to human bodies," noting that race is both historically contingent and socially constructed, racial classifications being a by-product of bias that is variable over time.[145] Physical characteristics play a role in how dividing lines among humans are drawn, despite race lacking a biological or genetic underpinning.[146] How physical appearance is *viewed* is itself a learned social skill that constructs race.[147] Stephen Cornell and Douglass Hartmann note that "the selection of markers and therefore the construction of the racial category itself . . . is a choice human beings make."[148] With racial definition comes the chance to rank order groups. As an "axis of conflict," race implies a power relation, which leads to the conceptualization of the relationships among racial groups as a "racial hierarchy," groups arranged according to degrees of privilege and oppression.[149]

I refer to Latinos as a racial group because they are treated as a unitary group by outsiders and any assertions about national origin or ethnic group are glossed over by a racial categorization. A long history of racial-ization of Latinos predates and justifies my terminological decision, from labor recruitment to occupational queuing and deportation programs based on race.[150] The Mexican-origin population, the national-origin group making the largest contribution to the Latino category, has been treated distinctly since the United States colonized northern Mexico after the Mexican-American War, which ended in 1848 and marked the origin of Mexican Americans as a racial group.[151] This history of conquest and colonization feeds into contemporary legal definitions of Latinos as a separate group that qualifies for federal programs for disadvantaged racial minorities, further legitimizing understandings of Latinos as a racial category.[152] This history of racialization informs how U.S.-born Latinos see themselves: later generations self-identify as Hispanic/Latino, in addi-tion to their national origin, more so than as American, reflecting racial-ized exclusion.[153]

In contrast to race, I understand ethnicity as referring to "culture and descent," where "culture" refers to "religion, language, 'customs,' nation-ality, and political identification" and "descent" means heredity and group origins.[154] In other words, ethnicity is "not biological or primordial [but rather] . . . it involves a great deal of choice."[155] Ethnicity is voluntary and subjective; individuals electively claim group membership that refers to a "distinctive connection" based on "common descent."[156] I use the term "ethnicity" to refer to national origin or heritage (for example, Mexico or Peru), which are smaller divisions within the Latino category. I call "inter-ethnic" marriages "cross-national" marriages (for example, a Mexican-origin person married to a Bolivian-origin person, irrespective of nation of birth) to move away from the confusion over whether Latinos constitute a racial or ethnic group.

AN OVERVIEW OF THE CHAPTERS

This book moves from considering intermarriage to intramarriage. Chapters 2 through 4 concern racial intermarriage. Chapter 2 focuses on a key question for Latino and white intermarriages: How do people account for exogamous marriage, from the perspectives of both partners? This chap-ter explores the reasons why people out-married, teasing apart the influ-ence of preferences as well as "supply" or demographics. A chief finding is that Latina women who suffered domineering Latino fathers assumed that all Latino men shared this trait and therefore rejected all Latino men and favored white men who "looked" different than their fathers. Class is also operative here as Latina women fused race, class, and gender to perceive white men as desirable on these grounds. From the whites' perspective, a discourse of multiculturalism facilitated intermarriage and operated alongside imagery of Latina women as domestic. Racialized experiences, gender ideologies, class status, imagery, and multicultural discourse all construct romantic desire. These preferences combine with population demographics to produce Latino and white intermarriage.

Chapter 3 continues the focus on Latino and white intermarriage, asking: How does intermarriage affect identity, culture, and racial consciousness? Assimilation theory views intermarriage as evidence of successful integration and predicts that the minority partner will shed minority group attachments. Contrary to this assumption, the "breaking of ties" is only one of many outcomes for these intermarried families; multidirectional biculturalism is the chief cultural result. I theorize variations of biculturalism and examine how intermarriage foments racial consciousness in whites, with white women in particular adopting and perpetuating their husbands' heritage. Interviews with Latino-white mixed-race children illustrate that proximity to Latino extended family members is crucial to sustaining Latino cultural ties, especially in the predominantly white Kansas context.

In chapter 4, I look at Latinos who are intermarried with non-Latino racial minorities—namely African Americans, Asian Americans, and Native Americans. Like chapters 2 and 3, this chapter addresses the rationales for and ramifications of a union that crosses racial boundaries, this time with a non-Latino minority. Focusing on dual-minority partnerships, this chapter charts the desire for an interracial minority partner among those who not only rejected Latinos (or did not find them to date) but also excluded whites from their dating pool, believing that white privilege would make such partners fundamentally unknowable to one another. Through "shared marginalization," these couples discovered in each other a common experience with a *different* nonwhite category that legitimized their racialized experience. The California-Kansas comparison is germane here: in California, couples considered themselves a reflection of their multiracial environment, whereas in Kansas, cross-racial minority partners emphasized the experiential parallels of their marginality. A shared racially subordinate perspective is central to these marriages, and racial empathy with someone from a different minority group is vital to their bonding.

Chapters 5 through 7 center on Latino intramarriage and move from couples who are most dissimilar in nation and generation to those who are the most similar. Chapter 5 is devoted to cross-national (also known as "panethnic" or "interethnic") Latino partnerships: unions between people with ancestry from two different Latin American countries. These marriages are spurred by a preference for cultural commonality, a desire not to have to explain one's background, resistance to a familiar brand of patriarchy, and escape from whites' stereotypes of Latinos. Latinas who struggled against patriarchal fathers but otherwise appreciated their culture sought out Latino men who hailed from a different nation in order to find a racial and gender haven. Marrying a Latino with a different national origin is an attempt to avoid the problematic elements associated with a national-origin community yet maintain broader Latino cultural elements. For Latino men, notions of cultural compatibility, which rule out white women, are at work. The consequences of these unions include cultural exchange, pan-Latino cultural blending, and women's upkeep of a husband's national culture through her gendered efforts at maintaining the home's cultural life.

In examining Mexican-origin, mixed-generation, endogamous marriage (for example, a Mexican immigrant and a third-generation Mexican American), chapter 6 covers five key themes: transnationalism, "assimilation" within mixed-generation partnerships, the political-legal consciousness of spouses of immigrants, upward mobility coexisting with solidarity, and Latino men's feminism. This chapter unveils the cultural and structural mechanisms that foster these relationships and exposes variations within the supposed monolith of racial intramarriage. The range of experience these partnerships encompass proves the multifaceted quality of racial endogamy. Relatedly, Latino men's feminism is not exclusive to this marital type but is discussed here to show the elasticity of gender norms.[157] Latino men's family-of-origin experiences with patriarchy and their heterosexual romantic involvements with women inspire them to revise their enactments of masculinity. Interviews with children show how families shape but do not overdetermine the next generation's identity and performance of culture.

Chapter 7 profiles Mexican-origin couples who share the same generation status (intragenerational intramarriages) and their children. Focusing on the California case, these endogamous parents and their children use social-distancing racial strategies to avoid race-based negative stereotypes. In the Latino- and immigrant-dense context of California, rejecting or downplaying their racial status is a primary way in which interviewees strove to gain upward mobility and obviate treacherous stereotypes. Gender is operative here in terms of who is most castigated and therefore most invested in resistance: Mexican-origin men were especially subject to low-class and gang stereotypes and reactively most engaged in social-distancing strategies. In-married parents in this category diminished racial ties in favor of striving for class advancement, which they perceived as incompatible with nonwhite ethnicity, and children tended to utilize the same racial strategy. This strategy, practiced by those striving for middle-class status, reveals that in-marriage does not equate to cultural retention but can instead lead to redoubled efforts to attenuate ties to a group that threatens economic ascent.

Chapter 8 steps away from rationales and consequences to examine the uncertain process of dating, the decision to marry, marital tensions, divorce, and remarriage. While some of these issues are present in earlier chapters, this chapter uses the search for love as its centerpiece to ask questions about process. Given that this book focuses on currently married couples, chapter 8, in offering an honest appraisal of how and why people get in and out of relationships, rounds out the book by accounting for life as a long-running sequence of experiences. Although I interviewed respondents at one point in time, their retrospective accounts show their lives playing out more like movies—occurring over a period of time that provides room for growth, change, and decisions—than static photographs.[158] Conflicts about gendered responsibilities in the home and sexual fidelity fomented marital tension and led people to either live ambivalently in a marriage or separate. Extended families in earlier chapters provided a connection to Latino culture, but here meddlesome parents-in-law could interfere with a couple's happiness and, by not allowing them to negotiate a mutually agreeable family life, move them toward divorce. Complicating the pairing of happiness with marriage and unhappiness with divorce is the finding that some people remained married but were unhappy, reluctant, and unsure. And other people who fled problems through divorce were happier unmarried. The couples who reported the greatest long-term happiness were those who carefully selected their spouse by *quality-coding*, that is, identifying personality characteristics that they needed in a partner and screening dates until they found someone who offered the right palette of qualities.

The concluding chapter, chapter 9, summarizes lifetime partnerships as the result of negotiated desire that takes into account intersectional concerns stemming from racialized, gendered, and classed life experiences. Marriage is an intersectional critical juncture: people construct romantic desires in response to intersectional concerns and select partners whom they believe are good bets to fulfill their most crucial needs. Personal experience, cultural notions of race, gender, generation, and nation, and the demographics of a place all bear on family formation. As such, the preferences versus opportunity debate in the marriage literature is based on a false dichotomy; this chapter reminds us that preferences shape opportunities and vice versa. Additionally, marriage choices can have both anticipated and unexpected results. Marriage has repercussions in racial awareness, racial strategies, cultural practices, gender ideologies and strategies, class mobility, and national residence. Chapter 9 reminds us that using a lens of family offers an important optic on some racial boundaries proving to be more readily crossed than others and on the modest reconfiguration of the racial hierarchy through family life.

This book contributes to our understanding of meanings and interpretations that drive marital pairings involving Latinos and their consequences. By taking a life history approach and intersectional perspective, I trace the ways in which personal experience—patterned by racialized, gendered, classed, regional, and national experiences—inclines people toward either intermarriage or intramarriage. Rather than take marital formations as given, I unearth the reasons that lie behind those patterns and accumulate into negotiated desire.

As people craft their chosen families, they are making racial choices and influencing race relations. Even if race is not their top priority, their marital life reshapes understandings and enactments of race, culture, and identity. The racial choices made in marriage and the intimate life lived therein make marriage an especially fruitful site for examining why people choose the families they do and how they chart their course as Americans.

Chapter 2 | Latino and White Intermarriage: Preferences and Convenience

How CAN WE understand people's rationales for intermarriage? Some people out-marry for very well-conceived reasons, others have latent desires that lead them to out-marry, and still others seem to fall into intermarriage. Race, including the "cultural/ideological meaning[s]" associated with racial groups, is central to why people out-marry.[1] Race is always present in marriage, for even marriages facilitated by structural factors (such as population demographics) are influenced by a place's racial history (such as immigration streams resulting from labor market recruitment). This chapter demonstrates how cultural expectations around race, gender, and class, in addition to structure, inform romance.

This chapter's organizing question about the factors driving intermarriage requires the examination of how individuals define what mattered to them in choosing a lifetime partner. Love matters as a prerequisite to marriage, and yet my angle on family formation is to theorize the background features that informed what people sought—what mattered most to them and why— in their search for love and companionship.

People can be articulate about their preferences, and yet my job, as a social scientist, is to discern how their personal experiences and preferences and their local contexts guide their actions. In using the terms "preferences" and "rationales," I am referring to the foundational desires that take form in action. Social structure, referring to more rigid social arrangements such as population demographics, the legal system, and the labor market, does not work independently of personal preferences but instead shapes them. Structure imposes constraints—such as population composition—yet it also offers opportunities.

Specific rationales rooted in personal experience culminate in preferential intermarriage, which I analyze by race, class, and gender. Three rationales drive Latinos' preferential intermarriage: Latina women's concern about gender equality; a desire for upward class mobility; and racial policing, which values whiteness and denigrates blackness (see table 2.1). Three logics influence whites' preferential intermarriage: imagery of Latina women, previous romantic relationships with Latina women, and multiculturalism.

Intermarriages can also be "convenient," not driven by strong preferences. For Latinos in predominantly white areas, demographics play a key role in intermarriage. A small supply of coethnics can lead to out-marriage for Latinos who may prefer in-marriage but are outnumbered by whites; constricted opportunity overwhelms their preference. Whites' rationales for intermarriage in largely white contexts are actually *preferential* since effort is required to pursue an out-group member in a milieu abundant with same-race possibilities. Among Latinos facing a limited supply of potential endogamous partners, as in the Kansas context, not all nonwhite racial groups are ranked equally, and some respondents expressed anti-black prejudice to preserve their relative privilege. For intermarriages promoted by population demographics, an order of priorities was relevant as people sought partners who matched their class status or religion.

This chapter is based on interviews with thirty adults who were part of a Latino-white intermarried couple. Fourteen married couples are represented (I interviewed both people in the pair) as well as two people who were divorced. Of the thirty interviewees, sixteen were Latino/a (ten women, six men) and fourteen were white (five women, nine men). Although Latina women and men out-marry with whites at relatively similar rates, the sample here included more out-married Latina women than men: ten couples

Table 2.1   Preferential and Convenience Rationales, by Race

	Latinos/as	Whites
Preferential		
	Gender goal–oriented	Imagery (sexy, suitable)
	Class calculations	Previous romantic relationships
	Racial policing	Parental teaching of equality; multiculturalism
Convenience		
	Demographics (in majority-white areas)	None

Source: Author's calculations.

were Latina women and white men pairs, and six couples were Latino men and white women.[2] Two divorced Latinos were included: one woman and one man.

This chapter examines preferential intermarriages, followed by convenience intermarriages. Within each section, I focus first on Latinos, then whites. Preferential intermarriage offers an interesting gendered trend in that out of eleven people, six were women, *all of whom were Latina women*. By race, seven of eleven preferentially intermarried individuals were Latino and four were white, *all preferentially out-married whites being men*. Convenience out-marriages are almost evenly split between Latinos and whites (nine Latinos and ten whites) and between men and women (nine women and ten men).

PREFERENTIAL OUT-MARRIAGE: LATINOS/AS

Gender Goal Orientation

In response to their personal experiences and natal family systems, Latina women who deliberately pursue out-marriage view intermarriage as a way to avoid the negative experiences or traits they associate with Latino men, usually epitomized by a domineering Latino father. Oppressive family-of-origin dynamics predispose Latinas toward out-marriage. As Maria Root finds in her study of multiracials, "some participants . . . who had been treated cruelly by a parent, or who saw that parent treat other people cruelly, *color-coded* this experience and stayed away from people who resembled that person racially."[3] This logic castigates an entire racial and gender category of people over prior bad experiences with certain individuals. Gender goal–oriented Latinas who aim for greater gender freedom cast the net widely in an effort to avoid any characteristics that *might* be related to a specific gender and racial category. This sweeping logic makes sense in light of the research finding that fear of being saddled with a harmful "cost" (such as a domineering mate) more directly determines the choices people make than calculations of possible "rewards."[4] "Color-coding" that is fueled by a desire to avoid potential costs is a useful way of thinking about how natal family experiences inform a person's responses to people who physically resemble family members who negatively affected him or her at earlier life stages.

Color-coding is a mechanism of negotiated desire that rests on an emotional and mental bargain meant to placate prior hurt and defensively approach the future. Color-coding is also a reaction against childhood socialization. Socialization theories focus on how early relationships, especially with parents, develop gender identities. A central goal of this literature is to uncover the unconscious and role model processes of mimicry that reproduce social relations, gender schemas, and gender inequality.[5] A critique of socialization theory is that it does not account for social change; it only explains how the social order continues intact. Emphasizing how "motivations and capacities . . . once instilled in childhood . . . lead adult men and women to recreate their parents' pattern in their own lives," socialization theory misses an opportunity to theorize dynamism and social change.[6] The human experience is not destined simply to reproduce the status quo. Kathleen Gerson's critique of socialization puts it eloquently: "By focusing upon *reproduction processes* rather than *change,* socialization theories underestimate the human capacity for development beyond childhood."[7] Socialization theory freezes the possibility for change over time, presuming that childhood is the unalterable blueprint for development into adulthood. My research disagrees. By attending to childhood experiences in the natal family system as well as extrafamilial experiences, this book honors human agency and capacity for change throughout the life course. And by drawing links between childhood experiences and adult choices but refusing to mechanically hinge the two and predict a singular direction, this book identifies multiple connections between personal lives and personal choices without becoming deterministic or universalistic.

Rather than condemn adults to the fate of unwittingly replicating past patterns they witnessed in childhood, color-coding is instead a *reaction against subordination.* Color-coding does not fuse futures to pasts, as socialization theory would do, but instead allows for the possibility that people learn, adapt, and apply lessons from their past to their future, and it recognizes people's power to unshackle themselves from oppression or critique unearned privileges. A behaviorist approach to decision-making informs us that people become conditioned to associate certain stimuli with certain outcomes, such as rewards and positive feelings or punishments and negative feelings.[8] When considering punishments, this link between stimuli and results transmogrifies into "learned inhibitions . . . [that] are often reinforced by internalized fears and anxieties."[9] Women are especially attuned to gender issues, but rather than become habituated to violence and silencing, women can become catalyzed by their fears to react against subordination in an attempt to claim greater freedom.[10] As we will see in the narratives of Celeste Collins, Sylvia Nava-Kelly, and Cynthia Herrera-Redgrave, many Latina women who had domineering fathers generalized this trait to all Latino men and avoided it by turning their attention to whites, whom they assumed would be safer bets.

Celeste Collins acted on a color-coded and gendered rationale for exogamy, her out-marriage choice being grounded in her concern about gender equality. Celeste identified as Latina, although technically she was half Native American, through her mother, and half Mexican American, through her father. For Celeste, intermarriage was a motivated choice: she out-married to avoid the gender-stifling attitudes and behaviors exhibited by her patriarchal father. She painted a picture of her natal family household: "We had a very traditional household. My dad was a traditional, strong male figure, and my mother was *clearly* the nurturing [one] . . . managed the house, took care of the dishes . . . the cooking . . . the cleaning and . . . the care of the children. I was very much raised that that was my role also." She did not date much in high school and college: "I had a couple of boyfriends—they were all Caucasian, I was attracted to Caucasian men, and I met my husband when I was twenty-one." When I asked about the preferences she expressed in her dating history, she elaborated: "This sounds terrible, but I did not want to marry anybody like my dad. He's too domineering, and everything had to center around him, and I didn't want to—that was very not attractive to me. So I think I consciously did not want to pursue anyone that looked like my dad."

Thus, Celeste, who "consciously did not want to pursue anyone that looked like" her father, color-coded her father's domineering nature with his physical appearance. Not all Mexican American men are domineering like her father, and not all non-Mexican men are gender-egalitarian. Yet Celeste self-protectively excluded Mexican American men from her dating pool to guard against the domination that she associated with her father and the entire racial and gender category to which he belonged. Having fused domineering masculinity with Mexican American men, Celeste made the motivated choice to out-marry.

In addition to this conscious intent, population demographics played into Celeste's dating options in Lawrence, Kansas, where she attended the University of Kansas (KU): "When I came to KU, I lived in a scholarship hall and it was predominantly Caucasian. . . . I was not with many Mexicans or Native Americans—didn't have a large pool to draw from. But . . . I knew I didn't want to marry anyone that seemed like my dad. . . . I didn't want . . . to be pigeonholed into a role like my mother. . . . I had a different path in mind."

Although being in a predominantly white college environment had limited her dating options, Celeste moved from commenting on the available "pool to draw from" to reiterating her resistance to masculinity like her father's, which "pigeonholed" her mother. Rejecting her father's male dominance and running in the direction of white men—all of her boyfriends were white—Celeste deliberately picked not just any white man but a "supportive" and "encouraging" white man. Unlike many of her Latina peers, Celeste did not generalize that all white men would not be domineering but instead selected a white man whose qualities fit with her value system.

Sylvia Nava-Kelly was another Latina with a challenging father whose negotiated desire targeted gender equality in marriage. Sylvia was a Cuban American from a suburb of Chicago: her father was a Cuban immigrant, and her mother was U.S.-born of Czech descent. Her father was "not mainstream anti-Castro," like most Cubans in the United States; he did not come to this country as a political migrant or exile but arrived prior to Castro's rise to power in 1959. As a medical doctor, he was a highly skilled immigrant who left the island because he wanted to earn a larger income. She "resisted" her Cuban heritage in her youth—primarily because of her father's "emotional roller-coaster" tendencies and the gender imbalance in the household, her brothers getting more privileges and fewer household duties than she did. These gender asymmetries and her desire for gender equity were the reasons why she out-married with a white man.

Using the strong language of "slavery," Sylvia explained the gendered household division of labor in her family of origin as well as her "rebellion" against that family arrangement:

Every Sunday the Cubans would come over.... The Cubans were loud, and it was all smoky. They were crazy, and they would eat a lot and stay up really late.... The women would clean up. And I was like, "No, that's not me." I was very rebellious. I couldn't deal with [it].... I gravitate to the Czech side because I'm like, "I am not a slave." The Cuban heritage was women were played down and I just rejected it. I rebelled against my dad so much.... My mom wanted me to cook for [my dad when she was on a trip], and I absolutely refused because she didn't ask my brothers also. I was like, "No way."

This gendered division of labor was supported by the family's Cuban friends. Sylvia recalled: "My mom divided up kitchen duties so we each had a day on the calendar to clean the dishes. I remember my dad's friends just being horrified that the boys would have to clean the kitchen."

Coming from a family where her "brothers were . . . put on pedestals," Sylvia "rebelled" against her family, rejecting the subservient role they expected of her: "I had no tolerance for it at all. So I was always assertive to make sure I was treated fairly." Preferring an out-group that was free from the weight of experience, Sylvia said, "I don't think I ever could have married a Hispanic, especially when [he] was *really* Hispanic, [and] wasn't . . . diluted. I just don't think I could have dealt with it." Using her personal experience to negotiate desire, all of Sylvia's previous boyfriends were white and "just very American." As a self-proclaimed "diluted Hispanic," Sylvia willfully "diluted" her Cuban side, aligning herself more closely with her mother's more serene manner, which she associated with

Czech heritage and whiteness. Sylvia protected her gender identity in her choice to out-marry.

Sylvia recoiled from her father's strong emotionality and his strict gender expectations, saying, "I went the other direction." The roadmap for her internally negotiated desire was clear: she did not want a husband with her father's dominant personality traits. Putting negotiated desire into practice, she color-coded overbearing male power, rejected Latino men, and married a "Wonder Bread white" man:

> I mean, there was so much conflict with my dad. My husband is Wonder Bread white. . . . His nickname my dad always called him was blanco [white]. He is so white. It was a funny name. It wasn't meant to be offensive at all. He always called him blanco. It was so funny. My dad was pretty dark-skinned. I remember several times just being . . . so frustrated with my dad. I was just like, "I'm marrying a white guy." Plus, he was very emotional. . . . I remember thinking, "Is it just 'cuz he's Cuban?" . . . There's a lot of Cubans that aren't like that, but . . . that's the way I associated it.

Sylvia color-coded high emotionality as a Cuban male quality. She even checked herself, understanding that emotionality and Cuban identity are not tightly fused, and yet she nonetheless "associated" the two. When she was directly asked, "What were you trying to avoid?" Sylvia replied, "The high emotions was a lot of it. . . . I don't know if I . . . really consciously said 'Cuban,' but [I wanted] someone who was not controlling or . . . emotionally a roller coaster." Having heard this knee-jerk reaction of color-coding before, I asked Sylvia whether she might run across white men who were emotional roller coasters. She acknowledged this possibility more than other interviewees: "[As a lawyer,] I work with a lot of women who are victims of abuse. And most of their husbands are white, because we are in this white community. . . . So it wasn't like I thought white guys were . . . more emotionally in control." Unlike other Latina interviewees, Sylvia was aware that any man could inflict abuse. Yet, with her father in mind, she too veered away from Hispanic men as a precautionary measure, concluding, "I don't even feel that I'm attracted to Hispanic men." Eyeing greater gender freedom, Sylvia's negotiated desire diverted her attention away from Latino men and flat-lined her attraction for them.

Natal family dynamics do not wholly predict marital choices; dating experiences also shape desire. Cynthia Herrera-Redgrave did not grow up with a domineering father and did not color-code patriarchy with Latino men. Despite this absence of male dominance in her natal home, Cynthia's notions of gender freedom and her hopes for socioeconomic upward mobility exerted pressure when deciding whether or not to marry her Mexican fiancé, the father of her first child.

As a child in Lawrence, Kansas, she lived in a Mexican American neighborhood, where she observed that, "if you didn't marry a Mexican it was . . . frowned upon. . . . [Therefore,] when I was younger, like high school, I probably [thought] I was gonna marry somebody who was Mexican." Once in college, Cynthia met different types of people and considered dating beyond her coethnic circles. She transitioned from assuming endogamy to opening up to exogamy:

> It . . . wasn't even that I was looking for Mexican guys to go out with. I just . . . figured that's who would ask me out or I would go out with. Once I got to college . . . you get that experience of seeing different people and talking to different people and just going, "Oh my gosh, there is a whole different world out here." . . . [There are] even different Hispanics than, you know, the Mexican little community I'm used to. There's a lot of difference out here now and . . . I'm going, "This is just a different world."

For Cynthia, exposure to a racially diverse community and a variegated Hispanic community in college opened up the possibility for interracial and interethnic bonds.

Unlike Celeste and Sylvia, Cynthia had no preexisting desire to outmarry to "protect" her gender identity. Cynthia did not complain about an overbearing father whose masculinist behavior she wanted to avoid. Not engaged in color-coding behavior, Cynthia evaluated her relationship with her Mexican fiancé and decided to discontinue the romance to avoid a patriarchal relationship. She explained:

> I just think we were coming from different mind-sets, you know. . . . My dad just always . . . had me set for . . . "You . . . just get a career. You're gonna have a house. You're gonna just aspire to keep moving up and on. . . ." I don't think that was [my fiancé's] mind-set. . . . I would rather just drive a junky car and have a really nice house, where he was more in the mind-set that a car is that big thing and your house may be not so great. . . . I'm the opposite.

Concerns over gender and class overlap here. Fearing conflict over money and disregard for her opinions, Cynthia detailed the race, class, and gender complexity of her apprehensions: "Plus I had gone to college and he didn't. . . . He had that machismo kind of thing where it was kind of hard that your wife is . . . [traveling] and meeting new people. I was making more money than he was making." A clash of gender expectations plus discord around financial priorities contributed to their breakup. Her issues around gender relations and class mobility were obviated when Cynthia, as a working woman, met her husband, Mitch, at the computing company where they both worked.

Many Latina women featured in this chapter made gender goal–oriented choices to out-marry. The overwhelmingly dominant pattern was Latina women feeling compelled to out-marry to escape patriarchy, as first embodied by their fathers and then as generalized to Latino men. Secondarily, some Latinas experienced gender inequality in romantic relationships that they sometimes dissolved before turning to white men in their expanded dating pools, who, they believed, embodied a different set of characteristics. Latinas who saw intermarriage as a way to attain their gender goals color-coded their Latino fathers' domineering masculinity as a Latino male trait rather than as a characteristic specific to their fathers or one potentially possessed by non-Latino men. Through this mental fusion of Latino men with women's subordination, gender goal–oriented Latinas castigated the entire category of Latino men, excluding them from their dating pool for fear of gender oppression. This self-protective maneuver homogenized Latino masculinity and did not allow Latino men to prove these assumptions wrong, since they were eliminated as dating partners.[11] In sum, the priority these women put on their gender freedom justified their decision to out-marry.

Class Calculations

Those who made "class calculations" to out-marry considered socioeconomic status gain to be paramount. I have no examples of men who attempted to improve their class situation through intermarriage, nor do I have examples of whites who used this class-based strategy for intermarriage. It was Latina women in particular who were focused on class status and who observed that socioeconomic status is changeable over the life course and variable owing to a spouse's economic situation. The intersection of race, class, and gender "triple oppression" embodied by less economically privileged Latina women could create a preference for white men, who were associated with race, class, and gender privilege.[12] This is a constructed preference: the structure of occupational niches and pay scales positions white men economically ahead of Latino men. In class-calculated out-marriages, group-level socioeconomic status differentials play into partner preference. A Latina preference for white men based on class status reflects the structural constraints of the labor market and the racism in economic markets—the invisible hand behind romantic predilections.

Chiefly concerned with socioeconomic upward mobility, Rowena Cooper prioritized socioeconomic advancement on her wish list of attributes in a lifetime partner. In her story, a class calculation to out-marry informed her racial choices. Born in Texas but raised in California as one of seven children, her labor contractor parents struggled financially: "We were poor. We . . . didn't have a lot of money. . . . What do you have when you're that many in the family? We lived in a two-bedroom house with seven children in that house. . . . [We had] a little bit of meat and a lot of potatoes, a lot of rice and beans. That was it; a treat once in a month. Once a month was fried chicken. . . . We really didn't know that we were, per se, poor."

Rowena's parents worked in Kern County, California, and they lived outside of Bakersfield, in "a little town that you blink and you pass." Rowena grew up seeing labor stratification, her parents occupying a middleman minority position between the white farm owners and the Hispanic farmhands.[13] She learned about a labor system stratified by race just by observing her surroundings: "The Caucasians were . . . the farmers. The Hispanics were the worker bees." Her own family's class status was marginal:

> Did we have hard times? Yeah, we had hard times. We did. We shared seven dresses between two girls. There were four girls in one bedroom. As we got older I wound up sleeping on the floor, but we still had our own room. Did I feel bad about it? No. Do I blame my parents? No. They did the best they could with what they had. My mom kept saying, "I want you to do better than we did. I want you to go get your education. I want you to go do this. I want you to have better than me."

Given her upbringing with meager financial resources, Rowena valued financial security. One way to "have it better than her mother" was to marry someone financially secure.

In response to her marginal class status, Rowena creatively increased her economic standing by bargaining with her parents to let her keep her earnings to buy clothes. As early as age thirteen, Rowena was concerned with her "presentation of self" and how her attire could reflect her upwardly mobile class status.[14] Rowena's determination to climb the socioeconomic ladder and her presentation of self affected her dating options, both in terms of who found her attractive—Caucasian men were attracted to her, while Mexican men thought she was haughty—and whom she found appealing:

ROWENA: My sister and I were talking about that . . . : "Why is it [our dates are] always Caucasian?" I said, "I never thought about it. . . ." It just happens. Maybe it's because they're the ones that are showing the interest. . . . More so than the Hispanic[s]. . . . I think they [whites] feel more confident to approach us than the others.

AUTHOR: So white men feel more confident to approach you than Hispanic men?

ROWENA: Yeah.

AUTHOR: I wonder why?

ROWENA: Growing up in the small town that I grew up in, they said that we were up here [*raises her hand to indicate a high level*]. We weren't, because we talked to everybody. We didn't care who you were. We always were friendly. But we dressed better. When I worked in the fields at age thirteen, I approached my mom and dad and I said, "If you let me keep my check I will buy us girls . . . school clothes." . . . My parents jumped on it and said, "Okay." So I did. . . . I would buy the clothes, and we would share them. . . . So guess what? We bought nice clothes. I think we were unapproachable.

By using her own earnings to purchase new clothes, Rowena showed the value she placed on presenting an upwardly mobile appearance. By using her hard-earned resources to dress well, she displayed herself as moving up the socioeconomic ladder; as a result, Mexican young men found her "unapproachable" and Caucasian young men pursued her. By design, Rowena positioned herself to appeal to white men. This type of search for whiteness, in concert with Kelly Chong's research on inter-married Asian Americans—whose "desires for 'white identification' to avoid racism . . . [were] typically accompanied by attraction to Caucasian boys from a young age"—can persist throughout the life course.[15]

Using a theory of homogamy, or "like attracts like," Rowena described the class dynamics of her dating and marriage choices and those of her sisters.[16] If class mobility aspirations inspired her earning and spending choices, they were also central to how her dating and marital "tastes" developed:

AUTHOR: The Caucasians who were interested in you—were they equal or higher in terms of class?

ROWENA: They were higher; they were already up there. We were doing this [*indicates an upward move with her hand*]. They saw us as moving up. . . . The Hispanic guys . . . stayed the same. That's the only thing I can think of. *If you dress less than, what do you attract?* You know how the saying goes: "You are who you associate with." . . . How do you look? How do you dress? Do you look like a chola [a working-class Latina]? We didn't look like cholas at all. The ones that were cholas felt intimidated because we dressed better than they did. So that's probably why it was so natural for us to marry Caucasians I guess. They were the ones that came around.

Key to this rationale for "dressing up to date up" is her rhetorical question: "if you dress less than, what do you attract?" Using "you are what you wear" logic, Rowena and her sisters distinguished themselves from their modest circumstances through the strategic use of clothing. The structure of the dating marketplace also affected their decisions: in a racially stratified context where "Hispanics were the worker bees" and Caucasians were ranked higher racially and socioeconomically, each category had its advantages and disadvantages. In a context where a Latina woman might end up with either a Hispanic or a Caucasian, effortful action to secure romance with a white man increased the chances of rising in the ranks of race and class. Through their purchasing power, Rowena and her sisters aimed to appear higher-class; by fashioning themselves to appeal to Caucasian men who were "already up there," or class-advantaged, it became "natural" for them to marry Caucasians. Rowena discursively naturalized her class and race ascension, disguising the effort embedded in her intermarriage with a middle-class white man.

At the time of the interview, Rowena was four years into her second marriage; her first marriage, from which she had two sons, lasted twenty-five years. Uncoincidentally, both husbands were white; her prospects for class mobility had remained a factor in whom she married. Rowena's story contrasts with an earlier study on intermarriage that found that Latino partners do not "expressly associate marriage with a white partner as a route to upward mobility."[17] In contradistinction, Rowena was in pursuit of a higher-class, white suitor. Careful shopping and attention to her attire allowed her to *appear* higher-class than her bank account or family assets would have shown. Her calculated "presentation of self" made her appealing to those who found middle- and upper-class styles attractive and who could afford to dress well themselves as well as support Rowena's expensive taste.

The sociology theorist Pierre Bourdieu informs us that "tastes" are socially constructed and are indicators of class status.[18] Taste unites members of a social class and helps them distinguish themselves from other classes. Preferences are products of upbringing, education level, class background, and social standing, and they function to mark class membership and boundaries.[19] Thus, tastes are encoded with class markers. Bourdieu writes: *"Taste classifies, and it classifies the classifier.* Social subjects, classified by their classifications, distinguish themselves by the distinctions they make."[20] With this class-inflected definition of taste in mind, we can see that Rowena's emphasis on a fashionable presentation of self that overestimated her class status was a calculated way to attract upwardly mobile men.

Bourdieu's theory of cultural tastes assumes that the non-elite classes accept their status: "Dominated agents . . . tend to attribute to themselves what the distribution attributes to them, refusing what they are refused."[21] Rowena's conscious attempts to improve her class station through marriage with a higher-status man, however, contrast sharply with this theory. Instead, social exchange theory offers insight into Rowena's class calculations. Social exchange theory posits that lower-status racial-ethnic groups trade resources such as wealth, education, or beauty for a mate with a higher racial-ethnic status as they engage in what is colloquially known as "marrying up."[22] Social exchange theory helps us understand how Rowena traded on her youth and beauty for the racial and class privilege of a white, middle-class mate.

In a marriage market in which the ability to perform attractiveness to whites is based in part on physical appearance, lighter-skinned Latinas have greater cachet. Skin color affects not only how Latinos are treated in the dating market but also how *they* treat and select others.[23] At sixty-two years old, Rowena was an attractive woman with light skin who obviously still put care into her appearance. She wore her reddish-brown hair short and styled in large waves. Gold and green eye makeup showed off her lighter brown eyes and paired nicely with her pale skin. According to her, she "used to have quite a trim figure in younger years and was the envy of her first husband's business partners and their wives." She had physical attractiveness and sexual appeal to "trade" for a white, middle-class income–earning spouse. Lacking a college degree, she capitalized on her beauty to achieve her goal of financial security and racial privilege.

In the United States, the class stratification system maps onto a racial hierarchy, with racial minorities historically and currently disadvantaged in comparison to whites.[24] Given this social structure, Rowena's romantic "taste" for white men (which we know from Bourdieu was class-inflected and marked distinctions) revealed a desire for socioeconomic and white racial privilege. The desire for class and racial privilege undergirded not only her dating patterns but her marital choices, both her first and second husbands being white.

Trying to attract middle- or upper-class white men was a successful strategy in Rowena's family: "Believe it or not, out of four sisters, three married Caucasians and one married a Hispanic," she noted. Rowena met her Caucasian first husband while working at a bank where she was a teller and he was a customer. In Rowena's description of her attraction to her first husband, a Bourdieuan reading of taste is once again relevant as a signifier of class status. When I asked, "What would you say were the main qualities that you were interested in?" Rowena responded: "We thought about the same things. We talked about the same things. . . . We liked the same things. We had goals. . . . We were married for twenty-five years. . . . Our tastes were the same, so there was a lot of commonality there between the two of us. . . . If [I] wanted to purchase something, he would say, 'Oh, I like that.' . . . We enjoyed nice things. We saved money to get what we wanted." For Rowena and her first husband, who both had a penchant for "nice things" and used their combined earning power to purchase coveted items, financial objectives were paramount.

Latina women gave a great deal of thought to socioeconomic standing when contemplating long-term partnerships. Mexican American Bianca Stroeh, a longtime resident of predominantly Hispanic Pico Rivera, California, initially preferred to date Mexican-origin men, but then she realized that her list of desired qualities in a mate ran longer than someone who spoke Spanish, was Catholic, and could dance. Bianca had a Mexican Catholic boyfriend when she first met her husband-to-be at work, at which point she decided that the boyfriend "was a loser. I was like . . . 'You meet these requirements, but you don't meet these other qualifications. . . . I'm just going to have to let you go.' " Noting his financial stability, Bianca's family was supportive of her relationship with Chuck, who converted to Catholicism for her:

> Believe it or not, it was actually my family who liked him. He had a job, and he had a car. "Bianca, go out with him!" . . . As far as . . . the respect issues that you might find in Mexican culture, he already had those . . . manners. . . . My family [liked that] he had a job and a car. The boyfriend before him didn't, so they saw that as more like . . . the basic requirements.

In theory, Bianca preferred in-marriage, but her exposure to non-Latino romantic possibilities in college and her requirement of socioeconomic stability led her to her white husband. Initially put off by the idea of dating her husband—she told him, "You're not Mexican and you're not Catholic, and only one of those can be changed"—she married him once he embraced Catholicism.

In "class calculation" out-marriage, Latina women position themselves for romance with white men as a way to consolidate class and racial privilege. Financial standing can either be a preexisting priority or emerge through the dating process, becoming increasingly important as they evaluate their dating and marital options. Latina women who desired a higher class status and perceived white men as having a dramatically higher standing in the racialized labor market oriented themselves toward white men. To be clear, Latina women with a desire for long-term financial stability also in-married with Latino men, but they also told me that they filtered their dating prospects on qualities such as whether they were "goal setters," were "educated," or had a "work ethic." Such class concerns were gendered: alongside their Latina counterparts, white women were also concerned with the financial prospects of a partner. Nevertheless, aside from the singular white woman in this study who grew up in poverty, the white women's concern about the impact of marriage on their socioeconomic trajectory was muted relative to that of the Latina women. Class mobility via marriage is a focal point for women but not for men. Anxiety over socioeconomic status is a gendered burden: women anticipate that they are tying their economic future to their husband, and men expect to be the primary breadwinner for the household.[25] This gendered perspective arises from a variety of sources. For some, it is a holdover from earlier times when marriage was more definitively about men's consolidation of landholding and women's dependence.[26] For others, it arises from women's lower earning capacity relative to men in the paid labor market, and for still other women, paid employment is precluded by their desire to be primarily responsible for the private domain.

Race remains a front-running feature of dating and marriage even where class is paramount because cross-racial intimacy with whites is a strategy to improve class standing. Race is present in class calculations because knowledge of the racialized labor hierarchy and wealth distribution affects the appraisal of potential romantic partners. Interracial intimacy is a way for the less privileged to achieve class advantage, race being salient in how economic prospects are inferred and marriage being seen as a way to solidify or improve class standing.

Racial Policing

Sexuality tends to be viewed "as 'natural' and 'private,' even though it is simultaneously an arena of constant surveillance and control."[27] Racial policing of romantic boundaries, or "border patrolling," is a chief way in which Latino families respond to the possibility of losing racial status.[28] In America's racial hierarchy, racial groups are invested in maintaining their social distance from lower-status groups. The "group threat" theory of racial prejudice holds that prejudice is fundamentally about a "sense of where the two racial groups *belong*."[29] The aim of racial prejudice, then, is to maintain a sense of group superiority.[30] Group threat theory explains that interracial conflict is spurred on by the risk of territory and income loss.[31]

Among Latinos, group threat inspires antiblack discrimination stemming from fear of status loss. Latino intermarriage with whites is therefore not singularly about closing social distance with whites but also about increasing social distance from blacks. Antiblack discrimination, deployed to preserve Latinos' relative group privilege, pushes blacks further away.

Nathan Lucero espoused antiblack prejudice, as modeled to him by his father. Making romantic decisions in a context wherein whites were afforded the highest racial status, Nathan married a white woman in pursuit of racial status achievement.[32] Yet Nathan's agenda was not only to decrease his social distance from whites but also to *increase* his social distance from blacks. He tried to ensure his interracial family's racial status as closer to whiteness than blackness by disapproving of his daughter's choice of dating black men. His "racial project" of racial aggrandizement was at stake in his children's courtship and marriage choices, so he followed a historical pattern of providing (unsolicited) advice in the hopes of influencing romantic outcomes.[33] Nathan hid behind his father's bigotry as he established dating ground rules for his daughters:

> I tell both my girls, "You know, girls, you can marry anywhere between Mexican and white, Asian, or whatever you want to do. It's up to you." But I'm concerned with what can happen with the genes. . . . I know if the girls happen to marry a black, it's gonna upset [my father] very much. I told them that I'm very open, but just remember the genetics. I have to look at it that way.

Saying that he himself was "very open," Nathan pointed to his father as the one who had strong antiblack prejudice that would be inflamed if one of his granddaughters married a black man. In this convoluted advice, Nathan drew on a biological understanding of race to justify antiblack prejudice. In the list of options he offered his daughters, he endorsed Mexicans, whites, and Asians and excluded African Americans and Native Americans; in other words, he delimited their dating options to the middle and upper ranks of the racial hierarchy. A black-nonblack divide has arguably come to typify contemporary American race relations.[34] Access to resources, privilege, and romantic partners now depends on whether one falls on the "black" or "nonblack" side of the divide.

Nathan would not permit his daughters to marry "down" and racially policed his teenage daughter who had a penchant for blacks:

> I had to sit [my daughter Haley] down, and I said, "Haley, you've got this wide range; you know Asian, Indian [Asian subcontinent], and white. You have this whole range. You're telling me you can't find anyone in between

this range? It has to be black. It's gonna be your decision but . . . once you get the reputation. . . . I'm not saying you can't. I'm just saying be careful. . . . If you're asking me would I prefer anywhere between Mexican and white, I would. . . ." And she says she's . . . attracted to the half black instead of full black. . . . The baby would [be] half white, a quarter Mexican, and a quarter black. I don't know what that's gonna look like.

Nathan outlined a dating "range" for his daughter. He was preoccupied with racial status, reputation, and the aesthetics of racial mixing, all of which was bound up in his daughters' dating choices. Once subject to racial policing himself, Nathan now indulged in that behavior with his daughters, cautioning them against blacks and urging them toward Mexicans and whites. Nathan viewed dating and marriage as a "life transition" that "amplifies racial and phenotypic hierarchies," and he exerted paternal power to keep his daughter Haley within an acceptable "range."[35] Through racial policing and "border patrolling," he promoted either a racial status quo (endogamy with Latinos) or racial status achievement (exogamy with whites).

The intersection of region and gender in Kansas led Latino families to strongly caution young women against "downward" racial mixing. The state has a large nonblack population, and Latino families viewed cross-racial dating with blacks as an avoidable norm violation. Latina women faced stronger counsel against dating blacks than men because of their procreative capacity and their presumed role as the "carrier of culture."[36] Here we see how "regimes of sexuality shape ethnic relations, conflicts, and boundaries . . . [and] how the construction of . . . boundaries depends on the establishment and enforcement of rules and regulations governing sexual demeanor, partners, and reproduction."[37] Forty-three-year-old Lorena Cota, from Kansas, dated a black man covertly against her family's wishes: "I [wasn't] able to tell my family that I was dating an African American. . . . My dad . . . wouldn't have approved. . . . Social pressures [were] to date more Caucasian and Hispanic . . . only." Another Kansas Latina in her forties, Cassie Hoffman, who was previously married to a black man, had been "a little nervous" about informing her parents of her engagement because, she confessed, "he was black and I didn't know . . . if they would approve or not."

Families have a strong hand in setting guidelines for how their children negotiate desire. Parents can intervene in their children's lives to exercise antiblack prejudice, as when Noelle Puente's father transferred her to a Catholic high school in Topeka to remove her from African American peers. Defensive moves such as this show how racial boundaries are reinscribed and how "racial group-making entails prescriptions and proscriptions about different forms of intimacy."[38] Boundaries against black men were clear to Noelle: "I knew that dating somebody black wasn't gonna . . . go anywhere. . . . I ended up at a bar that my uncle . . . showed up [at] and my uncle actually followed us [out]. Then he tried . . . to beat [my date] up. Then I was confronted by my dad: 'You have a choice. You either choose your family or you choose him.' " Noelle never dated the black man again. This formative family experience lay behind Noelle's assertion that "I knew that I would not marry somebody African American." Yet her "knowing" that she would not marry a black man did not occur in a vacuum: the threat of being ostracized by her family silenced her dissent, first in high school and then later in her choice to marry a Latino. Despite structural opportunities to find a cross-racial mate, family pressure to form in-group liaisons and antiblack prejudice help explain why people become less likely to be in an interracial relationship as they age.[39] Noelle's negotiated desire for a coethnic spouse was grounded in her decision to outlaw black men rather than risk family excommunication.

Latino men in the study also discriminated against blacks to cling to relative racial privilege. Although families' racial policing of Latina women's dating was more rigorous, because of their reproductive capacity and their status as women whose reputation had to be defended in a patriarchal society, the families of Latino men also exerted antiblack discriminatory pressure on them. In California, where the prospect of dating blacks was a foreseeable option, antiblack messaging in these families was more crucial than in Kansas. Thirty-four-year-old Mario Bermudez concealed his cross-racial romances from his immigrant parents and eventually married a woman with Mexican American and white heritage. Mario likened interracial intimacy to homosexuality, underscoring the transgressive quality of the pairing: "When I used to bring home . . . a black girl . . . I would never bring her around . . . my whole family. . . . It's almost like you're gay, kinda. Like . . . you're 'coming out.' " It was "a big deal" for Mario to date non-Mexicans, and in his belief that dating a black woman was tantamount to being homosexual, he was invoking another identity that is highly policed in the Latino community.[40]

Latinos who occupy a middle position in the U.S. racial hierarchy discriminate against blacks to safeguard their relative racial privilege. To the extent that romantic preferences are not always expressions of an attraction to a particular racial group but a way of seeking social distance from other racial groups, "personal preference . . . normalize[s] racism."[41] Associating with whites and racially policing against romance with blacks are complementary processes of status achievement. In combination, these race-inflected logics encourage Latino and white intermarriage and inhibit Latino and non-Latino minority intermarriage (which does happen, though less frequently; see chapter 4). Although Latina women are most strongly affected by their families' racial policing owing to their position as literal and figurative reproducers (of children and culture), Latino men are not immune to this policing. Finally, where there is an ample supply of whites, such as in Kansas, narratives of antiblackness are stronger, and dipping into the black dating pool is viewed as avoidable and anathema.

PREFERENTIAL OUT-MARRIAGE: WHITES

Imagery and Previous Romantic Relationships

Popular images influence sexual preferences, which in turn affect dating and marriage choices.[42] Racialized, gendered, and classed images have staying power and can direct people's desires. Moreover, imagery has history. For example, white men's attraction to Latina women originated in the early days of conquest in the Southwest when Anglo-American male travelers would denounce Mexican men but exempt "Mexican women . . . whom they described as far superior in industry and character."[43] Racialized and gendered depictions of Latina women are now encoded in mainstream media, which represents Latinas as embodying "desirable femininity, domesticity, and the heteronormative family."[44] Imagery of the "other" can shape sexual desire and notions of who is a desirable partner.

Such imagery and the associations that white men have with Latina women lead to a sexualized preference for them. White men interviewees consistently discussed Latina women as beautiful, sexy, and possessing virtues that made them good wives.[45] Kent Guthrie was unsure of the origin of the notion that dark-haired, dark-skinned women are good wives, yet it had piqued his interest in phenotypically dark women:

> Maybe it's because of stereotyping from growing up through TV or jokes. I just thought a darker-haired gal would be more of a wife material, a better partner for me. I just always thought . . . the dark-haired gal . . . would be more [of a] fit for me and would be a better spouse. . . . I just [had] that vision in my head. I like smaller girls with dark hair . . . particularly Hispanic and Asian. I had that thought in my head when I was growing up that blondes are fun but darker girls would be more stable, more prone to family life.

Kent linked his attraction to physically dark women with virtues such as "wife material," "better spouse," and "more prone to family life." The media homogenizes Latinos and Latinas, "hegemonically taming" the racial category by reproducing "dominant norms, values, beliefs, and public understandings."[46] Media representations of Latinas fomented the "appreciation for darker-skin females" that directed Kent's dating patterns and marital choice. "Heteronormative sexual stereotypes" had infiltrated Kent's thinking as he evaluated the moral value of the differently racialized romantic options before him.[47]

Beyond the media imagery and discourse that construct desire, prior satisfying relationships with Latinas can fuel white men's desire for them. In a "cumulative causation" logic whereby a trend becomes self-perpetuating, white men who date and have positive experiences with Latinas continue to date Latinas.[48] As we saw earlier in this chapter regarding some Latina women's refusal to date coethnics in order to avoid patriarchy, certain attributes become color-coded.[49] For white men intimately involved with Latina women, popular imagery and prior satisfying relationships with Latinas set persistent desire in motion. Kent described his dating patterns:

> I dated blond-haired gals when I was growing up. It just didn't ever seem to work out. . . . The long-term relationships [were] always [with] the dark-haired gals. . . . I think a lot of blond-haired gals are beautiful. I just always leaned toward the dark-haired gals. . . . Maybe it was because I did have relationships that were always long-term with the darker-hair [women]. I don't know if that has anything to do with it, but those always seemed to work out. I just found something that worked for me and went with it.

In the spirit of cumulative causation, once Kent found a "type" of woman who "worked for him," he did not question the pattern but "went with it." He restricted his dating pool to dark-haired women, his romantic successes cementing his predilection for brunettes.

Despite this pattern of preferences, it takes the wind out of the sails of a love story to identify the reasons that spark a romance. Injecting love back into the story of how he met his wife, Kent highlighted emotion and caprice: "I just happened to be living my life, and we just ended up falling for each other at the same time. I think it was just opportunity and chance." This perspective tells part of the story, but it does not tell it all: people are primed for particular kinds of love as the result of their experiences and how they apply lessons learned from those experiences in the local dating realm. For Kent, the future he had imagined with his wife had panned out: "She's been perfect for raising our kids. I have no complaints whatsoever. All my expectations were met on her being a mother, a wife and partner."

Demonstrating that prior successful relationships with Latinas perpetuate desire for Latinas was Shawn Downing, whose "first love" was a Latina woman. "At a certain level," he thought, he might have "associated that really intense overwhelming" feeling with Latinas. However, he did not rule out options based on race: "After that [breakup,] I would date white chicks . . . you know, whoever I was attracted to, and race really didn't play a part [in] it consciously, I don't think." Nevertheless, Shawn's fusion of love with Latinas had shaped his dating preferences:

> I think that maybe on a certain level it was my preference to date a Latina girl. . . . I'm thinking maybe . . . I associated [a Latina] . . . [with that earlier] awesome time in my life. [That] may have actually kind of carried over. . . . If someone were to ask me when I met Liz [his wife], "What's your preference?" I probably would have said, "Yeah, I am more attracted to Latina girls than most others." So I think that might have actually played a part in us initially getting together . . . looking back on it. . . . She sort of fit that mold. . . . Maybe on some level I was looking for that. . . . It's kind of hard to say. Because I was young and horny at the time too.

The idea of a Latina "fitting a mold" recalls both Shawn's prior loving relationship and popular imagery, and his comment about being "young and horny" opens the door to a discussion of Latinas being viewed by white men as exotic and erotic.[50] However, he may simply have been referring to raging hormones that do not discriminate based on race.

What types of images of Latina womanhood fostered Shawn's desire for Latinas? When asked what attracted him to Latina women, he referred to both culture and attraction:

> I think it was two things. . . . When I had briefly been exposed to that culture, I thought it was cool . . . [and] interesting. . . . Physically, I was attracted to Latinas more. I think there might have been a mystique about their culture that I just found attractive for some reason. I, I, I knew that, for the most part, I would be getting with a girl that uh . . . I'll stop on that one, 'cuz I wasn't really quite sure where I was going with that . . . what was the question again?

Between the "cool" culture, his physical attraction to Latinas, and his "first love" being a Latina, Shawn was predisposed toward Latinas. When expounding on why he found Latinas especially attractive, he stuttered and declined to say more, asking to be redirected. It was unclear whether he stopped in mid-thought because he simply was unsure where he was headed or because it was awkward to discuss issues of sexual attraction to Latinas with a Latina interviewer.

Previous romantic relationships with Latinas encourage white men to seek other Latina women to date once one relationship ends. Popular conceptions of Latinas as appealing and wifely spark white men's initial interest and positive intimate relationships with them instantiate that desire, at least among white men who ultimately marry Latina women.

MULTICULTURALISM, PARENTAL TEACHINGS OF EQUALITY, AND A GLOBAL PERSPECTIVE

The current political climate in the United States of ostensibly valuing diversity and multiculturalism opens the door to multidirectional cultural shifts. In earlier times, such as the 1920s, "Americanization programs" put a great deal of pressure on immigrants and nonwhites to conform to a white standard of American identity.[51] In contrast, by the 1990s diversity policies in business and higher education had become common, taking the form of multicultural requirements, voluntary ethnic organizations, and diversity initiatives and trainings.[52] The logic undergirding diversity policies also shifted, from affirmative action programs targeting injustices to newer diversity management styles predicated on the notion that differences are inherently valuable and lead to greater productivity.[53] In higher education, the pro-multiculturalism motto became "excellence through diversity."[54] Americans' attitudes have shifted accordingly: their stated tolerance for diverse ancestries has increased over the last century—with the caveat that attitudes toward immigrants did not improve over the last decades of the twentieth century.[55] This is the greater cultural milieu in which the interviewees operated—the youth being steeped in a generally more tolerant environment, with the exception of the lightning-rod topic of immigration. A criticism of multiculturalism, however, is that it not only reifies and exaggerates the importance of cultural distinctions but elides structural power differences.[56]

Multiculturalism, parental teachings of equality, and a global perspective acquired through military service all shape preferences by expanding the area of socially sanctioned desire. For people steeped in an environment that values diversity (at least formally), interracial romance becomes a possibility. An ethos of racial tolerance that approves of cross-racial connections can heighten dormant desire or create desire anew, linking macro-level discourse to the institution of family. The ideology of both progressive parents and the U.S. military, which prioritizes multiculturalism, paves the way for interracial romance.

Parental endorsement of equality, or at least the lack of overt racial prejudices, stimulates openness to interracial relations. A sampling of statements offered by intermarried white respondents follows:

[My parents discussed how you] treat everybody equal and people deserve respect not based on color or appearance or class but the person themselves. . . .

I was taught to view people as individuals as opposed to assigning one to a whole group. (Ryan Carlisle)

One thing I give my parents a lot of credit for is we were brought up around all kinds of people. . . . My parents . . . used to bowl in a bowling league . . . [that] had African American people, white, Asian, Hispanic. . . . You could almost call it like a United Nations bowling league. . . . I feel fortunate that we weren't sheltered from people of different races or ethnicities. (Chuck Stroeh)

[Hispanics] were just another shade of brown. I happen to be a very, very light brown. I have always thought of it that way. My parents never said anything. (Trudy Ybarra)

My parents were pretty straightforward: as long as . . . the girls were nice people, I don't think my mom or dad had a preference as to what color they were. . . . There [were] no stereotypes. (Mitch Redgrave)

Multiculturalism had most profoundly shaped the views of white interviewees. From active discussion and demonstration of racial equality to tacit racial messages based on the absence of negative stereotypes, their white parents had inculcated in their children racial lessons that bore on their intimate lives. Espousing multiculturalism is a privilege of whiteness. The white privilege of white interviewees' parents allowed them to advocate for racial equality from a position insulated from racism. In contrast, Latino interviewees' parents instructed their children on how to navigate social terrain riven by racial politics.[57] For whites, multiculturalism stemming from parental teachings or the U.S. military had opened them up to interracial romance, broadening their options for sexual partners.

For Sheldon Hoffman, a fifty-four-year-old white man who was born in Kentucky but had lived all but one year of his life in Kansas, his parents and his religion had instructed him on equality: "Christian background . . . taught that [Hispanics and blacks] are no different than we are and that they have the same rights. . . . I think my folks made it a point that . . . they are no different than we are. It was always easy for me . . . to have friends of different race and backgrounds." The civil rights movement had also critically shaped his views on tolerance. Sheldon attended Lawrence High School during the race riots of 1970, when civil rights and antiwar activists burned down the University of Kansas Student Union; afterwards Lawrence would be called "the Berkeley of the Midwest," indicating that it was a hotbed of progressive political activism.[58] Sheldon also conversed in high school with teammates of other races who taught him that, "if you take the time to make friends and socialize, you'll find out that they have the same needs, the same concerns, the same misconceptions that you do. So it's having that opportunity to reach common ground and to really see other races as human." Parental teaching, Christianity, and his high school sports participation during the civil rights era all led Sheldon to believe in human equality—a belief that increased the chances for his intermarriage with a racial minority.

Multiculturalism values diversity and is a foundation for more tolerant racial attitudes.[59] Multiculturalism not only helps make Mexican ethnicity "a desirable and even a rewarding aspect of identity for Mexican Americans" but can make nonwhite ethnicity "desirable" and "rewarding" for whites as well.[60] As discussed in the next chapter, "ethnic sojourning," or "ethnic settling" and "affiliative ethnic identity"—signaling whites' migration into nonwhite racial and cultural territory—are permissible in an era of multiculturalism that endorses cross-racial intimacy.[61] Parental teachings that confirm multiculturalism advance the project of racial equality and make interracial romantic partnerships feasible.

In addition to the family, the military is another institution that can promote racial equality and a global perspective that decenters a whiteness and Americanness that typically go unnamed.[62] Others have documented that military occupations lead to sexual encounters, "war brides," and migration streams from the occupied to the occupying country.[63] Acquiring a global perspective from military service and from working collaboratively alongside people of different races and nationalities can be a democratizing force and erode stereotypes.[64] Monica McDermott's study of black-white interaction finds that "a lack of contact affords no opportunities for stereotypes to be challenged or for commonalities of experience and outlook to be realized."[65] The two white men who discussed their military service declared that the formal dogma, heterogeneous work environment, and international deployments mandating interracial cooperation taught them racial equality. Despite a distribution of "goods and burdens [that] sometimes disadvantage racial minorities," working across racial lines and in foreign countries while in the U.S. military fosters a tolerant perspective, opening the door to later romantic connections with diverse populations.[66]

Two tours in Iraq as a U.S. Marine amplified Ryan Carlisle's preexisting belief in human equality. Stationed in Iraq, where he was a racial minority for the first time, Ryan worked alongside civilians who were Arab, Turkish, and Iraqi. The global perspective provided by the military reinforced Ryan's earlier familial and religious cautions against making group-based judgments instead of evaluating people individually. Working alongside people from different nations and seeing their common human concerns strengthened Ryan's core belief in human equality. He discussed what it felt like to be a white male U.S. Marine stationed in Iraq during wartime and the assumptions of his wealth that he encountered:

> I was in boot camp when I was eighteen. . . . I had my twentieth and twenty-first birthdays in Iraq. . . . We worked with a lot of native Iraqi interpreters that would be from there or other . . . [Arabic]-speaking countries. . . . Workers were from the [Philippines] . . . or were Turkish. . . . So it was people from all over the place. . . . I had been exposed to people [who were not white], but the focus was more on *them* because I'm in my society and I'm white and [they] are the minority here. But being on the *opposite side* where they have perceptions about you. . . . One of the things that cracked us all up is: we're all low-ranking, especially my first tour, and make maybe $30,000 a year, and they were like, "You guys are all rich." And we were like, "No, we're definitely not." They would ask us to . . . talk to the president. And we were like, "We can't do this. What are you talking about?" It was interesting to see how they view us. They perceive us as white Americans, like you have a lot of power and authority. And we were like, "No, we really don't." That was different for me. I think that would be the first time . . . I saw how other people perceived me, it made me more aware of that sort of thing.

As a white man in Iraq surrounded by Arabs and imported Filipinos and Turks, Ryan had a glimpse of what it is to be a numerical minority. His experience was notably different from that of racial minorities because whiteness is associated the world over with power, colonialism, privilege, and cosmopolitanism.[67] Nevertheless, Ryan's international experience gave him a unique opportunity to confront racial and class-based stereotypes and become more empathetic to racial minorities in the United States, whose experience is replete with racialized assumptions. I inquired as to the connection between Ryan's military experience in Iraq and his view on race:

AUTHOR: How would you say that being in the Middle East during your two tours of duty and being among . . . people from different nations . . . affected your perspective on race?

RYAN: You kind of have this mind-set that we are the good guys and these certain people are bad guys and it's like a black-and-white line. Where, really, it's like there's probably as [many] bad guys in the U.S. as there are in Iraq or Iran or anywhere like that. . . . Especially being over there, [among] predominantly Arabs, I've learned that they are all individuals too and there are families that have the same values as I do. Just because they're a different race or ethnicity doesn't make them any different than me. It was harder to deal with when

> I got back here because people would just lump everybody
> into [one group]. . . . You hear a lot of times people being
> really extreme, "Oh, we just need to nuke the whole country."
> It's upsetting to me, because I've built relationships with
> these people that I would consider better than a lot of the
> people I know here. More hardworking and caring.

In this thoughtful answer, Ryan made a direct link between his service and friendships in Iraq and seeing beyond racial, national, and political differences to find shared human concerns. Ryan learned that "they are all individuals too," and that many of them "have the same values as I do," a discovery that, for him, crippled stereotypes and created an openness to intermarriage. Returning stateside, Ryan found that his realization about the overriding common humanity of all people rendered race, nation of birth, and undocumented status unimportant when he fell in love with Glenda and married her. As we will see in chapter 3, however, as their intermarriages catalyzed Ryan and others around race, trivializing racial differences in a way that lowered barriers to marriage did not equate to dismissing racial inequality altogether.

Kent Guthrie corroborated Ryan's account of how "serving with all types," being indoctrinated with the creed of service and sacrifice, and taking formal diversity classes minimized racial differences in the military. Kent was from a military family, and he followed his father's lead by also enlisting. He talked about military service reducing interpersonal prejudice through the diverse environment, the pursuit of common work objectives, and antiracist "army values":

> I've been in the military, and I've served with all types. I've served with
> African Americans. I've served with Hispanics. A good friend of the unit
> was killed when we were in Iraq, and he was Hispanic. We never thought
> of him as a Mexican American or anything like that. He was just a friend. . . .
> I know my dad served with all kinds of races, but he never said anything.
> It was just, "This is Sergeant this, Captain that." It was just a person, not
> categorized by race.

The military's strict hierarchy of authority based on nonracial criteria socialized Kent, as did his military father, to obey the chain of command. Kent experienced the military as a democratizing agent, even though it has been documented that race can play an insidious role in rankings, job assignments, and interactions in the military.[68] I asked Kent to expand on the instruction he received from his father and his official military training that the common goal must override any division that could hinder military success:

> AUTHOR: Could you say a little bit more about the military? How does that work in terms of teaching you or not teaching you about race?
>
> KENT: You don't get a choice of who you get to hang out with. Your roommate could be black, white, Asian, whatever. You just got along. It wasn't about what they looked like, just what they can do to help you out or what you can do to help them out. They drill it into you. . . . They always have these classes you have to go to every year about accepting others. Racism is not an army value. You have to get over that. I've never personally seen [racism], and I've been in twenty-three years. I know it's out there. I've heard of stories, but I've never personally seen it.

Kent was not oblivious to the possibility of racism in the military, but he insisted that racism is not "an army value" and he had never witnessed it. The racial equality fostered in his military family and during his tenure in the armed forces combined with his images of Latinas to result in his marriage to a Latina. An ethos of multiculturalism, parents who instruct their children on racial equality, and a global perspective achieved through international military experience can make intermarriage a conceivable— even preferable—option for whites.

CONVENIENCE OUT-MARRIAGE: LATINOS

Demographics

Out-marriage based on opportunity rather than preference is often a function of demographics: people have opportunities to meet their future spouses when Latinos and whites circulate in racially integrated settings or Latinos reside in predominantly white spaces (as in Kansas). Racial demographics bear strongly on Latinos in white spaces, where they are the numerical minority and whites are the most prevalent option for romance. Since I did not conduct interviews in majority-Latino areas with few whites, whites in my field sites were not constrained by demographics to date Latinos. In my sample, owing to the racial composition of my field sites, only Latinos engaged in convenience out-marriage since whites were the most "convenient" dating partner in mixed or largely white settings. Whites chose to marry Latinos based on factors other than demographic supply, making their marriages preferential in ways detailed earlier. My use here of the term "convenience out-marriage" draws from the social science term "convenience sample," which refers to a strategy for recruiting research project participants based on ease of availability.[69] This notion of demographics making some populations more "convenient" or accessible than others points to the fact that, absent taking extra measures, people are bound to seeking partners among a supply of individuals located in a particular place.

Matthijs Kalmijn's discussion of network theory, or supply and demand, is helpful in explaining how demographics construct marriage pools.[70] Acquaintance, which is shaped by the local population, precedes any intermarriage:

> First of all, our possible contacts are constrained by the local settings in which we are embedded. Examples of settings are the family, the neighborhood, the school, and so forth. These settings make up the supply of contact. Second, within the more limited and typically more homogeneous pool, potential interaction partners may choose (not) to interact with each other. This is the demand part of the interaction, also called the choice part.

The supply or availability of diverse populations is a crucial precondition for any mixed-race pairing. One needs to be in a situation to meet and become acquainted with people of diverse backgrounds in order to intermarry. Kalmijn underscores the importance of the supply side or population demographics to intermarriage, but choice is also critical to the outcome of mixed-race family formation. People can circulate in racially integrated environments but still self-segregate or police racial boundaries. Both availability of racially diverse populations and a desire to interact across racial lines are required before dating and marriage can occur.

Convenience out-marriage happens when people live, work, and marry in an environment composed of racially dissimilar people. As Zhenchao Qian and Daniel Lichter note, "By definition, minority group size is inversely associated with rates of out-marriage to whites."[71] In a social context where Latinos are the numerical minority among a white majority, demographics make intermarriage the most obvious option. In convenience out-marriage, demographics steer marriage choices. Cassie Hoffman commented on the lack of a diverse dating pool: "I wanted to stay in this area [Lawrence], but . . . there were just maybe three guys that were Hispanic. There were not very many to choose from [laughs]." Fifty-one-year-old Nathan Lucero, who was related to two of the town's pioneer Mexican families, discussed how labor migration created the Mexican community in Lawrence: "The story goes that . . . in the early 1900s . . . [when] there were no Mexicans in Lawrence at that time . . . [the railroad company] asked for five families to volunteer to come over [to build the railroad from Topeka]. That's what started the Mexican community here." Starting from this modest base of five Mexican families, and absent a large in-migration wave since then, it made sense that "everybody knew each other." After an acceptable round of intermarriage among the pioneer families, their descendants became kin by blood or by marriage, which made in-group dating difficult for later generations.

Convenience out-marriage was common in Kansas because whites far outnumbered Latinos and the Latino community was small enough for inbreeding to be a valid concern. It was not preference that produced out-marriage in this case, but rather the simple demographic fact of a majority-white population. In convenience out-marriages, people enact constrained choice: they make marital decisions within situations that have certain limitations, such as a low supply of coethnics. Liz Downing offered an example of convenience out-marriage and constrained choice due to the lack of in-marriage possibilities in Lawrence, Kansas. I asked her, "So was it important or unimportant to you to date someone of a similar ethnic background?" Liz referred to population in her response:

> LIZ: No, it wasn't at all important to me. . . . It'd kind of be a joke that I couldn't date any people that were Mexican in Lawrence, because we were related to most of the Mexican people in Lawrence [*laughs*].
>
> AUTHOR: Really? So it wasn't just an exaggeration?
>
> LIZ: No. Also, by marriage we would be related to somebody— that was still a no-no for me anyway—because a lot of my brothers and sisters married some of the other Hispanics that did grow up here. My brother married somebody [Mexican] that was also from Lawrence and . . . [that] just connected other families by marriage.

Liz's negotiated desire was grounded in her limited Latino dating pool. Liz may have been open to, or even preferred, a Latino partner, and yet her local context, with few nonkin Latino options, foreclosed endogamous possibilities.

Given that Lawrence's population in 2000 was 82.0 percent non-Hispanic white and 5.7 percent Hispanic (of any race), Latinos have far greater opportunity to meet whites there than other races.[72] Living in a largely white context similarly affects the dating lives of those who are younger and currently unmarried, like twenty-one-year-old Paloma

Lucero, who was born and raised in Lawrence. Paloma touched on how family relations made dating within the local Latino category impossible: "I have probably over twenty [cousins] here in Lawrence. . . . You walk down the street . . . and you can run into a cousin. I went to Hy-Vee [the grocery store] last week . . . and ran into a cousin." As Myra Lucero quipped, "It's . . . weird to date somebody your own race 'cuz you're related to so many of them. [*laughs*] 'Cuz you're in Lawrence. [*laughs*] . . . Brown people I knew were just family . . . so they weren't even an option." Seventeen-year-old Caleb Redgrave shed light on the need to be cautious and find out whether someone he had a crush on was a relative:

> It's kind of hard for me, 'cuz when I develop crush on a Mexican girl . . . I have to find out first if I'm related. . . . I don't know who all I'm related to, 'cuz I've met a whole bunch of cousins in the past few years I never even knew I was related to. So you have to go through that process, and you've got to make sure everything's okay there before you can finally move in or try anything. That's usually a big problem.

In a small Mexican American community, the incest taboo looms large for these native Lawrencians. Even putting aside the very real concern about mistakenly dating someone who is a blood relation, population demographics can propel a penchant for whites, according to nineteen-year-old Ava Gonzalez: "Most of the people that I've dated throughout adolescence . . . have been white. . . . Living in Lawrence, I can count on one hand . . . all the Mexican people that I've known well. [Friendships and dating have] just been a sort of thing defined by circumstance." The demographic makeup of an area can define or redirect desire.

The constraints of Kansas's population demographics equally affect women and men, both younger and older. Forty-nine-year-old Roland Flores reported: "[I dated] a lot of white girls back then because there were more. . . . I can count . . . the [Mexican] ones. . . . There may have been ten girls that would have been my age. I had a [high school] class of six hundred people." Julio Herrera revealed how racial policing and demographics could operate simultaneously: "As kids we were always told, 'Try to stay in your race. . . .' But when you grow up in Lawrence, Kansas, you're related to all the Mexican girls here. So you can't date any of them. . . . You have to go to Topeka or Kansas City, or you date outside the race, which is what we did." Nathan Lucero illuminated the awkwardness that can unfold when one unknowingly becomes interested in a coethnic who turns out to be cousin:

> When I first started dating, they were usually Caucasian. . . . It was very tough for me to date in my own background. [Once], I met this girl. I was

in a bar. I saw this girl that I was really attracted to. She was Mexican, and I went over there and talked to her and bought her a beer. Her sister comes over, and it's my cousin. So she was a cousin that I didn't know. . . . I was always related [to local Mexicans] . . . as a second or third cousin. So it was very difficult for me to date because we didn't have much diversity with the families. . . . I'm related to the Lucero family and the Romero family [two of the original Mexican-origin family lines in the town]. I didn't know the Chavez girls. I'm not related to them, but none of them were my age. . . . So it was just kind of hard to date [other Mexicans].

The demographic reality of a predominantly white environment combined with restrictions against dating Mexican-origin youth for fear of being related nearly demanded that these Kansan Latinos date and marry interracially. Demographics tip the scales in favor of Latino-white intermarriage in spaces where whites are the majority and the Hispanic population is not large enough to sustain numerous endogamous marriages. Numerous respondents from Kansas noted how demographic opportunity—and concern over unwittingly breaking an incest taboo in the small Latino community—steered them toward dating whites, whereas not a single respondent from California registered this complaint.

Rationales related to race, gender, and class, in addition to demographic imperatives, show that people approach relationships with a hierarchy of desires. Class status and religion top the list of non-race- or gender-related reasons people are steered toward each other. True to the noted trends in marital homogamy, wherein people usually marry within their own social categories (race-ethnicity, education level, class status, religion), most interviewees sought partners who shared their class status (or offered the possibility of upward mobility) or their religion.[73] A desire for socioeconomic aggrandizement can drive out-marriage when upward mobility is believed to come in the form of whiteness, as seen in class calculations. Notably, achieving class status similarity—as opposed to seeking a higher-ranking spouse—was a priority for many. Among the middle and upper classes, such similarity facilitated intermarriage and assuaged family concerns about racial inequality. Among higher classes, partners appreciated class similarity because it bespoke—and cemented—their privileged lifestyles and grafted an economic similarity onto a racial dissimilarity. For lower- and working-class respondents, class homogamy, coupled with evidence of a hearty work ethic, was an important foundational quality. In marriages with a white partner and a Latino partner who had both grown up in meager circumstances, both partners valued money and endurance through hardships, and the white partner converted class empathy into racial empathy.

Although interviewees often listed religion as a top priority, they also cited the importance of having "values" in common, even if they did not conceptualize those values as religion. At least two whites (one man and one woman) converted to Catholicism because of their spouse's religious commitments, and two Catholic Latina women sought out a Catholic for their second marriage owing to conflict with a non-Catholic first husband.

Convenience out-marriages are not devoid of preferences. A hierarchy of desires delimits the field of options and helps people make choices about romantic partnerships.

A Hierarchy of Preferences

Religion was high in people's "hierarchy of preferences" for what they sought in a romantic partner, reflecting its importance as a socializing institution.[74] Bianca Stroeh saw Mexican heritage and Catholicism as intimately bound: "To me it was almost automatic. I honestly don't think I had met a Mexican who wasn't Catholic until college. I almost thought the whole world was Catholic when I was young. . . . I was used to crucifixes and the rosary." Similarity of religion was a high priority for Bianca, and it facilitated her marriage to Chuck, her white husband: "When I took a look at what I wanted in a husband . . . he met the other *deeper levels*. His grandparents were [Catholic], and he used to go to mass with them." By "deeper levels" she meant "the same values and the same priorities," reflecting a connection to shared norms and practices. She asked Chuck to take Catholicism classes so they could marry in the Catholic Church and share their faith. Bianca recalled these discussions: "I was like, 'Okay, well, you know you're going to have to [convert] if we're going to get married in a Catholic church because that's part of the requirements. It's a sacrament.' It wasn't just like going to Vegas or going to city hall." Chuck took the requisite classes and converted to Catholicism, and the couple's children now attended Catholic school.

Another couple, Roland and Courtney Flores, shared their conversion story. Roland was straightforward with Courtney about his religious faith when they were dating: " 'I'm a Catholic forever.' That's what I told her. I wasn't willing to give on that. 'But,' I said, 'you can be Methodist. But I'm gonna go to my church on Easter.' " Discussing religion opened the door to outlining other priorities, such as the centrality of family: "When we first started dating, I said, 'God is number one to me, but my family is number one in this life I live. It's important to me. It's important for me to be around them, and we're very close. We hug. We kiss. So if you don't want any part of that, it ain't gonna work.' That was a quality . . . I did look for."

Courtney converted to Catholicism of her own accord, yet noted her husband's influence: "I wouldn't be Catholic if it weren't for Roland, because I wasn't Catholic before. . . . I was always drawn to the Catholic faith. . . . So when I started dating Roland and we started going to church at St. John's, I just felt at home. It was like this was kind of meant to be. So it was easy to make the decision to switch." Their four children attended Catholic elementary school.

For the faithful, specific nuances of religion became a measure of compatibility. Cynthia Herrera-Redgrave reported that she and her husband Mitch shared a *Mexican* brand of Catholicism: "We celebrate Our Lady of Guadalupe. . . . My kids have always participated in the mass. Mitch just stepped right [in]. I mean, I don't even think he thought twice about it. He just . . . knew this is what we did, and he just has always stepped in. . . . The big joke is [when people say], 'Oh, we just thought you guys were Mexican.' "

Cynthia's natal family had long attended mass at the local Catholic church and taken on leadership positions at the church's annual fiesta, which featured Latino food and dance. Although originally a Latino-oriented event that appropriated space and created a sense of belonging for Catholic Latinos in a predominantly white Kansas community—a strategy also employed by Catholic Latinos in other Midwestern towns—the fiesta had gained in popularity and now drew a racially heterogeneous crowd.[75] The family joke that positioned Mitch as an honorary Mexican pointed to the close association of Mexican identity with Catholicism. It also underscored the role of women in perpetuating culture in the family—in this case, in shepherding the family along a religious course.

Religion and region interact in an important way for families. Even for families featured in other chapters, the local Catholic church functioned as a "nucleus of community events" and "de facto ethnic institution" in Kansas in a way that was not emphasized in California.[76] An impressive number of families in Kansas noted the weekly masses and annual fiesta hosted by the local Catholic church as a touchstone for not only their religious identity but also their Latino identity. In an area with a sparse Latino population, religious events doubled as racial community functions. Paloma Lucero made this connection: "The weekend for the St. John's fiesta is [when] everybody comes together for one big event. The entire Lawrence Mexican community comes together for that. Other than that, St. John's does . . . masses in Spanish on Sundays. Besides going there, I think that places where everybody in [the] community can get together is limited."

Many of the Kansas Latino respondents portrayed the annual fiesta hosted at the church as the main public Latino cultural activity for the year.

They talked about volunteering to organize, decorate, and provide services at booths at the event as a family activity. In small-town Kansas, this
religious event, in concentrating a racial community, provided a chance
to become reacquainted with family who also volunteered or attended.
Paloma continued: "My uncle [takes food] orders. And my cousin . . . did
that as well. Then . . . you walk into the food booth and you're like, 'Oh,
hey, I know you. I think you're a cousin.' " Summer Flores, age nineteen,
concurred about the extended-family-oriented nature of the annual event:
"Our church has the Mexican fiesta. The whole family is part of that. My
dad does security. My aunts and I and cousins decorate. My grandma and
aunts cook. It's . . . a family deal that we all hang out at."

Contrast the Kansas field site, where the local Catholic church concentrated the local Latino community, with the California field site, where
the racially diverse environment prevented religious institutions from
playing the same pivotal role in assembling Latinos. The claiming of a
religious space seen in Kansas was so regularly performed in California
that it had been normalized and went unremarked upon. In Kansas, the
annual church-based fiesta was a consistent topic of enthusiastic conversation, whereas religion and its social function were less remarkable features
of everyday life in California.[77]

In multiracial California, a diversity of people were members of the
Catholic Church, diluting its identification with Latinos exclusively. Bianca
Stroeh, who worked at the church where her family worshiped and her son
attended school, remarked on the racial diversity of the Catholic school:

> [My kids have] only known California. . . . A lot of the friends and families
> that they go to school with are either Filipino or Mexican. . . . If you look at
> them alphabetically, the child before them is [Salamat], which is Filipino.
> And the one after them is [Suarez], which is Mexican. . . . The only thing that
> ties the Salamat, Stroeh, and Suarez together is that we're Catholic. We all go
> to the same school. We all go to the same church.

The Catholic Church served a unifying function in California too, but in this
case the reference group was other Catholics, regardless of race, whereas
in Kansas the Church was seen as a rallying point for Catholic Latinos.

Although religion functioned differently in Kansas and California, it was
a consideration before marriage for respondents in both regions. Religion
was an important organizing institution in binding partners that helped
them articulate their beliefs and collective practices. Even convenience out-
marriages, which occur because of population demographics and lack of
race or gender rationales, are not devoid of preferences. Rather than rest-
ing on a preference for or against one's own racial group, marital choice

can be steered by a hierarchy of preferences. Among interviewees, religion ranked high in many people's order of preferences as a factor that helped them delimit their field of options as they chose romantic partnerships.

CONCLUSION

Using the concept of preferences to explain the construction of romantic desire and the concept of convenience to illuminate how population demographics drive marriages, this chapter has distilled the chief reasons for Latino-white intermarriage. For Latinos, color-coding based on gender concerns, class calculations, and racial policing stimulate out-marriage. Latina women who crave greater gender equality or class-related security explicitly desire intermarriage. A racial hierarchy that privileges whiteness and degrades nonwhiteness also produces exogamy through racial policing and anxiety over racial status achievement or loss. For white men, images of Latina women as attractive or suitable domestic partners and previous romantic relationships with Latinas encourage their romances with Latinas. Parental teaching of equality and a multicultural discourse (also promulgated by the U.S. military) make intermarriage acceptable, if not appealing, for whites.

In contrast to preferential intermarriage, convenience out-marriage results from choices that are constrained owing to demographic limitations in majority-white areas where Latinos are numerical minorities. Out-marriage is an obvious choice for Latinos in places where whites comprise the majority of the dating pool. In contrast, whites' many endogamous options in those same majority-white areas make their choice to date interracially a clear preference. Convenience out-marriages are also formed by using a hierarchy of preferences that captures nonracial qualities that both Latinos and whites seek, such as religion similarity.

This chapter has satisfied questions about why Latino-white interracial partnerships occur, from the perspective of both partners, using an intersectional perspective to address the formation of preferences while also speaking to the constraints of structural factors. A natural companion to this chapter on rationales, the next chapter explores the consequences of Latino-white intermarriage in terms of cultural and racial consciousness. Since culture and race are dynamic, how do romantic partnerships affect the attitudes and behaviors of the intermarried?

Chapter 3 | Consequences of Latino and White Intermarriage: Biculturalism and Racial Consciousness

So what happens *after* Latino and white intermarriage?[1] How do cultural practices shift? How do understandings of race change? To provide a glimpse of the variety of answers provided in this chapter, here is a sampling from three respondents:

> [My husband] wants our son to grow up knowing his Mexican culture and the language. . . . Ryan's favorite food is Mexican food. He loves my mom's chile rellenos. He loves all that stuff. So, because of that I feel like I can definitely embrace every part of my Mexicanness because he loves that side. Because he encourages and embraces that, it just makes me feel like I can take it and run with it. (Glenda Carlisle, Mexican-born immigrant)

> [I have] more interest and . . . more compassion toward . . . social issues. . . . It was an . . . interest gained because . . . [I] came . . . from a white background. . . . I [am] interested in other cultures and more Mexican than other cultures because I [am] with a Mexican woman. (Shawn Downing, white)

> I drew closer to whiteness as this relationship was . . . growing up. . . . I definitely didn't get any more Hispanic. . . . I tried to salvage some of my Hispanic [heritage] by trying to cook more. . . . I still get this nostalgia. . . . Married to [my white husband], I'm more partially white. (Sylvia Nava-Kelly, half Cuban American, half white)

These excerpts range from intermarriage that heightened Hispanic heritage for both partners, owing to one partner's "embrace" of the culture, to

69

growing compassion, to drawing closer to whiteness. Intermarriage itself does not have a decisive influence on culture and identity; personal sentiment, spousal support, and social context all bear on culture and identity. This chapter addresses the consequences of cross-racial marriage for both Latinos and whites and finds that intermarriage results in a diversity of bicultural outcomes as well as bimodal understandings of race, from minimized to heightened. I first explain how the concept of assimilation has been used in the past and outline its shortcomings; I then answer the guiding questions with a section on biculturalism and a section on racial consciousness.

INTERMARRIAGE: ENDPOINT OR STARTING POINT FOR CHANGE?

Since 1970, the number of Hispanics married to non-Hispanics has tripled, reaching over 1.5 million in 2000.[2] By 2008, the intermarriage rate for native-born Latinos was 52.5 percent, and 90 percent of those marriages were with whites.[3] Using intermarriages between minority and majority groups as a gauge of successful integration, assimilation literature tells us that minority persons will move away from ethnic identification and toward mainstream identification. Cultural attachments are predicted to follow suit: in an unrealistically zero-sum game wherein one either does or does not have ethnicity, natal culture is shed as the host culture is holistically adopted.[4] The assimilation literature focuses on change *between* generations (for example, between the first and second generations) rather than *among* Latino-white intermarried couples. Integration studies have always focused on change by *Latinos*, rather than by whites, missing an opportunity to assess change in whites.[5] Finally, assimilation literature largely assumes that intermarriage is a culmination of change and overlooks intermarriage as a *starting point* for change. Although some scholars have nodded at this possibility, there has been little empirical assessment of intermarriage as an engine of social change.[6] I take this opening and, rather than view intermarriage as a mark of "successful" integration, I flip the assumption and interrogate how intermarriage is a departure point for changed racial attitudes and behaviors.

Intermarriage is considered an especially important component of assimilation because it indicates acceptance of the minority group by the majority group. The classic assimilation theorist Milton Gordon posited that intermarriage, or "marital assimilation," was the "inevitable by-product of structural assimilation." In Gordon's words, the "entrance of the minority group into the social cliques, clubs, and institutions of the core society at the primary group level inevitably will lead to a substantial amount of intermarriage."[7]

Gordon argues that, following marital assimilation, the minority group member will stop identifying as ethnic. This claim requires empirical assessment; it does not leave room for two-way acculturation where hybridity or biculturalism—"dual cultural socialization"—may result.[8] The notion that intermarriage produces a "breaking of ties" with one's ethnic community needs to be analyzed.[9] Determining whether intermarriage works *counter* to assimilation theory's prediction of whitening and instead generates awareness of race and racial progressivism is an important empirical question.[10] Rather than intermarriage signaling an overcoming of race, perhaps instead it foregrounds race and racial issues in new ways.

Assimilation theory assumes that both the white partner and the minority partner want to minimize attention to race.[11] Narrowly viewing intermarriage as evidence of the "success" of assimilation, assimilation theory does not take into account the possibility of race cognizance, or a heightened awareness of race, that can occur when whites realize that their minority partner is treated worse than they are. Eileen O'Brien argues that "cross-racial/ethnic intimacy," in either the family of origin or the family of procreation, can lead to a racially progressive stance.[12] Racial progressives approve of racial intermarriage and affirmative action and declare the reality of racial discrimination.[13] This notion that intermarriage may produce race cognizance, as opposed to the minority partner folding into whiteness, contradicts the view of intermarriage as an indicator of assimilation. Assimilation theory's suggestion that an endpoint of similarity between previously distinct social groups is desirable misses the fact that some people hold strongly to their ethnic culture, finding it inherently valuable, especially in the age of multiculturalism.[14]

Intermarried whites are entirely absent from assimilation theory. Left unexplored is the possibility of a white partner migrating into Latino culture or being catalyzed about race after exposure to a different racialized perspective. This chapter corrects the typical conception of assimilation as a unidirectional process and conceives of it instead as a two-way process, one in which whites and Latinos both are susceptible to cultural shifts and ethnic explorations.[15]

Interracial relationships destabilize racial boundaries owing to "boundary blurring": as two people create a household together, the "social profile of the boundary . . . become[s] less distinct."[16] Boundaries are blurred when ongoing social relationships are maintained across boundaries. One mechanism of boundary blurring is what Joane Nagel calls "ethnic settling or sojourning," which involves those who are "permanent or long term resident[s]" in another ethnic setting.[17] Similarly, "affiliative ethnic identity," as a knowledge-based enactment based on "ethnically linked symbols and practices" (such as "cuisine, language, art, holidays, festivals"), blurs ethnic borders.[18] Ethnic settling or sojourning and affiliative ethnic identity are the means by which whites identify with and practice a Latino/a spouse's ethnic culture. Whites who engage in these borrowing and blurring tactics are often called "honorary Latinos/Hispanics/Mexicans" by those who recognize their deep connection to a culture and history not inherited from their family of origin but adopted after marriage.

This chapter examines the most common exogamous dating and marital pairing for Latinos: Latinos and whites.[19] This chapter draws from forty people representing sixteen families. The sample of forty includes thirty adults (fourteen married couples and two divorcées) who were in Latino-white intermarriages, plus ten children from those relationships.[20] The adult couples were the same as those profiled in chapter 2.[21] The ten children from these couples ranged in age from fifteen to twenty-one, and all but two college students were dependents, living with their parents. Thirteen families hailed from northeastern Kansas and three were from California.

This chapter presents two main findings regarding the cultural and racial consequences of intermarriage. First, I find gradations of biculturalism that I theorize on a scale from "leaning white" to "everyday biculturalism," "selective blending," and "leaning Latino." The preconditions of biculturalism include nearby Latino family, especially in Kansas, and a white spouse who supports Latino culture. The second finding concerns racial consciousness, or ways of understanding race. On the one hand, intermarriage prompts race cognizance relative to public sphere discrimination, enhancing whites' understanding about the salience of race, while, on the other hand, conjuring color-blindness, or the tendency to minimize race in the private realm.

CONSEQUENCES OF LATINO-WHITE INTERMARRIAGE

I theorize biculturalism as four "ideal types" — heuristic devices to organize abstract concepts that help make sense of what is happening in the world.[22] The four ideal types are "leaning white," "everyday biculturalism," "selective blending," and "leaning Latino." *Leaning white* refers to whites or Latinos who continue an affiliation with whiteness that began prior to, and was unchanged by, their marital union. Latino culture is acknowledged but ranks a distant second to whiteness. *Everyday biculturalism* is an intermixing of cultures that occurs with little intentionality as people live their lives. Cultures are calmly intermingled, and everyday biculturalism is the product of laissez-faire attitudes toward one's own and one's partner's ethnic culture. An intentional form of biculturalism is *selective blending*, wherein the two partners consciously choose cultural elements from *both* of their backgrounds to continue or discontinue. *Leaning Latino* is an intentional, undiscriminating embrace of most of the Latino elements brought to a relationship. Leaning Latino prioritizes Latino identity over whiteness, more strongly identifies with Latino heritage than everyday biculturalism does, and more holistically embraces Latino culture than selective blending does. These variants of biculturalism demonstrate that Latinos and whites are both affected by intercultural contact and that cultural intermixing is multidirectional.

In applying these categories, I use individuals as the unit of analysis and focus on the adult partners. I sprinkle in data from the children in the findings sections to show patterns of consistency and variation across generations. In most couples, both partners substantially agreed in how they described their cultural inclinations. Yet since individuals can be captured by more than one ideal type, I coded each person according to the one or two types of biculturalism dominant in his or her life. Of the thirty adults, six leaned white, fifteen displayed everyday biculturalism, five engaged in active selective blending, and ten leaned Latino (see table 3.1). One in four Latino respondents leaned white, demonstrating the fluidity of cultural borders. The least intentional of the forms of biculturalism, everyday biculturalism described half of the interviewees. Selective blending, a product of conscious intent, described 17 percent of the interviewees. One-third of the respondents leaned Latino; the fact that half of the whites leaned Latino speaks to the porousness of boundaries and shows that marital lives are vehicles to becoming an affiliated ethnic.

The two forms of racial consciousness, race cognizance and color-blindness, do not correspond to cultural activity but instead refer to whether respondents deemed race relevant in their life or their spouse's life. Surprisingly, since these two categories are ostensibly opposites (race viewed as important or not), these categories can coexist. Whites were

Table 3.1 Types of Biculturalism in the Subsample, by Individual (Adults Only)

	Latinos (n = 16)	Whites (n = 14)	Total[a]
Lean white	25% (4)	14% (2)	20% (6)
Everyday biculturalism	63 (10)	36 (5)	50 (15)
Selective blending	8 (2)	21 (3)	17 (5)
Lean Latino	19 (3)	50 (7)	33 (10)

Source: Author's calculations.
[a]Percentages add up to greater than 100 because a maximum of two types of biculturalism were coded per person.

highly represented in the race cognizance category: the intermarriages of ten of fourteen whites (71 percent) and five of sixteen Latinos (31 percent) enabled them to experience race cognizance. For whites, intermarriage with Latinos illuminated race because they witnessed how being nonwhite differentially affected their partner. Forty percent of adults reported that their intermarriage had minimized race in their lives. Those who expressed color-blindness might have seen the reality of race outside of their relationship, but they downplayed it in private life and felt that they had surpassed racial barriers in the personal realm.[23] Data on the children of the intermarried show that family orientations toward biculturalism and racial consciousness shaped but did not overdetermine the practices and perspectives of the next generation.

The Four Types of Biculturalism

Leaning White: Affiliation with Whiteness   A minority of adult respondents (six of thirty—four Latinos and two whites) continued or increased their identification with whiteness. They were not totally rejecting Latino identity but rather emphasizing whiteness. The predisposition to lean white often preceded and informed marital choices. For Mexican American siblings Myra and Nathan Lucero, forty-nine and fifty-one years old, respectively, affiliation toward whiteness was the result of *prior* assimilation. For the Lucero siblings—who were born and raised in Kansas, where demographics made out-marriage with whites common—their out-marriages resulted from their parents' upward mobility: they had been relocated to the predominantly white "west side of town—the better side of town," as Myra put it. Myra remarked on the lack of Mexican culture in their family of origin: "When I was growing up, it was more [about] assimilation than trying to stay Mexican. . . . We just assimilated. . . . We are white Mexicans, so to speak. . . . I don't really see any difference between us and any other average American home." Yet, since race is best understood relative to other racial categories, it is useful to consider the interconnectedness of the local racial groups and their associated meanings.[24] Intermarriage with whites offers proximity to white privilege, yet out-marriage with whites also offers a departure from other racial groups that are lower on the racial hierarchy. Myra described her sense of her romantic options and the meanings associated with each group: "We knew that we were not going to date a black. . . . Indians around here were just seen as drunks—so really that was . . . not seen as an option. Asians weren't even around. So it was pretty much you were just going to marry brown or white." Myra had a clear understanding of the local racial hierarchy in Lawrence, Kansas. Viewing "brown or white" as her only socially sanctioned options—racial status quo or racial ascension—her marriage to a white man was driven not only by her parents' encouragement of identification with whiteness but also by the low supply of coethnics, the absence of Asians, and the even lower status of Native Americans and blacks.

Myra and Nathan's parents, Magda and Joaquin, who are both in their seventies, promoted an affiliation with whiteness. In addition to moving out of the Mexican neighborhood, they shored up their relative racial privilege through antiblack prejudice, a shunning of blackness that has a history reaching back to colonialism.[25] Joaquin cautioned his children and grandchildren, "I don't want you to run around with just blacks only." According to Joaquin, marriage with blacks was out of the question because mixed-race children would default to blackness, owing to the one-drop rule: "Because your kids are black . . . they've got to go with black because other races won't mix so easy." This family affiliated with whiteness and drew a boundary against blackness in order to preserve their status.

Families' racial ideologies powerfully socialize younger generations on race issues.[26] Paloma, Myra's daughter and Magda and Joaquin's granddaughter, reported on her family's strong influence on her dating preferences: "I was . . . told growing up you don't date a black person." My earlier interview with Paloma's grandparents had provided occasion for them to debrief her about the interview and to reassert their antiblack prejudice. Paloma told me, "My grandma told me a little bit about her interview with you. . . . [She said] my grandpa said something like [blacks] were lower-class and [he] wanted [me] to move up in class and not down. And I was like, '. . . There's also a lot of really successful black people out there.' [But] I wouldn't date a black guy. . . . I don't want grandpa to be mad at me." After mild protest, Paloma acceded to her family's edict against dating black men. She also relied on population size to further justify the likelihood that she would continue to affiliate with whiteness through mate selection: "I think that, given the numbers, the chances of marrying a white American are a lot higher than marrying a Mexican American." While "relationships are increasingly likely to be interracial the later they are formed in historical time," this increased tolerance does not apply equally to all racial groups.[27] In Paloma's case, family sanctions and the local opportunity structure had generated her preference for whites.

Splitting away from the older generation's racial prejudices, Haley, Paloma's cousin (Nathan's daughter and Magda and Joaquin's granddaughter), was dating a mixed-race black man, to her family's chagrin. Embodying the increasing tolerance for racial diversity and interracial romance in the United States over time, seventeen-year-old Haley prioritized certain qualities over race in a prospective partner.[28] "I honestly could not care what background they have," she said. "I want them to have a good family. . . . If I like them, then it doesn't really matter what their race is." Personality, closeness of family relationships, or peer groups may explain the variation between the cousins, yet this latitude in opinions also reveals how racial viewpoints and dating behavior are influenced but not overdetermined by family.

Latino-white intermarried couples who lean white deemphasize but do not completely disregard Latino culture. The Guthries, who identified as a "middle-class white family," acknowledged Latino culture but left it to the Latino partner to maintain.[29] Kent, a forty-one-year-old white man, described his mixed family as a Caucasian one that occasionally engaged in activities that suggested Latino influence: "[Our family] probably leans more to the Caucasian side; however, she converted me to Catholicism. . . . I go to all the fiestas . . . the folklore-type stuff. . . . I wanna support her, whatever she wants to do. If you look around the house here, you couldn't tell that there is a Hispanic person living here. . . . I think of [us] as a middle-class white family."

In Kent's description, middle-class status, his own whiteness, and his children's mixed-race status justified the family's "middle-class white" appellation. Scholars have noted that changes in identity claims can lead to a "loss" of Hispanics, which makes it impossible to accurately chart gains and causes the problem of "unmeasured progress."[30] Here, Kent's reduction of his mixed family to "white" obscured their interracial status, rendering invisible his wife's Latina heritage. Adriana's background was itself mixed, however, as she was half Mexican American and half white. Though she identified as Hispanic, one could see how the logic of "rounding up" made Kent's summary of his mixed family as white accurate. As Mary Waters found in her study of white ethnics, married couples tend to emphasize their ethnic commonality rather than difference.[31] Not only was Caucasian Kent's own racial status, but it is more highly valued in society and was the common denominator between him and Adriana.

Despite the Guthries' predilection to lean white, their daughter Kaleigh offered that her dad "started off as Christian, but he transferred over to Catholic." Removed from his Southern roots and living near his wife's Catholic extended family, Kent converted to Catholicism and supported Kaleigh's baptism at the local Catholic church. Although the national trend is for Latino Catholics to become Protestant over generations in the United States, the opposite—white Protestants converting to their Latino spouses' Catholicism—can also occur.[32]

Family orientations can shift over generations. For example, Kaleigh had moved toward the middle of the bicultural spectrum of options, away from leaning white. Staying true to her background, Kaleigh refused to pick only one race when asked, saying: "I've never picked before. It's always together. I say Mexican American: half Mexican, half white." She participated in mainstream environments, such as school, in addition to ethnic organizations, such as a Latino organization. Since only those who self-identified as Hispanic could participate in this program, I asked how her white background fit when her Hispanic background was the focus. Her mixed identity was unproblematic to her: "I guess it just kinda flows with it. I don't see it as separate. It's just one." Kaleigh exhibited cultural fluency in both white-dominant society and a Latino community, a biculturalism that befit her "half and half" identity: "I don't see [my backgrounds] as separate at all. I don't think about, 'I'm doing this for my Mexican background. If I'm doing this, it's for my white background.' I just think, 'I'm doing this.' "

A preexisting inclination toward whiteness can shape what people teach their children about race. Recall that Rowena was a Mexican American whose two marriages were with white men. Rowena's desire for socioeconomic aggrandizement predisposed her to intermarriage with white men, a classic example of racial-beauty exchange theory wherein women of color "trade beauty . . . for a higher racial caste mate."[33] Despite her identification as Hispanic, Rowena promoted affiliation with whiteness and distance from Hispanics. Complicit in supporting white superiority by perpetuating Latino stereotypes, Rowena cautioned her sons: "Don't you bad-mouth or talk back to a Hispanic because they are one mean son of a gun."[34] Her mixed-race children picked up her cues and claimed that they were "more Caucasian." When Rowena rebutted, "Excuse me? You're half," the kids foregrounded their whiteness, saying dismissively, "No thanks, Mom." Rowena's generalization that whites are middle-class and Hispanics are lower-class (obscuring her own reality as a middle-class Mexican American) steered her family toward whiteness.

For intermarried Latinos, leaning white often preceded intermarriage, predisposing them to partner with whites. Most couples in which at least one partner described himself or herself as "leaning white" consisted of Latina women and white men. Hypergamy theory—the idea that males of the dominant group "visit their sexual attentions upon females of subordinate groups"—tells us that women exchange virtues such as beauty, sex, and fertility for men with a higher-ranking racial status.[35] People lean white to achieve white privilege, a status viewed as synonymous with economic stability, and thus leaning white is principally a story about race and power.

Everyday Biculturalism: A Laissez-Faire Approach The most frequent ideal type evident in these intermarried couples was everyday biculturalism, which engages both partners in a casual two-way cultural exchange. Everyday biculturalism requires little intent and organically grows out of two people sharing their lives. Requiring little decision-making, everyday biculturalism arises in partnerships in which neither individual is particularly committed to their own, or the spouse's, heritage.

Bianca, a forty-one-year-old Mexican American woman, and Chuck Stroeh, her forty-four-year-old white husband, live in Southern California, claim an American identity, and give little thought to their respective heritages. As Americans first and Mexican- or European-descent a distant second, Bianca and Chuck are bicultural with little effort. U.S.-born Bianca noted that her everyday biculturalism contrasted with the tendency to lean Latino among her immigrant neighbors:

> I still consider myself Mexican American, though I think, being here in California, I'm probably not as Mexican as some families are who are immediately from Mexico. I would say we're more American as far as some of our practices and . . . traditions. . . . For Father's Day we're going to barbecue carne asada [barbecued beef]. That's my husband's choice; that's his favorite. I do see myself as Mexican American, but I have a German [married] last name. . . . I identify more with American because I don't have a really strong connection to Mexico. I don't see it like, "Viva Mexico" ["Long live Mexico"]. So I identify with American and California.

In the immigrant-heavy context of California, Bianca compared herself to immigrant Latinos. That she did not necessarily connect her white husband's choice of Father's Day food, carne asada, to traditional Mexican cuisine showed how much cultural blending had already occurred. To her, unless she declared "Viva Mexico," she was not very Mexican American.

Everyday biculturalism is bidirectional: Bianca adopted her husband's German last name of Stroeh, and Chuck requested carne asada for a celebratory dinner. Chuck, as a white man, might have matched the expectations of Bianca's assimilationist upbringing ("my parents just didn't pass on [traditions] to us. . . . [We experienced] assimilation by just being here"), yet she was not oblivious to her Latino culture and indeed imparted some aspects of it to him. Chuck remarked: "She jokes that I become more and more Mexican all the time. Because I like the food—which I always have." Pointing to nearby family, which is important in California but even more so in Kansas, Chuck discussed the influence of grandparent-grandchildren relations: "I think the kids have learned a lot from Bianca's dad, spending time with him. . . . [My son] Tito will go over there and they'll watch a movie . . . in Spanish. . . . I think that exposure's been good." In the two-way street of everyday biculturalism, an effortless cultural mix is the outcome of an intermarriage in which neither partner has preservationist or revisionist instincts.

Fifteen-year-old Tito Stroeh, son of Bianca and Chuck, was placidly multiracial. Reporting that race did not matter to him in his life, he noted that his mixed-race status and heterogeneous social setting, which included whites, Hispanics, and Filipinos, might have made him more empathetic toward other minorities. Showing a "symbolic ethnicity" style—that is, ethnicity as "a nostalgic allegiance . . . that can be felt without having to be incorporated in everyday behavior"[36]—Tito remarked that "the most traditional part is the food. It's usually rice and beans and hot dogs and carne asada." Holding on to neither Mexican nor white ethnic (German and Irish) culture, he reported: "I don't really think about it that much, 'cuz it just doesn't really come up." He suggested that this orientation stemmed from his family, who didn't "really focus on [race] that much."

Fifty-seven-year-old Mexican American Luke Ybarra, of Kansas, was married to a fifty-eight-year-old white woman of Irish descent from St. Louis, Missouri. He discussed what is a hallmark of everyday biculturalism— the casual intermixing of their backgrounds: "Before our relationship, I don't know how much exposure [my wife] had [to Mexican American culture]. But I think that she does appreciate it, and she's learned to make enchiladas. . . . Being married to her probably has enhanced my appreciation of the Irish holidays and food. So I think it's been good in both directions."

Everyday biculturalism engages ethnicity symbolically through practices such as "holidays and food."[37] Luke and his twenty-six-year-old son Duncan talked in terms of having the "best of both worlds" in their home, yet this only translated to food in their examples. Duncan linked a distinctive cuisine with each side of his family: "My dad's entire family is Hispanic, so whenever we go to Chanute, Kansas, it's Mexican food . . . and when we go to St. Louis to visit my mom's family, we're talking turkey and spiral-cut ham." Duncan summarized the noncommittal nature of the everyday biculturalism his parents charted: "Between my mom and my dad there is not a whole lot of stuff that is trying to be passed on. . . . We are fairly open-ended on things. . . . I guess we are kind of making [traditions] up as we go [*chuckles*]."

Luke's wife and Duncan's mother, Trudy, answered my question about whether biculturalism described her family:

Biculturalism—that's a great word. Yeah. I never even really thought about it. . . . I always told [my children] they're Mexican. They are Irish. . . . It's just kind of a blend. . . . It's not pinning two against [each other]. It's just [like] blending the Germans with the Irish, or the French with the Polish. It's really no different than that. It's kind of fun.

Everyday biculturalism combines two cultures without much delib-
eration. If there is conscious thought, it is about striving for a "middle
ground" or a "blending," without particular regard for which elements
are to be either preserved or altered, a de facto blending rather than intentional "selective blending" (described next). Trudy "never even really
thought about it," since in the course of everyday life her heritage and
Luke's heritage easily combined. Pointing to a history of European nation
intermixing, Trudy likened the experience of her Latino-white family to
the history of the European cultural blends that resulted in today's white
ethnics in the United States, tacitly pointing to the compatibility of cultures in her family.

Everyday biculturalism is the result of the conjoined ethnic lives of two
partners who "meet in the middle" and do not conscientiously transmit
cultural knowledge to their children. Sources of support for biculturalism
vary by region: families in California emphasized their racially diverse
communities, whereas families in Kansas pointed to their nearby extended
families as sources of culture. Across families, consumption practices and
food choices provided evidence of combined cultures.

Selective Blending: Retaining and Discarding Cultural Elements   As
immigration scholars have noted, "The culture of any ethnic or racial
group is continually formed and reformed in the United States."[38] It is
through selective blending that we can best witness cultural dynamism.
Assimilation literature incorrectly assumes that all traits associated with
an immigrant culture will dilute over time.[39] Yet, in reality, some cultural
attributes are guarded while others are jettisoned. People make choices to
selectively blend cultural traits from their own background and their partner's background. These personal, agentic preferences creatively blend
cultures and produce a new amalgamation.

Celeste Collins, a half Native American and half Mexican American
forty-three-year-old woman from Kansas, exhibited selective blending.
Although this chapter focuses on the consequences of intermarriage,
Celeste's *rationale* for her out-marriage was directly tied to the *consequence*
of selective blending. Recall from the previous chapter that Celeste's reasoning concerned gender: she selected out the trait of male domination
(which she experienced with her father) in her choice to marry an emotionally sensitive white man. Celeste refused to marry anyone who "looked
like" her dad and also specified the character trait she wished to avoid.
Celeste avoided strict gender expectations by marrying a sensitive white
man who displayed "gender flexibility," that is, a willingness "to share
power, child care, and household chores with women."[40]

Celeste and her white husband, Doug, consciously changed the gender norms with which she had been raised, revealing how choices around intimate life produce cultural change.[41] She described cultural and economic shifts that had occurred since her marriage, as well as Doug's reinforcement of select elements associated with her Mexican-origin family:

> I had moved away from *my* background a little bit, in the traditional roles of the home. Because I am . . . a dominant part of . . . our economic life. And my husband takes up more of the home life than my father ever did. I think we're more distant from the traditional roles [of] my . . . Mexican American culture. But we continue to have the larger family dynamics, where family is important. [Doug] definitely *loves* that part of my family, that we are close and affectionate and fun-loving, and that we get along. His side of the family, unfortunately, does not have that closeness. He likes very much the music and the food of our culture . . . we have retained that. . . . It's . . . a different home life than what we grew up with.

Family dynamics, such as how close a family is, are subject to selective blending. Doug appreciated his wife's affectionate family and re-created that in his marital home. In explaining Doug's motivations for change, Celeste noted that he was creating a home life that he wished he had had in his early life: "As a child, he didn't get a lot of his parents' attention, and I think he's trying to veer away from that. He's trying to not repeat that. He's very involved with both my son and daughter. . . . His family . . . [didn't] express their love very openly, [whereas] he sees my family and how we greet each other . . . and he very much respects and admires that." Selective blending allows for the conscious retention or removal of both cultural and familial characteristics. Natal families serve as models to be altered, as in Celeste's desire to avoid male domination and traditional gender scripts and Doug's wish to have loving relationships with family members.[42]

Selective blending runs bidirectionally, applying to both cultures in a partnership. Ryan Carlisle, a white man, discussed how he and his Mexican-born wife Glenda selectively blended cultures in their home. Ryan equally condemned rigid gender norms that reigned in Glenda's youthful household and America's "dog-eat-dog" culture. Ryan and Glenda engaged in selective blending geared equally toward Mexican and American cultures. They tempered attributes they viewed as negative in *both* national cultures: patriarchy in Mexican culture and self-centered individualism in American culture.

Unlike Celeste, Glenda did not fuse the notion of Latino men with patriarchy but rather associated *all men* with patriarchy. Thus, despite the fact that she married a white man—which was precisely what Celeste did in order to *avoid* domineering masculinity—Glenda's upbringing taught her to associate all men with emotional distance. Ryan recalled a time when his Mexican mother-in-law counseled Glenda not to cry, saying that "men don't like that." He rebutted this advice, assuring her that he wanted her to express herself freely: "I'll say something that disagrees with . . . her opinion, so she'll just back down. I'm like, 'No, I want to discuss this. I want to know what you really think.' . . . I'm not in charge of all of our decisions; it's more of a family thing than one individual that makes all the choices."

Selective blending applies not only to Latino people and culture but also to whites and their natal culture. Evenhanded in his social criticism, Ryan faulted U.S. society—in particular capitalism—for promoting selfishness, an attribute that ran contrary to both his Christian beliefs and the collectivist orientation he learned in the U.S. military. Ryan condemned American capitalism for breeding rampant selfishness and cut-throat individualism:

> The American dream is all focused on *me*, and this is to benefit *me*—you see that a lot in capitalism. I . . . want to instill that you are not the end-all-be-all in the world. . . . In [the biblical book of] Romans, we're called to be "living sacrifices." Which means, if I have a chance to sacrifice my desires . . . to help better you or a group, then that's the path that I should take. . . . It's not about making the most money. It's not about being the most powerful. . . . Part of that comes from my military background too. It's instilled in you that your life is something that you can use to the benefit of others. In boot camp, when you're doing these exercises, they'll read all of these Medal of Honor citations about so-and-so jumped on a grenade and lost his life but he saved ten other people.

For the Carlisles, selective blending centered on gender issues and capitalistic selfishness as they strove to recalibrate gender power imbalances and orient their family toward the collective.

Selective blending is a conscious crafting of a bicultural atmosphere in which *both* partners in a couple carefully select elements of their natal cultures to retain, discard, or improve upon, according to their own priorities.

Leaning Latino: Active Biculturalism   Leaning Latino is a deliberately engaged form of biculturalism that is more wholehearted and less critical than selective blending. Active biculturalism is aided by a supportive non-Hispanic partner and geographically proximate Latino family members. Especially in Kansas, leaning Latino required effort, since Latino culture was less concentrated there than in majority-minority regions. The families profiled in this section demonstrate the unreserved embrace of leaning

Latino, and their interviews highlighted the supporting roles of non-Hispanic spouses and proximate Latino family members.

Courtney Flores, a forty-six-year-old white Kansan, rebutted the idea of out-marriage producing a "breaking of ties" with Latino culture: "In our case, it's been the opposite." Courtney depicted her family's lifestyle of leaning Latino as an active "choice" in a space where whiteness can overtake minority cultures: "We've definitely kept [Latino culture] and in some instances have even made it stronger than what Roland grew up with. We've had to make the choice. Do we want to participate in this event, or do we want to teach this value that comes from his family? . . . The Hispanic is more dominant in [our] relationship." She speculated as to why her family leaned Latino: "Maybe it's because the non-Hispanic person is non-native to Lawrence [where we live]. Or maybe because I'm a mutt and he's a purebred. So it's that majority-minority kind of thing." Courtney touched on two issues repeated by other respondents who were accounting for why they leaned Latino. First was the proximity of Latino family who reinforced this identity, and second was that her husband was "a purebred." Echoing others' sentiments, Roland's "purebred" Latino identity was easily identifiable, whereas her "mutt" heritage was fractional. In their "purebred" and "mutt" pairing, Roland's easily identifiable, 100 percent Latino background outweighed hers, tipping the family culture in that direction.

Courtney and Roland's two teenage children, Summer, nineteen, and Shane, seventeen, had adopted their parents' orientation toward Latino culture. Speaking to whiteness as a conglomeration of national identities that made it challenging to identify with, Shane remarked: "[My mother] is four different things; German [is] the main one. I can't remember the other three. . . . We go to the Oktoberfest every year and get some German food, but there's not much that we're holding on to from her background." The family had distilled Courtney's whiteness, composed of multiple heritages, into one. As Mary Waters found in her study of white ethnics, such "simplification" is common, some ancestries becoming "hidden."[43] Without an ethnic community to supply resources that can support an identity, outside of an annual Oktoberfest, white ethnic heritages recede to the background.

Summer's elective affinity with Mexican identity was a reaction to her Caucasian background being amply represented in the majority culture. She had to work to maintain Latino culture, as seen in her effort to take Spanish classes and her aspiration to study abroad in Mexico or Spain in the hope that she would "be able to learn some things and bring that . . . back into our family." Similarly understanding whiteness as a backdrop of society that does not need to be asserted, Shane picked "Mexican" on official forms if he could choose only one option: "I would pick Mexican. . . . White is more common . . . in America. . . . I like being unique and being different." In contrast to California, where Mexican ethnicity was far more readily associated with negative stereotypes such as low-class status and gang membership (as discussed in chapter 7), in majority-white Kansas there was no such pervasive stigma. Shane's associations with Mexican heritage stemmed from his family, leading him to express pride in his background and connect it to positive values such as family togetherness.

White women's affiliative ethnic identity can encourage an interracial family to lean Latino, their cultural work sustaining their husband's heritage, especially in the Kansas context. Both Latino and white respondents were aware of the role of the non-Latino partner in the continuation or diminishment of Latino culture in the family. Ignacio Gonzalez, a forty-seven-year-old Mexican American living in Kansas, would agree that supportive spouses who are "affiliative ethnics" are crucial in maintaining or revivifying Latino culture:

> I think that the person that reminds me the most that I'm Latino is [my wife] Deirdre. . . . She reminds me that we have to speak to the kids in Spanish. . . . We cannot have . . . children who won't speak Spanish at all to their children and within two generations that language is gone from "Gonzalez." . . . Deirdre said, "How can you give your son a name like Ignacio Gonzalez and have him not be able to speak Spanish?"

White women who affiliate with their husband's Latino heritage, like Deirdre Gonzalez, can promote that identity through actions ranging from "reminders" to skill-set acquisition.

The experience of whites who have an "affiliative ethnic identity" and who maintain an ethnic culture acquired through their Latino spouse runs counter to assimilation theory.[44] While the racial classification of these whites does not change, the cultural content of their lives does. Nineteen-year-old Ava Gonzalez said of her affiliative ethnic mother: "My mom is someone who married into a family with cultural practices she knew nothing about, but she's worked really hard to try to get to know that side of my family, especially with learning the language." Shane Flores similarly described his mother's affiliative ethnic identity: "She's different in . . . color . . . but basically she's another one of the family, basically another Mexican. . . . My mom speaks . . . some Spanish, she's learning to cook some . . . Mexican food. She cooked the sopa [soup] that you ate tonight. She's learning a lot of the Mexican ways. I mean, she's becoming one even if she isn't one." Her close relationship with her husband's family, Shane observed, had led to his mother "being let in on some of the

Mexican secrets" that supported the family's Mexican identity. The Flores family shows us that racial boundaries are indeed permeable, and that the white category does not always "win" or exert the most gravitational pull.

Julio Herrera said that his white wife, Susan, had "adapted more to my family than I have adapted to her family." Both historically and in contemporary times, women have been "constructed as the cultural symbols of the collectivity . . . and as its intergenerational reproducers of culture," the family members responsible for feeding the family, maintaining kinship relations, and transmitting ethnic culture to children.[45] Adding a twist, the culture that a mother passes on to her children might be *her husband's* ethnic culture. This was true for white Susan, an "ethnic settler" who had an "affiliative ethnic identity."[46] Susan's mother-in-law was a valuable cultural resource concerning quinceañeras (a coming-of-age ritual at a girl's fifteenth birthday): "[My husband's] mom . . . gave me ideas. . . . She went to México and got items. If [she] lived out of town, I don't know that we'd have [the quinceañera]." The proximity of Latino relatives propelled them toward that culture, Susan reasoned: "I think it leans more towards his family just because . . . they're here in town." With an affiliative ethnic white woman at the helm of the Herrera household, plus cultural resources delivered by the Mexican American mother-in-law, the children received cohesive cultural messages.

Julio and Susan's fifteen-year-old daughter Camille followed her parents' lead and leaned Latino. Having her Mexican grandparents living nearby, with no German American enclave nearby to represent her mother's heritage, made this cultural predilection easy. Proximity to her extended Latino family and her affiliative ethnic mother supported Camille's leaning Latino: "My mom has shown that she cares about me being Mexican. . . . She was really into planning [my quinceañera] . . . and learning all of the things you have to do . . . and what it means. . . . She knew bits and pieces of it, but . . . we learned a lot together. . . . [She got information from] my grandparents, books, the Internet, my cousins."

Older generations are a wellspring of cultural information for intermarried partners and their children, especially where there are no large Latino populations to supply cultural resources. Non-Latinos who learn and transmit cultural elements that they were unacquainted with until the point of marriage demonstrate the porousness of racial boundaries. Intermarriage may socially *brown* whites just as it may socially *whiten* nonwhites.

Supportive non-Hispanic spouses who express an affiliative ethnic identity are crucial in maintaining or enhancing a family's connection to Hispanic culture. Both white women and men can lean Latino. Seven of fourteen (50 percent) of the white spouses interviewed leaned Latino (four women and three men). Despite this near-parity, women remained primarily in charge of cultural maintenance in the home. The white women who leaned Latino actively immersed themselves in their husband's Latino culture, whereas white men supported or reinforced the cultural proclivities of their Latina wives, taking a more passive role as their wives took charge of the family's cultural life. As Derek Nava-Kelly pinpointed, "I really came to like black beans. I often will ask for them now. But imagine if that weren't the case—if I were resistant to it—the impact that that could have on culture. So there [are] reinforcement issues that become important."

Women, as "symbolic bearers of collective identity," play a particular part in the continuation of ethnic culture, even if it is not part of their lives until marriage.[47] Women as wives and mothers take (or are charged with) responsibility for the cultural life of the family. Counter to assimilation theory, white partners who adopt and maintain a spouse's ethnic culture show that racial boundaries are indeed permeable and that "white" cultures do not always win out over nonwhite cultures.

Racial Consciousness

I use the term "racial consciousness" to refer to how people comprehend race; it is an umbrella term that captures perspectives from "color- and power-evasiveness" to "race cognizance."[48] Among the respondents, racial consciousness was altered in two distinct ways upon intermarriage. First, whites developed race cognizance, understanding in new ways the salience of race as a social fixture. Second, both whites and Latinos found that racial difference was reduced in their personal lives. The context in which these two understandings emerged is important: race cognizance is prompted in the public realm in response to racial discrimination, whereas race is minimized in the private sphere when it is rendered innocuous. This section concentrates on intermarried adults and also draws from their children to show how racial consciousness in the home socializes youth, who may nevertheless develop their own, alternative understanding of race.

Race Cognizance   Whites overwhelmingly reported a heightened awareness about the salience of race as a consequence of intermarriage with Latinos. Research has found that "heightened racial identity salience is prevalent among groups that have been historically underrepresented, [whereas] White[s] are less likely to think about their own race—an attribute of White privilege."[49] Accordingly, while Latinos discussed their awareness of race, their race cognizance preceded marriage. Ten out of fourteen white interviewees (71 percent)—and an equal number of men (five) and women (five)—reported that intermarriage increased their awareness of race in the world. This finding suggests that sharing a life with someone of a different—lower—racial stratum can transform racial consciousness. Race cognizance among whites in the study contrasted starkly with intermarriage literature's prediction that race will become less important in the lives of the intermarried.

Interracial relationships can destabilize racial boundaries. Ruth Frankenberg has found that, by taking on the perspective of a black partner, white women can momentarily sympathize with a less privileged racial position.[50] A "rebound effect" of racism occurs when whites adopt the position of their black partners and feel wounded by the racism they witness. That intermarriage may produce a *heightened awareness of race* contradicts assimilation theory. If intermarriage can increase rather than decrease awareness of nonwhite racial realities, then intermarriage fails as an indicator of assimilation. The conventional "brown becomes socially whitened" image of intermarriage denies cultural dynamism and obscures the possibility of intermarriage fostering racial progressivism in whites. Intermarriage may serve as a starting point from which to freshly conceive of race rather than an endpoint that buries racial differences.

White spouses experienced a heightened awareness of race by sharing their lives with their Latino partners. Fifty-eight-year-old Trudy Ybarra, the white spouse of Mexican American Luke Ybarra, recounted a time when she and her husband were served "extraordinarily slowly" in a way that he felt was discriminatory. Since that incident early in their marriage, Trudy had been more sensitive to incidents tinged with racism: "Now, instead of trying to come up with reasons . . . why they are taking so long, I would say, 'Come on, let's just go. This isn't worth it.' So it's like learning from him." In keeping with the notion of a rebound effect of racism, Trudy remarked that "I do feel slighted when he's slighted. Racism is very subtle. Luke has taught me a lot about it." Intermarriage unveils racism and precipitates whites' race cognizance, a far cry from downplaying race.

Even for whites whose spouses were affiliated with whiteness, such as Scott Cooper, race cognizance still developed sometimes. This reveals that the racial title a spouse claims ("Spanish," in Rowena Cooper's case) can conflict with others' assessment of his or her racial category.[51] Scott reflected: "I think [intermarriage] opens my eyes to people of different cultures, people of different backgrounds, and how they're treated and how they're viewed." Here we see the limits to elective affiliation with whiteness, Rowena's racialization as nonwhite having incited Scott's awareness of racial power dynamics.

It is by looking through a loved one's eyes that whites learn about the reality of race as experienced by nonwhites. Feeling a "rebound effect" of the racism directed toward her husband after hearing about his poor treatment on the job, forty-six-year-old Courtney Flores remarked: "I just didn't know anything about the Latino culture growing up. I wasn't exposed to it. . . . So it's just been . . . an educational process for me." Courtney learned from witnessing her husband undergo racism: "I feel . . . a real strong sense of indignation. . . . Not only am I processing it for me, but [I am] also creating an awareness that this crap is still out there and helping other people to be aware of it [so] maybe we can change it."

"Helping people" is how white Deirdre Gonzalez worked to achieve equality, an aim that predated but had been enlivened by her marriage to her Latino husband. A social worker, Deirdre worked at a college assistance program for Southeast Asian and Latino migrants. She spoke to the link between her intermarriage and her career in education: "I guess . . . because I was married to Ignacio and we had biracial kids [and] I feel connected to his side of the family, I thought I could connect with these students. I think I might be able to do something for them." Familiar with the documented migration history of her parents-in-law and thankful that they promoted her husband's education, Deirdre was sympathetic to immigrants and their children, and aware of the barriers they face. For Deirdre, race cognizance was sweeping, her knowledge of race and immigration transferable from one population to another.

Familiarity with migration and legal status issues as vectors of a racialized experience can spur race cognizance. Since Ryan Carlisle married his Mexican-born wife Glenda, he was far more attuned to the ways in which Mexicans are derogated by the legal system and in public discourse. I asked Ryan, "Does your increasing knowledge about [your wife's] family increase your awareness of the importance of race?" In his answer, he expounded on the relationship between corporations, class status, immigrant reserve armies of labor, and race:

> I think a lot of people have this . . . misconception that . . . anybody can work hard and get up to this status. It's really not true. . . . It's obvious that minorities are closer to the bottom and whites are closer to the top. I'm having to explain to people that the system is set up so that it continues. So I've definitely been made aware of that, especially with her situation [as a visa overstayer]. . . . It makes me really mad to see the two-faced [stuff]. . . . It's like, "illegal immigrants are taking these jobs." First, they're not taking any jobs that you would want to do. Second, you always hear about raids on farms or meat plants. You hear about all these people who get deported, but you never hear about the consequences of the people that are taking advantage of this and employ these people. . . . There are different things that I've looked at now that I wouldn't have considered before just because, sadly enough, I think when things don't directly affect us, then we don't think about them as much.

Informed by his wife's position as an undocumented immigrant (a visa overstayer who arrived at age three with her documented parents), Ryan offered informed ideas about immigration reform, keeping central immigrants' need for legal entrance into the United States and for jobs with living wages. As he phrased it, "when things don't directly affect us, then we don't think about them as much." It was through marrying a foreign-born woman that Ryan had come to understand the salience of race in the United States and how both race and nativity either enhance or undermine life opportunities.[52]

Whites married to Latinas who were not undocumented immigrants experienced less striking race cognizance; most commonly, they became more aware of racism and racial joking. Shawn Downing stated, "If a stranger . . . expressed racism towards her race . . . if there [are] some teeth behind it . . . I would . . . make note of it in my brain." Even respondents who deemphasized racial distinctions in their marriage, like Sheldon Hoffman, were alert to racial joking: "I'm much more sensitive to the ethnic jokes now," Sheldon said. "I will now say something as opposed to just letting it fly by." Intermarried whites' acquired sensitivity to race makes them increasingly uncomfortable with racial joking—which "not only reflects but also reproduces racialized systems of domination."[53] Race-cognizant intermarried whites are no longer willing to "go along" with racist jokes.

Intermarried whites are not alone in experiencing race cognizance: their mixed-race children do too. An immigrant family history is sufficient to inspire race cognizance in mixed-race youth, even in families that downplay race. Consider the teenage Herrera-Redgrave brothers, Caleb and Tristan: their Latina mother expressed aspirational color-blindness, suggesting that her children were the harbingers of a mixed-race future in which, she hoped, race would carry less social significance. Yet the boys' comprehension of their family's racialized immigrant history led them to race cognizance. Caleb's familiarity with his grandparents' immigration story lends insight into the contemporary national conversation on immigration: "My grandpa will tell me about how he came over and how he had jobs picking cotton. . . . It gives me a little bit of a sense of what immigrants today go through." Caleb's greater understanding of racialized topics such as immigration—which at its heart concerns who is envisioned as racially suitable for inclusion in the nation[54]—was a sign of race cognizance. He added that being mixed-race had increased his empathy for others and given him a personal connection to public debates on race: "I feel like being more ethnicities . . . helps you understand more [about] other races. It helps you judge them less. I feel like it's easier for you to not judge something badly when you *are* that something. So, when you're more of the races, you don't judge all of the races as much."

Skin color also promotes race cognizance.[55] Caleb (skin-color code 1) did not touch on this theme, but his brother, naturally tan Tristan (skin-color code 3), was adamant about having to "represent Mexicans" because they "get a bad rep[utation] with stereotyping." When Tristan talked about "changing people's minds" about Mexican stereotypes, he linked this challenge directly to his grandparents' struggle for survival during their migration journey; in his case, an immigrant narrative and skin color had influenced his race cognizance. Despite the boys' mother, Cynthia, advancing a hopeful color-blindness, Caleb's and Tristan's understanding of race as imbued with social meanings and consequences piqued their race cognizance. The context in which these divergent forms of racial consciousness occurred was important: color-blindness prevailed in and described the racial tenor of the Herrera-Redgrave home (Cynthia's perspective), whereas race cognizance was a reaction to how race differentially privileges and oppresses in the public domain (Caleb's and Tristan's perspectives). A parental perspective that is inclined to minimize race in the home does not preclude race cognizance. Several factors shape mixed-race children's race cognizance, including darker skin color and racialization as nonwhite, the experience of racism against themselves or family members, and familiarity with forebearers' immigrant history.

Race cognizance was a common consequence of intermarriage, experienced by most intermarried whites. By sharing life histories and daily life with their Latino spouses, whites virtually experienced or actually witnessed differential treatment or hardship that they perceived to be due to race. By vicariously experiencing their Latino family members' race-related difficulties, intermarried whites freshly comprehended the social weight of race. As the saying goes, stepping into the shoes of another—in this case, a loved one—enables those in intimate cross-racial relationships to discover the power of race.

Color-blindness   Color-blindness—"the belief that racial group membership should not be taken into account, or even noticed"[56]—turns a blind eye to race and racism. Color-blindness is a product of a climate in which it has become politically impolite to focus on racial divides, the fallacious hope being that turning attention away from racial issues will make them dissolve. Color-blindness is presently theorized as racist; Eduardo Bonilla-Silva, for instance, defines color-blind racism as discourse that "explains contemporary racial inequality as the outcome of nonracial dynamics."[57] A linchpin of color-blind racism is white "transparency": the tendency of whites not to think of themselves in racial terms or to consider their norms, behaviors, experiences, or perspectives as white-specific.[58] This phenomenon has also been called "color- and power-evasiveness," a discursive strategy that conceals inequalities and emphasizes cross-racial similarities.[59]

Humans, of course, do not actually *not see* difference. In a conceptual sense, everyone "sees" race, for it is "encoded into individuals through iterative social practices."[60] In the post–civil rights era, "new racism" involves the replacement of overt forms of racism with "structured racism" or "color-blind racism," which keeps white privilege deeply embedded in the organization of society.[61] To change unequal power relations, whites must transcend their "transparency" and recognize their racial identity and privilege. Intermarried whites may be better poised to do this than others. The question is whether the color-blindness expressed among intermarried couples is the same stifling brand as previously documented in non-intimate domains.

The color-blindness literature oversimplifies racial consciousness by conceiving of it as dichotomous: one is either race-conscious or color-blind. This bivariate conceptualization of mental constructs around race is unrealistically sharp and nullifies the possibility that people view race as a powerful principle of social organization in certain circumstances but not in others. I found that intermarried couples invoked color-blindness *optimistically, locally* (within their marital families), and *futuristically*, signaling a future moment when race will not inhibit relations or bespeak inequality.[62] Intermarried spouses and their children who expressed this hopeful version of race relations viewed their families as a blueprint for race relations; they did not lack critical engagement with race, but instead envisioned a future when racial inequality will be mitigated.

Julio Herrera, a Mexican American of Lawrence, Kansas, emphasized "everyday" life to underscore commonality over difference:

> I think once you start living with somebody every day, you really notice that . . . there's not that big of a difference. . . . My sister and [her husband] Mitch: Mitch is Italian-Irish. . . . The Italian community is so similar to the Mexican community. . . . His mom will talk about being Italian and . . . you're like, "Gosh, you could put my mom's name in that story and it would be totally believable."

Julio pointed to his sister's intermarriage to draw similarities between two sets of foreign-born ancestors. Also seeing similarity was Julio's wife Susan, who quipped, "I think with everyday living [race doesn't matter]. We all get up and brush our teeth."

Cynthia Herrera-Redgrave, Julio's forty-six-year-old sister and the mother of Caleb and Tristan, looked to her mixed-ethnicity children as a harbinger of a multicultural future. In this case, both cultural and phenotypic intermixing had led to the minimization of race. As blurred intermediate zones expand, rigid racial categories become less relevant. Cynthia saw the future in her five children (one, her oldest, with a Mexican ex-boyfriend and four with her white husband), who ranged in skin tone and hair color from light to dark:

> When I was younger, I thought more about being Mexican. Most of my friends were Mexican. . . . Before, you just kind of [thought], "I know you're one of my people." Now, you can't really tell anymore because we've all just intermixed and intermingled. . . . I just don't notice race all the time . . . as much. . . . It's almost like I don't have a prejudgment of people anymore. . . . My kids, they're all five so different-looking that you wouldn't be able necessarily . . . to tell exactly what a couple of them are.

Intermarriage and "boundary blurring" was prevalent in her generation, as Cynthia observed: "We're getting all so intermixed." With racial intermarriage, the focus on "authentic" identities decreased; biculturalism was the reigning theme in these mixed households.

"Cultural" or "international" differences are a softer way to distinguish people from one another than the hard-line category "race."[63] Courtney Flores used the word "culture" to distinguish between herself and her Mexican American husband because it is a lighter word than "race," which is too harsh, or "ethnicity," which is imprecise. To her, the word "culture" honored the fact that she and her husband are both American. Courtney highlighted shared traits over differences:

> Roland will tell me . . . some of the struggles that [his] particular family has been through. For me, I think it has just really solidified that we are all individuals that are God's children. We're still human beings, and we all struggle day to day with various things. What might be a struggle to me isn't to somebody else. Everybody is the same, but we're different. . . . I know there's a cultural piece to it, but for me it's just still that individual and family makeup. . . . We're all the same, but yet we're different.

Courtney's focus on "culture," the "individual," and "family makeup" is a way to address basic commonality, but with unique variations. Minimizing difference by emphasizing that we are all "God's children" with an inherent "sameness" is a color-blind way to highlight connection, yet it misses the connection between some tribulations and race. In also expressing race cognizance, Courtney showed that these categories are not mutually exclusive. Importantly, race cognizance often emerges in reaction to public discrimination, whereas color-blindness is evoked in response to shared experiences in the private realm.

Sheldon Hoffman, a fifty-four-year-old white man, shared that his intermarriage with his wife Cassie, a forty-six-year-old Mexican American woman, had made race "less daunting." His family was now composed of people with varying racial backgrounds, including Cassie's large Mexican-origin extended family and her mixed-race black and Hispanic daughter from her first marriage. This multiracial exposure had made Sheldon less likely to think of someone racially and to emphasize family relationships instead of race:

> I don't think of them as Mexican. I just think of them as family. . . . I just think of her as my wife and best friend and she just happens to be Mexican. [Now] I think that I'm probably less likely to think of someone as a particular ethnic background. I'm probably much more accepting. . . . Race seems to be even less daunting. . . . Her first husband was African American, [so my stepdaughter] is African American, and . . . I have been able to meet with that side of the family . . . and develop relationships there. . . . It's just broadening my horizons, broadening my opportunities.

Through sustained relationships with his extended family—Cassie's Mexican American family of origin, her ex-husband's African American family, and his black-Mexican biracial stepdaughter—Sheldon deemphasized race in service of highlighting common human interests.

The race relations literature has shown that working closely with others from different racial backgrounds can reduce antagonism, break down stereotypes, and underscore a common human condition that transcends racial distinctions.[64] Since race no longer determines the types of relationships that groups can have with one another, owing to relaxed legal sanctions, race can feasibly be left in the background in personal relationships. Yet, while color-blindness among the intermarried is progressive in that race is not prohibitive to these personal relationships, it does not acknowledge the still-powerful effects of race and the injustices perpetuated along racial lines.

The Children of the Intermarried   The children of intermarried parents toggled between race cognizance and optimistic color-blindness. Their inclination to minimize racial difference was not rooted in denying race but rested instead on advocating equal race relations. Parents and children cited religious teachings as the foundation of their belief in human equality, a writ to treat people without regard for physical appearance.[65] Kids who attended Catholic school discussed human equality as a moral law prescribed by the Bible. Caleb Herrera-Redgrave noted that his religious instruction legitimized a fundamental equality:

> It was kind of hard for me to notice [race] at school because I went to a Catholic school. Our teachers . . . pushed equality. They didn't really treat anyone different. . . . Jesus . . . treated basically everyone the same no matter who they were, whether they were good people or bad people. [Teachers] incorporated that a lot. You never really saw them favoring children; you saw them trying to help everyone and be nice to everyone. . . . You didn't treat anyone different by race or anything.

Camille Herrera, who attended the same Catholic school in Lawrence, Kansas, drew a link between religion, equality, and color-blindness: "I think the Bible . . . taught us a lot about everyone is the same. Everyone is God's child. . . . We are all equal, and no one is better than anyone." Camille's mother, Susan, chimed in at this point in the conversation to add, "They always say treat others how you want to be treated." Religion grounds a belief in human equality that people translate to color-blindness. Church is a strong socializing institution for children, especially those enrolled in religious education classes. Religious teachings undergird the belief that everyone is equal and should be treated as such. Color-blindness among the intermarried and their children is aspirational in nature, a way to advocate for a progressive transcendence of race that, unlike conservative deployments of color-blindness, *recognizes* race and decries racial inequalities in the public sphere.[66]

Race cognizance and color-blindness are not mutually exclusive categories. Many people oscillated between these two ideas about race, their race cognizance brewing from observations of racism in public and their color-blindness springing from their innocuous experiences with race in the private realm. In vacillating in how he thought about race, Duncan Ybarra recognized and resisted race simultaneously:

> There are some points where I just don't see it [race]. . . . I only saw people for who they were, not what color they were. Because that's really superficial. [*chuckles*] . . . If I'm going to like you or dislike you, it's not because of where you come from, it's about who you are as a person. . . . If you are really nice at the get-go, I'll answer any question you ask me. [*referring to me, the interviewer*] . . . In the real world, everybody is like, "Yeah, we got to look outside of race, everybody is a human being." . . . Even though everyone is striving toward everyone of all races and creeds being able to live together

equally, it'll never happen because people are so prejudiced. It's a double-edged sword: yeah, it'd be nice if things were like that, but it will probably never be like that.

Duncan's words and chuckle indicated his awareness that "color-blindness" is a politically correct term that clashes with his belief that "in the real world" society is largely structured by race.[67] He considered equality an unrealistic utopia that will never come to fruition because "people are so prejudiced." One reason people like Duncan toggle between race cognizance and color-blindness lies in the disjuncture between philosophy and the "real world." A second reason for multiple understandings of race is that people observe discrimination against Latinos in public and yet, in their mixed-race homes, they see "races" reduced to "cultures" that meet on a bicultural middle ground.

Linking Biculturalism and Racial Consciousness

The four brands of biculturalism and the two types of racial consciousness are not mutually exclusive. Approximately one-quarter of the adults discussed in this chapter used multiple, "adjacent" forms of biculturalism. Those who deployed more than one brand of biculturalism always utilized neighboring middle categories (everyday biculturalism and selective blending) or a middle category in combination with one extreme (leaning white or leaning Latino), but never two extremes. In short, no single person ever leaned white *and* leaned Latino. Similarly, people can experience both race cognizance and color-blindness. These understandings are provoked in different contexts: race cognizance is stimulated by the public domain, whereas color-blindness is evoked in the private sphere. These different contexts suggest that, among interracial couples, race remains a prominent social feature in public space even as it is minimized in private space.

There is no overriding relationship between type of biculturalism and racial consciousness. Everyday biculturalism is equally associated with race cognizance and color-blindness, and there is no clear relationship between selective blending and racial consciousness. But an association emerges at the tail ends of the biculturalism spectrum. Nearly all who leaned Latino developed race cognizance, whereas, oppositely, all who leaned white also expressed color-blindness. Although men and women were equally inclined toward race cognizance, the finding that about twice as many men minimized race begs the question as to whether male privilege makes racial inequality less visible; this observation is in line with other findings that working-class white women are likely to be "race traitors" and to not endorse color-blind ideology.[68]

A REGIONAL COMPARISON

Kansas Hispanics relied heavily on nearby Hispanic relatives to support their Hispanic identity, whereas dependence on family was not crucial for California Latinos, who had abundant resources outside their homes and families to bolster their identity. Comparing the perspectives of two teenagers is useful to illustrate how their disparate contexts either required reliance on family (Kansas) or did not because they had abundant other resources to draw upon (California).[69] Kansas teenager Ava Gonzalez quipped, "I think because [whiteness is] what I'm surrounded by, I rarely think of it as something that needs to be preserved because it's already so prevalent. . . . A lot of the things that I've experienced in terms of Mexican culture have been with my Mexican family." In her largely white social context, whiteness was the obvious "standard."[70] Thus, her relationships with geographically proximate Latino family members were indispensable in supplying Ava with cultural knowledge. In contrast, California teenager Vanessa Ornales noted the omnipresence of Latinos in her circles: "[At] school . . . everyone's last name [is] Gutierrez or Hernandez." This ready supply of Latino people made Latino culture—from coethnic friendships to her traditional Mexican dance troupe—an everyday experience for Vanessa. The comments of these two teenagers suggest that the upkeep of Latino culture requires more effort in predominantly white areas than in areas that are home to a sizable Latino population.

The teenage Flores siblings of Kansas agreed that family was their strongest connection to Mexican ethnicity. Summer opined on the physical proximity of Latino family members inspiring her desire for cultural knowledge: "I've always just wanted to learn more about the Mexican side than the German side or Swedish. . . . I think just being around . . . my Mexican side of the family has made me wonder more and be more curious." The proximity of family members inspires cultural curiosity. Moreover, maintaining Latino heritage in majority-white contexts is especially reliant on extended family as sources of knowledge and support. Unlike in the California field site, the younger interviewees from Kansas exhibited a desire to learn more about their Latino identity. In disproportionately white Kansas, a focused effort to sustain a nonwhite heritage is required if it is not to be at risk of fading.

Absent Hispanic-dominant towns or cities in northeastern Kansas (though there are such neighborhoods), Kansas respondents referred less to a community than to their proximate family as cultural resources. Personal relationships with extended family served as "unmediated resources" to connect with their Hispanic ancestry.[71] Blair Lucero, a white woman, learned and practiced her husband's Hispanic culture with the help of her parents-in-law: "My girls are extremely close to their grandparents that live here that are Hispanic. My mom and dad . . . [have] just never been as involved. . . . [My husband's parents are] a part of who we are as a family. [My daughter has] been able to be more involved in that culture because of . . . them. And because I wanted my children to be [involved], I became involved myself." Lacking strong cultural ties herself, Blair invested in her husband's cultural legacy and participated in family relationships to transmit a culture that was not readily available outside of personal networks. Grandchildren in Kansas perceived that their grandparents were an important link to culture. Fifteen-year-old Tristan Herrera-Redgrave put it succinctly: "I can go to the source, like my grandparents' house. It . . . informs me more. My mom will tell me stuff, but . . . when I'm at my grandparents' house, they just tell me everything about them[selves]. . . . So I just go to the source." Tristan tied his Hispanic identity to his nearby relatives: "Hispanic definitely is the strongest [part of my heritage], and then Italian and then Irish. Just 'cuz we grow up with the family all around us, that's the only reason I think Hispanic is represented higher." Although the importance of family as a *value* crosscut the two field sites, it was only in Kansas that respondents highlighted the significance of family relationships in sustaining Latino culture. In California, where Latino cultural resources are plentiful, family relationships did not serve as a centerpiece of Latino identity the way they did in Kansas.

In addition to proximate family, the Catholic Church, in regularly assembling local Latinos of the same religious faith, served a crucial cultural function in Kansas. This is not to say that the Catholic Church is not a stronghold for Catholic Latinos across the nation, but in a locale with few Latinos, this institution serves as an important central meeting point for the religious within a racial community. Other racial-ethnic organizations can serve this function, of course, but the lack of a strong Latino population deters the creation of such groups. The Catholic Church fills the gap by hosting weekly English and Spanish masses and activities.

One indication of the importance of the Catholic Church as a bridge to meeting local Latinos was the difficulty in connecting to Latino culture in a predominantly white space for those who were not Catholic. For Sylvia Nava-Kelly, lacking a community of people equated to lacking culture outside the home: "A missing part is that we don't have this Hispanic community." Living far from her natal family, not being Catholic, and being a Cuban American in a town where the largest share of Latinos were Mexican Americans ("I've always felt like I couldn't connect very well with the Mexican community"), Sylvia felt culturally isolated. Seeing the Catholic Church as a central meeting place in town, Sylvia marked religion as a dividing line between herself and other local Hispanics: "I didn't grow up with any religion. . . . I think that is a huge thing that separates me from the Hispanic community. . . . There's always events at St. John's [Catholic Church], but I am just not [Catholic]. . . . Most of the Hispanics I've come to know, they are so religious. . . . I just can't connect."

In a predominantly white space where Hispanic resources are scarce, important pillars of Latino identity are found in proximate family, the Catholic Church, and spouses interested in Latino culture. In sum, across marital types, connection with and continuation of Latino identity was much easier in California (see chapter 7, however, for a discussion of the downsides). In Kansas, Latinos needed to rely on extended family, religious institutions, and a supportive partner to avoid feeling "whitewashed" by their environment and maintain a tie to a nonwhite history, culture, and perspective.

CONCLUSION

Assimilation literature proposes that minorities' intermarriage with whites leads to identificational assimilation, shifting minorities away from ethnic self-descriptors. In Milton Gordon's classic formulation, cultural assimilation is the first type of assimilation to occur and may occur indefinitely.[72] After cultural assimilation, there may be structural assimilation, which involves the entrance of minorities into cliques, clubs, and institutions in the host society. This integration at the level of societal institutions paves the way for intermarriage, which, in turn, is hypothesized to lead to the loss of ethnic affiliation and self-descriptors. This "straight-line" pathway is linear to a fault and overly focused on the minority component of race relations. Assimilation theory has four chief flaws: first, the assumption that culture and identity are dichotomous (one can only be American *or* ethnic) and that the transition of the intermarried is universally toward whiteness; second, the exclusive focus on ethnic minorities, eclipsing how intermarriage may affect whites; third, the view that racial distinctions and awareness are necessarily reduced; and fourth, the assumption that intermarriage is the endpoint of change rather than a departure point for change.

This chapter has rectified each of these four simplifications by taking a broader race relations approach. First, the vast majority of intermarried respondents charted a bicultural course, eschewing dichotomous notions of culture. Moving toward whiteness captures only one of four bicultural possibilities. Second, I have detailed how whites are affected by and participate in intermarriage, correcting the theoretical bias that minorities are the only ones who (should) alter their attitudes and behavior. Third, contrary to assimilation theory, this chapter has shown that whites can experience race cognizance as a direct result of intermarriage with a minority, remedying the erroneous notion that race must be "overcome" and reduced prior to intermarriage. And fourth, the discussion in this chapter of intermarried partners in Kansas and California has demonstrated that intermarriage is too narrowly conceived as a culmination of race relations rather than as a launching pad for revised cognition, behavior, and interracial relations.

Latino-white intermarriages do not unilaterally produce the social "whitening" and minority culture detachment that assimilation theory predicts. The most common outcome of intermarriage is biculturalism, not absorption into whiteness. Theorizing biculturalism shows an array of behavioral options that range from low to high identification with the minority culture. Although leaning white is one possible consequence of intermarriage, that tendency is often a continuation of a pre-established affiliation with whiteness based on socialization by the family of origin to value whiteness. Everyday biculturalism is a by-product of cultures intermixing as people effortlessly live their cultural lives. Selective blending is a deliberate process of bidirectional cultural change; families engaged in selective blending have ideological reasons (such as gender concerns) for retaining, discarding, or revising certain cultural elements. Partners who lean Latino foster Latino heritage because they find it to be an easily identifiable culture compared to fractional white ethnic heritages. Living in close proximity to extended Latino family and having an affiliative ethnic spouse supportive of the upkeep of Latino identity aid biculturalism as the two partners in these interracial couples, both of them inclined to explore new racial territory, discover that cultural boundaries can be porous.

Not impassive or untouched by interracial relations, whites actively participate in and are affected by their interracial marriages. Indeed, white spouses can be fundamentally changed by intermarriage and are involved in all the brands of biculturalism detailed here. White women are particularly prone to becoming "ethnic sojourners/settlers" or "affiliated ethnics." These "honorary Latinas" adopt and transmit the Hispanic culture that they first became intimately acquainted with through their Latino husband. Beyond cultural knowledge and practice, intermarried whites comprehend in fresh ways how race structures lives in public realms yet can be minimized in personal spaces.

Counter to assimilation theory, which assumes that whites want to pay less attention to race, intermarriage does not necessarily reduce racial distinctions and racial awareness. A color-blind narrative about commonality outweighing difference is only one possible outcome; another is greater race cognizance. Intermarriage is not a measure of "successful" assimilation so much as a vehicle for race cognizance in whites who have not been privy to the power of racial status. From becoming acquainted with a minority's life history to experiencing the "rebound effects" of racism, intermarried whites grow aware of how race shapes life experiences. As couples chart their lives together, countervailing types of racial consciousness develop: race is simultaneously viewed as a profound feature of social life and an overlay atop human equality.

Intermarriage can be a starting point for change, upending the long-standing assumption that it is merely the endpoint of change. Intermarriage is not the culmination of a race relations process whereby people with different racial statuses become increasingly similar, but rather an intimate relationship that brings different racialized experiences into close quarters and sparks change. Far from marking a triumph over racial differences, interracial marriage heightens contrasts in racial statuses and attendant inequalities. By placing racial statuses in relief, the intimate context of intermarriage can bring to light the real-life consequences of racial difference and cast a spotlight on rather than obscure the social reality of race. Intermarriage is not a finish line for race relations but rather a starting line for two people now given the opportunity to see race from a loved one's perspective.

Parents' biculturalism and racial consciousness influence but do not overdetermine children's cultural behaviors and racial attitudes. Virtually all Latino-white mixed-race children in this study were bicultural, matter-of-factly proclaiming both sides of their identity. Latino grandparents, as "key conduits of ethnic culture," are instrumental in nourishing their grandchildren's cultural life and are wellsprings of information for their non-Latino in-laws.[73] Whether children submit to or resist their forebearers' edicts around race, familial relationships set the stage for children's cognition and behavior around race. Most Latino-white mixed-race children display a mix of race cognizance, stemming from the differential treatment of various family members they have witnessed, and aspirational color-blindness grounded in having dual heritages that "meet on equal footing" (Caleb Herrera-Redgrave). It is interesting to ponder the extent to which these children may foreshadow future race relations in the United States. Even as racial history continues to shape the present, the children of the intermarried exhibit dynamism, awareness, hopefulness, and empathy around race that suggests a reformulated racial future.

This chapter has revealed how culture and race function in the most common Latino out-marriage pairing: Latinos and whites. In examining a less frequent intermarriage combination, Latinos and other racial minorities, the next chapter illustrates how privilege and oppression contribute to nonwhite cross-racial intimacy.

Chapter 4 | Cross-Racial Minority Pairings: Latinos Intermarried with Non-Latino Racial Minorities

THIRTY-SEVEN-YEAR-OLD Darnell Korteweg, who resisted using racial labels, choosing "none" or "all" on official forms requesting his racial category, ended his interview with me by using his son as an example of multiracialism:

> My oldest son's name is Enrique. There's always going to be that aspect of who he is. And his middle name is Alejandro. Then his last name is Korteweg. That's the part that I love. So his name is Enrique Alejandro, which is a beautiful Spanish-sounding name, then Korteweg. I love that because it's like, "Your name is Enrique Korteweg?" . . . His name represents a lot of what I stand for. It should throw you for a curve. If you think you know who he is because his name is Enrique, that's sad.

Darnell railed against racial classifications and the social construction of race.[1] He opted out of racial schemas by saying, "My ethnic background is whatever you say I am because it changes even in that our definition socially changed." He eventually answered my racial identification question using a hyphenated amalgam of his genealogy: Euro-Afro-Native-Asian-American. His biological father had African ancestry but also claimed Native American, and his mother was Dutch, part of her family hailing from Indonesia, which was once a colony of Holland. Darnell was raised in part by his white stepfather in a Latino-dominant area of New Mexico. Darnell used naming his son to toy with language and trouble assumptions about monoracialism, the idea that people belong to one unitary race.[2]

Darnell's wife Inez was a thirty-seven-year-old woman who emigrated from Mexico when she was ten years old. As an immigrant, she was especially aware of her racial-ethnic and immigrant status during times of heated political debate concerning Latinos, such as the run-up to passage of Arizona Senate Bill 1070 in 2010.[3] She too skirted race-related questions, saying, "I like to think of myself as a human being." Claiming a "Mexican American" identity, with the caveat that she did "not always fit in," she asked, "Am I really Mexican when I go to Mexico? And I'm not really American, obviously, by the way I look. I think I'm a combination of both." Born in Mexico and having lived in the United States for nearly three decades, Inez did not neatly fit the national imaginary of either nation. She wanted to be judged on nonracial terms: "Applying for college, I didn't want to be accepted because I was meeting a quota. . . . I wanted to be admitted because I was capable." Even as they downplayed race, it was still at work in Darnell and Inez's relationship, yet it did not tell the whole story. Gender told part of the story as well. As we saw with Latina women intermarried with white men, Latinas who disliked their domineering fathers often chose to marry non-Latino men.

Since racial intermarriage does not always involve the dominant racial group, this chapter complements the prior two chapters on Latino-white intermarriage by examining Latino–non-Latino racial minority intermarriage. These pairings include a Latino who was born in the United States (or, if foreign-born, who arrived in the United States by age twelve) and a non-Latino racial minority (Asian, black, or Native American). I argue in this chapter that intersectional concerns—especially Latinas' understanding of Latino masculinity as tantamount to gender oppression—spur outmarriage. Their initial critique is the same as that of Latinas who married whites, and yet their choice of marital partner differed. Latinas who married non-Latino minorities excluded whites because of their all-too-different racial location and presumed lack of understanding of a subjugated racial position. Subordination was so central to these couples' lives that they felt the need to share marginalization. In terms of consequences, these couples engaged in cultural exchange, transmitted nonwhite cultures to their children based on attitudes toward natal cultures, and (for those whose background was vacant or displeasing) experienced affiliative ethnic identity.

The experience of race is quite different from lower strata on the racial hierarchy than from the top. Patricia Hill Collins argues that being an "outsider within"—someone who is marginal to yet inside the larger social structure—allows for poignant critique of the system.[4] In this chapter, the notion of "outsiders within" comes alive as a lived experience for nonwhite racially heterogeneous couples.[5] While being an "outsider within" can be a catalyst for sociopolitical insight, can it contribute to marital choice? How do interracial minority couples—who are similar in their marginality but dissimilar in their racial status—comprehend race? How do interracial minority couples practice culture?

Prior scholarship has not shed much light on interracial minority couples, most research focusing on black-white couples and Latino-white couples.[6] Intermarriage scholarship chiefly concerns measures of "social distance" or changing rates of intermarriage over time. In contrast, this chapter uses cross-minority pairings, an overlooked demographic reality, to delve into the reasons behind marriage trends as well as their ramifications. Just as race and gender experiences inspire these unions, these same features remain prominent as couples either perpetuate or reject cultural representations in their homes.

This chapter draws from twelve individuals (six couples): five U.S.-born Latinos, one Mexican-born Latina, and their non-Latino partners: two Chinese Americans, one Native American, two multiracial black-white individuals, and one Japanese American. Of the six Latinos, five were Latina women and one was a Latino man. Correspondingly in these heterosexual pairs, five of the non-Latino minorities were men and one woman. Three couples resided in California and three couples in Kansas. No children of these couples were interviewed; either they were too young to participate or I was not granted an interview. While no children's perspectives are represented, I asked the parents about their parenting styles and their children.

Racialized and gendered experiences influenced the marital choices of my sample. The chief reasons driving intermarriage with another minority group member were women's desire to escape patriarchy through out-marriage and a nonwhite minority-minority connection. Class status was a more subtle factor, an issue more on the minds of women than men. As for the consequences of cross-minority marriages, interracial teaching and learning between two nonwhite partners was predominant. Sharing a non-white status but belonging to different racial groups opened the possibility of overtly race-oriented discussions among these race-conscious individuals, hence the utility of Collins's notion of "outsider within." These couples discussed race, gender, and culture as they transported historical and contemporary issues into their everyday conversations. Although they varied in the emphasis they placed on Americanness in combination with their minority identity, most of the couples were race-conscious and cultivated both an American identity and racial minority pride. Most cross-minority couples did not want to forfeit one identity for the other and hoped that they were harbingers of a multicultural and multiracial American future. The *multi*racial focus of their perspective animated a critique of the dominance of whites and whiteness in American race relations, history, and imaginings.

THE RATIONALES FOR LATINO AND
RACIAL MINORITY PARTNERSHIPS

The people in my sample often called on race and culture when relating their reasons for marrying their spouse. Four of the five Latina women had preferred to out-marry, citing their desire for more freedom as a woman than they experienced in their family of origin. Four people (two men, two women; two Latino, two non-Latino racial minority) had preferred either in-marriage or another minority individual. The unanimous reason for this inclination toward coethnics or other racial minorities was the under-standing issuing from a similar racial minority social location. Only non-Latino minority men (four of five) claimed that race was not important in their dating and marriage decisions. It is feasible that those for whom race was not an obvious factor in their union downplayed race in order to "empower" themselves and prevent race from acting as "a constraint on individualism," as Erica Chito Childs has found among black-white intermarried couples.[7] Relatedly, Julie Dowling finds that some Mexican Americans strategically minimize race, for "acknowledging the imprint of racism in their lives would undermine their claims to . . . American iden-tity."[8] For the couples in this chapter, even if the impetus for marriage was not race, the "margin is at the center" in their married lives—that is, their status on the racial periphery is central to their unions.[9]

Gender Issues: Motivated Marital Choice
and Child-Rearing

As in the chapter on Latino-white intermarriage, some Latinas in this chap-ter made the motivated choice to partner with someone who did not racially or ethnically resemble their domineering father. By color-coding a negative experience with dominant masculinity, some Latina women rejected stern male authority and excluded Latino men as prospective long-term roman-tic partners.[10] Their moratorium on romantic links with Latino men froze masculinity in the image of their father and foreclosed the opportunity to become familiar with Latino men who enacted different forms of masculin-ity. Latinas who out-married with the intent of finding a heterosexual part-ner whose gender ideology more closely matched theirs did this to create a secure home environment for themselves and their children. In contrast to Latinas who out-married with white men, Latinas who out-married with non-Latino minorities did so because of their need to be racially understood in ways they felt only minorities are capable of.

Penelope, her mother, and her sisters were unhappy with her father's omnipotence in the house. She described her father as a disciplinarian who had "a really bad bark." As soon as he entered the house, "things changed . . . things got really strict." Penelope resented the uneven distribution of duties in the home: she and her sisters were saddled with work, while her brothers were not. She "rebelled against that thinking" and likewise rebelled against Latino men as potential marital partners. Penelope began to cry as she considered her late mother's advice: "She wanted us to be strong and independent and not have to rely on a man, and so I kinda turned off the Mexican side and the *macho-ism*. I've really felt more comfortable within the Native culture." Despite the fact that her mother (Ojibwe) and her husband Travis (Lakota) belonged to different tribes, their cultural commonalities as Native Americans overrode their tribal differences.[11] Penelope escaped the brand of masculinity she resisted in her youth by steering both away from Latino culture and toward Native culture: "I just feel better, identifying and raising my family as Native." Her reaction to her father's dominance—color-coding behavior she deplored— had intergenerational consequences as she raised her daughter as Native.

Although Penelope dated men from a variety of backgrounds before Travis, she "never dated a Mexican man" because she "just didn't want it," referring to the male authority she associated with her father. Prior to meeting Travis, whom she described as a "really humble, gentle person," Penelope engaged in racial exploration: "[As] I grew more interested and learned more about my Native culture, I started being more attracted to Native guys. . . . I felt like Native men were humble, funny, and they 'got me.' " Her racial journey involved attending Kickapoo pow-wows at the reservation near her hometown and then working for the Office of Multicultural Affairs at the University of Kansas. By the time she met Travis at a pow-wow, "it was by choice" that she preferred to associate with Native Americans and learn more about her Native heritage, so she had "put [herself] in that . . . scene" where she met her husband. Penelope's dual cultural backgrounds provided her with two cultural avenues; she rejected the one she saw as based on male dominance in favor of the other. This rejection and favoritism set the stage for her racialized affinity with Travis.

Penelope carried forward her vision of a strong minority woman as she raised her four-year-old daughter. Travis was a resource for Penelope as she learned about and resurrected her mother's "buried" Native culture, which had been nearly extinguished by boarding schools and rampant anti-Indian racism, and endowed it with positive affect for her daughter. She stressed the importance of raising her daughter to be a strong woman of color: "I think that probably the biggest gift I could give to her is to give her a strong self, [a] strong sense of who she is. . . . Right now . . . we're trying to do that through the Indian culture. . . . I think it's hard to be a . . .

woman of color in this world. . . . There's still just a lot of . . . tension around race . . . so I want her to be able to be strong and be sure of herself."

Penelope provided her daughter with a nourishing cultural environment, upheld a nonwhite tradition of spirituality, and retained a nonwhite understanding of history and the social structure. To combat "the masculinity thing, the *macho-ism* of Latino culture," Penelope immersed her daughter in Native culture, teaching her songs, tribal languages, dances, and prayers. Because of her experience with patriarchy—her Mexican-origin father dictating that "a woman has her place"—Penelope emphasized "the matriarchal part of . . . Ojibwe culture." Even here, however, she employed a selective reading of culture, as tribal communities have also been critiqued for sexism.[12] Nevertheless, for gendered reasons rooted in her natal family experience, Penelope had chosen to marry a Native American, a choice also reflected in her parenting strategies promoting minority womanhood.

A shared racial minority background was not crucial to all cross-racial couples. Hailing from different racial categories, Inez and Darnell Korteweg agreed that deemphasizing both patriarchy and race was important. Inez's story was similar to Penelope's: she also preferred out-marriage to a partner who was not patriarchal like her father. In answer to my question about the relevance of gender in her life, Inez launched into her reasons for marrying outside of the Latino group:

> I think the reason why I married out of my culture is because I didn't feel that I could work out with someone born [in Mexico] or have the mentality of a [Mexican] man. I don't fit that traditional role. My dad always said I needed to learn to cook and clean . . . so that my husband would be happy with me. I hated it. I hated that he would say that. . . . I didn't want to be my mom. . . . I didn't want to be submissive. I didn't want to be taken advantage of. I wanted to have a voice. I don't think that my mom had that.

Critical of both her parents, Inez not only wanted to avoid a man like her father but did not want to turn into her "submissive" mother. Inez's father "was very abusive emotionally, physically, psychologically," getting "really upset" and "smacking" her mother if she neglected to put an appropriate utensil on the table. Referring to these emotional and physical outbursts, Inez said, "It was things like that I associated with Mexican men. I guess you call it machismo. He also cheated on my mom. . . . I didn't want that disrespect."

She found her match in Darnell, who conveyed his egalitarian gender ideology:

> I'm not a machista [macho man]. . . . I wash dishes and I don't care. I'll carry my wife's purse and I don't care. . . . I don't see it as a male role or a female

role. I'm not raising my boys to think that cutting the lawn is a male thing and washing the dishes is a female thing. They see their dad wash the dishes all the time. . . . I'd like them to see that. Valuing both mom and dad's voices is important. . . . It's not me being like, "I'm the man of the house." I'll ask them, "What did Mom say? If Mom said no, the answer is no." It's not like I'm going to trump her because I'm the man.

Distinguishing himself from a "machista," Darnell shared household duties and valued Inez's "voice"—the very term she used to describe how she wanted to be respected. Gender played an important role in the Korteweg home: Darnell and Inez co-created an emotionally stable and gender-egalitarian household that was in stark contrast to Inez's natal family.

As prominent as gender ideologies were in forming Inez and Darnell's partnership, attraction, culture, and race were present as well. Illustrating marriage as a social arrangement that creates order and meaning ("nomos-building"), Darnell served a "validating" function for Inez.[13] Honoring the fact that humans are sexual beings, Darnell began by describing his physical attraction to Inez before moving on to his cultural openness that validated her experience:

What I found attractive about her was *her*. She's one of those women that . . . anybody that knows her loves her. It's her energy. It's her heart. It's all those things. She is beautiful. If she was physically beautiful and not all of the things that I just described, I wouldn't have been attracted to her. I've actually met physically beautiful women that I found very unattractive because of who they are. . . . I do think that if I hadn't studied in Mexico that I would have had less of a chance of ending up with her. I think the fact that I picked up Spanish and had a larger understanding of Mexican culture changed the dynamic of our relationship—not just with her but also with her folks. Being able to communicate with her mother who only speaks Spanish . . . I don't think it would have killed the opportunity, [but] I just think [my Spanish facility] lent itself in that [positive] direction.

Darnell described the ineffable qualities about Inez that captivated him at first, but that was just the start. His cultural sympathies facilitated a cultural connection between him and Inez, a bond supported by her approving parents. This cultural fluency was both practical and emotional: it allowed Darnell to sustain Inez by validating her experience and participating in shared practices, despite their differences.

Philosophically in agreement on rejecting racial descriptors, Inez and Darnell focused on "humanity" rather than divisions. Rather than describe herself as a member of a racial or national group, Inez said, "I like to think of myself as a human being," and Darnell answered my race-ethnicity question with, "I would say I'm human." These remarks reveal, *not* that race was unimportant to them, but that they resisted it as a means of classifying and ranking. Given their emphasis on "humanity" and their direct challenges to racial classification systems, race was present in their lives as a system they were trying to dislocate.

Nearly all of the interracial minority spouses told tales of their youth that were inflected with an awareness of race as a category that divides people into groups. Being on the nonwhite side of the divide, minority respondents did not experience their race as the taken-for-granted standard, as whites typically do.[14] (Even for interviewees who were half white biologically, including those who were seen as fully white, their nonwhite heritage carried significant social weight.) Not being situated at the top of the social hierarchy affords "situated knowledge" derived from one's particular vantage point.[15] Most intermarried minority men and women cited their connection on racial minority grounds as important to them as a couple.

Latina women who had been subjugated or abused by their Latino fathers expressed the added incentive of seeking a nonviolent, non-macho (and therefore, in their minds), non-Latino husband. In earlier chapters we observed Latina women color-coding such negative behavior and avoiding Latino men by marrying white men, but for the Latinas in this chapter, whites lack a perspective they valued: that of a minority man who comprehends the power of race. In this formulation, Latina women critique both Latino men for aggression and white men for lacking a sympathetic perspective on race and power. In her theorizing on black women's perspective on white men, Collins could also be speaking to the situations in which Latina women in my sample found themselves when she observes: "It should come as no surprise that Black women's efforts in dealing with the effects of interlocking systems of oppression might produce a standpoint quite distinct from, and in many ways opposed to, that of white male insiders."[16] For these Latinas, marriage with a non-Latino minority man was the answer, provided that he was also nonviolent and race-conscious (or, less commonly, invested in downplaying race). Telling a woman-centric story, women who experienced gender inequality early on specifically sought men who they felt would be non-oppressive husbands and fathers. This finding links early life experience to rationales for marriage, emphasizing how accumulated experience shapes belief systems and, in turn, family formation.

While using a gender lens uncovers how gender structures lives—how a gendered past informs choices in the present—in the next section we see how minority men and women determine racial marginality to be foundational to a lifetime partnership.

Minority-Minority Connection:
Shared Marginalization

Although there are group-level power dynamics in Latino–Asian American, Latino–African American, and Latino–Native American race relations, an important commonality is their nonwhite status and their (often critical) view of dominant society. Even as U.S. society becomes increasingly multicultural, whites remain the power elite, advantaged by laws and practices and holding a disproportionate amount of income, wealth, and political power.[17] Interracial minority-minority partnerships are founded on a nonwhite connection that facilitates a color-conscious critique of U.S. racial history and race relations.

Two couples—Penelope Rio and Travis Strong, and Trinity and Rodrigo Valencia—were fervent about the comfort they felt with a marital partner who shared their racial subordination. As a marriage partner, a spouse is ideally "the nearest and most decisive co-inhabitant of the world."[18] The comfort that issues from the marriage union is emblematic of the validation that marriage partners give to and receive from each other. To understand each other fully and be immersed in a shared world, these couples felt that they needed to share an "outsider within" status. This was clearly articulated when I asked how they "clicked" as a couple. To be a racial minority in the United States is to lack privilege. Among these interracial minority couples, a primary source of bonding was the dialogical process of discussing subjugation from their cross-racial viewpoints and discovering their shared marginalization.

Penelope Rio, who was Mexican American and Native American (Ojibwe, otherwise known as Chippewa), and Travis Strong, who was Native American (Lakota), shared Native ancestry and had grown together in that direction since their marriage. By both accounts, Penelope and Travis felt a great deal of cultural commonality because they were both nonwhite. Despite being Native American on her mother's side, Penelope had identified as Mexican American in her youth owing to a complex array of factors: her Mexican American father's extended family lived in town, and her Native American mother downplayed her Native heritage because it was even *worse* to be Native American than Mexican American in Kansas when she was young.

Travis, as full Native American, expressed a deep and dear connection with Mexican people, saying, "We are all brown people," as he rubbed his index finger along his arm to indicate his brown color.[19] He was highly sensitive to historical oppression, including the forced removal of Native Americans, and this subjugation was the primary reason he felt a bond with Mexican Americans. Travis grew up off-reservation in Colorado and

South Dakota, where Native-Mexican mixed families were part of the racial landscape: "A lot of Lakota families married into Mexican families. A lot of Lakotas have Mexican last names. . . . But they were also a big part of the Native community too. . . . They mingle in like that, marriage-wise." Travis took cues about the compatibility of Native Americans and Mexican Americans not only from his own observations of intermarriage patterns but from leaders in the community, such as medicine men:

> Talking with a lot of the medicine men—the spiritual leaders—we are all the same. We don't . . . call Mexicans "them." In *our* eyes, the Lakota eyes, they are our brothers and sisters, they are no different—they're Indians too. That's why a lot of our medicine men treat spiritually the Mexicans now, for healing. You can take an individual, let's say Joe Rodriguez . . . to the medicine man, and he'll say, "Yes, come bring him in my house." So we look at them as the same, there's no difference.

When the reference point is racial minority status (as opposed to abstract liberalism that supports color-blind ideology), "we are all the same" is a color-conscious affirmation that brings the margins to the center. One reason for Natives' acceptance of Mexicans as "brothers and sisters" is historical. "They're Indians too" harkens back to the historic origins of Mexicans as the descendants of the Spanish conquering forces of Hernán Cortés and the Aztecs of Montezuma's empire in the 1530s. Aztecs and other tribes in what is now Mexico were indigenous to the Americas, just as Native Americans are to the United States. Further, the incorporation of significant parts of what used to be Mexico into the United States with the Treaty of Guadalupe Hidalgo (1848) makes deterritorialization a common theme between Native Americans and people of Mexican descent. Knowing this history, Travis grounded his contemporary intercultural connection with his Native American and Mexican American spouse in indigenous origins, colonization, and shared cultural features such as "the extended family," "celebration [of] their dead," "child-rearing," and "taking care of their elders." The overlap between racial histories that undergirds Travis's emphasis on the interracial solidarity of "brown" people illustrates that "racial categorizations constantly evolve, and groups may develop a panethnic consciousness that transgresses 'official' designations."[20] If colonialism erases intragroup differences by imposing racial categories on previously distinct groups (for example, the tribes and bands collapsed into "Native American"), colonialism also is foundational for cross-group solidarity, a unifying theme that yokes groups with similar histories.[21]

Travis made a deliberate choice to marry someone with whom he shared Native ancestry and nonwhite experience. Travis had dated only Natives prior to meeting Penelope: "I always admired the brown person. I've never touched a blond hair!" Despite the availability of blond women, Travis wanted to date someone "with some *culture!*" In prioritizing Native American or "brown" culture, Travis's thought process negotiated his desire away from whites and toward brown people. His dating history was not the result of demographic constraint but the expression of a *preference* (for "someone with *culture!*"): "Because I think . . . culture . . . makes you become a better person. . . . You don't get stuck in this everyday rut of 'dog eat dog world' if you've got culture. You can always activate the culture button and everything will be okay after that, you know?" Travis not only valorized his own culture for its values (family cohesion, spirituality, and reverence for elders) but critiqued white society for being "dog eat dog." His white brothers-in-law "never say *anything* about their background— never!" For Travis, culture was grounding—a "button" that could be "activated," after which everything would be "okay." As my collaborator Christopher Wetzel and I discovered, Mexican Americans' and Native Americans' discursive valorization of minority culture and their critique of white society can serve to reinvest these derogated groups with esteem.[22]

Penelope Rio agreed with her husband Travis that their minority-minority connection was a source of bonding. She was raised in Horton, Kansas, knowing nothing more than the simple fact that she was half Native on her mother's side, racism having taught her mother shame. As a girl, Penelope's mother was sent by her poverty-stricken family to attend a Native American boarding school. Indian boarding schools were established in the United States during the late nineteenth and early twentieth centuries to educate Native American youth according to Euro-American standards. Originally established by Christian missionaries, the Bureau of Indian Affairs (BIA) created these assimilation-model schools that over 100,000 Native Americans were forced to attend.[23] Native children were removed from their families and communities to rupture racial identity and solidarity. Immersed in European-American culture, Native American children were forbidden to speak their native languages, their traditional dress and haircuts were changed, and their given names were replaced by Anglophone names. Boarding schools were a heavy-handed approach to Anglo-conformity; destructive to Native American identity, they inflicted what has been called a "soul wound" on Native American peoples and cultures.[24]

Penelope explained this period of cultural stripping and Americanization that drove her mother to "bury" her Native American identity:

> She went to boarding school in South Dakota. . . . Because her parents were really, really poor . . . the best way they thought to handle that was to let the

kids go to boarding schools. . . . She told her parents . . . around eighth grade that she was going to commit suicide—that they needed to come get her. So they came and got her and decided to bring her to Horton. . . . And then she . . . and my dad met and married and had us, our family.

In the local racial hierarchy in small-town Kansas, Native Americans were positioned below Mexican Americans. Given Penelope's mother's aggrieved experience as a Native American, her choice to marry a Mexican American was a move up and away from her debased racial category. Mexican Americans were not rejected as thoroughly as the Native Americans in Kansas during the 1940s and 1950s, making out-marriage with a Mexican American appealing as an escape route from Native American degradation. As Penelope explained it, her mother "took on" her husband's culture because her experience as a Native American woman had been nearly unbearable: "As I look back, I can see it [Horton, Kansas] as being pretty racist. They had the [Kickapoo] reservation right there, so they were really down on Indians. They . . . went so far as to having signs in the windows of the . . . local Dairy Queen . . . saying No Indians allowed. . . . That [was a] pretty bad experience for her, so she . . . took on my dad's culture."

Penelope's mother adopted her husband's only slightly less aggrieved culture, which she endorsed with her children: "My mom pretty much buried everything. She didn't talk about her Native culture at all. She really took on the traditions of my dad." Even as the oppression of Native Americans kept Penelope's mother ashamed of her Native heritage—until she reclaimed it (through Penelope and Travis) at the end of her life—Penelope's Mexican American father was not immune to racism. Penelope recalled: "When [my dad] was in high school, he was a big basketball stud . . . a real big important part of the team. They went to state [championships] . . . his senior year, and the hotel they stayed in wouldn't allow him a room. He had to stay in the boiler room. Yeah, as a high school kid."

The specific histories of the destruction of Native American and Mexican American lands and cultures may differ, but oppression is their overriding similarity. Penelope and Travis bonded over being on the losing end of power struggles with the U.S. federal government and white-dominant institutions. History was present in their contemporary racial lives. Being "outsiders within" together with highly attuned racial consciousnesses makes minority-minority pairings a place of comfort and understanding.

For cross-minority couples who espoused the power of race, finding another minority partner was a clear preference. For those sensitive to their racial group's oppression, the desire to be understood as racialized beings was paramount. I call this "racialized affinity," that is, the desire to be understood as a racialized person by another racial minority in a way that draws people together. As Anthony Ocampo notes regarding Latinos and Asians, "despite linguistic, socio-economic and cultural differences . . . groups develop panethnic [and panracial] consciousness by . . . *emphasizing cultural commonalities or highlighting shared racial experiences.*"[25] This logic is a basis for racialized affinity that is foundational to minority-minority pairs who regard racialization as central to their experience.

Illustrating racialized affinity, Trinity and Rodrigo Valencia felt that racial subordination and class disadvantage played so central a role in their lives that they needed to share this foundation to feel intimately understood. Trinity Valencia, a biracial black-white woman, said, relative to her dating history, "I was always attracted to men of color—even though I was surrounded by white men. . . . My choices had always been . . . men of color." Trying to specify the cause for her attraction, I asked, "What draws you to them?" Trinity linked her experience of being a racial outsider to her preference for men of color: "Just feeling like [men of color] would understand what it's like to be an 'other' and that experience. Not always feeling comfortable in white culture. . . . Yeah, shared experience and someone who understands being an 'other.' " The experience of being a racial "outsider" or "other" was so fundamental to some minority respondents that it was essential for them to share this experience with a loved one if they were to comprehend one another more completely.

As seen with gender and race in natal family systems, experiences with race and class outside the family also shape how people see the world and influence their marital decisions. Considering all marital types, racial minority respondents were more attentive than whites to legacies of racial, class, and gender oppression as well as immigrant stigma. Trinity Valencia's ruminations on her intersectional subjugation as a woman of color were laced with history. When I asked about her experience as a woman of color, Trinity spoke passionately about the positionality of black women in America:

> This entire nation was built on the backs of black women. . . . Black women go through all this struggle and they still provide for their families and they're still this strong rock. . . . A lot of time people count me out because I am a woman of color. . . . I . . . really identify with the Maya Angelou poem "Still I Rise." . . . Sometimes when I'm feeling . . . marginalized or invisible, I recognize that I've played a strong role, or people before me have played a strong role, in creating the country and getting us where we are today.

With her sharply gendered racial consciousness, the long history of racial and gender inequality was very real to Trinity. By ushering history into the present, Trinity unveiled how present-day marginality did not suddenly crop up but instead was evidence of the "sedimentation of racial inequality" that has accumulated disadvantage over centuries.[26] And by centering black women's "struggle" in slavery and commemorating their persistence as "strong rocks," Trinity identified the value of perseverance. Moving to the contemporary moment, she said that she is "counted out" as a minority woman, a modern slave of a gender and race hierarchy in which black women (as she referred to herself here) are at the bottom. As a spokesperson for multiculturalism in both her personal and professional lives, Trinity credited historical figures who had worked for equality. As we saw, Trinity selected her life partner based on shared marginalization (someone similarly racialized and occupying a class-disadvantaged position), and their agreement about how race and class contour advantage and disadvantage was critical to their relationship.

Rodrigo, Trinity's Mexican American husband, preferred the company of Mexican Americans or blacks because of shared marginalization—what he called their "life experience" similarities—despite the work he invested in claiming an "American Mexican" identity. Flipping the customary term "Mexican American" into "American Mexican," which prioritizes Americanness, Rodrigo leveraged this term as his "operating identity"—the "mental construct . . . [that is] enacted and communicated via symbolic interaction."[27] By inventively switching the order of a commonplace ethnic label, Rodrigo was symbolically and rhetorically bringing to the forefront his primary identity: "I would be more comfortable being known as an 'American Mexican,' just because . . . when people think of 'Mexican Americans' they think, 'Oh, you must be first generation . . . from Mexico.' And I have no problem saying, 'No, I was *born* in this country, and my parents and grandparents were born in this country.' " Despite his birthright and his preference for identifying himself as "American first with Mexican ancestry," Rodrigo's racial marginality was fundamental to the bond he shared with his wife.

Rodrigo and Trinity met working for a college preparatory program that served high school students from low-income families and families in which neither parent held a bachelor's degree. Even the place where they met—a summer job helping low-income and minority students gain admission to and succeed in college—reveals the extent to which they were sensitive to race and class. Rodrigo explained his rationale for choosing a racial minority life partner: "The people I was *interested* in . . . would be either Mexican American/Hispanic or maybe black. . . . [When I met Trinity] I thought, 'Well, she's biracial.'Both of us have similarities in life, not so much *culturally*, but just life experiences" [Rodrigo's emphasis]. "Life experiences" captures both race- and class-related positions of disadvantage. For interracial dual-minority couples, it is critical not so much to mirror one another's racial background but to stand on the racial periphery together and share that marginal perspective.

A Half-and-Half Connection

Caroline and Bryce Wu, like Penelope Rio and Travis Strong, shared half of their ancestry. Caroline and Bryce were both half Caucasian, unlike the Rio-Strong couple, whose ancestry overlap was Native American. Despite being half Caucasian and having claims to whiteness, Caroline and Bryce felt marginal to mainstream U.S. society, and this common outsider status was a source of bonding for them. Despite both being half white, their "half-and-half" status figured prominently in their lives. Even the self-designation of "half-and-half" suggests that they were not entirely accepted by the wider U.S. community; otherwise, their mixed-race status would have gone unmentioned. It was the racialization of the nonwhite portion of their identities that had made this couple's "half minority" background salient.

U.S. racial categories have historically been rigid and dichotomous, and the census practice of providing a multiracial designation (checking two or more races) did not even begin until the 2000 census.[28] Blackness was long defined through hypodescent—the "one-drop rule"—which made whiteness "tainted" if mixed with blackness.[29] This logic underlies whites' "possessiveness" of their whiteness and the privilege that accompanies it.[30] The rule of hypodescent—applied, most obviously, to blacks—lends insight into how U.S. society looks upon interracial families. Regarding mixed-race children born out of black-white interracial partnerships, whites "seem to object to the creation of 'black' children . . . who may be inferior or 'pollute' the white race."[31] Many whites have "invested" in their position of relative superiority: they oppose racial mixing because of the threat of status degradation.[32] Since nonwhiteness is a durable dividing line in the United States, sharing nonwhite backgrounds can be a platform for a powerful bond.

Caroline Wu was a thirty-one-year-old woman who was born to an Ecuadorian mother and an Anglo father from Texas. Born in Redwood City, California, she had moved with her family to Lawrence, Kansas, when she was three. She had pale skin, short light brown hair, hazel eyes, and a narrow nose. Caroline said that she was perceived as "100 percent white all the time" and that people expressed surprise when she spoke Spanish or claimed a Latina identity. She received her first racial lesson when people did not recognize her biological relationship to her Ecuadorian mother. Such inability to recognize mixed-race families shows how deeply embedded the notion of racial homogamy is in U.S. society and how people police others based on the expectation of same-race families.[33] Caroline's first racial lesson included racial questioning:

> I do remember when I was five years old . . . coming home from school and someone had told me that I was adopted because I didn't look like my mother. And I had to have the proof. They had to . . . get out the baby books and show me the pictures of my mom holding me when I was new. . . . This friend acquaintance . . . really had convinced me that there was no way that I could be not adopted because I didn't look anything like my mother. So I think that's probably the first time I was really kind of aware . . . of . . . physical differences that have to do with race.

Not only elementary school friends in the United States but Ecuadorians during a month-long trip to her mother's hometown perceived the mother-daughter relationship inaccurately. Even Ecuadorian shoppers questioned Caroline's biological relationship to her mother. She recalled the tale, now a joke in the family, of local shoppers at the market thinking "that I was . . . out with my maid. 'There's the little gringita [white girl], out with her . . . servant, her nanny . . . [or] the housekeeper.' " In the two countries to which she has a birthright or ancestry tie, mixed-race Caroline had trouble claiming family relationships because people did not acknowledge racial, cultural, and familial complexity. Instead, both societies enforced her peripheral status.

Like Penelope Rio and Travis Strong, Caroline felt a comfort in discomfort, taking solace in sharing mixed-race status with her husband Bryce. She described her first reaction to the half-white, half-Chinese man who would become her husband: "[What] I did like about him right away . . . right off the bat . . . was that he was half just like me. . . . I really latched on to that [as] something that we had in common. . . . We have this one major thing in common, which is growing up . . . with one foot in each culture in Kansas." For interviewees in Kansas, being a racial minority or mixed-race was more remarkable than in California owing to this population's underrepresentation in the Midwestern state. For Caroline, being "half" and not fitting into neatly bounded racial categories was so central to her life experience that she instantly felt a visceral connection to Bryce.

Interracial minority couples can be creative in delineating their common ground. Just as Travis Strong saw both himself and his wife as phenotypically "brown" people, Caroline did the same between herself and Bryce:

> My cousins say he looks more Latin than I do. . . . [laughs] It's the black hair. . . . Besides the obvious, like physical characteristics, there's the food. . . . You know, eating things that aren't . . . part of the regular day-to-day American

diet . . . things that are steamed or . . . wrapped. He's a very adventurous eater, and I grew up being an adventurous eater, and not knowing that I was an adventurous eater, because that was just . . . my norm.

In her reference to physical features, Caroline challenged the fallacious assumption that racial categories are discrete. In fact, biologists and sociologists have demonstrated that there is more genetic variation *within* than *between* so-called racial categories.[34] For Caroline, the experience of being half white and half nonwhite was very similar. In her perception, being half white made both Bryce and herself simply nonwhite. She summarized: "We do realize there's a lot of similarities. [*laughs*] Often we joke . . . that Chinese and Ecuadorian people really are the same race [*laughs*]."

Although it might seem amusing to think of Chinese and Ecuadorians as the same race, Caroline's comment underscores the socially constructed quality of race: since racial groupings are not natural but human inventions, why should Caroline Wu *not* consider herself and her husband as belonging to the same racial category? The predominantly white local context in Kansas made it even more logical for this dual-minority couple to assert commonality—even sameness—in their nonwhiteness. In a social context where whiteness prevails, varieties of nonwhiteness become fused into a more general nonwhite sameness, even as some people understand points of difference. Illuminating this phenomenon among dual-minority couples is Robert Smith's term "conjunctural ethnicity," which "recognizes that ethnicity emerges in historical and social conjunctures and contexts . . . and . . . focuses on the local, historical, and life course contexts . . . seeking to capture dynamic and sometimes unanticipated processes that affect racial and ethnic experiences."[35] In a local context where racial minorities are few, nonwhites in Kansas seek out nonwhite similarity at critical junctures in their lives, such as marriage. The life course angle is relevant here because contemplating marriage encourages people to assess their priorities, wants, and needs. When racial marginalization, if not sameness of racial identity per se, tops the list, partnering with another nonwhite minority makes sense. With local demographics latently encouraging people to look outside of their numerically small racial group, racial minorities in Kansas find each other, discover comfort in their shared experiences of marginalization, and come to highlight their sameness of marginality over their difference. Declarations of unification come from representatives of groups that are typically viewed as distinct—"we are all brown people," for example, or "we really are the same race." This rhetoric highlighting shared marginality is a strategy to unite formerly disparate groups.

Bryce Wu had a Caucasian mother and a second-generation Chinese American father. He had pale skin, dark hair, and a slim face with high cheekbones. He was the lone Asian student in his elementary school in an affluent Kansas City suburb. Bryce's paternal grandparents emigrated from China, and two generations later Bryce was raised speaking English and using certain Cantonese phrases only sparsely, such as Cantonese titles for family members. Like his wife, Bryce recalled white peers who pointed out racial difference in elementary school: "One kid . . . would . . . tease me about bringing eggrolls in my lunch . . . or dumplings. . . . I'm just like, 'Why? What are you talking about? No, I've got peanut butter and jelly. It's like what'd you bring.' " Bryce felt a bond with Caroline because she struggled with issues of race and acceptance as he did:

> Caroline's mom . . . spoke Spanish, she was from Ecuador . . . and her dad was [from] Texas, Oklahoma, Kansas. [That] kind of mix . . . I think really . . . was intriguing for me. It's like, 'Oh, here is someone who . . . went through some of the same self-realization that I went through, but not the same culture.'. . . There were common experiences with a different twist. . . . I was intrigued by that. That was kind of fun.

Bryce suggested that being mixed-race is qualitatively different from being monoracial. I asked him to explain what he meant by "self-realization" with "a different twist." He responded:

> Just the . . . traditional U.S. holidays . . . trying to . . . explain exactly . . . why the Fourth of July is such a big deal. . . . Her mom understood but didn't necessarily feel compelled to celebrate to the same level. . . . I . . . saw that as well. Also . . . the language barrier. . . . She understood going to family reunions and having all the older generation speaking . . . Spanish. I would go and they'd all be speaking Chinese.

Many other interracial minority couples echoed Bryce's comment that "support and understanding [comes from] having gone through some of the same things." Although "outsider within" experiences can be uncomfortable, sharing those experiences can be grounds for bonding.

Cross-minority pairs are founded on racialized affinity developed from marginalized status on the U.S. racial scene. Historically, nonwhiteness has been the dividing line for privileges, including citizenship, property rights, and job acquisition.[36] Respondents in dual-minority marriages see as an essential element to their relationship the "common racialized experiences [that] allow people of color to validate each other's struggles to deal with everyday racism rather than invalidate experiences through colorblindness."[37] In cross-minority pairs, racial subordination was a unifying and transcendent theme.

THE CONSEQUENCES OF PARTNERSHIPS BETWEEN LATINOS AND NON-LATINO RACIAL MINORITIES

The main consequences of these cross-minority intermarriages were inter-racial cultural exchange, race-consciousness that saw history as alive in the present, and debates around cultural preservation.

Intercultural Exchange, Affiliative Ethnicity, and Honorary Identities

Two-thirds (eight of twelve) of the cross-minority intermarried respondents engaged in intercultural exchange. This finding transcends reasons for intermarriage as well as gender.[38] Three of the eight people who were intercultural learners claimed to be *more* closely affiliated with their spouse's racial background than their own. The three people who adopted their spouse's heritage over their own had preferred to out-marry from their racial community because they did not fit in (Trinity Valencia) or were reacting against their racial group owing to concerns that they attributed to culture, such as gender inequality (Penelope Rio and Sharon Cheng). Feeling ill at ease with their own racial community had led to out-marriage, which then facilitated the "affiliative ethnic identity" they acquired at the point of marriage (as discussed in chapter 3).

The remaining four cross-minority intermarried respondents reported different outcomes: two reported a strengthening of their own racial identity, one reported a more "American" identity, and one reported no change. The two who experienced a stronger racial identity now than before their intermarriage were *intercultural teachers* to their eager spouses (the Valencias and the Chengs). In the process of intercultural teaching, these men emboldened their own racial identity. As they dug into their own racial histories and cultural repertoires in order to educate their spouses, they became more acquainted with their own backgrounds and strengthened their racial claims. Rodrigo Valencia explained: "She may have a question about 'what does *this* mean?'If I didn't know it, I would want to go and find out. . . . I think [my racial identity] has definitely gotten stronger. And that's because of *her* genuine interest as well." As explored in chapters 3 and 5, supportive spouses are crucial to racial identity maintenance or amplification.

Most interracial minority couples engage in intercultural exchange. The intercultural teaching and learning process is more obvious in these couples than in Latino-white pairs because, in Latino-white couples the teaching is unidirectional, flowing from Latino to non-Latino. Whiteness does not need to be taught because it is pervasive in U.S. society. In contrast to Latino-white couples, for whom ethnic culture flows one way, for interracial minority couples a bidirectional cultural exchange was the norm. Their dual-minority relationships provided them with opportunities to teach and learn about nonwhite history, culture, and perspectives and opened up space for "outsider within" unity.

These respondents viewed the exchange of cultural knowledge as part of the process of desire. Caroline Wu pondered the consequences of her interracial marriage: "When we first met, I wondered how different things would be if I had found someone who was Latin American, because then I would have . . . reinforced my cultural heritage instead of . . . expanding. . . . I feel that my life is pretty rich now, having this whole other country to explore, this other culture." As many others remarked, interracial relationships "expand" one's knowledge of the world and of racialized perspectives. From Bryce Wu's perspective, teaching his wife about his Chinese culture had strengthened his Chinese American identity while also exposing him to another culture: "I've learned more about her background, [and] it has sparked a curiosity to learn more about my own."

Beyond intercultural exchange between two people whose cultures stand on equal footing, interracial relationships offer the possibility of affiliating with an ancestry not one's own. Trinity Valencia, a half-white and half-black woman, did not easily fit in with whites in predominantly white St. Joseph, Missouri, and she was rejected by the small black community in college. Her uncles told her white mother that they had no desire for a biracial child in the family; she was the target of race-related property damage and aspersions by whites; and she was disqualified from the black student union in college for failing to be black enough. When she experienced the "minority-minority connection" with her Mexican American husband Rodrigo, Trinity became an "affiliative ethnic" — that is, she became culturally Latina. This brief exchange at the beginning of our interview makes it clear that she claimed a biracial identity and then overlay it with a voluntary Latina identity:

AUTHOR: How do you identify?

TRINITY: Biracial. My mother is white, my father is black.

AUTHOR: Any Latino/Latina?

TRINITY: No—until I got married. [*laughs*]

Trinity answered my question by referring to what Ian Haney López would call her "bio-race," which is seen as "solely about ancestry or morphology" and does not include socioeconomic status or personal preferences.[39] Yet race is multidimensional, involving both objective/ascriptive and subjective dimensions.[40] "Self-definition" rests on one's internal judgment, whereas how one is treated points to external racial ascriptions. In her answer, Trinity moved from objective racial classification ("biracial") to her subjective identity ("Latina").

Romantic partnerships can consolidate subjective racial identities. Trinity veered away from her bio-race and gravitated toward the category Latino/a, already a racial admixture, because of the discomfort she had experienced in white and black communities.[41] Rejected by white and black populations, she could claim identity as Latino, a social group to which she had no bio-racial claim, and be released from authenticity challenges. Trinity joined a Hispanic student group on her college campus prior to meeting her husband and became more active in it as they began dating. Trinity mused on how she culturally leaned toward her Mexican American husband:

> I wonder if . . . because I didn't have my own culture . . . I adapted and picked up his culture so quickly. . . . In the car we'd listen to reggaeton and . . . then I'd go to his mother's house and . . . she would fix [Mexican food]. It was never *not* a part of our life together. We were both in HALO [Hispanic American Leadership Organization] . . . so it's a part of our relationship. Me learning about his culture, through all the things we did together, me *taking on* that identity . . . [was] a foundation of our relationship.

I asked why she grew toward Hispanic culture. "I think initially it was the shared experience," she responded, "but . . . also, nobody questioned why I was in the group. . . . Nobody said, 'You can't do this,' or, 'We don't think you're Hispanic.'" In contrast to her rejection by the black student union, Trinity was accepted by the Hispanic organization, a space that provided her with room to explore race without critique and that bolstered her minority-minority connection with Rodrigo.

Rodrigo was jubilant about Trinity's embrace of Latina identity: "I joke with her, I say, 'And now I made you an honorary Hispanic [*laughs*], a Latina!'" He justified her "honorary Hispanic" stature by her knowledge about his culture and family, saying that, in comparison, she "doesn't know . . . *anything* about her father's side, which was her African American side," and her mother's white family did not promote any culture other than "American." While most couples' cultural exchange was reasonably even, this couple's was not for the principal reason that Trinity, being shunned by both the black and white communities, preferred to adopt her husband's culture over sharing hers with him.

Intercultural exchange was common among dual-minority couples. For those with a meaningful minority-minority connection, intercultural exchange was a source of bonding that reinforced identity and a race-conscious worldview. People engage in affiliative ethnicity if they see their partner's race as preferable to their own, as a resolution to racial problems, or perhaps as neutral. Like the cross-national Latino pairs profiled in the next chapter, intermarried minority pairs viewed their relationships as racial havens. Within these relationships, two people who had both experienced racial marginality could grieve for and recover from racial wounds, rail against racial inequities, and ponder potential racial futures. As these pairs co-constructed a home life together, they created a racial and cultural environment that they perceived to be safe, shared, and liberatory.

History Alive in the Present

Perceived similarities between racial minority groups around pervasive racial discrimination shape a Latino identity and sympathy that is inclusive of other nonwhites and can be a basis for a marriage.[42] Oppression is remembered and discussed more frequently among dual-minority pairs than among Latino-white pairs, and most cross-minority pairs point to racial subordination as a significant bond.[43] Contemporary issues of race and racism were discussed by couples of all marital types, but conversation concerning historical eras of racial injustice was prominent among interracial minority couples. In cross-minority pairs, we see an evaluative process of comparing subjugation across nonwhite racial groups and, upon identifying parallels, concluding that shared marginalization is a firm foundation for a love match based on understanding. The margins become the center in these marriages. Knowledge-making is accessible to everyone, and these cross-minority partnerships spur on the critique of unequal power relations.[44]

History was alive in the present in cross-minority couples in their overt discussion of historical racial oppression. Historical events and power differentials informed interracial minority couples' views on contemporary racial issues, group histories of race-based domination being a connective theme. Cross-racial minority couples, including half-whites, are "outsiders within" who possess two *different* racial minority perspectives, and they cast a bright light on how the nation has systematically used race as a tool to privilege some and oppress others.[45]

Travis Strong worked in building maintenance at Haskell Indian Nations University in Lawrence, Kansas, a university with an enrollment of one thousand Native American students from 130 federally recognized tribes. On its web page, Haskell announces its location by replacing the name "Kansas" with "Kansa" (otherwise known as "Kaw"), the Native American tribe that inhabited the area prior to and during white settlement. Operating since 1884 and originally a residential boarding school for American Indian children, Haskell serves the "educational needs of American Indian and Alaska Native people from across the United States."[46] Haskell attracts Native American students from various tribal nations in the United States. Travis, who called Haskell the "largest Native University," was on the board of the university's Cultural Center and saw himself as a "mentor" to younger Native Americans. He offered a striking example of history being alive in the present. In relating the following encounter, Travis demonstrated how Native experience with colonialism at the hands of the U.S. federal government is alive in, and casts a pall on, the present day:

> There was a person that came to Haskell, a white guy. He had something in a box, and he said, "I'm lost, can you direct me to somebody? I need to give these to somebody." Well, what is it? . . . He unveils it. He goes, "My grandfather gave me these years ago. He used to use these. . . ." It turned out to be a little kid's handcuffs. Handcuffs. His grandfather would gather all these Indian kids and bring them to boarding schools. Forcefully. It just tore you apart, because they were made for little wrists, they were scaled down. He said he couldn't live with those handcuffs no more. . . . Man, we freaked out. We had to have [cleansing] ceremonies. It just tore everybody up. . . . It's a good reminder, though, of what went on.

In this encounter, Travis saw the inner workings of domination and, in witnessing "white power demystified," came to know "that it was not the intellect, talent, or humanity of [whites] that supported their superior status, but largely just the advantages of racism."[47] The white power techniques of the boarding schools had not been left in the past but resonated in the present in the form of handcuffs, ghosts, and the loss of culture and language. "Haskell is still Haskell from years ago," he remarked. "It is very much alive. What I mean by that is the past still makes its presence." He cited a current example of an apparition caught on camera that the Cultural Center director confirmed wore the dress and haircut of the boarding school days. The past being "very much alive" is also seen in Haskell's effort to preserve memories and artifacts. There is a graveyard on Haskell land as well as in the nearby wetlands, and the Cultural Center keeps historical records, lest history be forgotten or repeated.

For as long as he could remember, Travis had been acutely aware of race and his racial group's subjugation. I asked him to recall his first memory of the idea of race. He spoke of racial violence thick with historical significance: "Oh yeah. . . . Probably when my mom pulled a .22 out of her purse back during the Wounded Knee siege. . . . When you see your mom pull a .22 out of her purse, you know! Divisions, all right. . . . You could find [that] very much so in any border town on the reservation. The division of race."

Travis was referring to the 1973 incident at Wounded Knee, South Dakota, on the Pine Ridge Indian Reservation, where he grew up. On February 27, 1973, approximately 200 Lakota occupied Wounded Knee to protest the U.S. government's failure to satisfy its obligations as set forth by treaties with Native American tribes. Living on tribal lands during his youth, Travis had an informed perspective on Native-white clashes over geopolitical boundaries, the allocation of resources, and racial antipathy: "I noticed the difference between races in the border towns on the reservation through violence."

Travis's attention to history had led to his understanding of contemporary race relations and his frustration with people who do not comprehend how history has shaped present-day race and class relations. Whites, he said with a sigh, "have this idea of free . . . they think we get everything for free . . . stuff handed to us. Little do they know, it's all in the treaties. . . . It's stuff that they owed to us, and they're giving it to us that way, free medical care and stuff like that. . . . It says it in the treaties." He was referring to the Johnson-O'Malley Act, passed by Congress in 1934 to subsidize the education, medical services, and other services provided by the state of Minnesota to Native Americans.[48] For example, Travis related, in elementary school other students had to pay fifteen cents for milk whereas he was given free milk and lunch.

Indian-white tension existed alongside white-against-Mexican strife, which Travis observed through dynamics affecting his Mexican classmates. He saw the similarities between the Native and Mexican group histories as reason for interracial coalition and a basis for marital harmony. As I closed the interview with Travis, I asked if he had anything else he wished to say. His concluding remark reemphasized interracial connections: "I just like the fact that . . . we consider the Mexicans as our brothers and sisters now. . . . A lot of boundaries went down: we need each other as allies, this is our, Mexican and Native lands, you know. . . . We are coming back as brown people. . . . And we are going to be much smarter than a long time ago."

His use of the term "brown people"—referring to skin color more than to political movements (Brown Power and Red Power were two distinct movements during the civil rights era)—rhetorically *unified* Natives and Mexicans. Highlighting their similar dispossessed histories, their non-white phenotype, and issues such as "violence, drug runs, land disputes, water rights . . . the 'haves' and 'have-nots,' " Travis enumerated the reasons for the two groups to act as a coalition. He tacitly invoked the notion of "linked fate," the concept of taking political action in pursuit of group interests that are seen as a proxy for self-interest.[49] He argued that forming a coalition of groups that identify as "brown" owing to their shared marginalization would be a powerful way to combat race-based inequality not confined to one group. Here "brown" is cast as a "master frame" that defines inequality by encompassing multiple subordinated groups, a way to forge solidarity and collective action.[50] At a personal level, this interracial solidarity that brought the margins to the center provided a solid experiential and ideological foundation for Travis's marriage.

Most interracial minority couples were race-conscious in their mate selection and discussed racial issues in their married life. For race-conscious couples from two different nonwhite racial groups, history reverberated in the present as they unearthed the similarities in their marginalization, which served as an important bond. Sharing a nonwhite position of marginality was essential to the couples who were aware of how race and other intersecting axes of oppression contoured history, their own lives, and contemporary societal dynamics. This race-consciousness kept a critical race perspective alive in these families where the historical processes of racialization and links to the present were openly discussed.

Women and Men as Carriers of Culture: Cultural Revivification or Deemphasis

Both women and men in these couples saw themselves as transmitters and tailors of culture. The women took on the obvious roles of cultural transmission, such as arranging festivities and learning how to cook ethnic food, whereas the men varied in the level of their involvement, from being actively hands-on themselves to being supportive of their wives taking the cultural lead in the family. Both women and men were involved in the transmission of culture or the cessation of culture, a process that, either way, affects both older and younger generations in families.

Caroline and Bryce Wu were both hands-on teachers of their five-year-old daughter, teaching her to speak English, Spanish, and Chinese. Caroline commented on her family's acquisition of Chinese culture for the benefit of the daughter: "We had our first Chinese New Year party last year. . . . We [had] . . . some people over and [had] special foods . . . the whole thing." The birth of their daughter ignited Bryce's yearning to preserve his cultural roots. He described being raised with a "behemoth of culture" that he now re-created for his daughter:

> I grew up comfortable in who I was and knowing that I had a rich cultural background. . . . I knew there was this . . . behemoth . . . of support and . . .

culture and history and tradition. I would see . . . [it] through spending time with my grandparents or . . . hearing stories about my family. . . . It's one of the reasons why we really want . . . to pursue the whole trilingual language thing. . . . It really makes a difference in acknowledging the cultural difference.

Parents revivify culture as they acquire cultural knowledge to pass on to their children, as Bryce and Caroline did in (re-)learning Chinese to support their daughter's learning. In answer to my question as to what prompted his increased attachment to his Chinese culture in adulthood, Bryce responded: "With [my daughter's] birth . . . it was . . . a conscious question of, what are we going to teach her . . . to know from the Ecuadorian side and . . . what do we need to do on the Chinese side?" In providing cultural roots for his daughter, he had strengthened his own roots and been engaged in intercultural teaching and learning with his Latina wife.

As Travis Strong and Penelope Rio learned about each other's Native American bands, they both taught their five-year-old daughter about Native American heritage. Through Native languages and dance, Travis and Penelope developed their Native American identity that they passed on to their daughter. They were teaching their daughter English, Spanish, Lakota, and Ojibwe as well as Native dances, including a spiritual " 'jingle' dance . . . [from] around the Great Lakes Area." Travis considered his position as a husband and a father: "When it comes to culture—song and dance—it's rejuvenating. . . . You can learn . . . a little bit more about your spouse through song and dance and your culture. And then it's even more beautiful when you have a kid: you get to show your child culture and [see] how they grab hold of it and *they* run with it." For Travis, song and dance were cultural processes of discovery and creativity that crosscut generations. As a husband, Travis shared with his wife, and as a father he instructed his daughter in cultural ways; for this couple, family was a place where culture was rejuvenated.

While women are often viewed as the "carriers of culture," men also carry culture.[51] Women certainly perceive men to be carriers of culture because the very idea of men possessing cultural and gender ideologies is precisely what steers them away from or toward prospective romantic partners. Downplayed as transmitters of culture because they have traditionally been less prominent in household labor and child-rearing, men nevertheless have a robust ability to carry culture. Although the men I interviewed talked less about being cultural ambassadors than the women did, they did not dismiss culture; they simply deployed culture differently. The men were less self-conscious about possessing and passing on culture than the women were. Some men left *explicitly* cultural activities (such as cooking and rituals) to their wives. Many men who wanted to pass along their cultural inheritance took a backseat to their female spouse (who often learned customs from a female in-law) or took on leadership positions for the benefit of the community (see the Herrera family featured in chapter 3). In both tendencies, gender divided what men and women viewed as their cultural responsibilities.

We typically think of teaching and learning as running across channels within the same generation (between friends, peers, or spouses) or from older to younger generations (from parents to children). However, knowledge can also move from younger to older generations.[52] Parents often intentionally pass cultural knowledge to their children, but children can also act as conduits for their parents. In the Strong-Rio family, recall that Penelope's Native American mother was sent to a boarding school that stripped her of her Native American culture. Penelope's mother revived a positive sense of her Native heritage through Penelope and Travis, an example of what families are actually doing beyond discussion to repair history in the present moment. With both men and women as carriers of culture in this case, cultural transmission could work its way "up" the generations from younger to older. Since Penelope grew up with a dearth of Native culture, owing to her mother's aggrieved experience, Travis played an essential role in supplying both Penelope and her mother with information about their Native American history and culture. Penelope choked up as she told the story of how Travis introduced a positive image of Native American life to her mother:

> One of our first social events [as a couple] with the family was . . . my great-niece's . . . first birthday party. Travis is a flute player, so . . . he took his flute out and played her a song. . . . My mom cried and said, "When I die, I want you to play at the funeral. . . ." She really clung on to Travis. And he brought so much to my mom during her last few years. . . . [cries] I think he's kind of woken up everybody in my family about, it's okay to know things about your Native side and to celebrate it. . . . Right after that song he played, she was diagnosed with cancer, so she only lived two more years.

In the Strong-Rio family, Travis, as a husband, father, and son-in-law, was a vital cultural resource who passed knowledge and healing along to all three generations, even assuaging race-related "soul wounds."[53]

Not everyone wants to communicate culture to their relatives. The Nakamura and Korteweg families offer counterexamples in that they maintained an assimilation orientation. Because of their concerns about male domination and class status achievement, these couples did not transmit ethnic culture to their children beyond a few foreign-language words. These families with aggrieved family histories emphasized the achievement of an unqualified "American" identity. As we will see in chapter 5, these respondents saw American identity and the possibility of socioeconomic advancement as diametrically opposed to a racialized nonwhite identity.

The Kortewegs accentuated Americanness and family traditions. Mexican-born Inez emphasized her Americanness in order to feel a part of the United States. In teaching her young sons, she focused on the United States and placed her natal country of Mexico on par with other foreign countries: "I think [being American is] my priority. . . . I think I would bring in the Mexican culture just the same way that I would want them to learn about China or about Africa." Darnell concurred that they had family rituals detached from heritage: "I'm really not a very ethnically conscious person. Inez wants to create rituals and traditions, but I don't know if that's necessarily ethnic. Several years ago I started baking gingerbread cookies on Christmas." Making gingerbread cookies at the holidays was not linked to either of their backgrounds but instead was a family ritual.

The Kortewegs may have deemphasized race as a family, yet society keeps racial issues alive. Inez cited how political controversies over race and migration made her want to ensure that her kids did not "grow up feeling like victims." She reported first telling her children that they were Mexican in response to "chatter about Latinos" that her son overheard relative to Arizona Senate Bill 1070, the law legalizing racial profiling. Inez answered my question about whether she was trying to pass on any culture to her children: "I want my kids to be good people. . . . I want them to be active in their country, in their city, and in their school. . . . We're not trying to do that [teach culture]. We want them to feel that they're gifted, that they're bright, and they're Americans." As a reaction to her immigrant status, Inez highlighted her children's Americanness. Minimizing race and immigrant status was strategic, a tactic that Julie Dowling found among her Mexican American respondents, who used color-blind racial ideology in an effort to shore up their claim to American identity because they feared that acknowledging race would undermine this entitlement.[54] Even as Inez and Darnell rejected racial categories, their parenting strategies conceded that racial status and nationality filter people either into the center or onto the margins of the U.S. national imaginary.

Why are some families intent on passing on or even reviving nonwhite culture and some are not? The self-esteem associated with the racial group is the critical difference. In a social psychology study, Hispanic college students "who evaluated their group negatively lowered their identification with the group, whereas those students who felt positively about their group showed an increase in identification."[55] This logic rings true here: those who transmitted culture to other family members steered away from a heritage they had negative associations with and pivoted toward a heritage they had positive associations with. Those who declined to pass on cultural trappings had had negative experience with the culture. Those who did not want to pass on ethnic culture prioritized socio-economic advancement, were against racial categories as a matter of principle, or were first-generation immigrants who wanted to steep themselves in American society. Those who chose to perpetuate ethnic culture were U.S.-born, had had positive experiences with culture in their youths, and did not view ethnic culture and upward mobility as antithetical.

CONCLUSION

This chapter began with questions about whether a racial minority status promotes cross-minority pairings and how race works within those relationships. Being an "outsider within" is a catalyst for sociopolitical critique, and those who are race-conscious are inclined to partner with a minority. Gender enters the equation in that Latinas with domineering fathers do not want to replicate that dynamic in their marital life and so they steer away from Latinos. These Latinas who are not seeking Latino partners because of oppression at the hands of Latino men in their youth are also rejecting whites because of their need to connect on the point of racial marginality. In these priorities that build a preference for non-Latino minorities, we witness how negotiated desire involves using decision-making around marriage to improve one's life. These gender-sensitive Latinas experience a Goldilocks moment when they come to see Latino men as too macho, and white men as too racially dissimilar, but other men of color as potentially just right. Theirs is a critique not only of Latino men but of white men as inadequate partners. These Latina women's experiences are distinctive because of their strong concern over gender subordination and their desire for a minority-minority connection with a spouse.

Nonwhite cross-minority pairs are founded on experiences of racial oppression. Their "special standpoint on self, family, and society," based on an "outsider within" location, leads these minorities to prefer to marry other (non-Latino) people of color.[56] Romantic racialized affinity is developed out of an experience of shared marginality in the U.S. racial scene. This vital connection is founded on experiences with historical or contemporary oppression that foster emotional attachment and allow race-conscious partners to feel that they are understood in fundamentally important ways. The interviewees in this chapter picked mates whose level of concern about race matched their own. Most of these dual-minority couples were race-conscious, and they used race-consciousness as a measure of compatibility with a prospective partner. Similarly, the few people who minimized or rejected race selected partners who were an ideological match.

The chief reason why racial minorities partner with other racial minorities flows directly from the idea of family as a racial sanctuary. There is a coalitional aspect to this type of intermarriage, Latino–non-Latino minority partners explicitly creating supportive relationships that they perceive to be absent from mainstream (white) society. Unlike Latino-white partnerships, cross-minority intermarriage does not lead to a heightened awareness of race precisely because these spouses were already cognizant of the power of race before their marriage.

There was no one way in which the interracial minority couples interviewed for this study thought about race. Racial consciousness was pervasive, but their racial discourses ranged from heightening racial consciousness to downplaying race. Racial outlooks directly informed parents' wishes to perpetuate, change, or cease ethnic culture in their children's lives (which I explore in depth in chapter 3). A small fraction of families encouraged a diffuse "American" culture or a non-ethnic "family" culture, feeling a tug-of-war between "American" and "ethnic" culture. The variety of stances they held toward either amplifying or downplaying ethnic culture while *simultaneously* being committed to living in the United States shows the importance that these couples placed on being considered "American," even as some were devoted to a minority identity.

Intercultural exchange was a common consequence of cross-minority marriages as couples explored new cultural terrain while also sharing their own. Relative to racial identity, some people strengthened their racial identity, others were unchanged, and still others embraced a spouse's heritage. This variability shows the dynamism of racial identity and how marriage and family life can (but do not always) have a decisive impact on racial identity claims. Those who had strong racial identities before marriage either remained the same or had their identities enhanced by taking on an intercultural teaching role vis-à-vis their interracial spouse. Those who had encountered racial strife were the most likely to affiliate with their spouse's heritage.

Multiracial families, especially in California, saw themselves as the future. Even multiracial families in Kansas saw themselves as commonplace, despite their overwhelmingly white environment. So, while race-conscious individuals were more likely to select a minority partner who they felt would understand their racialized perspective, this choice did not redouble their "minority" status but rather increased their coalitional understanding as they pointed—from the periphery of mainstream America—to the racist policies that produce racial disparities.

These cross–racial minority couples' rhetorical and cultural maneuvers were a response to the extant racial hierarchy. Dual-minority couples built their families in reaction to racial, gender, and class inequalities and in search of support, solace, and a compatible perspective on race. We can see that their natal family systems, personal experiences, and social context all bore on their family formation processes. Considering marriage as an exercise in "nomos-building," or the construction of social codes or cultures that endow lived experience with meaning, we see how people respond to myriad social experiences as they make decisions about their intimate lives. People transport their pasts into the present as people try to defy, change, or build from their personal histories by way of their romantic relationships.[57]

Chapter 5 | Cross-National Latino Marriages: Racial and Gender Havens

Alicia Duarte was born in Mexico and immigrated to Whittier, California, with her mother and younger sister when she was two years old. They lived in a preschool building for a few years because they "had no money and nowhere to go." When her dad left her mother, they divvied up the six children: two girls would live with their mother in the United States, three older boys with their father in Mexico, and the youngest boy with their maternal grandfather in Mexico. Alicia, now forty-two years old, described her brothers who were raised by her father in Mexico as macho men who adhered to narrow notions of masculinity and femininity: "[My brothers] were typically macho. They worked, and the women stayed home and got pregnant and had kids. . . . They will say that I'm whitewashed, and I'll say that they're old-fashioned." Attributing their differences to the national contexts in which they were raised, Alicia rejected the type of Mexican masculinity embodied by her absentee father and traditionalist brothers: "I wanted somebody who was not going to be a typical Mexican type of man: somebody who is not educated, somebody who is very machismo. . . . I hate to say [it], but that's . . . my brothers. So I totally wanted to be opposite." Because of her natal family relationships, and in spite of variation among individuals within national cultures, Alicia associated Mexican men with lack of education and the preservation of male privilege. She wanted to avoid both of these attributes in a spouse.

Gender, nationality, and class status are interwoven in Alicia's story. Given her understanding of Mexican men, rooted firmly in interactions with her philandering father and uneducated, conservative brothers, Alicia had ruled out this type of potential partner. She envisioned a partner who was "probably born here [the United States], raised here, who adapted

132

to the culture, to the American life." Seeking to live beyond narrow gender scripts and financial constraints, Alicia married cross-nationally—her husband was a U.S.-born man of Peruvian and Costa Rican descent. Given her indigent background, Alicia described her husband: "I married an American who's an engineer, who has a career. Who, like myself, wants more." This is not to homogenize Mexican-origin people or overlook the rising middle class and changing gender norms among Mexican Americans, but instead to show that previous life experience drives individuals either toward or away from their national-origin group.[1]

Cross-national couples are those spouses who are either U.S.-born or foreign-born and have dissimilar national origins—for example, a Mexican married to a Peruvian.[2] This chapter asks: how do conceptions of gender and race-ethnicity facilitate marriage with someone within the Latino category but with a different national-origin heritage? In my earlier book, *Mexican Americans Across Generations* (see chapter 4), I examined how gender ideologies figure into marital choices for U.S.-born Mexican American men and women. This chapter looks squarely at how gender—both prior experiences and ideologies—informs men's and women's marital choices. How gender attitudes, beliefs, and norms steer romantic decisions is a new angle on union formation that sheds light on the experiential tools that people use to make life-changing decisions.

Those in cross-national pairings have both racial and gendered reasons for their marital choice. Some who appreciate aspects of their Latino culture—those cultural traits encoded in the notion of Latino authenticity, namely, "roots, values, and cultural toolkits" (including food, language, and religion)—may wish to retain its positive elements.[3] Gender inequality experienced at the hands of fathers, brothers, and boyfriends or husbands may squelch the desire of some Latina women for conationals. In contrast to Latina women who out-marry, as seen in prior chapters, these women appreciate Latino culture, broadly defined, and because the dating choices of those who are Spanish-dominant are constrained to Spanish-speakers, they end up with Latino spouses, language skills and demographics having outweighed cultural preferences. Cross-national marriage may also look more attractive to those who have encountered whites who impose gendered racial stereotypes on Latino men and women. In reaction to being placed in a distastefully restricting racial and gender "box," they choose to "stick to one's own," the opinion being that another Latino will understand and suit them better.

Cross-national partnership, standing midway between racial intermarriage and same-nation-of-origin intramarriage, is a window into how prior gendered experiences and beliefs steer lifetime partnership choices. My argument is that cross-national marriage serves as a consciously self-protective device—a way to avoid gender and racial stereotypes coming from both other racial groups and one's own national-origin group. Latinos who marry other Latinos *with a different national heritage* do so to avoid the in-group stereotypes they believe are upheld within a particular national-origin group but not within all Latino groups. It is not that gender and racial stereotypes are nonexistent in these unions, but simply that the partners chosen are judged to be less threatening and more in concert with self-perceptions. Cross-national marriages are sites for adjudicating among gender, racial, *and* national-origin concerns.

This chapter is based on interviews with nine respondents—six women and three men—representing six couples; five of the couples were currently married. (I interviewed both partners in three couples [six people] and two people whose spouses were not interviewed. The one person from the sixth couple was divorced.) Of the six couples, three were from California and three were from Kansas. Based on these interviews, this chapter starts by analyzing rationales for cross-national marriage, discussing first gender and then race, before moving on to the ways in which cross-national marriage reshapes gender and ethnicity and the roles of women, men, and national context in these outcomes.

THE GENDER RATIONALE: ESCAPE FROM PATRIARCHY

Latina women's fear of patriarchy is developed in relation to close family figures, most often a domineering father or husband. Numerous Latinas married to Latinos with different national ancestries reported having had trouble with their father, who controlled their lives with strict rules concerning appropriate behavior for men and women. Alicia's story highlighted her father and brothers; in Valentina Arroyo's story, it was her father and her first husband who were gender-oppressive and drove her migration to the United States.

Valentina was a fifty-year-old Colombian woman from a town near the Venezuela border that was ravaged by guerrilla warfare. She described her father as "very strong, very demanding, [and] very strict." Her first husband, a Colombian, exhibited the same controlling "psychological" behavior as her father, using intimidation to keep women obedient: "My dad was controlling, controlling, controlling, and my first husband was controlling, controlling, controlling." Valentina and her first husband's relationship was fraught owing to his manipulations meant to psychologically dominate her, sequester their financial assets, and circumscribe her social circles. She had selected a controlling man as a mate because it was familiar behavior: "Because my dad was that way, I got somebody the same way. . . . You are not comfortable except in the way that you know. . . . You know that kind of life, and you get somebody that puts you in the same situation." Because she made no concerted effort to change, Valentina repeated the pattern of male domination. Yet upon moving to the United States, the protections from harm offered women by state and federal laws buoyed Valentina's courage to divorce her first husband soon after she won her legal case for asylum in the United States.

"Color-coding" her oppressive experiences with her Colombian father and first husband, Valentina did not want to partner with another Latino man:[4]

> I told Ernesto [her Mexican American second husband], if I had to marry again, I don't want to marry a Latino. Latinos are very impulsive, possessive, and you have to be a strong woman to put them in their place. . . . If not, they're [running] over you all the time. . . . I tried all the time to stand up [to my first husband], but he was over me all the time putting me down.

Finding herself in a national context where women's rights are supported was critical to Valentina's ability to defy her second husband's authority: "Here [in the United States] I'm free. I can talk. I can say no. . . . I know that I'm free here. I know that I have my rights. I know that I can say no. . . . I know my rights in the United States. . . . If you do something to me, I call [the police]." Because refugees are incorporated through the welfare state and receive resettlement assistance, they feel entitled to care and protection from the state.[5] In addition to laws protecting women like her against intimate partner violence, Valentina felt especially entitled to state care as an asylee.

Valentina was steadfast in her opinion of Latino men: "I don't prefer to be with any Latino. It's going to [be] fighting again." Nonetheless, she ultimately remarried with a Latino man, contradicting her own wishes, because of her Spanish-dominant Latino networks in California. Her Spanish monolingualism restricted her to Spanish-speaking Latino networks. She met her husband, Ernesto, through her search for work. Valentina wove together her settlement and love stories:

> I'm an interior designer and . . . I already had my papers to work. I had everything, and I started contacting different companies. But I always called in English . . . and I got interviews, but my communication was not good. . . . An interior designer told me, "You need to go to an . . . office where they can talk in both languages. Then you can work with somebody you understand and you can learn." I checked in the [phone]book, and I said, "Well, this looks like it's in Spanish." And I called Ernesto.

Lacking English-language skills, Valentina looked in the phone directory for people in her profession with Hispanic surnames. Ernesto explained how he met Valentina "from the profession. . . . Because her English was atrocious . . . she wanted to work for a Spanish-speaking interior designer." He became her boss and then her husband.

Alicia's and Valentina's stories show how gendered experiences within one's family of origin and in prior romances shape marital choice. They deduced from personal experience with fathers, brothers, and first husbands that patriarchy was a pervasive trait in their *national-origin group* and therefore rejected all men in the group on that basis and chose to partner instead with a Latino from a different national-origin group. Women who make this kind of self-protective move, in seeing patriarchy as a characteristic of men from a particular national-origin group, may miss its association with men more generally. Moreover, Valentina, as an adult immigrant, was chiefly concerned with financial stability. She could temper Ernesto's strong personality, but her economic and linguistic reliance on him (recall that he was her bilingual employer) left her in no position to be selective about a mate, especially after an unplanned pregnancy.

Whether the original root of resistance against patriarchy is a father, brother, boyfriend, or husband, the Latina women in this section used cross-national in-marriage to find more gender freedom. Even Valentina, who struggled with gender issues in her marriage with Ernesto, experienced *relative* improvement in her gendered home life; that was progress, even if she had to do "emotion work" to manage her problems.[6] The men did not articulate concern over gender issues in their marriages, but they did reveal how antipatriarchal concerns inspire egalitarian behavior at home and work (as seen in chapter 6), and motivate migration, as seen with Miguel Moya later in this chapter.

SEXUALITY

Sexuality is certainly far from absent in marriage decisions. Although it can be difficult to tap into one's own thoughts on sexuality and the deep desires that can guide one's actions, sexual desire does inspire romantic pairings, and some respondents were able to tell me about that process. Valentina's sixty-three-year-old second husband, Ernesto Arroyo (also on his second marriage), made it clear that sex appeal was foundational to his romantic relationships. We can see in his story that, in addition to physical attraction, family pressure and social networks steered him into both his first and second marriages. By paying attention to how Ernesto summarized his two marriages, we can witness the process of getting on and off the "marriage-go-round" of serially monogamous relationships.[7]

The fact that he met his first wife, Belinda, at a beauty contest and arranged for a first date at a pool indicates the premium Ernesto placed on sex appeal. Ernesto and Belinda, a Mexican national, met through international social networks. Living at the time in Montebello, California, a middle-class Mexican American neighborhood, Ernesto's politician father was invited to parties attended by elites in both the United States and Mexico:

> My father was a politician here . . . [and] became a prominent person . . . a community leader. He was the president of [a local organization]. . . . My father would have parties at home where . . . state senators . . . and mayors would come. . . . [A] committee that my father was [on] would host the Miss Mexico in Los Angeles contest. [My brother suggested we go to the] . . . beauty contest . . . [saying], "[There's] going to be girls, come on, let's go!" So I went. . . . Belinda was one of the girls that was . . . a contestant. . . . We watched them walking down the ramp . . . in bathing suits and dresses. Very nice. And then afterwards there was . . . a VIP cocktail [party] . . . and that's where I met her. And right there I asked her if she wanted to come swimming at my house. She said, "Oh, okay." And so she did. And then we started dating and dating and dating.

It is telling that Ernesto met Belinda at a beauty contest, where he had little to judge her by other than her physical features. This is Ernesto's story, of course, but it is interesting that he accorded Belinda little agency, giving her only a single line of assent ("Oh, okay") in reply to his pool date invitation, a place where they were guaranteed to be scantily clad. Again underscoring Ernesto's laser-focus on sexual attraction, he interrupted his tale to interject that he "had another girlfriend, a beautiful girl, [with] black hair, five-foot-six, and really gorgeous!" This succinct description also points to the physical as the main starting point for Ernesto's relationships. Other respondents—both men and women—were not so blunt about the role of sexuality in their romances, but for Ernesto, physical attraction was foundational to sexual partnerships.

Families of origin shape people's ideas about the kind of partners who are suitable for them (in terms of race-ethnicity, sexual orientation, class, religion, and so on).[8] Families provide coaching not only on *who* is an appropriate marital partner but also on *when* one should get married. Once Ernesto and Belinda began dating, Ernesto's parents stressed that it was time for him to be a family man:

> I was already thirty-three years old, and my parents kept putting pressure, "When are you going to get married, man? What's going on? . . . Are you going to be a bachelor forever?" Keeping that pressure, that pressure.

And . . . then, [from] her side, the same thing. "Look, I don't believe . . . in long [courtships]," my father would tell her. . . . So there was pressure from both ends, and so eventually . . . I proposed to her and tied the knot.

Modern marriage may no longer be about submitting to family decrees aimed at creating political alliances and consolidating wealth or land, as in the past, but families are far from inconsequential in marriage decisions.[9] Families impose restrictions, offer advice, and even exercise violence or threaten children with expulsion from the family if they "choose" incorrectly—"choice" under such conditions of constraint or duress being hardly an exercise of free will but rather a selection from a set of options preapproved by family authorities.

Succumbing to family pressure about his having reached an appropriate age to marry, Ernesto married Belinda. Yet immediately after telling me that they "tied the knot," Ernesto added that "we were different as night and day." Repeating twice that she was "a very, very beautiful girl," Ernesto summarized his first marriage: "We became lovers before we became married. . . . We bought a home, we lasted twelve years, no kids." Eventually he became dissatisfied with her heavy work and travel schedule in the fashion industry. But time apart was not the only tension: Ernesto realized that he had yielded to family pressure to marry in the first place. Keying into his emotions, he recounted:

I felt empty. . . . I married her without really being in love with her. For the wrong reasons. [I had thought], "Maybe I should [get married]. She's a nice gal . . . she's pretty . . . she's smart, she was a regional manager. . . ." And one day . . . I told her I didn't want to be married anymore. And, uh, it cut her like a bomb. . . . Long story short . . . we sold the house, we divided the money in half. . . . We sat down like two mature adults that made a mistake, and there was no hatred. . . . We were estranged from each other. We started drifting apart; she started taking, as a hobby, flying lessons. . . . I was out of that loop, you know? . . . We were doing things away from each other, and I said, "This is nonsense."

Wrapped up in this narrative are two competing but compatible notions of why Ernesto and Belinda divorced. First is that they were the wrong match to begin with and had rushed into marriage without love. Second is that they drifted apart, owing to her work travel and their separate activities. These two rationales for divorce are complementary. By his own admission, Ernesto had superficially focused on Belinda's beauty. By consistently calling her a "girl" (or "gal"), Ernesto minimized Belinda's maturity and ability to be an equal in a partnership; ironically, it was her work travel, based in her employment and intelligence, that physically removed her from him and became a problem in the marriage.

In addition to sexual attraction, one might wonder what Ernesto wanted in a marriage. What he attained in his second marriage with Valentina that he did not have with Belinda was a wife who was dependent on him. Ernesto's understanding of masculinity entailed providing for, and being necessary to, his spouse. In addition to Valentina's beauty and their sexual compatibility, which resulted in a son, Ernesto valued feeling more indispensable than he had in his first marriage because of Valentina's initial linguistic dependency on him and her continuing economic reliance on him.

Ernesto was single for twelve years before remarrying. His tale of meeting Valentina stressed their sexual chemistry, first in her ability to talk him into giving her a job and second in their capacity to conceive a child:

> [Valentina] was to be my employee. . . . She was recently here from Colombia. She . . . looked at the yellow pages to see architects with Spanish-sounding names. . . . That's how she called me. She wanted a job, but I kept telling her, "No, no, no." . . . [She kept calling, and] I [finally] said, "Oh, okay, come on in for an interview. . . ." Then when she opened the door, I said, "Wow!" I was stunned. She was really, really pretty, you know?

Beauty functioned here as a form of social capital: Ernesto created a job for Valentina that she insisted she wanted and that he, up until seeing her, had maintained he did not have available.[10] The turning point in her quest for employment was their meeting: Ernesto promptly hired her so that he could be around her, with the thought of a sexual liaison likely on his mind. Moreover, given Ernesto's desire for a partner who would be physically near him, as became clear when his first wife began traveling a great deal, hiring Valentina as an employee who would be linguistically and financially dependent on him would make him essential to her in a way he was not to Belinda. Despite these differences between his first and second wives, one similarity was that he met both women through social networks—Belinda through family social circles and Valentina through a Spanish-speaking Latino community.

While Ernesto was sexually attracted to both his first and second wives— both of whom he showered with compliments on their beauty—he declared that he had "sexual chemistry" with Valentina, meaning that they gave birth to a child, which never happened with Belinda: "Valentina got pregnant. . . . It was like a joy because I thought I was . . . shooting blanks with my other wife, but I think our chemistry was not compatible." He noted that his ex-wife later married another man and had a child with him, proving that neither of them had been physiologically incapable of conceiving. With

Valentina, Ernesto succeeded in being a man according to his definition—one who is virile and capable of having a family whom he provides for and who rely on him.

THE RACE RATIONALE: STEREOTYPE TRADE-OFFS AND CULTURAL COMPATIBILITY

When Xochitl opened the door to her Kansas City suburban home, she warmly greeted me as if we were old friends, exclaiming, "Jessiquita!" Her conversion of my first name into a diminutive form in Spanish expressed familiarity and racial solidarity of the sort that connected Xochitl with her husband—and now with me. Xochitl and Enzo Velasco were a cross-national Latino couple who had been drawn together because she wanted to avoid the gendered and racialized stereotypes of Latina women held by white men, and he sought cultural commonality with a Latina, which he had missed when married to his white first wife. They were attracted to one another because they offered a racial and gender haven to each other. They helped each other "feel at home in the world" by validating each other's "identity and place in this world."[11] In their union they avoided outsider stereotypes and benefited from cultural understanding. Xochitl strongly identified as Mexican American (she was half white and half Mexican American), and Enzo was a Bolivian immigrant with dual citizenship. Their cross-national Latino intramarriage was preferential: she wanted to marry a Latino because of the gender and racial understanding she hoped to secure, whereas he was seeking the cultural and linguistic traits he associated with Latinas.

Thirty-nine-year-old Xochitl was born and raised in Oakland, a Mexican American neighborhood in the state capital of Topeka. Community life centered on the Catholic church, Our Lady of Guadalupe. According to Xochitl, "that's where all the Mexicans . . . resided because that's where the Santa Fe railroads were." Raised by her white mother, who was a Mexican American affiliative ethnic, and her "super Chicano" father, Xochitl and her three siblings were steeped in Mexican Catholic traditions: "We always celebrated Christmas, but we . . . [also] celebrated Las Posadas"—a neighborhood celebration in which Joseph and Mary's pilgrimage in search of lodging in Bethlehem before Jesus's birth is re-created. Xochitl's community celebrated birthdays with "piñatas and big parties" and hosted Cinco de Mayo and Mexican Independence Day celebrations and a big fiesta every summer. Mexican culture was "always . . . incorporated" in everyday life in her youth.

Xochitl's parents supported her strong Mexican American identity. Her Mexican American father attended civil rights marches in California in the 1970s and brought back "Frida Kahlo books . . . [and] Aztec coloring books" for the children. Like the women discussed in chapter 3 who performed cultural work to perpetuate a cultural heritage that had not been a part of their own experience until they married, Xochitl's white mother was supportive of her husband's ancestry. Xochitl attended the University of Kansas and became the president of the Hispanic student organization. Her mother was encouraging, never saying, " 'Well, why aren't you president of the Irish organization?' . . . She was . . . proud of the fact that I was a Latina and that I took pride in that." For Xochitl, her Mexican American identity derived not only from her ethnic community but also from her physical features and surname: "I've never been mistaken for being 'just white' ever in my life. And I've always had the [Hispanic] name. [It's] always been like, 'You're a Borges [maiden surname]. We know you're something else [nonwhite].' " How others racially perceive and treat people affects their racial identity claims.[12] Interpolating outsiders' conception of her, Xochitl had always claimed her heritage and taken pride in it, supported by her Mexican American father, her white mother, and her Mexican American neighborhood.

From an early age, Xochitl learned lessons on the racial hierarchy in the United States and her place in the "racial middle."[13] As detailed in the opening of this book, discourse about race conveyed messages about whom she should marry to increase her racial status and whom she should not marry to avoid devaluing her racial status. To recap, whites were "a sign of success," African Americas represented "trouble," and Mexicans were "status quo." Aware of societal and familial preferences that encouraged marrying white, Xochitl nonetheless developed a clear preference for Latino men based on her cultural comfort with them and cultural discomfort with white men.

Central to Xochitl's negotiated desire was her quest for racial and gender freedom in a Latino partner. Through endogamy, she wanted to escape a problematic set of stereotypes about Latinas held by white men. Having dated whites and blacks, Xochitl determined that Latino men were more suitable for her because they offered a refuge from disconcerting stereotypes of Latinas as exotic or "other":

> I always . . . knew I wanted to be married to a Latino. I always was partial to Latinos, boyfriends and everything. . . . I grew up with Mexicans, boys and girls; I just always felt really comfortable. . . . It wasn't until I went to college and started dating a white guy would I see differences between him and I. . . . Some white men that are married to my Latina girlfriends . . . they like the "Latina spice." . . . They make fun of her accent. They think it's cute. . . . They like that exoticness. . . . I didn't ever like that. I don't want to

be treated as an "other" in my relationship. I knew with Latinos there was never that "other" factor. . . . I was just Xochitl Borges and there was nothing particularly Latina about me—I [did not] have to put on this Latina-ness or take it off. . . . I could just be myself and be really happy.

Xochitl's negotiated desire for Latinos derived from having grown up in a Mexican American community and from wanting to avoid the distasteful stereotypes held by white men. Reflecting on her Latina friends' experiences with their white husbands, Xochitl was offended by the prospect of being "treated as an 'other' " in an intimate relationship.[14] The white men whom Xochitl mimicked held a white normative perspective "in which whites are both privileged and seen as normal, neutral, and regular, and everyone else is defined against [whiteness]." From this white normative stance, racial others merely "add flavor" in a way that reduces American diversity to cultural consumption by whites who "exoticize, criticize, trivialize, and compartmentalize" people of color.[15]

Besides circumventing stereotypes, Xochitl also sought identity freedom through endogamy. To her, the term "Latina spice" combined sexual promiscuity, gender, and race in a way that reduced Latinas to objects of desire rather than subjects with the power to act. "Complimentary othering," as I discuss elsewhere, reduces the "other" to a foreign object of desire.[16] This bias involves what social psychology refers to as a "category-based response," that is, "reacting to another person as an interchangeable member of a social group," most often a group to which one does not belong.[17] Category-based responses to out-groups (including stereotyping, prejudice, and discrimination) are typically more negative than responses to one's own group. To escape category-based responses, Xochitl insulated herself within her own in-group by marrying a Latino with whom she felt identity freedom.

Xochitl's intramarriage preference as a way to skirt stereotypes of the "exotic other" was forecast by her ease in predominantly Mexican towns: "In Brownsville, Texas . . . and then Guadalajara, [Mexico] . . . I just felt free to be Xochitl Borges. . . . [There was no] 'That's your Latina-ness talking.' It was just being me. I liked the comfort . . . the familiarity of it and just being free. . . . It feels really free." In a bilingual, largely Hispanic environment, Xochitl was not hemmed in by biases or made to feel as if she was representing her entire gender and racial group. Indeed, she resisted being expected to represent those categories: "Brownsville, [Texas] . . . and Guadalajara, [Mexico] . . . it's all Mexican American there. And people can speak Spanish and English. . . . So you just don't stand out. . . . Because of that you can just be yourself. You have that freedom just to be you, make mistakes, say stupid stuff, or do great things, and *it has nothing to do with you being Latina or not Latina. It's just the way you are* [emphasis added]." In coethnic environments, there was no pressure to feel that "mak[ing] mistakes," on the one hand, or doing "great things," on the other, would reflect on the groups to which she belonged. Coming from her own experience, Xochitl's negotiated desire to be understood as an individual apart from race and gender was foundational to her preference for a Latino spouse.

Her comfort in Mexican American towns led Xochitl to believe that she would obviate category-based responses like stereotyping and prejudice by marrying a Latino. She judged white men as unsuitable because the white men married to her friends alienated their Latina partners. The fact that hers was a cross-national marriage mattered less to her than that her husband shared Latino heritage. Unlike the women discussed earlier in this chapter for whom it was crucial to move out of their national-origin group, Xochitl did not push away Mexican American men so much as resist white men before she met and married a Latino from a different national-origin group. Given the slower in-migration flow into Kansas, the state experiences less "immigrant replenishment," or restocking of Mexican immigrants, than the border states do, and this demographic trend circumscribes the dating possibilities.[18] Although cross-national Latino men are not devoid of their own images of Latina women, these in-group understandings of Latina women as cultural keepers, as we will see with Enzo and Xochitl, may be consistent with women's own self-perception.

Enzo, thirty-eight years old, grew up in Bolivia and began college in Argentina before moving to the United States to complete college and earn a master's degree in business administration. Spending less time discussing his family background, Enzo focused instead on the traits that he associated with white women. His image of white women and his failed first marriage to a white woman had led Enzo to define white women as incompatible with him. He attributed the hardships in his first marriage with a white Kansas woman to their cultural differences: she had been irritated by the numerous family gatherings he attended, and she had also felt excluded, not being bilingual, by the Spanish conversations that took place among extended family. Enzo explained the trouble in his six-year marriage with his first wife: "You have the closeness to family and . . . in the beginning . . . you don't realize those things. . . . We could not attend everything, but we always got invited. . . . At some point it was like a burden [to her]. . . . [Whereas] I'm so used to being with my family." Enzo cited a family orientation as a cultural distinction between Latinos and whites. Differing obligations to and rewards drawn from family caused friction in Enzo's relationship with his white first wife, and family activities he enjoyed she found burdensome. He drew Xochitl into the conversation, highlighting their compatibility around exactly these issues:

> Xochitl enjoys my family. . . . She doesn't have a problem with me . . . visiting my family. . . . The other part . . . is . . . the language. My mom and my aunt . . . are older ladies, so their default language is Spanish. . . . They will revert to Spanish . . . [and] once they start going, everybody else speaks . . . Spanish. I think that also caused some problems. . . . I think it was maybe seen [by my first wife] as . . . a lack of care.

Time with extended family and language became wedge issues between Enzo and his first wife.

Upon divorcing his first wife, Enzo was inclined to partner with a coethnic whose traits fit his lifestyle. While he "wasn't necessarily looking for a particular nationality or ethnic group," he nonetheless mapped qualities onto certain racial groups, associating affection with Latinos and independence with Americans.[19] Enzo also desired someone who was well traveled and cosmopolitan, so that she could understand his international experience. He depicted his ex-wife, a white Kansan, as ill-fitting: "People . . . [who] haven't traveled and explored other cultures—let's say a pure American girl from the middle of Kansas—didn't have certain other attributes that I liked . . . such as appreciate[ing] things in the Latin culture." Enzo also cited family togetherness, saying that impromptu family gatherings and cariño (affection) were vital parts of his life. He exclusively dated Latina women after his divorce.

Prior failed romances had led both Enzo and Xochitl to prefer Latinos, and yet they ended up in a cross-national partnership more by chance than specific desire, unlike Alicia and Valentina. Their involvement in Latino networks and events led to their meeting: they were introduced through a mutual friend who hosted a party after a Hispanic Chamber of Commerce function. Even how they met bespeaks their mutual emotional investment in the Hispanic community and their upward mobility. They "hung around the same circle," became friends, and then dated for two years before marrying. Now married to Xochitl for four years, Enzo had found a good fit in her:

> In my family we are very huggy [and] kissy. . . . I noticed that was a big difference . . . with the . . . people that hadn't been exposed to other cultures. . . . I didn't like that so much. . . . I decided that the ideal situation would be somebody that . . . appreciated family and being close but at the same time had . . . independence. . . . That's one of the good things about my relationship with Xochitl. That's why I picked her. Or maybe that's why she picked me.

The right balance of qualities Enzo was looking for included affection, valuing family, and independence. In picking each other as mates, Enzo and Xochitl both achieved what they wanted: cultural comfort and understanding that they felt could only come from another Latino.

Cross-national couples see the category of "Latino" as a bounded group whose members have comparable values, beliefs, and cultural practices. Women (and children) who struggle against patriarchy judge their entire national-origin category as potentially patriarchal and therefore migrate or marry out. In this way, we see how people view the groups to which they belong as *concentric circles of likeness* that increase in size yet still make up a bounded collectivity growing in size from their national-origin group to the category of "Latino." As the bounded group moves from more specific to more generalized, people consider both what they would lose in a potential mate (traits they associate with their national-origin group) and what they would gain (characteristics they believe are shared among Latinos but not whites).

Cross-national partnerships are predicated on two elements: a rejection of whiteness and an embrace of pan-Latino identity. In interviews with Latinos in this chapter, category-based responses—ideas about groups—appear in three ways. First, interviewees perceived that whites used category-based responses in interaction with Latinos. Second, Latinos utilized category-based responses as a logic to reject those same whites whom they judged to be incompatible. And third, category-based responses are the basis for a positive evaluation of their own group. No one identified as problematic the contradiction that they were rejecting and accepting groups of people using judgments about entire categories. I suspect that interviewees failed to reflect on this because once the logic had worked for them—it had helped them decide whom to marry and they were happy with that choice—they had no pressing need to interrogate their earlier judgements, reactions, and decisions. In essence, they saw category-based responses or group stereotypes as harmful when these were used against them, but as reasonable shorthand when they used these stereotypes in their own decision-making.

Dissatisfying experiences with whites had convinced Latino men and women who valued their cultural heritage to retreat from interracial relationships. By marrying endogamously and cross-nationally, these Latino individuals deemed their chosen partners to be their cultural match, and one predicated on the rejection of whiteness. Latinos who had suffered discrimination in dating and valued their culture had determined that they would only be properly understood and treated well by a coethnic. Latinos who found race to be central to their experience desired endogamy, and diverse Latino networks presented the opportunity for cross-national partnerships.

GENDER CONSEQUENCES

Gender Wishes Come True:
Women Who Get What They Want

Many women who explicitly sought out gender equality in marriage got their wish, most often by avoiding specific personality traits, not simply a particular national-origin group. This outcome involved choice and agency. Women, lacking privilege relative to men, spoke assuredly about wanting to move toward gender equality in their marital lives. Men, as members of the more privileged gender category, were relatively silent about desires to maintain or redistribute power along gender lines.

Alicia Duarte, introduced in the beginning of the chapter, avoided Mexican-origin men yet remained mindful of the type of masculinity that she wanted to dodge in any man:

> Sit down and eat at a table together, I don't think they [my brothers] do that. Everybody's in front of the TV. Typical Mexican family: the mom is cooking in the kitchen while everybody is eating already. And that's still going on at my brothers' place. My sisters-in-law are serving everybody, and they're eating and she's still cooking. . . . It's kind of like putting yourself last as a woman. Literally and figuratively.

Alicia's brothers provided a point of national comparison, epitomizing a distasteful version of masculinity that she mapped onto Mexican-born men. Both "literally and figuratively," Alicia did not want to come in last. Gendered experiences in one's natal family can shape desire for certain styles of gender performances in a marital union.

Alicia got what she wanted with her husband in terms of gender equality. She wanted someone with acculturated gender sensibilities, so she filtered for this characteristic as she dated. I call this "quality-coding": a mechanism of the negotiated desire process whereby people who are on their romantic journeys target personality traits they desire in a mate as well as undesirable characteristics to avoid. In an affirmative twist on color-coding, quality-coding (discussed in more detail in chapter 8) divorces nefarious characteristics from a particular racial group—rather than damning an entire group—and seeks the positive, inverse quality instead.

As a happy consequence of her romantic search based on quality-coding, Alicia's relationship with her husband was very different from the relationship between her parents:

> I wanted somebody who was going to be there for their kids. . . . Tradition in my house now [is that] we eat dinner every night together. When we were

younger, we never did. [My mom] was never home. Or she would make dinner and then she was so tired she'd go to bed. . . . She . . . made a comment just the other night: "Wow, [your] husband sits there and talks to the kids about how their day went." . . . We do that all the time. We didn't realize until afterwards: she's never seen that before. . . . I didn't realize that that's really amazing for her to see that there's a man there.

Her dissatisfaction with her absent father and her belief that men should not be privileged and women relegated to a service-oriented secondary position had formed Alicia's desire for a man whose ideas about gender equality and family unity would match hers. By seeking out these qualities, Alicia got what she wanted. Note that in her two narratives she repeated the theme of meal preparation, food consumption, conversation, and the bonding that occurs at mealtime. Knowing that women tend to be in charge of family meals, Alicia was suggesting that a focal point for her was to bring women out from a service role and have men occupy more supportive roles as family members.[20] Class status and family form were also relevant to the gender shift Alicia noted: her mother was a single mother who worked menial jobs and was depleted of energy by the end of the day, whereas she and her husband had middle-class standing and were part of a two-parent household in which they jointly cared for their children.

Xochitl's wish for gender and racial freedom also came true. She referred to her desire to in-marry as a vehicle to find freedom from gender and racial stereotypes when she responded to my question about the consequences of her relationship with Enzo:

Well, it confirmed for me why I knew I wanted to marry a Latino. . . . I enjoy the freedom of being [with] another Latino who doesn't stereotype me for being a Latina or even Mexican. He just accepts me as I am. So I feel very free with that. He's . . . the perfect mix of being affectionate, cariñoso, but because he never had it easy coming from Bolivia, he's always had to work hard. He has that strong work ethic that I appreciate. . . . That's what I always imagined it would be like if I married a Latino. All that other . . . stuff would be gone and I would fit in and it would just blend all really nicely.

With Enzo, Xochitl found what she desired: freedom from stereotypes and acceptance. Not blind to his other characteristics, she also found other items on her wish list fulfilled in Enzo's affectionate nature and strong work ethic. Her carefully selected in-marriage was unfettered by "other stuff" like stereotypes and cultural conflicts.

Sharing a Latino identity, more so than a national-origin-specific identity, was important to Xochitl because she could engage it without explanation or justification. As a result of her union with Enzo, Xochitl's already strong Latina identity had become more robust. She compared her husband and a prior white boyfriend, underscoring the racial freedom she experienced in her marriage:

> I think it's gotten stronger. With him [Enzo], I'm able to really celebrate it [Mexican culture]. And I don't know if I would if I had married the white American I dated in college. He was always kind of like, "Calm down.... Don't say those things when you come to my parents' house." Or, "My friends won't get that." There's none of that. There's none of that caution. . . . Just . . . be yourself. I was able to hang up my Frida Kahlo . . . and . . . Emiliano Zapata stuff, write my [Latino-oriented] stories, and go [to] my Latino readings and be really happy with all of that. I don't have to hide any of those things.

Xochitl's comments here ring with the freedom of cultural expression. Through in-marriage with a culturally attuned husband, Xochitl avoided being instructed to "calm down" or informed that her cultural knowledge was out of place in white company. Mentioning both Mexican-specific and broad Latino themes, Xochitl did not have to be "cautious" or "hide" her cultural proclivities. As a strongly identified Latina woman, Xochitl's solution to the conundrum of gender and racial freedom was to marry a like-minded Latino who supported her quest for living a true-to-herself life.

How National Context Frames Gender Expectations

Among couples who do not share compatible outlooks on gender, conflicting gender ideologies can lead to marital discord and divorce. What happens if a woman wants an escape from patriarchy (a gender haven) in a marriage but does not achieve this goal?[21] Moreover, how does national context either support or undermine gender equality? And how does national environment become visible in marriages and in women's understanding of the liberation they can achieve?

Sarah Crosby's life story illustrates how national context matters a great deal in defining what types of gender relations are acceptable. She married a Brazilian man who held more rigid understandings of gender than she did, and she therefore dealt with conflict around gender once married. To her dismay, Sarah unwittingly replicated her parents' model of male dominance and female submission. Although comparisons between nations can be overblown and can overlook the variation within nations, national contexts do influence gender norms.[22] As migration literature points out, migrant families often confront changed gender expectations in their host country, which can lead to conflict, followed by adaptation.[23] Changes in gender norms across national contexts can either be successfully negotiated within a marriage or result in marriage dissolution.

Born in Colombia to a father who was an executive in an international corporation, Sarah had lived in several countries. Divorced from a Brazilian man, she had lived thirty-one out of her fifty-three years in the United States. Her mother was Dutch-descent white, and her father was mixed-ethnicity white and Mexican American. Sarah's story illustrates the strength of national context in supporting or condemning gender relations that privilege men. In her experience, male privilege was normalized in Brazil, but when she and her husband relocated to the United States, her understanding of gender norms in the country led her to expect to achieve gender egalitarianism. Sarah was not alone in perceiving varying levels of gender equality based on nation. A Pew Research Center report found that the United States and Brazil are on par with the belief that women should have equal rights (97 and 95 percent, respectively), but that the gap widens when supporters of equal rights are asked whether more changes are needed. In the United States, 64 percent thought that more liberal changes are required to reach gender equality, whereas 84 percent in Brazil thought so, indicating the perception of greater gender inequality in Brazil.[24] In Sarah's case, framing her expectations for gender equality on national context failed her. When no changes in her intimate life followed her move to the United States with her husband, marital dissatisfaction ensued, culminating in divorce.

Like other Mexican-origin men of his time, Sarah's father had a "very strong concept of masculinity and femininity," she said, and maintained a "very traditional viewpoint." Her mother enacted what she called de la casa (literally, "of the house") femininity, or marianismo, the subservient counterpart to male dominance.[25] She bore five children in eight years and reigned over the domestic sphere, including cooking, knitting, and making decorative lace. Sarah was estranged from her father because she disagreed with the way he flouted his male privilege by going on alcoholic binges and having extramarital affairs. Believing that "a girl should be a girl and a boy should be a boy," he forbade Sarah from working at a refugee camp in Thailand after college, but she did so nonetheless, asserting her independence.

Having lived in Colombia, Spain, Holland, and Japan by her senior year in high school, Sarah was cosmopolitan and sought out different cultures when in the United States. In her youth, she dated a variety of men, including white, Asian, and Latino men; she "loved learning about culture and language and ethnicity" through her boyfriends, she said. Attracted to Brazilian culture, Sarah lived in Brazil for seven years and married a Brazilian. She explained a complex "attraction-repulsion" with her ex-husband: she embraced Brazilian culture for its vivacity and its family form, yet repudiated the male dominance.

National context shaped both the gender dynamics in her marriage and what Sarah was able to accept. In Brazil, she tolerated gender inequality owing to the prevailing gender norms and the socioeconomic status she enjoyed with her husband, which allowed them to have domestic help. (In Brazil being able to afford domestic help is the middle-class norm.) She muffled her gender egalitarian philosophy in Brazil because not only was gender inequality widely condoned, but she and her husband out-sourced the domestic work; if they had not been able to afford to do so, she would have been saddled with that work, and it would have been a daily reminder of inequality. In contrast, in the United States her husband's dominance clashed with the prevailing gender expectations and her own expectations in that national context. Married for five years, Sarah and her husband divorced because of conflict around gender issues.

Sarah described how class status and national context allowed for an agreeable way of life in Brazil that was not sustainable in the U.S.:

> SARAH: He . . . was . . . very authoritarian in the marriage, which worked well in Brazil, but didn't work well in the U.S.
>
> AUTHOR: But you were the same woman, so how did context matter?
>
> SARAH: Brazilian culture allowed me to be what I needed to be as far as a wife in Brazil and still have lots and lots of time to do professional things. Whereas in the States, because I was so busy . . . working . . . I didn't have time to do the wifely, housewifely things, and so that created a lot of problems. . . . In Brazil we could have a maid.

Being a professional woman with hired labor to aid her in home responsibilities was normal in the Brazilian context and allowed Sarah to avoid carrying the burden of the "second shift" of household labor.[26] "It worked in Brazil and was comfortable in Brazil. . . . I think it works for [my friends there] still. . . . They're lawyers and . . . dentists and . . . doctors, but they have maids and cooks." Part of the global care chain, Sarah and her husband achieved the class privilege of a pleasing balance of work and leisure by hiring lower-class women as domestic workers. This "globalization of care work" is based on income inequality and intensifies stratification as women from poor countries provide low-wage domestic assistance to families in wealthier nations.[27]

Upon their move the United States, Sarah and her husband engaged in a "role reversal": while she attended graduate school, he was unemployed and took up the domestic tasks. Reflecting on this "difficult period," Sarah recognized that gender tensions, exacerbated by the shifted national context, led to marital conflict and divorce. Sarah's story of marriage and divorce shows how people can alternatingly approve and disapprove of gender relations in their own marital lives based on differing national contexts.

Nations not only frame expectations for gender behavior but also provide differing structures that support or oppress women. For instance, Valentina viewed the United States, with its laws prohibiting battery against women and supporting their equality, as a gender haven relative to her home country of Colombia. Backed by these federal and state legal protections, she felt empowered to assert herself in her marriage and defy her husband if his interests opposed hers:

> Here [in the United States] you can talk and say "no." There [in Colombia] you can't talk because there's nobody. . . . In Colombia, to call the police— they will not come to your house. . . . It's not a law like here when you call 911 somebody comes to your house. There's nobody to call. There's nobody to defend you. If you talk loud to him, he's going to hit you. Nobody is going there to defend you and the kids.

Determined not to turn into her submissive mother, Valentina divorced her first husband and challenged her second husband when necessary. One ramification of national context for Valentina was how much braver she felt in the United States than in Colombia because of U.S. laws and police presence. She herself was legally authorized to be in the United States, yet she was sensitive to the predicament of undocumented Latin American immigrant women who might suffer spousal abuse out of fear of going to the police and having their unauthorized status discovered: "They are quiet because . . . they have no papers." Valentina was pointing to an example of "legal violence": undocumented migrants being harmed by the effects of a law that could not only "obstruct or derail immigrant incorporation" but also have an impact on their personal safety.[28] Suspicious of male dominance, Valentina did not believe that American men were qualitatively different than Latin American men, but she noted the difference that national context makes for women's rights: "I don't know about American [men]. . . . I don't know how they play with their wives. I think they have affairs. They fight the same. . . . They're the same . . . because they are men. The only difference is that women in the United States already know how to defend themselves." Laws and legal organizations that support women are plentiful in the United States, whereas in Colombia, Valentina reported, the police do not make site visits for a domestic disturbance emergency call.

In a supportive national context, Valentina was more assertive in her second marriage with Ernesto, a man who was less oppressive than her first husband but who could still be jealous and aggressive. Valentina performed boundary work with Ernesto, tempering his dominance through calm interpersonal interactions. Valentina tried to have open dialogue with her husband, but because frank discussions could be uncomfortable, she had other tactics to quell volatile situations. Given her prior experiences with men, she had a mental script for how these conversations would unfold: "You say, 'Sit down. We need to talk.' It's uncomfortable. They try to push me down because they like making the decisions. Latinos try to bully you. You're going to get intimidated and they start yelling." At this juncture, Valentina would interrupt Ernesto as the pitch of the conversation escalated:

"Why are you yelling? We can talk." He tries to pass the line, but I can't let him pass the line. . . . I told him, "It's better to talk in a public place because that way you behave. At home, the men only act like boys and you're only going to raise your voice." He's very aggressive. "If you want to talk, it's better to go to a restaurant. Do you want to have a dinner and we can talk?" I do it like that because he raises his voice.

Having important private discussions in a public place was Valentina's governing device, a strategy for enforcing decorum suitable for public viewing and avoiding interpersonal eruptions.

Ernesto, Valentina's sixty-three-year-old, 1.5-generation, Mexican-origin husband, agreed that Valentina moderated his male dominance. Ernesto described his family of origin as patriarchal and acknowledged that Valentina "put brakes" on him when his attitude or behavior conflicted with her sensibilities:

I grew up in a patriarch[al] household. . . . So there's a certain part of me that's very macho. . . . I grew up with being spanked. . . . She doesn't like . . . children to be hit. So when I'm going to be spanking my kid, she kind of holds me back, says . . . there's a different way of . . . approaching [our son]. So she has kind of . . . influenced me in that regard, so I'm . . . not the way my father used to be. . . . She's put brakes on me. So in a way she's molded me a little bit to be more understanding of kids. My father's attitude was children should be seen and not heard. . . . We're different with [our son] because . . . he's our pride and joy. . . . So, in that regard, I have changed.

Valentina's history of domination by men sheds light on how prior experiences intersect with national context to shape women's actions in their adult romantic relationships. Having successfully wriggled out from under the authority of her Colombian first husband, in the United States she interacted with her second husband more assertively because of the legal support the nation offered her. Valentina vigilantly defended her own and her son's interests in a context that supported her rights, showing how "institutions, especially laws, make some actions . . . much easier to realize than others."[29]

Ernesto was less articulate about the impact of national context on his behavior, in part because he arrived in the United States with his parents at age five and had little basis for comparison. That does not mean, however, that U.S. laws and codes of conduct around gender and domestic issues had no effect on him. Nevertheless, he credited his wife with promoting change in his behavior. His initial inclination was to approach his son with the model he observed from his own father, who relegated children to relative powerlessness. Although he expressed no dissatisfaction with having been "seen but not heard" as a child himself, he was receptive to Valentina's "molding" him and now treated their son as their "pride and joy." Ernesto demonstrated that men use their own fathers as models or anti-models for how they will parent, replicating the strengths and rectifying the limitations of the fathering they received.[30] A crucial link in this process is the awareness spurred by the women in their lives.[31]

Like women, men can perceive national context as an important dimension of women's liberation. Marriage choices aside, gender concerns can be cause for migration when male family members see gender inequality through the eyes of beloved women. The immigration of Miguel Moya, a forty-year-old Mexican-born man, was precipitated by concern over gender inequality that was damaging to his mother. Miguel first lived in the United States with his maternal grandmother when he was eleven years old, then moved back to Mexico for three years. When he was fifteen, his older brother masterminded a plan to move their mother and siblings to the United States to escape their abusive father, who was "getting out of control. We found out that he had another woman . . . had a second house. . . . [My brother's] plan was to get everybody moved here and to have a better life. So it wasn't because of financial needs." Thus, unlike many Mexican immigrants, Miguel's family migrated not because of economic deprivation but to remedy an oppressive family situation. The two brothers found a four-bedroom apartment and then invited their mother and their remaining five siblings for a visit. When they came, the brothers revealed that they wanted them to stay. Upon entering the house for the first time, Miguel's older brother unveiled his plan:

> "This is your new house. Welcome." . . . She started fainting. . . . "Mom, this is your new house. You're not going back to Mexico. . . . Forget about my dad—forget about your husband. . . ." In the meantime my brother waited about a week and called my dad and told him: "You lost your family, they're not going back." My brother was old enough to realize that it was a dangerous situation for us in Mexico.

Surrounded by all seven of her children, the mother "accepted it right at that moment." Miguel teared up as he detailed the intricate, months-long plan to wrench their mother away from a "dangerous" family situation. This harrowing story shows that perceptions of gender expectations being framed by the national context are not limited to women. By reflecting on their own oppression or borrowing the perspective of female loved ones, men can comprehend how different nations offer varying prospects for gender freedom. Miguel mused on the connections between human agency, migration, and changing one's destiny:

> I tell my kids all the time: you have the power and ability to change your destiny anytime you want to. . . . Why? Because I saw how we changed our destiny. I saw how my brother changed mine, and I changed my sisters', and my mom changed mine when she left me here [when he was eleven], and then I changed hers when she became [a] United States citizen. So we all have the ability to change it. It's up to us.

Migration is a resounding theme in this narrative about changing one's destiny. Many migrants are seeking to improve their economic fortunes, yet people migrate to secure better non-economic futures as well.

National context matters in terms of how women and men view the possibilities for gender equality. Divorce is an option when a marriage does not meet a desirable type of gender relations (considered in greater detail in chapter 8). In the United States, Latina immigrants, seeing that federal and state laws protect women's rights, are emboldened to be vigilant about policing gender boundaries at home. Through interpersonal interactions, women influence men's behavior, placing limits on tyrannical behavior. In this way, the macro-level context of the nation influences and intersects with the micro-level interactions between partners, empowering women to assert themselves within a generally supportive sociopolitical environment. Men, privileged in society at large, take cues from their wives if they care to preserve their marital relationships. National context therefore works indirectly on men through the efforts of their emboldened wives or simply by virtue of living in the United States, which provides legal protections for women.

ETHNIC CULTURE CONSEQUENCES
One National Culture Adopted, the Other Eschewed

In cross-national partnerships that were grounded in a woman's desire to escape patriarchy, it was common for the couple to emphasize the national culture that was not closely associated with patriarchy. Even if a husband was in fact patriarchal, this mattered little so long as he was perceived as *relatively less patriarchal* than what his wife had previously experienced with a father or intimate partner. Many of the Latinas who sought out a cross-national intramarriage in part because of gender concerns chose to adopt the husband's national culture and jettison their own owing to its association with patriarchy.

Alicia Duarte, whose story opens this chapter, was happy to learn how to become Peruvian for multiple reasons: she did not associate it with domination, she did not comfortably fit among her Mexican American peers, and her husband's family was both more upwardly mobile and more tight-knit than her own family. These reasons combined to inspire her to adopt a Peruvian identity to replace her Mexican identity. Alicia never felt fully accepted in her Mexican American community, and because of her acculturation and desire for upward mobility, her brothers and peers derided her as pocha, or "whitewashed."[32] In reaction to her discomfort with the Mexican American community and her view of it as patriarchal, Alicia's household claimed her husband's Peruvian culture and dismissed her Mexican heritage.

For as long as she could remember, Alicia had wanted education and upward mobility. Her impoverished beginnings inspired her desire for mobility: "I knew I didn't want to do work in the fields, picking whatever, like my brothers did. I just remember when I was little, I was poor. . . . I did not want to be poor." She saw an avenue out of a manual labor fate in her husband, who came from a middle-class family and was an engineer. When asked how she got out of her economically deprived position, she said simply, "I got married. I got a job."

Beyond his educational credentials and career path, Alice was attracted to her husband because he came from a more financially stable and united family, two qualities her family of origin lacked.

We came from totally different parents. My mom was the first-generation Mexican. . . . And his parents were Peruvian; in Peru they came from . . . [the]

middle class. So they came over here with some money. . . . I've seen pictures of his parents, and they're nicely dressed in suits. . . . My mom barely had sandals on . . . totally opposite. And I think that I [am] attracted to my husband because of his family. His family is very tight-knit.

Coming from "different countries, different classes," their parents shared a generational status in the United States, but not much else. Her husband's family and Peruvian culture were a welcome alternative to Alicia's fractured family, economic stress, and gender oppression:

Our family gravitates to his side, meaning my two kids and him. I think it's because of family stability. He didn't come from [an impoverished] family like I did. My children [will] never see what it [is] like to take cereal to school in a box. He never had to do that. I see pictures of him when he was little [with a] little tie. [laughs] . . . I just don't want my children to go through . . . what I did growing up. . . . Plus, he's there for my kids. He's there in the family. . . . I'm gravitating more towards the Peruvian culture because it's more stable. It's not broken. . . . It feels better.

Alicia moved away from her Mexican culture because, while not true for all Mexican-origin families of course, she associated it with hardship, poverty, and family separation. Her husband offered her a solution in the form of middle-class status and family unity. For her, these class and family structure characteristics became typecast as "Mexican" and "Peruvian." According to this logic, "Mexican" was reduced to gender and class oppression and ruptured family forms, while "Peruvian" was perceived as class privilege and family unity. With these family-level experiences serving as cognitive maps, it is no wonder that Alicia jettisoned her Mexican heritage and adopted her husband's Peruvian heritage.

What did leaning in the Peruvian direction and away from the Mexican heritage look like in their home? Alicia and her husband had adopted the style of "symbolic ethnicity": ethnic difference was not instrumental in their lives, and they wore their ethnicity lightly, parading it mostly at ethnic festivals or at mealtimes.[33] Alicia discussed her modified cooking habits, learned from her mother-in-law: "Predominantly, I adapted to cooking. I cook more Peruvian dishes than I do Mexican dishes at home. My kids eat more bread. In South America that's what they do. In Mexico they eat more tortillas." Like other women who perpetuated their husband's ethnic culture more than their own, she acquired specific cultural knowledge through her mother-in-law, a source that reveals the gendered responsibilities behind family culture.[34]

Alicia's adoption of her husband's Peruvian culture broke the cycle of patriarchy she linked with Mexican culture. Yet this rupture in patriarchy entailed the loss of other cultural attributes, such as a taste for Mexican cuisine:

> Breaking the cycle comes with the consequences or repercussions . . . [like] my kids not liking . . . typical Mexican food. . . . My mom's like, "Why don't you like it? . . . You're Mexican. You're supposed to eat Mexican food." . . . Or [my mom will] make Mexican rice. And my daughter doesn't like it; she likes white rice. On the Peruvian side, that's what they eat.

A taste for "white rice" as opposed to "Mexican rice" bespeaks a larger cultural orientation, food marking the boundaries of ethnic cultures.[35] Alicia was one of the few women who talked about the cultural shifts (or costs) that occur as a result of moving away from Mexican culture. Most Latina interviewees who married across national-origin lines or married non-Latinos neither acknowledged nor regretted the unintended loss of ethnic culture. For most of these women, avoiding patriarchy was a reward that justified other forms of cultural diminishment.

Perceptions of patriarchy are relative. One's cultural and natal family background becomes the baseline against which other national cultures are judged. For Alicia, Peruvian culture was an escape from Mexican culture, whereas for Valentina, Mexican culture was an improvement on Colombian culture. Patriarchy is in the eye of the beholder: these women based their judgments on prior experiences that they self-protectively generalized to an entire national-origin group.

Valentina and Ernesto oriented their lives toward Mexican American culture because of Valentina's understanding of Colombian gender relations as patriarchal and unchecked by a weak nation-state. Given Valentina's experiences with guerrilla warfare and patriarchy in Colombia, she did not maintain a connection with her homeland. She had not returned to Colombia since her arrival in the United States fourteen years earlier. Reacting against the war and gender oppression pervasive in Colombia, she was not eager to pass on a Colombian identity to her eleven-year-old son. From the perspective of symbolic ethnicity, she taught her son only a few simple and symbolic things about her country: "I told him that Colombia is a beautiful country; the coffee that we have, the colors of the flag, and the music. . . . I only tell him about the positive; that you have a family, you have a lot of cousins [there]." Valentina strengthened her connection to Mexico, her husband's homeland, to fill in the cultural void left from rejecting her homeland: "I am getting a stronger relationship to Mexican because I know more about Mexico now. . . . I'm not interested in going back [to Colombia]. I don't want to take Ernesto [and our son] to meet my family. Why am I going to put them at risk to go to Colombia?"

Acting from a nexus of gender, race, and immigrant status, Valentina raised consciousness about gender issues among her Colombian women family and friends. She was an advocate for women compatriots, providing abused women with information and resources so that they could better their lives, as she did. Referring to a female talk show radio personality who "teaches the value of self," Valentina helped other Latina women focus on their own needs rather than the needs of their husbands. She ascribed to a "you first" ideology: "I'm teaching my sister the value of herself, to be more about you. Not everything for your partner or your husband. You need to take care of you first. Don't let people pass over you or treat you bad." Having learned from personal experience, Valentina was a champion of women's rights and spread messages of empowerment—made easier in the U.S. legal context—to her sisters and other immigrant women. And she traded her gender-oppressive Colombian culture for Mexican American culture, which she experienced as less patriarchal.

Given Valentina's rejection of her natal culture, the cultural scale then tipped in Ernesto's Mexican-origin direction. Ernesto learned superficial details about Colombia but otherwise continued his ethnic identity uninterrupted: "It hasn't changed at all. . . . My Mexican-ness does not come from who I'm with. It comes from within me. . . . I'm not less Mexican because I'm married to a Colombian." Without another national culture vying for attention at home, Ernesto, whose "identity was already strong" prior to marriage, continued his Mexican identity undisturbed. Unlike the couples in chapters 3 and 4, biculturalism was not the outcome for Ernesto and Valentina. Because of the rejection of one culture for gender reasons, one national culture was represented in their marriage and the other was left behind.

In these two examples of cultural rupture predicated on patriarchy, both featured women as the rejecters of their own heritage who then adopted their husband's relatively less patriarchal national culture. In cross-national marriages, men may adopt the culture of their wife's natal country (as opposed to blending two cultures), but in my sample they did not do so. When patriarchy was the paramount concern, women led the voyage of cultural redirection, since they were the ones to benefit most from a reorientation.

Cultural Work at Home as Women's Work, Men as Revisionist Fathers, and Panethnicity

Xochitl and Enzo's home would be suitable for the cover of a Pottery Barn catalog, with the notable addition of ethnic decor hailing from both

Mexico and Bolivia. Boasting a pristine look, the living room wall behind the L-shaped couch where we sat featured several framed photographs of their wedding. Indicative of their equal representation of both cultures were photographs of the bride, the groom, the couple together, and the guest gifts at each place setting: a Bolivian figurine and a Mexican decorative metal gift box adorned with calla lilies. Multiple pieces of artwork were displayed: a large, brightly colored painting from Bolivia as the centerpiece above the fireplace, a vase from Bolivia, a large chess set with carved wooden indigenous Bolivian figures, a clay Mayan calendar purchased in Mexico, an indigenous Mexican mask, and a picture of Mexican artist Frida Kahlo.

Mexican and Bolivian artwork and culture were also equally represented in the Velasco home. Xochitl decorated their home and hosted celebrations that featured both cultures, taking a cue from her mother on how to represent a national culture that she knew little about until marriage. Xochitl learned about and represented her husband's heritage, just as her own white mother did with her Mexican American father. In the household division of labor, women's work includes cultural work. Women are "often the centre of family networks and the support system for family-based ceremonies."[36] In the absence of reasons for cultural distancing, such as patriarchy, Latinas represent their own and their husband's ethnic cultures, a homegrown panethnicity, or groupness, that "maintain[s] subgroup distinctions while developing a sense of metagroup unity."[37]

Xochitl discussed her mother's display of affiliative ethnicity:

> My mom . . . is white American. And my father is Mexican. For her it was just really important that we stayed at Our Lady of Guadalupe [school] . . . from kindergarten to eighth grade. . . . She played in . . . an all-female mariachi band . . . in Topeka. . . . She played a big guitaron and . . . a trumpet. Every birthday we would get serenaded with las mañanitas [Spanish birthday song] at some ungodly hour of the morning. . . . It . . . was just a natural thing to us.

Interethnic or interracial intimate relationships, such as with romantic partners or children, can inspire cultural allegiances other than one's own ancestry.[38] Xochitl's white American mother, she said, "naturally" participated in and perpetuated Mexican American culture through community involvement, musical tradition, and family custom. Xochitl's mother acquired these cultural tastes from her Mexican-origin parents-in-law when she lived with them after she got pregnant by their son (whom she married) at age seventeen: "She moved in with my . . . Mexican grandparents, mis abuelos. . . . She spent most of those years with my abuelos [grandparents] learning their food. . . . I think they made a big impression on her." Being cared for during and after pregnancy by her Mexican parents-in-law fostered her knowledge of and interest in Mexican food and customs, which she carried throughout her married life. Xochitl learned lessons about the relation of women to ethnic identity—including a husband's ethnic identity—from her affiliative ethnic mother.

Xochitl carried on both her own national culture and her husband's. They engaged in cross-cultural exchange and panethnicity, their panethnic identities being complementary to their subgroup identities.[39] Enzo described what he had learned from his wife and how she celebrated his background:

> I've learned to appreciate . . . the Chicano movement and things like that. . . . Through her I feel like I've learned more about [the struggle of . . . the Mexican American people]. . . . The fact that she's particularly passionate . . . as a person . . . highlights it more. Then, my Bolivian culture, I don't think . . . has changed much other than I just appreciate . . . that she appreciates it as much as I do. . . . She's probably more: "Hey! Let's celebrate Bolivian Independence Day." I'm like: let's celebrate it because we're gonna have friends and family together. But she'll go the extra mile. . . . She created a crossword puzzle of Bolivian trivia. She really went all out.

For the "Bolivian festival" they hosted, Enzo's aunt, inspired by Xochitl's enthusiasm, taught her how to cook salteñas, a Bolivian baked empanada. Enzo complimented Xochitl as he drew a comparison with other cross-national married couples:

> It takes that special person that's really open to learning, open to their [spouse's] culture, and who really feels passionate. I've heard other people that say, "Yeah, I enjoy other cultures and I'm open." But quickly it's tested when you mention something that's a little bit out of the ordinary. It's like, "Oh, yeah, that's a little weird. I'm not gonna go that far."

In cross-national (or cross-racial) couples, both attitude and behavior must undergird multiculturalism if it is to feel authentic.

Both partners can participate in cross-cultural exchange, yet it tends to be women's work in the home that perpetuates ethnic culture, including the culture acquired through marriage. In Kansas, where the Latino population is small and the Bolivian population is even smaller, these demographics make Latinos reliant on the work of families to infuse Latin American cultures with meaning. Enzo remarked on the tiny Bolivian community: "I'm from Bolivia. . . . The Mexican community here . . . [the] celebrations . . . [or] customs, to me, were very foreign. . . . . There's not a

strong, big Bolivian community . . . [so] some of the customs are . . . lost."
Noting the function of family in propping up cultural activities that are
not present in white or non-Bolivian national-origin Latino subgroups,
Enzo commented: "Because I have a little bit of family here—my mom
came and I have a couple of cousins who . . . live in the area—we've tried
to maintain . . . the closeness of our family because there's not a large
Bolivian community." Carnival is very popular in Bolivia, but there is no
community-sponsored carnival celebration in Topeka owing to the small
size of the expatriate community, so Xochitl assumed the responsibility
to learn about and replicate this cultural event. Given that Xochitl looked
to Enzo's female kin to acquire this knowledge, we see how in a space
composed largely of whites and other national-origin Latino subgroups,
cultural work at home became women's work.

Brazilian Larissa Jaramillo and Mexican Miguel Moya pursued panethnicity as they blended cultures in their home. Some background on this
couple is in order. Immigrant status and acute sensitivity to race were factors that predisposed Larissa and Miguel to marry each other, with panethnicity a natural outcome of their wedded life together. Larissa Jaramillo,
a forty-year-old Brazilian immigrant who moved to the United States
for doctoral studies when she was twenty-six, and her husband Miguel
Moya, a forty-year-old Mexican immigrant who moved permanently to
the United States as a teenager, met in California before they moved to
Kansas. They both viewed "Latino" as a bounded group that shares meaningful characteristics, despite differences, two similarities being cultural
overlap and lack of connection with whiteness. Their mutual immigrant
status played a hand in how they met: when Larissa sought out a Latino
immigrant network immediately upon relocating to the United States, she
met Miguel within the first two weeks after her move. She shed light on her
conception of Latinos as a group brought together by similar perspectives,
experiences, and lifestyles:

> I connect myself so easily through the immigration experience. . . . I found this
> group of Latinos, Colombianos y Mexicanos [Colombians and Mexicans], and I
> just—I loved it! I felt, "This is my group, my people." . . . [Non-Latino] people
> had no idea about Brazil, where it was, [that I speak Portuguese]. . . . You're
> like, "We have nothing in common, what can we share?" And then you find
> this other [mixed national-origin Latino] group, [and] in five minutes you're
> hugging and talking and laughing and crying, and you are like, "I feel at
> home! I'm not at home, but this makes me feel closer to home."

In the concentric circles of likeness, Latinos, regardless of national origin or
immigration status, share an experience of segregation, similar treatment

by dominant groups, and similar behavioral orientations. This was borne out by Larissa, who said that Latinos have a knowledge base, cultural similarities, and a common nonwhite experience in the United States that made her feel "at home" when she was among them. This understanding of Latinos as a group bonded by culture and treatment in the United States mattered to Larissa for both friendship and marriage purposes: without it, she asked rhetorically, "What can we share?"

A preference for Latinos directed Larissa's marriage choice. Unlike other Latinas, she did not marry cross-nationally to avoid traits she had experienced in others from her national-origin group; instead, she sought the attributes she saw in the wider Latino category that felt "like home" to her. Larissa emphatically answered my question about whether Miguel being Latino contributed to her decision to marry him: "Oh yes! Because, again—you feel . . . at home. That's definitely, definitely, a hundred percent. And I have never, never, never in my life thought about marrying a white guy. Never. . . . Never even crossed [my mind]! I don't think we share . . . what would we share? [laughs]." Cultural compatibility was a central component of Larissa's decision to marry. Coming from Brazil, where an intricate skin color and socioeconomic ladder stratifies society, made it inconceivable for her, as a dark-skinned Latina, to marry a white man.[40] Racist experiences in Kansas (such as being skipped over for jobs despite her qualifications and people poking fun at her accent) had confirmed her social distance from whites and her vow to "never, never, never" think of marrying a white man.

For Miguel, Latinos constituted a group despite internal variation by national origin. He sketched out a portrait of the type of woman he was willing to date: "It was not really a preference to say, 'I want to marry Latino.' . . . For sure I would tell you that it wasn't going to be an American person—I mean like a blonde. . . . It could have been anybody from Colombia . . . Mexico . . . Nicaragua . . . Puerto Rico." Miguel excluded whites and articulated an affinity with Latinos of any national origin, whom he viewed as his racial community. As an immigrant, he was highly attuned to national origin, and yet he saw group bonds among Latinos hailing from different countries.[41] As nonwhite immigrants, Larissa and Miguel were socially located on the periphery of the mainstream; this location made them intelligible to each other and provided the basis for the kind of romantic connection they sought.

The couple's panethnicity and connection to both natal cultures were obvious immediately upon entering their home for an interview. Miguel introduced me to their Portuguese-speaking Afro-Brazilian housekeeper, as well as to their little dog, who bore a Spanish name. A large art piece depicting the Virgin Mary hung on the wall overlooking the entrance to the home; Miguel said that, as Catholics, they paid respect to it each time they left the house. In the downstairs family room, a sombrero that Larissa had brought back from a recent business trip to Mexico was on display. The Jaramillo/Moya couple shared elements common to their national cultures (such as Catholicism), and their home boasted cultural displays that were distinctive to their respective nations of birth. Larissa's purchase of Mexican cultural trinkets was indicative of the responsibility women typically take for the cultural work of the home, including representing their spouse's national heritage.

Larissa and Miguel agreed that over time they were becoming acculturated to the United States and less distinct as immigrants. Larissa remarked, "I came here a hundred percent Brazilian, in terms of my clothing, my styles, and then over time you just start letting those things go." Her sense of gendered responsibility for the cultural livelihood of the family led Larissa to steer the course of the family's cultural journey. As a highly educated working mother, Larissa found it "tough" to keep what she called her "Brazilian/Latina woman values," such as "cooking good food [and] providing for the family." Her response was to work the "second shift" at home, fulfilling her professional and family demands at the cost of her sleep.[42] "You just kill yourself, vacuuming the house at one o'clock in the morning. You wake up at four-thirty to cook, to make the beans—for me it's very important to have rice and beans every day on the table. You just . . . get into this crazy thing." She kept her demanding daily schedule because, as a mother, she felt that it was up to her to do the domestic work necessary to share her national culture with her family: "I do a lot because for me it's important to pass those things [on] for the kids. . . . Like the food: if I don't cook Brazilian food, where are they going to have Brazilian food?"

Like Xochitl with Enzo, Larissa contended that her cultural interests and event-planning efforts had brought Miguel closer to his natal culture. As we saw in chapter 3 with white women, Latina women can also perpetuate a specific brand of Latino culture that did not enter their lives in significant ways until they married. As a more recent immigrant than her husband, Larissa craved a Latino community, and when she built it, one effect was to enliven her husband's cultural affiliations and social networks. Larissa explained how her efforts in creating a Latino community had played out in her household:

> I think he is gravitating toward the Mexican because of me! [laughs] . . . I'm the one reminding him, "Tamales are great!" . . . I'm the one . . . who just enjoys [sharing] time with Hondureños, Colombianos, Salvadoreños, [that] . . . is where I feel good. And I bring this to him. . . . I go to Mexico more than he does—so then I bring Mexican things to . . . our house!

Larissa's effort to create a pan-Latino community in Kansas had provided Miguel with cultural resources and friendships that he had not independently sought out. Their twin eleven-year-old sons also illustrated the family's panethnicity: according to Larissa, the boys adhered to all of their identities equally: "They tell everybody that they are Mexican Brazilian Americans."

In considering their panethnicity, Miguel pondered what makes "Latino" a meaningful group category. Pointing to language (Portuguese and Spanish) and food as telltale signs of cross-national difference, Miguel remarked on the cross-cultural sharing that typified their panethnic Latino household:

> The food is different: tortillas do not fit in the Brazilian [cuisine]. Now, did I let the tortillas go? No, because I make quesadillas for my kids. When I make my own [Mexican] food, there's always tortillas on the table. . . . Larissa learned to eat tortillas, she learned to eat hot sauce. . . . She loves my country; I love her country. So yeah, we learned to put our two cultures together, we learned. . . . We share our lives [and] try to meet halfway.

Miguel and Larissa's willingness to combine their two cultures is reminiscent of the cultural negotiations between Latino and white spouses (chapter 3) that resulted in an "everyday biculturalism"—the daily habits of eating, speaking, and sharing lives that can produce a cultural amalgamation. Miguel viewed panethnicity as a positive contribution to his life: "I feel pretty lucky . . . being able to share two cultures in one household. . . . I've added more to my life."

Ideas about gender are cultural, and Miguel paid attention to his own deployment of masculinity as he parented his children, conscientiously trying to correct for the mistakes his father made. Prior research I conducted showed that men use their negative experiences with their own fathers as a benchmark to improve upon and that they try to father in such a way as to correct for the paternal shortcomings they endured.[43] In concert with this earlier work, Miguel wanted to be a better father than his father. He told me how he counseled his twin sons, his advice showing his commitment to cultivating caring father-son relationships:

MIGUEL: Don't be afraid of your dad. You can come to Dad for anything that you want. . . . So don't be afraid. Come and talk to me.

AUTHOR: Is that a change from what you felt with your father?

MIGUEL: Big, big change, absolutely. It was to the point that . . . anybody in my house [when I was young would] see my dad coming around the corner from the street [and say],

"Hide—go to your room." . . . [By contrast,] to this day [my kids] still . . . come to say good-bye when they go to school. They kiss me on the forehead.

This chapter argues that women take chief responsibility for cultural work, but men are also invested in doing cultural work—or making cultural change, as seen in Miguel's story. The difference in the division of labor of cultural work is that women take charge of reproductive labor, such as preparing meals and hosting social gatherings (often supporting their husbands' national-origin culture), whereas men either spend their cultural energies in the public sphere (as seen in chapter 3) or cherry-pick issues to invest in, such as certain family relationships (see chapter 6). In this case, Miguel was striving not to change national-origin cultural practices per se, but to tailor his own behavior so as to transform gendered interactions between himself as a father and his sons.

Among my interviewees, women continued to take primary responsibility for carrying forward their own and their partner's ethnic culture. The marriages among those who cared about their cultural background had resulted in cultural exchange and perpetuation supported by women's labor.[44] Men's efforts were not trivial, however, for while many were satisfied with simply being quietly encouraging, others selected cultural elements to revise, such as gender norms. Although cultural escapism predominated among those who were fleeing gender oppression, panethnicity was the cultural consequence among cross-national couples who had better early life experiences and who cared about preserving their Latino heritage.

CONCLUSION

This chapter has exposed two ways in which gender and race-ethnicity facilitate Latino cross-national marriages. First, Latina women who were oppressed by authoritarian fathers (or first husbands) color-code this experience and are driven to seek a romantic partner outside of their national-origin group. Unlike Latinas who reject all Latino men and out-marry with other racial groups, these women marry cross-nationally either because their appreciation for their Latino background leads them to select a Latino, simply with a different national origin, or because their language skill and a local Latino community have kept them immersed in Latino dating pools. Second, some Latino men and women see whites, the racial group with whom Latinos intermarry at the highest rate, as unsuitable for them based on prior dating experiences. These men and women discuss their avoidance of whites in terms of racial perspectives, cultural tradition, language use, family orientation, and values. People who employ these rationales for cross-national in-marriage view Latinos hailing from a different national heritage as an escape from an oppressive force. Cross-national in-marriage is also a means to preserve aspects of Latino culture that people find meaningful, even as a spouse's specific culture is a variant that may require cultural retooling.

The gender and racial-ethnic outcomes of cross-national in-marriage are as various as the rationales that led to these marriages in the first place. Latina women are far more vocal about their gender concerns than Latino men, who benefit from classical patriarchal styles. Thus, this chapter has focused heavily on women's efforts to seek relationships that suit their gender needs. Women in cross-national unions report three gendered outcomes of their partnerships. First, women who pursue men with attitudes about gender that correspond with their own are often able to find a gender haven in their partner. Rather than exclude all Latino men from their dating pool based on a stereotype, these women find that their selectivity works in combination with their eventual partner himself to make their gender wishes come true.[45] Second, women whose notions of gender clash with their husband's ideas experience marital conflict or divorce. Third, women's vigilance around gender oppression highlights their agency in protecting their rights, bodies, and voices. National context is also influential: nations with a police force and legal system that protect women boost women's confidence in drawing boundaries and safeguarding themselves in domestic partnerships.

Identity and cultural practices are dynamic—that is, they are apt to change. First, Latina wives who perceive cross-national marriage as a route away from male dominance adopt their husband's national culture and shed their own national culture. Ethnic culture is either grasped or jettisoned based on associated understandings of gender. Second, this chapter sheds light on the "general mechanisms by which groups become consolidated and forge alliances across ethnic lines," underscoring how marriage and family dynamics produce panethnicity.[46] Further, women act as preservation agents in the domestic and cultural spheres by performing much of the cultural work involved in perpetuating their own and their husbands' cuisine and customs.[47] That said, men are devoid of neither culture nor agency: some with problematic family histories enact change as they consciously parent their own children differently from the way they were raised (discussed in greater detail in the next chapter).

A search for a gender and racial haven that offers relative liberation from constricted definitions and enactments of gender and race can lead to cross-national pairings. The ramifications of these pairings fall in line: women either achieve their gendered aims with the help of a supportive national environment or, if not, encounter conflict. Cultural practices also follow suit with intentions: women who reject same-national-origin men in order to elude patriarchy embrace their husbands' national culture and are inattentive to their own roots. Depending on how closely women associate their national heritage with patriarchy, they either refute their national-origin culture or blend it with their husband's heritage into a panethnic Latino identity.

The cross-national families featured in this chapter were evenly located in California and Kansas, suggesting that despite stark demographic differences, residential segregation concentrates nonwhite populations, generating Latino dating pools that are internally diverse. For those who appreciate aspects of their Latino culture, intersectional concerns stemming from personal experience can spark the hope of fulfilling race- and gender-based desires through marriage to someone who is close, but not too close, to their own national-origin group.

Chapter 6 | Mixed-Generation Mexican-Origin Marriages: From Transnationalism to Feminism

OMAR ZELAYA WENT to Mexico to find a wife. Born to Mexican immigrants in Southern California, Omar judged the lifestyle in the United States to be too lax, "too unreserved," implying that American women would not suit his more traditional sensibilities. When he was ready for a significant relationship, Omar traveled to his parents' hometown in Mexico, a place he had regularly visited, to seek out a Mexican woman. The forty-eight-year-old man described his thought process in traveling internationally to find a wife:

> I said, "Hey, I got to start establishing something." So . . . I went on vacation to [Mexico]. . . . I should just try to find [a woman from Mexico], because maybe she'll understand me better. . . . I just want to raise a family. . . . It was mostly because of my upbringing. If my [Mexican immigrant] parents were a certain way, I think I could relate to a girl that was more this way.

Using his natal family experience as a guide, Omar negotiated his desire toward Mexican women, whom he idealized as "carriers of culture" to whom he could "relate" and envisioned as virtuous and capable of helping him "raise a family." This opening vignette typifies one of many possible beginnings to a marriage that involves mixed-generation (and, in this case, transnational) coethnics.

Since endogamy (racial-ethnic group members marrying each other) is so prevalent, in-marriage is routinely dismissed as normal and uninteresting. To the extent that coethnic intramarriages are even considered at all,

168

they are seen as consolidating racial power and privilege (among whites) or racial disadvantage (among minorities). Whites retain racial supremacy in part through endogamy, and minorities consolidate racial disempowerment through endogamy.[1] This chapter features couples whose ancestors come from the same nation—Mexico—but who themselves have different generational statuses (number of generations-since-immigration). For example, Omar was second-generation (his parents were both Mexican immigrants), and his wife Helen was first-generation (an immigrant herself). Examining such mixed-generation Mexican-origin intramarriages, this chapter questions the racial, gendered, and classed logics behind these couplings and explores what this group can tell us about Mexican ethnicity in the United States.

This chapter is based on twenty-two interviewees with eighteen presently married adults and four children, representing a total of eleven families. Of those eleven families, seven were from California and four were from Kansas. The chapter is organized into two sections based on marital type: marriages of immigrant Mexicans married to U.S.-born Mexican Americans, and marriages of U.S.-born Mexican Americans who varied in generation-since-immigration, such as a second-generation married to a later-generation (third-plus-generation). The section on immigrants investigates the theme of transnationalism as well as the keen awareness among immigrants of their legal status (especially the undocumented) and contemporary racial politics. The section on U.S.-born couples addresses upward mobility, as my sample lacked downwardly mobile couples; this may not be surprising considering that poverty rates in inner-city Los Angeles have decreased for all adult age groups. The vast majority of my California interviewees spent their childhoods in inner-city Los Angeles yet moved up and out to the suburbs in adulthood, reflecting the survey data finding that urban ghettos can serve as "launch pads" and not necessarily just as traps for cyclical poverty.[2] (There are no similar studies of urban poverty in Kansas.) I analyze upward mobility here as accompanied either by adaptation to the white mainstream or by ethnic solidarity. Socioeconomic achievement is not the death knell for ethnic solidarity, nor is ethnic loyalty found only among the lower class immersed in an ethnic community.

The final empirical section, on U.S.-born Latino feminist men, is thematic and deserves attention even if it is not tied to marital type. Women's feminism has been discussed throughout this book in the context of Latinas aiming to satisfy their gender aims through their marital choices. Men's gender norms shift when they want to correct for oppressive natal family dynamics, and these revised norms are often expressed through their marital relationships. Patriarchy affects not only women but men too. Even though adult men reap benefits from a system of male privilege, men who suffered domination as boys or witnessed violence or limitations thrust on their mothers or sisters can be inspired by those early experiences to rebalance gender inequalities. As seen in chapter 5, marriage can inspire shifts in gendered behavior as wives encourage their husbands to become more egalitarian for the sake of marital accord.

MARRIAGES INVOLVING THE FIRST GENERATION: IMMIGRANT MEXICANS AND U.S.-BORN MEXICAN AMERICANS

Transnational In-marriages

Transnationalism is "the process by which immigrants forge and sustain multistranded social relations that link together their societies of origin and settlement."[3] It is stimulated by colonization and global markets and spreads through social networks and communication and transportation technologies.[4] Transnationalism is supported by circular flows of people, information, and products between countries. Migrants' gender ideologies can be shifted (more significantly among younger people) when they live in the United States, yet their core sensibilities concerning what constitutes masculine and feminine behavior can be resistant to dramatic change.[5] Aside from Hung Thai's work on Vietnamese international marriages, this literature elides the role of transnationalism in the creation of family unions.[6] There remains a need for an examination of the way in which gender structures and is structured by transnational social ties.[7] I argue that transnationalism is both a *means* to achieve desired romantic relationships (transnationalism leading to marriage) and a *lifestyle* among middle- and upper-class families (transnationalism as a result of marriage).

Omar's impulse to travel to Mexico when he felt ready to settle down was normalized by his family history, his grandparents' transnationalism between the United States and Mexico having presaged his own. Omar's father migrated from Mexico in the 1940s, when he was eighteen years old, as a bracero—a worker authorized under the Bracero Program, a contract labor program sponsored by the U.S. government in agreement with the Mexican government, to enter the United States. Omar's mother's side of the family exemplified life on two sides of the border. He reported that his maternal grandfather "was born in Arizona. He was a legal U.S. citizen. . . . [When his] dad died, he ended up traveling back south into Jalisco, Mexico . . . where my mother was born. . . . He stayed in Mexico and he became a mayor." On both sides of the family, the international border was repeatedly crossed. In his youth, Omar spent several family vacations, lasting three to six months at a time, at his grandparents' residence. This understanding of the border as fluid and traversable made seeking out a marital partner across international lines probable. In a disruption of traditional notions of citizenship and belonging, Mexico was never a "foreign" country to Omar.

Mexico represented traditionalism to Omar. Like many intramarried men and women, Omar desired a cultural connection with his future mate. He craved cultural similarity and felt that traveling to Mexico offered him the best chance of finding a traditionally feminine Mexican woman. A critic of U.S. women, he assumed that a Mexican-born woman would be strongly oriented toward family. Omar did not discuss his mother until the very end, when I commented that he had not yet talked about her. He briefly described her as a woman dedicated to the home, children, and extended family:

> She was . . . a homemaker. She was always there for us, always sent us off to school, always had our meals ready, everything. . . . She was a homemaker. Our clothing was always washed. Everything was always ready. You can't complain about a mother who was always there. . . . She . . . was there to help out with my . . . dad's mother.

Social psychology suggests that mothers make an imprint on their children and serve as a model for a son's future spouse. Omar's mother was a constant figure in his life, yet she remained in the background and he took her for granted by virtue of her very constancy.[8] She was "always there," a homemaker whose sole responsibility was the home, and her appearances in public were further limited by the fact that she did not drive. Omar reasoned that he would meet someone with these same family values by seeking out a partner in his mother's country of origin. His logic resonated with the finding of a study on gender and sexuality in a transnational community that Mexican men associate U.S. women with loose morals, so "returning home [to Mexico] to marry was the only way to find a woman who would share their values."[9] Moreover, traveling to a parent's tight-knit hometown in Mexico was a sure way to verify a woman's reputation via social networks.[10]

His desire for a woman with a set of traits that he associated with Mexican women was not the only influence on Omar's dating proclivities. His understanding of the racial order in the United States also led Omar to rule out certain women. In answer to my question about his dating history, Omar expounded:

> I'm gonna be honest with you. I got along with white women fine. I had no problem with them. But I used to shy away from them a little bit more. . . .

I shied away from them . . . feeling a sense of cultural difference where I probably wouldn't be understood as well. . . . We couldn't be as readily acceptable to each other. . . . I noticed that some of these white girls, they didn't really pay attention to you. . . . You could . . . use the term "stuck-up" or "arrogant." . . . Maybe my accent gave me away sometimes, and some of them were not as friendly. The unfriendly ones had the tendency to . . . brush you off.

Omar moved quickly from asserting that he "got along fine" with white women to commenting on his own shyness in reaction to "cultural difference" and rejection from them based on race-ethnicity made perceptible through his accent. Omar summed up culture, race-ethnicity, and class by noting that he and white women were not "readily acceptable to each other." He perceived white women's disinterest in losing their racial power by "dating down" as arrogance. Learning about the racial hierarchy through repeated rejections by white women, Omar accepted his place in the hierarchy by self-segregating and "shying away" from white women.[11] He had internalized the racial order, and his negotiated desire for a Mexican wife stemmed as much from feeling pushed away by white American women as from feeling culturally pulled toward Mexican women. These two motions worked in tandem in Omar to produce his endogamous marriage.

Believing that he would be compatible with Mexican women, Omar went to Mexico to find a serious relationship with a woman who would share particular similarities with him: "Cooking. . . . Someone that could speak the language [Spanish] so your children could . . . learn a second language. But mostly because of the values. Values, food, and the culture in general. It's coming directly from there [Mexico], so it's going to be similar to yours."

As much as Omar was seeking a particular type of femininity in a woman, he was also seeking affirmation of his version of masculinity. In desiring a woman steeped in traditional, Catholic, racialized femininity, he simultaneously desired appreciation of and acquiescence to his traditional, Catholic, racialized masculinity. The sole breadwinner for a family of five, bringing in between $30,000 and $40,000 annually, Omar expected appreciation from his wife Helen, who had an eleventh-grade education and was economically dependent on him. Although it is problematic to juxtapose a sending country as a site of patriarchal oppression with a receiving country as less oppressive for women, people like Omar devise romantic strategies that perpetuate essentialized notions of immigrant femininity and class inequality.[12]

Helen's ideas about gendered responsibilities in the home meshed with Omar's. Now a housewife and mother of three children, the youngest an infant and the oldest sixteen years old, Helen was primarily in charge of home life, saying: "He can do better with the car; I can do better in the home." Like Omar, Helen had wanted cultural commonality with a mate, and she noted that she and Omar had "pretty much the same ideas" because they were from the same town (meaning his relatives' hometown in Mexico). After transnationalism—in particular Omar's travel to Mexico to find a wife—precipitated their romance, they discovered their compatible desires to retain culture, values, and the Spanish language, and so they wed. Even their wedding took place in two places: they were married in a Catholic church in Mexico and by the state in the United States.

In the context of Southern California, Helen found that it was easy to hold on to her culture and values because of the availability of Mexican materials, foods, and public events such as festivals:

> Here in California, they sell everything. . . . Here in California . . . the traditions like the Cinco de Mayo, the fifteenth of September, they're celebrated. So they're part of our tradition, and they continue here. I don't feel a large difference between there [Mexico] and here [the United States]. . . . They've exported a lot of Mexican products here that are common at home. I tell my mom, we have elotes [grilled corn with seasoning]. . . . It's not like people . . . say, "Ay, what is *that*?!" . . . Everything that is in Mexico is here as well.

In the Mexican-rich environment of greater Los Angeles, Helen did not need to change her daily food preparation practices or her habit of participating in annual celebrations. Despite her move from Mexico to the United States, the culturally consonant Southern California context required no change in her cultural practices because they were locally supported.

Transnationalism also reinforced the Zelaya family's gender traditionalism. Given Omar's intention of "finding a wife" in Mexico who exhibited the conservative feminine traits he valorized, it is not surprising that their home life was organized by a strongly gendered division of labor. By traveling regularly to rural areas of Mexico where the conventional styles of "ranchero masculinity" and "ranchera femininity" based on separate spheres and gender inequality predominated, the Zelayas buttressed their conservative perspectives on gender.[13]

Stella, Omar and Helen's sixteen-year-old daughter, had far more highly gendered family responsibilities than any other teenager I interviewed. When I was in their home for the interview, Helen asked Stella to check on her baby brother, bring him to her, and prepare his milk bottle. When Helen remarked, "Sometimes I feel like I don't have a third baby," in reference to Stella's assistance, she meant that as a compliment. I asked Stella if there were ways in which being a young woman, in her opinion, had influenced her experience, and she concisely replied: "The chores. Because

you are a Mexican [woman], you have to help out a lot more in the house."
When asked about her relationship with each of her parents, she described
how gender inflected her parents' treatment of her and her brother: "My
dad . . . mostly hangs out with my brother. I guess it's like 'man stuff.' . . .
With my mom, we'll go shopping, we'll . . . clean the house. I help her take
care of my little brother." Stella reported no shared time with her father,
and all three activities she and her mother jointly performed were domestic chores. Traveling to small-town Mexico, where similarly gendered
household divisions of labor were commonplace, supported the family's
gendered expectations, regardless of country of residence.

Helen, a Spanish-dominant homemaker without a high school diploma,
was economically and linguistically dependent on her husband. Omar's
breadwinning status was probably rewarding for him, since he was committed to gender traditionalism: this tilted husband-wife dynamic confirmed his version of masculinity as necessary to Helen and the functioning
of the household. And if fluency in the "legitimate" language (like the predominant language of a nation) is a mark of social distinction and a form
of capital or power, then Helen's lack of English fluency subordinated her
to Omar.[14] Noting that "he correct[s] me" to improve her English, Helen
told me, "My husband says, 'Why you not be American? [sic] You speak
so funny.' " Ironically, the man who explicitly traveled to Mexico to find a
wife now chastised her for not being sufficiently American linguistically.

Helen wished for different opportunities for her daughter Stella. Honing
in on finances, Helen did not want Stella to replicate her own situation of
economic dependence: "[I hope] that she can afford a place by herself. . . .
That she alone has a career, goes to the university, so she can maintain herself. . . . That she doesn't have to depend upon anybody else. That she has
wings large enough to fly very high." She contrasted her aims for her daughter with her own economic subordination: "If something were to happen to
my husband. . . . I would have a very difficult time." Not having attended
college herself, she knew little about the college application process, so after
my interview with Stella, Helen tried to boost her knowledge by asking me,
a university professor, about what would be involved in sending her daughter to college, from entrance exams and types of institutions to financial aid.

With two Mexican-origin parents who engaged transnationalism and
traditionalism, Stella anticipated that her romantic involvements would be
with people of Mexican descent. Stella drew on ideas of cultural compatibility and incompatibility as well as family approval to forecast that she
would probably engage in endogamous romance: "I think maybe [I want
someone ethnically] similar because I don't want to . . . clash with someone
who is not the same as me. . . . 'Cuz I want to make sure that we can get
along, because I don't want to end up divorcing them. I want to have a long

relationship." Much like the intramarried adults profiled in this book, Stella equated cultural commonality with understanding and a harmonious long-term relationship. She believed that her family would more easily accept a coethnic: "Our families can get along. . . . When they're similar, it's like, 'Oh, we understand what you're talking about.' " Her parents counseled her "to get married through the church. And . . . to try to find someone who is also from the same background. You want to make sure that you guys have a good relationship and a long-lasting life together." This formulation of shared religion and heritage serving Stella as a guideline for mate selection has directed partnership formation for centuries.[15] While the jury was still out on Stella, since she was young, her parents' and her own expectation for her future endogamous marriage was clear. Intervening factors that could shift Stella away from coethnic romance, however, included college attendance, which would expand her dating opportunities, and her own adult judgment about whether she wanted to replicate or repudiate the models of femininity and masculinity given her by her natal family.[16]

Transnationalism can be a *cause* of in-marriage and a means to preserve a way of life that maintains ethnic culture and male superiority, as in the Zelaya family. Transnationalism can also be a *consequence* of in-marriage, as in the Ornales family. Mexican-born Rosalinda's upper-middle-class status and professional occupation had facilitated her to travel to the United States, where she met her husband Gilbert. In this case, transnationalism was both a cause of an international in-marriage and a consequence as this newly formed middle-class family maintained a transnationalist lifestyle.

Rosalinda Ornales, fifty-three years old, grew up upper-middle-class in Mexico owing to her family's "very solid" financial background and land-holdings. Her own income was impressive: "I was making . . . four times more than [a] typical family over there." As a paid vocalist in an elite choir, Rosalinda was exposed to upper-class Mexico and travel to U.S. cities. She described how travel with the choir developed her cosmopolitan perspective:

> [With] the choir . . . we were able to travel all over the country [Mexico] and . . . be exposed to a different way of living . . . meaning the high class. If you went to sing for the president of Mexico, that means a plane especially for the group. . . . Going to [Puerto] Vallarta . . . every month . . . because the governor was there. . . . [It was a] very different experience than a typical girl from [the] pueblo [town]. . . . Having the freedom of . . . traveling . . . wasn't too common in town.

Traveling in style with the choir from age seventeen until thirty expanded Rosalinda's worldview and provided her with the chance to meet her husband in the United States.

Rosalinda was on tour with her choir when she met Gilbert, who had volunteered to house some male group members in his home. With her cosmopolitan lifestyle, Rosalinda had dated a Russian and an Asian before meeting Gilbert. With those other men, she complained, "something was missing in that connection." Gilbert, on the other hand, she described as "very romantic, very sweet, very respectful, a good son." Gilbert possessed the qualities dear to her, including his family orientation, which she referenced in calling him a "good son." Rosalinda drew a sharp line between what she viewed as Mexican family values and American ones: "I wasn't at all interested in someone from here [the United States] because of my experience of seeing two parents working and the kids by themselves. I wasn't interested [in] that. . . . In Mexico you get together at least for dinner. And you talk and talk for hours every night. And over here [in the United States], none of that was present."

In courting her internationally by traveling to Mexico every two or three months, Gilbert demonstrated his respect and family orientation. He brought his mother on one of those trips to introduce her to Rosalinda, allowing Rosalinda to see him as appropriately family-oriented. I asked how Gilbert captured her attention, since she was not seeking an American man. Rosalinda explained: "Talking to [Gilbert's mother], I learned that she was a housewife, she never had to work. . . . So I thought maybe we can choose to do that." By seeing in a new light how families could function in the United States (and how her suitor's family was organized), Rosalinda became receptive to Gilbert as a long-term partner. His values that matched hers won her over, irrespective of his country of origin.

In this love story, the couple had to jump through hoops to get the approval of protective family and friends. The literature on international migration pays little attention to the influence that people back home have on immigrants as they adjust to a new country. It is not simply the destination country that has an impact on immigrant adaptation but also the sending country and the existing social networks that migrants leave behind. Rosalinda's friends' criticism of her for leaving Mexico to marry an American was bound up with a suitor she left behind in Mexico:

AUTHOR: How has it been for you to be a Mexican woman in the United States who is married to a Mexican American? How has your relationship to your background changed, if at all?

ROSALINDA: . . . It was a little bit painful at the beginning, because going to Mexico with my American husband, my friends used to . . . criticize me. "How come you choose an American? We have. . . ." A couple of them stopped talking to me.

AUTHOR: So what was their issue, and how did you respond to that?

ROSALINDA: One of them, it's because. . . . He's a great friend. He
             wanted his brother to get married with me. His brother
             asked me. I said, "No way. You are like my brother.
             No." So he stopped talking to me for a couple of years.
             I was hurt, but I understood. This is my choice and it is
             my life.

It is easy to imagine the friend's statement "we have . . ." ending with ". . .
eligible men in here in Mexico too." Even the narrative by itself makes the
national comparison: Rosalinda chose to marry an American and depart
from Mexico even as Mexican bachelors sought her attention. With some
friends shunning her, it must have felt to Rosalinda as if the two nations—
not just men from the two nations—were competing for her loyalty and
affection.

Rosalinda clarified that her mystified friends were upholding Mexico as
a desirable place to live. Saying that "almost all" of her friends criticized
her decision to marry an American, Rosalinda noted that both friendships
and national pride were at stake:

ROSALINDA: I think [my critical friends were] being racist [read: nation-
             alist]. . . . Gilbert is a great man, and he was nice with all
             of them, and they loved him. But they didn't like the fact
             that I'm gonna marry him and leave the choir, the pueblo,
             the country. . . . [It was] more the idea of, "You belong
             here. He came and he's stealing you and taking you."

AUTHOR: How did you explain your decision?

ROSALINDA: I was almost thirty, so at that age you know what you
             want. I said, "You know what, I love you guys. . . . You are
             married, and you have children with your spouses. . . .
             I happen to live far away. That's the way that it is."

Rosalinda was resolute in her opinion that marrying Gilbert and moving
to the United States was not a rejection of Mexico or her life in Mexico
but a choice to develop her personal life. Her comment "I happen to live
far away" suggests that geographic location did not dictate her lifestyle,
friendships, or national pride.

In Rosalinda's tale, we see the process by which she elected to marry
Gilbert. Her international travel with her choir put her in contact with
Gilbert in the first place. Second, his value system meshed with hers: his
dedication to family was appealing to her, as was the role she might play

as his wife. Third, she had previously rejected the marriage proposal of her good friend's brother on the grounds that she viewed him more as family than as a romantic possibility. After wrestling with these complicated friendship situations, Rosalinda had come to a modern conclusion that highlighted her free will: "This is my choice, and it is my life."

The marriage of Rosalinda and Gilbert Ornales was made possible by transnationalism, and a transnationalist lifestyle that reinforced their Mexican ethnicity was the chief consequence of their international intramarriage. The couple owned several properties in Mexico, including a house in Rosalinda's hometown, and now had two teenage children. They had traveled to Mexico with their family for one or two months every summer for the twenty-one years since they married. In California, regular travel had reinforced their way of life, which they saw as more conservative and value-oriented than other American households. By traveling to Mexico, their kids could see a "pattern" that was consistent with the lifestyle they maintained in the United States. Rosalinda explained the linkage between travel and the values that she associated with Mexican households: "Traveling helps. . . . The things that I teach here and we try to live here, [the kids] see the same pattern over there. My daughter's cousins . . . have to ask permission [to go places], so she knows she's not the only one [with those rules]."

Transnationalism fostered positive self-identities for Rosalinda's Mexican American children, and their international experiences allowed her children "to be secure, to be confident," in a racially ordered society. The Ornales family's class advantage supported their annual travel and accompanying global perspective and bilingualism. Rosalinda acknowledged their fortunate class position and the benefits it could buy: "Thank God [we can] do it, because it's not an easy thing. You're talking a thousand [dollars] to get your tickets and spend a month over there. So far, we're doing it."

Underclass in his youth but now middle-class, Gilbert, a sixty-two-year-old Mexican American, was born and reared in East Los Angeles. He sympathized with the Chicano movement, and his identity as a Chicano was tied to the fight for equality: "When I was involved with the community in East L.A., this whole Chicano movement came about. . . . I was wrapped up in it, and I was proud to be part of it. . . . We were protesting against injustice, and we wanted equality and education." A conscientious objector during the Vietnam War, Gilbert was ordered to do "alternative service" at Colonia Designers, an urban planning organization that he helped establish whose name refers to the ethnic community (colonia means "neighborhood" in Spanish).[17] Colonia Designers was a way for Gilbert to use his urban planning degree to advocate for the needs of his community. Urban renewal projects that razed and displaced minority communities for public works projects such as highway construction inspired Gilbert to use his degree to speak for the interests of the lower-class Latinos of East L.A.[18]

Gilbert's rationale for endogamy was a simple calculation: "You basically learn that if you're a fish, you belong in the water, or you're stronger in the water." This philosophy also undergirded Gilbert's appreciation for his ethnic community and intense interest in aiding it. For him, intra-marriage was a natural extension of his established predilections for coethnic concern and camaraderie. In alignment with his intention, international in-marriage had resulted in cultural enrichment for Gilbert:

> It has definitely enriched me. It definitely has opened up my world. . . . It's just . . . another opportunity, as if you went to central California and saw something that you can relate to . . . or make it part of you, except that this is in Mexico. . . . When I go down there, I don't separate myself as being American. . . . In fact, I'm going to try to apply for a dual citizenship. I already talked to a lawyer.

In comparing Mexico to central California, a different region of his home state, Gilbert was depicting Mexico not as foreign but rather as familiar, and his plan to apply for dual citizenship also signaled his commitment to his family's transnationalism.

The Ornales' desire to move to Mexico full-time in the future was a more realistic goal than it is for many of those who romanticize a return to Mexico but become so deeply embedded in the United States that they never do so. Mexican culture was sustained in their family by Rosalinda's musical talents, by their daughter's ballet folklorico, and by Gilbert's construction of their second home ("the first California-style house in all of Jalisco [Mexico]"). Wherever they were residing—California or Jalisco—Mexican culture was a constant. Living in Mexico for one to two months each summer for the entirety of their twenty-one-year relationship was a consequence of their international in-marriage. All indicators suggest that this transnational lifestyle would continue in the next Ornales generation with nineteen-year-old Vanessa, supported by bilingualism, biculturalism, a home in each country, and a middle-class status to finance travel.

Vanessa estimated that she lived 60 percent of her life in the United States and 40 percent in Mexico. She was fluent in English and Spanish: "I just grew up speaking . . . Spanglish, like, 'Mommy, I want agua [water].' . . . On tests, they'd ask you, 'What's your first language?' And I'm not really sure, 'cuz . . . I grew up learning both at the same time." In mixed-generation pairs, one partner is a more recent arrival from the sending country and the later-generation partner is either drawn toward that ancestral country or pulls away from it. Referring to this dynamic, Vanessa credited her father with possessing a "passion for Mexican culture" that supported the family's transnationalism.

Indicative of her comfort with biculturalism, Vanessa caught herself when she began to say that she "appreciated" Mexican culture and switched to a more appropriate action verb: "[I am] Mexican American. It means that . . . I have Mexican roots, that I apprec— — . . . well, not appreciate, but I mean, I practice some Mexican culture, but I live in America. I also have influences from this country as well." Transnationalism led to Vanessa's biculturalism: she was "exposed to [both cultures] equally" and was therefore "in the middle." Despite this evenhanded experience of culture, her intramarried parents, much like Stella Zelaya's family, preferred that she date within her ethnic group, using ethnic similarity as shorthand for happiness: "Overall [my parents] want . . . the best for me. And . . . they know . . . [that] dating or marrying a Mexican is the best for me." Cultural familiarity would mean that her parents would "know what to expect" with her prospective mate. In contrast to her parents, Vanessa was more open-minded about dating across racial lines, but then she added, "What I look for in someone . . . [is] based off . . . what my race has taught me." Moreover, Vanessa's hometown environment of Pico Rivera, which she estimated to be "about 90 percent Latino and 10 percent everything else," had shaped her friendship networks and dating possibilities. Indeed, the Los Angeles area ranked number one in a study of Hispanic-white segregation in the fifty metropolitan areas with the largest Hispanic populations in 2010.[19] Vanessa's experience reflected this reality: "The places I've been [are] so . . . densely populated by . . . Latinos, so . . . [there's] more probability that I'm gonna be friends with Mexican Americans." In this Southern California context, Vanessa was positioned to continue "practicing" her Mexican culture, being friends with Latinos, probably partnering with another Latino, and even carrying on living transnationally.

This section has illustrated how transnationalism both facilitates in-marriages and is a consequence of in-marriage. Transnationalism, be it a cause or consequence of coethnic marriage among mixed-generation Mexican-origin couples, reinforces particular racialized understandings about race, gender, and family. Continued social ties in another country increase international exposure, bilingualism, and biculturalism and heighten the youngest generation's inclination toward endogamous romance.

Immigrants' Political-Legal Consciousness

Legality was a crucial issue for some immigrants and their spouses. These couples spoke emphatically about foreign-born status marking the immigrant as an outsider and the quandary faced by immigrants in trying to obtain legal U.S. citizenship.[20] This study does not explicitly concentrate on immigrants, since it required that one Latino/a in the couple was U.S.-born or 1.5-generation (foreign-born and having arrived in the United States by the age of twelve). Yet the experiences of the immigrants included in the study raised not only their own political consciousness but also that of their spouses.

Daria Fernandez, a sixty-one-year-old Californian who had spent her whole life in Los Angeles County, talked adamantly about politics having pushed her Mexican immigrant husband, fifty-six-year-old Chico (who declined an interview), to become a naturalized U.S. citizen. Daria spoke about the "boomerang effect" of politics: those targeted by legislation can become politicized. Even as Americans' prejudices have decreased over the last century, there has been no marked improvement in attitudes toward immigrants.[21] Immigration remains a hot-button political topic, and the issues of legality, illegality, and citizenship have a great impact on the lives and decision-making of immigrants.

Restrictive immigration policies encouraged Chico's naturalization. As "governments decide whom to let in and whom to keep out, they literally define the community that makes a nation-state."[22] Race-based legislation thus serves as a means to enact "membership exclusion."[23] Yet policy cannot predict how people will resist the restrictionist intent of legislation. Daria referred to the 1994 ballot initiative in California, Proposition 187, that established a state-run citizenship screening system and prohibited undocumented people from accessing health care, public education, and other social services:

> One of the reasons he became an American was because of [Proposition] 187. . . . I had always told my husband to become an American citizen. He said, "What for?" I go, "You could vote." . . . I [listed for] him all the benefits. It didn't matter to him. Then, when 187 [was being debated], he came home one day and said, "You know what? I went to the INS [Immigration and Naturalization Service], and I filed my papers so I could become a citizen." And I said, "Why?" He goes, " 'Cuz of [Governor] Pete Wilson." [*laughs*] You know, I think Pete Wilson's responsible for a lot of permanent residents becoming American citizens. . . . That's not what he intended. And then most of them vote Democratic 'cuz of Pete Wilson [a Republican]. So there was a boomerang effect.

A permanent resident for years since his immigration at age seventeen, Chico had been satisfied with that status until immigration came under attack in a wave of state initiatives in the 1990s.[24] Like many people who, politically threatened by anti-immigrant legislation, mobilized to achieve rights they had previously been unconcerned about, Chico engaged in "defensive naturalization" in order to protect himself from detention and deportation and to secure civic privileges. Joining what was a clear trend among Mexicans, Chico overcame his apathy about voting before the political maelstrom and became a citizen to legitimize his standing in the nation-state and guarantee his entitlements.[25]

Fast-forward to 2010 when Arizona governor Jan Brewer signed Senate Bill 1070 (SB 1070) into law.[26] A sweeping and strict anti-immigration law that endorsed racial profiling, SB 1070 was at the center of a public controversy at the time of our interview.[27] Like Proposition 187 in California in 1994, SB 1070 was an anti-immigrant initiative with racial implications. U.S. federal law requires all noncitizen inhabitants over the age of fourteen who remain in the United States for more than thirty days to register with the government and to possess registration documents at all times. SB 1070 makes it a state misdemeanor for noncitizen inhabitants to be present in Arizona without carrying the required documents and requires state law enforcement officers who suspect during stops, detentions, or arrests that individuals are undocumented to make attempts to determine their status. This anti-immigrant crackdown is racist because those most likely to be suspected of being undocumented immigrants are nonwhite. As Hector Amaya has observed, "citizenship is how we [as a nation] articulate the relationship of individuals to states, and therefore citizenship . . . is how we express ethno-racial supremacy."[28]

For Daria and her husband, she said, the "hoopla in Arizona" had made race and citizenship status a more important feature of their lives. The Arizona law encourages "ethnic lumping," the erasure of generational difference in favor of bringing ethnic group status to the foreground.[29] Because of their ethnicity, her husband's naturalized status, and the racially hostile political environment, Daria became attuned to race: "I think there's more of an identity as being Hispanic [for us] because we have a state that wants to treat Latinos different." The nation-state and individual states have been enforcers of racial inequality. National and state laws have an extended history of according privileges and rights to whites while withholding them from nonwhites.[30] Citizenship is often specifically at issue because it marks, visibly and symbolically, the boundary between inclusion and exclusion, creating an insider "us" and outsider "them."[31]

Daria responded to "ethnic lumping" with indignation, allying herself with all Latinos, irrespective of citizenship status. She was angered by the race-based unequal distribution of scrutiny and its linkage to the idea of citizenship as suspendable: "I wouldn't have a problem if everybody that goes to Arizona, every time that you get stopped you got to show a passport. . . .

But they're not doing that. It's only the Latinos . . . they suspect as being illegal." Using the term "we" to sympathize with all Latinos, regardless of documentation status, she explained her outrage:

> [Anglo] coworkers . . . don't think that we should feel bad because we're Americans, but they're not understanding that our status as an American is being called into question. . . . I tell them, "Well, you think different than I do because they're not gonna ask you to prove that you're an American. And they're gonna ask me and my husband to prove that we're Americans. And I don't think that that's fair. . . . " He went through a whole process to become an American.

The law, in challenging the Americanness of residents like Daria and her husband based on their race-ethnicity, enforces a particular (white) vision of the nation. This racial-ethnic meaning is invisible to whites (such as her coworkers), whose place in U.S. society is secure, safeguarded by both legal and social means. It was especially ironic that the required legal proceedings to become a naturalized U.S. citizen that Chico underwent might not protect him from race-encoded laws. Despite Daria's own undisputed citizenship, her husband's immigration and legal history had led her to identify with her Latino peers whose position was more tenuous.

All migrants must deal with legal issues, and so must their U.S.-born spouses. Immigration policies that "affect noncitizens have clear consequences for citizens."[32] When undocumented migrants face deportation for committing the civil infraction of crossing the international border without authorization, their U.S. citizen spouses must make the "impossible choice" between "your country and your family."[33] Jazmin Romo de Soto and José Romo were in exactly this position: being forced to make life-altering decisions about citizenship, residency, and family.

Jazmin grew up understanding the international border to be rather porous; she crossed it multiple times and lived for extended periods in both the United States and Mexico. An American citizen who was raised in both countries and fluent in English and Spanish, Jazmin did not necessarily see herself living in the United States for the rest of her life. She was married to an undocumented Mexican migrant, twenty-four-old José Romo, who came to the United States for work. José's undocumented status did not allow them to live a transnational lifestyle. He and Jazmin were attempting to regularize his status, a process that could take years. In the meantime, José and Jazmin existed in a space of "liminal legality" —a "gray [area] between documented and undocumented" that influenced their economic opportunities and shaped their membership in the host society.[34]

Jazmin, the more talkative of the two, recounted José's migration story, which included job precariousness in Mexico, downward mobility in the United States relative to his socioeconomic standing in Mexico, and family connections that pulled him to Lawrence, Kansas, in 2007. At a court appointment, José planned to "ask for . . . forgiveness for coming into the United States illegally and marrying an American citizen without actually having the right documentation to be here." If his petition was granted, he would have to stay in Mexico for two to eighteen months before being allowed back into the United States. If his application was denied, he would be prohibited from crossing into the United States for ten years, forcing decisions about where he and Jazmin would reside.

What effect did José's undocumented status have on their everyday lives? While other interviewees had more stressful reactions to their undocumented status (see Glenda Carlisle in chapter 3), Jazmin and José were taking the citizenship process in stride. Jazmin was willing to move to Mexico, a gesture made easier by her decade-plus past residency there. It was stressful, however, to be constantly trying to be as law-abiding as possible, in order not to draw attention to José's undocumented status: "He has to be careful. . . . If immigration comes by, any little thing can send him back to Mexico. . . . We're trying to make it right." Indeed, since the uptick in the criminalization of immigration in the 1990s, Latin American immigrant men have been deported at high rates for nonviolent offenses.[35] Caught in an extended moment of legal suspension, with paperwork in process, their lives and futures were uncertain: "We don't know where we stand. . . . We can't make future plans, really. You . . . kind of just have to go day by day. . . . Tomorrow he might not be here." This sort of dramatic precariousness is inherent in legal battles over citizenship and "territorial belonging."[36] Hoping to "get a job that actually is gonna pay me what I'm worth," José knew that being legally present in the United States would position him for higher wages and reduce his vulnerability to employers exploiting his deportability by underpaying him.[37]

In my study, immigrants and their native-born spouses were sensitive to current events inflected with racism, xenophobia, or anti-immigrant antipathy. Laws such as Arizona SB 1070 that foreground race-ethnicity and immigration heighten the sense of precariousness in U.S. society of Latino immigrants and their spouses. Even if the Arizona law did not directly affect my Californian and Kansan respondents, their political astuteness spoke to their awareness of the broader sociopolitical climate. Immigrants, especially the undocumented, have a heightened political-legal consciousness that inspires the same in their spouses and keeps both partners ever-mindful that the law can both censure and reward.

SECOND- AND LATER-GENERATION COUPLES: INTEGRATION WITH VARYING ETHNIC EXPRESSIONS

Coethnic in-marriages often differ in how many generations their families of origin have been in the United States. These "mixed-generation" coethnic marriages present an interesting case because they show how generation in the United States matters. Recognizing that "Latino" is not a monolithic category, my examination here of partnerships whose members vary in national origin (as in chapter 5) or generation-since-immigration provides a window into the formation of racial-ethnic identity *within coethnic couples*. Ethnic endogamy does not equal ethnic stasis. Mixed-generation couples with the same national-origin ancestry (Mexico) shed light on how cultural change happens and illustrate a wide variety of lifestyles. Two sections follow: the first discusses the "assimilation" by a later generation of a more recent generation, and the second analyzes ethnic solidarity. These themes are not exclusive to mixed-generation marriages but instead highlight the diversity of ethnic expression occurring alongside upward mobility. Latinos—even intramarried Mexican Americans—are a heterogeneous group with myriad internal dynamics. The variety of intramarried outcomes revealed here disproves ill-founded assertions that these immigrant ethnic groups are impervious to change, mired in the natal culture, unintegratable, and forever downtrodden.

Adaptation to the "White" Mainstream

Ana and Mario Bermudez were a prime example of a mixed-generation couple who were not culturally unmoving. Their interpersonal dynamics had pulled Mario, raised in Los Angeles and the U.S.-born son of two Mexican immigrants, toward white mainstream culture.[38] Mario's maternal grandmother, with whom he spent much time in his youth, lived in gang territory in South Central Los Angeles, across from a park where Mario was forcefully initiated into the gang through physical violence while on his way home one day. (He was not active in the gang by his late teen years.) He grew up in a racially segregated Latino and black neighborhood before moving to Van Nuys, a suburb where he attended a racially integrated middle school but felt racially profiled. Ana, third generation in the United States and raised in Santa Fe, New Mexico, was half Mexican American and half white. She lived "a very American lifestyle," spending time on school, sports, friends, and middle-class accoutrements like video games and having plentiful free time with few chores. Ana lived what I refer to elsewhere as "flexible ethnicity": she was equally adept at navigating different racial-ethnic social circles.[39] The interpersonal dynamics within this marriage had integrated the spouse of the more recent generation into the ways of the one from a more established generation.

Generationally distinct from one another, Ana and Mario grew up in different socioeconomic circumstances: she was from the middle class, while he was from the working class. Theirs is a story of intergenerational progress in wages, educational attainment, and occupation.[40] Their families of origin, with their different class statuses, had different views on money, travel, and place of residence. Ana's middle-class family could afford to send her to an out-of-state Catholic university and provide her with opportunities to study abroad. Mario attended Cal State Northridge and then Mount St. Mary's, never leaving Los Angeles. Mario compared his and his wife's experiences:

> She grew up with a family that was moving: going out and seeing the world is important. And that isn't something I was raised with. . . . My sister and I were smart kids . . . but [my wife and brothers-in-law] were encouraged to go as far as possible . . . and for us it was the opposite. . . . I received financial aid, I could live in a dorm, but my mom convinced me, "if you stay with me, you don't have to pay rent."

This parental encouragement to live at home during college was made in the interest of both pecuniary considerations and family cohesion. Mario drew the contrast between himself and his wife to make the point that they hailed from different class and culture backgrounds.

Teachers at the same school, Mario and Ana had met through work. Upon their engagement, Mario shattered his family's expectation that he would continue to live near them and moved to a nearby suburb of Los Angeles, promising Ana that he would eventually move to her hometown of Santa Fe. They were currently putting their "greater plan" into motion, Ana having recently secured a job that could be transferred, while Mario was working on his national teaching credential, which would allow him to transfer to any state. Mario and his mother "haven't gotten along well these last few years," he said, because his mother believed that his "philosophies have changed." His geographic mobility ran against his natal family's norm of close proximity: one sister lived two blocks away from their mother, another sister and her infant son lived with their mother, and an aunt and uncle lived with their grandmother. Despite having to break a family norm, Mario felt that residential mobility—moving "up and out"—made economic as well as marital sense for him.

Mario carefully balanced his upward mobility against his retreat from his community. He spoke about how Ana "gringo-izes" him and his twelve-year-old daughter from a prior relationship with a Salvadoran woman:

> We laugh, because she turned it into like the gringo house, you know? Friday night [is] family night: we pop popcorn and we watch a kid-friendly movie. My daughter and I laugh because before Ana came along, we were like camping out here . . . everything was kind of a mess, [there] was no structure. . . . Ana brought a lot of structure into this house. . . . She has changed . . . the way I look at things. . . . Sometimes you meet people [and] they kinda bring you down, and sometimes you meet people and they bring you up. After I met her, I went back and got my master's [degree].

Mario was already achieving socioeconomic upward mobility as a teacher, but Ana's philosophy and way of doing things had further propelled his educational goals and influenced his home life.

Assimilation literature assumes that Latino intermarriage with whites instigates incorporation; it overlooks that Latino in-marriage between people of *two different generations* can also prompt integration. I never use the hot-button word "assimilation" in my interviews, but Mario used the term unprompted to refer to his wife: "I think my wife is already on the third generation. She's already assimilated. . . . I think I've done a good job of assimilating, but I don't think I'm there, you know? . . . I think one way . . . was to marry Ana." In Mario's eyes, his later-generation, mixed-ethnicity wife was an agent of assimilation. He likened the integration of Mexican Americans into U.S. society to the experience of the Irish and Italians who arrived during the Great Migration at the turn of the twentieth century: "If you study the Irish Americans [and] the Italian Americans, I think . . . we are going through what they've gone through." Despite this view that Mexican Americans are following in the incorporation footsteps of those who are now considered "white ethnics," Mario expressed his opinion that he was "not there yet," adding, "The word 'assimilated'—the fact that I know about it or the fact that I'm telling you that I'm not assimilated just tells you where I am."[41]

Mario considered his later-generation, mixed-ethnicity wife to be assimilating him. In addition to geographic mobility and family movie nights, assimilation, to Mario, meant long-term financial planning and education: "Benefits, retirement, there was a lot of things that I never thought of before meeting Ana. It was like I didn't care, I was like, 'Well, when I die, someone can bury me.' . . . Now we have retirement. . . . It's a gringo [white] thing, you know? . . . The American culture [also] says . . . 'Where are you guys going to go to school [college]?' " Mixed-generation in-marriages can promote educational and financial values, otherwise known as structural and socioeconomic integration.

Mario envisioned integration as a mix of gain and loss: "At some point . . . every generation loses some of their culture. . . . You're losing a part of your culture, but without knowing, you're gaining . . . American culture." He did not feel that the process was value-laden, as in earlier historical times when immigrants experienced a heavy-handed push to conform to the white mainstream and there was less tolerance for cultural pluralism. Mario saw himself as becoming more American in his outlooks, goals, and allegiances. He explained the change in himself over time and the ways in which his wife had "sped up" the process of becoming American for him:

> It reminds me . . . of the movie *The Lord of the Rings:* it's like we're leaving one life and then starting another. . . . I feel like our time as Mexicans . . . is coming close to an end. And our time as Americans is beginning. . . . I think I'm in the middle, where[as] my wife, she's an American. . . . I think being in an interracial relationship speeds it up.

Cross-generational marriages can assimilate more recent generations. Even the distinction between intramarriage (my classification of this couple because they share Mexican heritage) and intermarriage, in Mario's term (based on their generational difference and her part-white heritage), reveals how complex intergenerational marriages can be.

Ana had dated both whites and Hispanics in high school and college, primarily because of "circumstance and opportunity." Not preferring one group over the other (but having "dated more Latin guys than white guys"), she dismissed race by saying, "It just happened that I met Mario and he happened to be Mexican." Ana reported that she remained largely unchanged by her marriage with Mario, beyond incorporating Mexican food that Mario cooked into their diet.

Life with Mario had underscored for Ana the ways in which her upbringing was influenced by her class status, generation in the United States, and mixed ethnicity. By comparing her life experience with his, Ana noticed that their family orientations were different: her family, for instance, had encouraged her to attend college in another state and to pursue a study abroad program in Spain, whereas Mario's family had emphasized staying local. As she put it, "I lived in Europe for a year, whereas Mario and his sisters . . . never lived anywhere beyond L.A." Ana attributed these differences to culture: "It made me think the way I was raised was more white or more quintessential American than the way . . . other Mexican families are raised. . . . His family is very dependent on him. . . . Whereas my family isn't dependent on me. . . . I talk to my family every day, but there's not that dependency." As had Mario, here Ana conflated "white" with "quintessential American," which she further equated to independence from family. Ana saw their respective orientations to family and the pressures that came with them as leading to "an interesting conflict" that would arise when their plans to move out of California became more concrete.

Racism also comes to light in intramarriages. In chapter 3, we saw that race becomes more salient to white spouses after seeing their partner undergo racism. Mixed-generation intramarriages can yield this same result. For those who are later-generation or light-skinned, witnessing racism against a loved one can be eye-opening. Ana was a fair-skinned woman with brown hair and a small physical frame, whereas Mario was a large, dark-skinned man with jet black hair. In response to my question about racial discrimination, Ana reported an increase in her consciousness of color after seeing her husband be racially profiled: "He's definitely racially profiled, and I didn't believe him until we were married . . . and I was with him when it happened. So, yes. He gets discriminated [against] and I don't." Ana's light skin had allowed her to skirt discrimination, but she felt a "rebound effect" of racism relative to her husband, taking personally his racialized treatment.[42] The interplay across generational statuses had made Ana more aware of the privileges and costs doled out based on race, color, and gender.

Mario and Ana's relationship played out as assimilation for him: Mario drew closer to the white mainstream by virtue of learning from Ana features of the mainstream that he associated with the dominant culture, such as education, occupational achievement, and financial independence. Mario's experience corroborated "new" assimilation theory's assertion that integration is a by-product of improving one's life.[43] Referring to the links between his wife, their mixed-generation status, and his assimilation, Mario remarked: "It's just something that happens with the territory." For Ana, the overriding lesson was about the continuing role of race and racism, even among the upwardly mobile. In mixed-generation couples like Ana and Mario, the later-generation individual can support the incorporation of the more recent arrival, who can bring racialization processes to light. These countervailing forces within cross-generational couples show how marriage intervenes in both assimilation and racialization projects.

Upward Mobility and Ethnic Solidarity

One does not need to have been immersed in a social movement to bear its effects: children of social activists possessed a political consciousness marked by their parents' influence. Lisandro Quiñones and Julia Vega were both Mexican American: raised in East Los Angeles, he was second generation, and she was the fourth-generation daughter of a woman active in the Chicano movement. The Quiñones-Vega couple showed that socioeconomic advancement can coexist with a strong ethnic identity.

Thirty-eight-year-old Lisandro was a professional artist who, in spite of his significant upward mobility, had not forgotten his roots, which he represented in both his artwork and his teaching. He and his wife Julia were a high-earning couple, with annual income between $150,000 and $200,000, and he seemed eager to participate in the interview for the purpose of increasing Latino visibility. He was referring to both himself and me when he opined that the community needed educated Latinos who gave back.

Lisandro credited his commitment to education to a youth spent observing his father's labor as a long-haul trucker: "I realized really soon that I did not want to be a truck driver. It was hard work [*laughs a bit*], and that kept me going to school more. . . . I kind of said, 'Well, I better study if I don't want to do this.' " Lisandro recalled "going to bed hungry, not just once, but a couple of times" during some "lean years." Despite strained finances, his mother provided him and his siblings with extracurricular education: "I remember [my mother] taking us to the children's museum on the bus . . . to Universal Studios on the bus, from East L.A. It took us like two hours to get there, but she said, '. . . Let's do it.' " As we will explore in chapter 7, this family was engaged in a version of "concerted cultivation," a term created with the middle class in mind; applied to the lower and working classes, the term "constrained cultivation" might be more apt.[44]

Although Lisandro was not a gang member, gangs were nevertheless omnipresent in his youth: "It was a pretty bad part of town. . . . There was a liquor store on the corner, and the owners would get shot every six to seven months. . . . The new owner would buy it, and he'd get shot, and then a new owner would buy it, and he'd get shot. . . . It was rough, you know." When a person was killed in their front yard ("I saw somebody, shot in my front yard, with three bullet holes in the head"), Lisandro's father moved the family out of East L.A. and into a suburb. With at least one cousin who was "in and out of penitentiaries," Lisandro took the path of education, calculating that "I could be like him or I could be like that person over there." Armed with "a different kind of thinking in the nuclear family" that avoided gang culture, Lisandro earned bachelor's and master's degrees at a University of California campus and was now a middle-class professional.

Lisandro and Julia started dating in high school in East L.A. They continued a long-distance relationship as they attended college in different parts of the country. Both coming from "pretty difficult neighborhoods" and attending top-tier universities, they were "focused on school" and understood each other's challenging college environment and the roads they had traveled to get there. They married in 1996 after they graduated from college. Their life experiences made them a good fit, Lisandro said: "We had a lot to talk about, a lot in common. When we got out of college, we were both expected to be professionals. . . . We've always had similar experiences or [demands] on our life." Traveling the same path from the same underclass urban area to prestigious universities made their marriage homogamous not just on race but also on class status, upward mobility, and educational achievement.

Despite Lisandro and Julia's different generational statuses, they both called themselves Mexican American, or Chicano. Julia described her Chicano identity as having begun before she was born. When Julia's mother participated in August 1970 in the Chicano Moratorium—a movement of Chicano activists in East L.A. protesting the Vietnam War and demonstrating for social justice at home by staging walkouts and marches—she was pregnant with Julia. Julia remarked on her identity: "When [my mom] would see the film [of the Moratorium] . . . in a documentary, she'd say, 'You were there. [*laughs*] You were there in my belly as I ran into a liquor store and put my head in the freezer to get away from the tear gas.' She said it was pretty bad. . . . I considered myself Chicano because she was Chicano."

Rooted in an earlier era of ethnic protest aimed at achieving first-class citizenship status, the term "Chicano" is about pride and empowerment. Lisandro concurred that he called himself Chicano because of its political connotation of self-determination, hybridity, and awareness: "To me, Chicano is specifically who I am, as a Mexican American person in the United States that likes Metallica and Juan Fernandez at the same time. It's not one or the other. . . . It's a political awareness, an identity awareness."

Having achieved professional success, Lisandro gave back to his ethnic community. Like other men in this study, his work was the chief way in which he remained connected to the larger Mexican American community. He was an art professor at two institutions in L.A. that had 50 to 75 percent Latino student enrollment. Lisandro contributed to structural diversity as a racial minority professor, and he advocated cultural diversity through his artwork. He was cognizant of his positive effect on his students in giving them an image of a successful Chicano:

> I believe teaching at [Hispanic-serving institutions of higher learning] really has a direct influence in terms of my community and how I get to expose them to art. . . . When my picture came out in the *L.A. Times*, my department chair put the [article] in a display case in the department lobby. My students really loved it. They ate it up. "Oh, man. He's the only Latino instructor in this department and he's [in a Los Angeles newspaper]."

Lisandro was also engaged in the community by showing his artwork in Chicano galleries, collecting Chicano art, and lending to galleries: "We collect almost exclusively Chicano art because that community speaks to us, and man, they need our help. . . . For a museum to ask for us to lend them a piece, that's pretty cool. . . . That's how we give back to the community." Being in an intraethnic marriage with a like-minded partner allows them to share concern for their ethnic community.

When upward mobility occurs alongside ethnic solidarity, ethnic cultural content does not necessarily remain unchanged. For instance, the gendered household division of labor was one social dimension that had been dynamically challenged in Lisandro and Julia's relationship. Jettisoning traditional roles that would place her at home and designate him as the breadwinner, Lisandro and Julia were flexible about who did what in the home. A gender-progressive couple, they had a household arrangement—with his flexible work schedule, Lisandro was home more often with their young son, and she was the financial breadwinner—that rebutted notions of coethnic unions as traditional or static. Coethnic couples' gender strategies are not distinct from the strategies employed in the rest of the United States. Shifts in gendered divisions of labor crosscut racial groups. On the distribution of responsibilities in their home, Lisandro said: "We make [decisions] together. There is no 'I'm the man, we do what I say.' " He saw his parents "negotiate all the time" and modeled that pattern. Lisandro spoke in terms of a gender role reversal as he described how flexibility was beneficial and functional for them:

> Macho and me don't get along. . . . I believe in the feminist cause. . . . Our roles are quite different than in the traditional sense. My wife makes money. She works for corporate America. For all intents and purposes, she's the man. I am the painter. . . . I'm more flexible. . . . I took [our son] to the doctor today. We went to go eat sushi.

Believing that "gender flexibility" is a healthy way to cope with unconventional work arrangements, Lisandro and Julia negotiated around home and child-rearing activities.[45]

With her very light skin and hazel-green eyes, Julia Vega could readily pass for white. She also had dark brown hair, a cherubic face, and an easy laugh. She grew up in East Los Angeles with a single mom. Her grandparents were U.S.-born Mexican American migrant workers, making her the fourth generation in the United States. Her grandparents had reacted to the discrimination they suffered by not teaching Julia's mother Spanish so that she would show no linguistic or accent difference that might provoke discrimination. They prepared Julia for racism by instilling ethnic pride: "The main thing that [my grandfather] and . . . grandmother wanted to pass on [was that] we should be proud of who we are, despite what society may tell us."

It was demographic opportunity—East Los Angeles was dense with coethnics—that led to Julia and Lisandro's meeting, as adolescents, in Jaime Escalante's calculus class. Escalante was a committed and enthusiastic teacher of lower- and working-class Mexican American students who was celebrated in the movie *Stand and Deliver*. Julia was the first person in her family to graduate from college, and she credited Mr. Escalante with giving her the knowledge and cultural capital to apply to, get accepted to, and attend a prestigious East Coast university: "He's the reason I got into Harvard. He brought [a world-renowned professor] from Harvard to our high school to talk to us. Before Escalante, [I] had no idea what Harvard was, so I didn't even think to apply." Her elite college education catapulted her into a high-income profession that helped her and her husband purchase their home in Montebello.

Similar to the minority-minority connection discussed in chapter 4 on cross-racial minority couples, Julia wanted a partner who understood her ethnic experience. Most racial minorities who want to be comprehended on a racial level judge whites as ill-fitting. Progressive whites may be intellectually understanding of racial plights, but minorities who marry other minorities crave an *experiential understanding* that can only be achieved firsthand. Who better to understand Julia's omnipresent feeling that she "had something to prove" and her being "overly sensitive to racial issues" than someone of the same background?

Opportunity and preference intersected in Julia and Lisandro's union. Having grown up in predominantly Mexican American East L.A., Julia concisely said, "I don't remember having friends that weren't Latino." Thus, the two teenagers began a romance owing in part to de facto school segregation:

> My options were pretty limited. [*laughs*] I didn't know anybody who wasn't [Mexican]. . . . It wasn't even a question. . . . I didn't think about race much because . . . we were all the same. [*laughs*] . . . It wasn't until . . . college, meeting people from other cultures . . . [that I was] like, "Oh wow, it really was Mexican. I didn't realize it." [*laughs*] So you don't notice until you're outside looking in.

Julia wanted someone who had had similar racial experiences. Because she felt generationally distant from Mexico, she sought a partner who could bring her closer to her heritage. Lisandro was able to teach her about her ethnic culture:

> I guess I did have a preference. . . . I liked that Lisandro was [second-] generation Mexican American. . . . I liked that because he had more connection to

his roots. . . . I wanted more access to a culture that I didn't really have access to. [*laughs*] . . . We didn't have that strong connection to Mexico, it was more to East L.A. . . . it was more the U.S. So I wanted to learn more about our heritage, which we kind of lost.

Living within a dense Latino community, Julia's "options were pretty limited." Although her social environment made dating across racial lines unlikely, she acted within this situation of demographic constraint to exert her preference for cultural knowledge and gender egalitarianism. Much like the intermarried Latina women in chapter 3 who engaged the "selective blending" form of biculturalism, Julia, in a mixed-generation in-marriage, exercised discretion and desire. She made choices within her limited opportunity structure: not just any man in the immediate vicinity would do, but only a man who exhibited traits she desired. Lisandro, two generations closer to the point of migration than Julia, provided her with "access" to their mutual heritage, which had dissipated in her family over time. Yet even as Julia desired cultural knowledge, she resisted a traditional gender division of labor, showing that intramarriages characterized by ethnic solidarity are not cookie-cutter: they do not always involve uncritical adoption of a cultural package. Instead, people in intramarriages judge and filter cultural content.

Julia's hope that Lisandro would reinforce her ethnic identity had been fulfilled: she had learned through her husband about their shared (if generationally distinct) culture. Her generational distance from Mexico was reduced in her mixed-generation marriage, as her husband supplemented her knowledge about their ethnicity. Encouraged by her mother-in-law, who spoke Spanish with her and her son, Julia had learned more Spanish, and she had also traveled to Mexico to visit Lisandro's extended family.

Although shared ethnicity was a priority, Julia also wanted a partner who believed in gender equality. Intent on going to college, she required someone who would support her educational goals: "[I wanted] someone who shared my views as far as how women should be treated. . . . As far as gender equality . . . [someone] that was going to be okay with nontraditional roles. Because I wanted to work, I wanted to go to college." Describing her husband as "very supportive," Julia reported that he convinced her not to forgo the opportunity to go to the East Coast for college.

The Quiñones-Vega pair were a mixed-generation Mexican American couple who exhibited upward mobility and ethnic solidarity. Contrary to much scholastic work and popular renderings, their socioeconomic advancement was not accompanied by a loss of ethnic identity, or "thinned attachment," as I discuss elsewhere.[46] Mixed-generation in-marriages come in many varieties, which in itself is a lesson: intramarriages are not universally the same but encompass multiple trajectories.

FEMINIST MEN

Latino men who advance feminist agendas—whether or not they call themselves feminists—deserve attention. I conceive of feminism here as an ideology concerned with gender equality, with specific attention to rethinking men's and women's socially prescribed roles. Several men in the study, regardless of their national origin or marital pairing, believed in gender equality or took measures to soften harsh masculinity. In prior research, I found that men used their negative natal family life experiences to evaluate the type of man they wanted to be; if they suffered from a domineering father, they tended, upon entering adulthood, to use that experience as an anti-model in need of revision.[47] The same was true for respondents in this study: oppression in their youth had led to their feminism, defined here as taking action to moderate the oppressive masculinity that inhibits the freedom and opportunities of women and children. Although not all of the male respondents had the same response to a childhood subjugated by an aggressive father, some of them were catalyzed by that experience to recalibrate gender dynamics and foster more caring relationships.[48]

Marriage intersected Latino men's feminist trajectory in two ways: first, as a platform to express changed masculinity in reaction to oppressive natal family dynamics, and second, as an influential factor motivating change. As mentioned earlier, some of these men not only personally suffered under strict paternal authority when they were boys, but also witnessed their mothers and sisters squashed under male authority. Recalling these boyhood experiences from a first-person or observer perspective was a catalyst for their empathy with women's oppression. And how do marital relationships motivate change that leads to feminism? By inspiring men who care about their wives to change so as to improve the quality of this intimate relationship. These two causes of men's feminism, both rooted in family, underscore the importance of family dynamics in both the persistence of gendered power relations and changes in those relations.

Mario Bermudez, discussed earlier, grew up poor, without an involved father, and spent a lot of time with his grandmother, who lived in what he described as "gang-infested" territory in South Central Los Angeles. A tall man with an imposing presence, he wore a short-sleeved button-down shirt open at the neck, where the topmost portion of a tattoo on his chest could be seen. The tattoo was a relic of his adolescent years as a member of a gang, which he directly linked to the lack of adult male role models in his life. Gang masculinity was the only version of masculinity available to Mario in his youth. Gangs were "normal," he said:

> I didn't have a man [around], so the men I looked up to were at the park. . . . Basically that's where I learned everything I learned: from the guys at the park. . . . And if they said, "Hey, let's get a tattoo," I'd do it. And they did. They put tattoos on me. . . . I lived that way for a few years. . . . Those were my role models.

Mario's is a classic story in that an absent father, a poor working mother, and a lack of public resources for youth led to his "street socialization"; his gang involvement was a reaction to social and economic marginalization.[49] The presence of Mario's uncles in the gang also normalized his gang participation—which ceased with the birth of his daughter when he was twenty. At that point, Mario elected to reorient his masculinity toward fatherhood and away from gang life.[50]

Lacking male role models in his youth, Mario, now a high school teacher, was both an educator and a mentor. Describing his father and stepfather as bigots, he said that neither man treated him or his mother with much care: his father left them when he was young, his stepfather was not emotionally supportive, and both men cheated on his mother. Reaching back a generation, both grandfathers were alcoholics and treated him "like shit." I asked Mario where he learned his vision of masculinity:

> I didn't have one. My grandfather treated me like shit, my other grandfather treated me like shit—they were all alcoholics. The only one who didn't really drink was my stepdad, but he never really took me out to a ball game. . . . My stepdad didn't really say, "Hey . . . let's go to a game," or, "Hey, here's a hug," or, "Hey, good job." . . . That's the one thing I think I don't have: any kind of a male role model. My dad—same thing. . . . My grand[fathers] weren't great either: I saw them treat my grandmothers like crap. . . . The masculinity thing I learned just through watching them. But it took a different effect on me. It just basically made me not want to be like that.

In those final sentences, Mario clarified that the dysfunctional men in his early life were anti-models who gave him an image of a man he did not care to replicate.[51]

Repudiating all the adult men in his life, Mario created his own definition of masculinity, fatherhood, and mentorship. As a teacher, he taught few classes in the summers, in order to spend that time with his daughter:

> I got to spend a lot of time with my kid. And I think that's the major difference. . . . I don't remember any man . . . ever actually talking with me and

teaching me something and spending time with me, you know? That's what I view as a Mexican father. It's just basically someone who pays for your . . . Catholic school. . . . I think things changed with my generation, at least with me. . . . I'm really involved in my daughter, in the school . . . [and] in her choir.

Mario's feminism was grounded in his attempts to be an involved father to his daughter. Although I doubt that he would call himself a feminist, his efforts to improve his familial relationships with women and girls resulted in more balanced gender dynamics than what he witnessed a generation prior. As a youngster, he conceptualized Mexican fatherhood as solely about economic provision.[52] He learned from his grandmother about providing a caring emotional and physical presence: "She would always show up. So it's kinda weird, but I think . . . I learned that from her." By gender-bending, Mario incorporated the "feminine" characteristic of providing an emotional bond, as modeled by his grandmother, into how he fathered his daughter. This type of changing masculinity over generations demonstrates that masculinity is not static but can be updated with conscious effort. Mario made deliberate choices about his expression of masculinity, in reaction to his deficient relationships with adult men in his youth.

Mario's feminism also played out in how he treated his wife and how he approached their household division of labor: "There are certain things I won't do with Ana. One is put her down or yell. I'm not above, 'Can you wash the dishes' [because] I usually wash, I usually cook." This might not qualify as full-blown feminism, but at minimum Mario's attitude was anti-macho, in that any effort to avoid macho behavior is an attempt to avoid behaviors that produce gender oppression. Anti-macho attitudes that might not qualify as feminism but trend in that direction underscore that change is a process and that viewing feminist expressions as a continuum rather than a binary allows us to see finer-grained progress.

Mario's burgeoning feminism spilled over from his family life into his professional life. A high school teacher in Los Angeles, he ruminated on his goals: "As a teacher, [my] main goal is to teach this kid . . . to be independent. To make choices, you know? . . . How can I make . . . a high schooler . . . make responsible choices?" Speaking fondly of his inner-city minority students, Mario became a teacher as a way to "give service back."

Feminism involving changed masculinity is also seen in flipping conventional gender roles. Recall that Julia Vega had a lucrative career and Lisandro Quiñones, who was also employed, took primary responsibility for their son. An artist, Lisandro had gained professional visibility in recent years; for instance, HBO had asked him for an interview for a documentary about Latinos. Despite a steadily increasing Latino population in the United States, Latinos' "inclusion in mainstream English-speaking media remains stunningly low."[53] If part of the media's power is to "construct our understanding of events, people, and places in our world," Latino underrepresentation is worsened by their stereotypical depiction as criminals, sexual objects, and low-wage workers.[54] On a social media site, Lisandro reported:

> Confession: Remember that HBO Documentary I told you guys about? Well, I did a "pre-interview" on Saturday and I didn't "test" well. They asked me questions about the role of the Latino male and I answered with words like "togetherness" and "inclusivity." Not what they wanted to hear. Turns out I'm a feminist. Good to know. So, sorry, no HBO Documentary for me.

By perpetuating racial stereotypes, mainstream media engage in "representational politics" that fortify narrow perceptions of racial groups.[55] In turn, "stereotypes, as hegemonic tools, reduce individuals to a single, monolithic, one-dimensional type that . . . is presented as natural and normal (read true and accurate)" and maintain the status quo.[56]

The media have a strong guiding hand in the "symbolic colonization" (the "manufacturing of race as a homogenized construct") of subordinate racial groups.[57] Even as the mainstream media participate in the construction and dissemination of imagery of Latinos, critical audiences can oppose these representations. "Symbolic ruptures" allow consumers of media to disrupt symbolic colonization through disagreement or challenge and not only to inject "moments of ideological instability" into the colonization process but even to "open up radical definitions of Latina/o identity."[58] Lisandro's reaction did just this.

By centering his perspective on Latino men on "togetherness" and "inclusivity," Lisandro "symbolically ruptured" the notions of machismo for which Latino masculinity is infamous, protested "symbolic colonization," and fractured calculated media stereotypes. The HBO film staff's request that he not "use academic words" and their subsequent rejection of him suggest that he was not in alignment with their (stereotypic) intent. In a message he later added to the online conversation thread, Lisandro said that the experience gave him new self-awareness: "The funny part of what transpired is that I learned something about myself, so in a way, it was good that I got rejected. The utility of failure." Through his "failure" to succeed at an interview for a documentary, Lisandro discovered his feminism and claimed the label. Moreover, Lisandro's friends who commented on this discussion thread were unanimously supportive of him and appalled at the filmmaker's objective to present so narrow a view of contemporary Latino masculinity. The experience affirmed for Lisandro and his friends that masculinity is dynamic and that men can actively "undo gender" by changing their gender performance and destabilizing mainstream media's "symbolic colonization" project in the process.[59]

The root of Lisandro's feminism was belief in gender equality, but most Latino men's feminism is a reaction to their childhood experiences under the shadow of an authoritarian or absent father. Yet for some Mexican American men, such as thirty-six-year-old Diego Assante, an additional impetus for adjusting gender relations in the household is their relationship with their wife.[60] Diego's father was emotionally distant, never verbally expressing love (until his deathbed). Diego, who called himself "anti-machismo," intentionally avoided male domination and emotional callousness in his own life. As a high school music teacher, he was determined to model responsibility and tolerance for his students, whom he affectionately called his "kids." Immediately after telling me about a white middle school teacher who discouraged him from a career in music (saying, "Why don't you just go try to fix cars?"), he illustrated how he modeled empowerment for his students. In a school that he estimated to be 98 percent Latino, Diego worked to "[give] back to the community and [open] people's eyes—I'm big [on] anti-machismo; [machismo] is oozing out of that school." Under his philosophy of "respect," Diego advocated tolerance for not only gender difference but also sexual orientation. He summarized the tolerance and anti-machismo he taught in his classroom:

> Respect your peers; don't judge a book by its cover. . . . There's definitely a high population of gay and lesbian in my school. Which, paired up with the machismo thing, is not good. Yet when you come into my group [of students], it's very mixed. . . . Everyone is welcomed, not judged. . . . [Students learning] how to be a good human being is my payoff. . . . That's pretty much what I teach them: how to become better people when it comes to talking to each other, acting like proper human beings.

Students working collaboratively in a multiracial educational environment or building an intergroup friendship can break down barriers.[61] A self-professed "anti-machismo" teacher, Diego felt that he successfully modeled respect and helped his students become "better humans."

At home, Diego was more verbally loving than his father: "My dad had a hard time saying 'I love you.' . . . I have no problem saying, 'I love you,' to my kids. I say, 'I love you,' to my wife." Despite this change, his wife expressed unhappiness at one point. In response, Diego voluntarily went to counseling and reconfigured his gender expectations, which had slipped toward his father's negative model. Diego explained that his wife Maya's unhappiness pressed him to rein in his macho expectations of a privileged position in the household: "When I first married Maya, I think that machismo was starting to creep up. . . . I had to get counseling for that. . . . She was just like, 'Where's the person I married?' . . . If I want to keep her for the rest of my life, this

[committing to change] is what I'm going to have to do." Diego had replicated his parents' stilted dynamics for a period: "I saw myself doing the same
thing my dad did. . . . That's what I saw . . . : Get home from work, take your
shoes off, and say, 'Where's my dinner?' " Empathy for his mother and love
for his wife inspired Diego's behavioral change: "Maya was doing most of
the work: she was cooking, doing the laundry. I [remembered], 'This sucked
for my mom.' " Nowadays, Diego and Maya shared household responsibilities, taking turns bathing the children, splitting cooking and dishwashing
duties, and each taking responsibility for cleaning certain sections of the
house. For Diego and Maya, natal family history and marital life combined
to prompt a rebalancing of gender relations in the home.

Diego unevenly employed equality: he forcefully advocated tolerance
among his students, to whom he was an authority figure, yet adhering to
gender egalitarianism was more challenging in his marital relationship. This
unevenness demonstrates that championing equality may be more easily
done in some spheres than others. For Diego, it was straightforward to push
an equality agenda in the professional realm, where he was a teacher with
an age and power advantage. In contrast, in the personal realm of marriage,
Diego slipped into replicating his father's macho patterns until his love for
his wife (and empathy for his mother) prompted change.

Marriage affects Latino men's gender expressions in two ways. First,
family is an arena where changed masculinity inspired by male domination in one's family of origin is performed in married families. Second,
marriage brings unhappy gender relations to light and can prompt men to
remedy these dynamics out of love for their families. Men's firsthand experience with oppression at the hand of an authoritarian father (and with
witnessing their mother's and sisters' domination) and their secondhand
understanding of their wives' marital dissatisfaction can spur change. Not
all Latino men had family relationships characterized by male domination,
and those who did were not always compelled to alter their own gender
performance. There are also differences in the degree and forms of Latino
men's feminism. In practice, Latino men may unevenly deploy feminism in
public and private realms because differences in age and authority make it
easier to advance a feminist agenda among younger people in schools and
workspaces, and feminist action in private lives requires communication,
reflection, and loving commitment.

CONCLUSION

In contrast to their scant treatment in research studies, Latino intramarriages are not uninteresting, even if they are the norm. Most endogamous Latino partnerships are mixed-generation, comprising Latinos who

have been in the United States for a different number of generations. This chapter has covered a lot of territory: from couples with one immigrant partner who live transnational or politically conscious lives, to U.S.-born endogamous pairs who are integrating into the mainstream while either adapting to so-called white norms or expressing ethnic solidarity. This chapter has also shown that Latino men can become feminists, like the women in their lives, and that culture, inclusive of masculinity and gender relations, can change as well. This wide range of themes is itself telling: cross-generational intramarriage is an incubator for a host of complex social functions. This internal heterogeneity challenges notions of ethnic cultures as homogenous and unchanging by reminding us that no particular outcome is predestined or immutable for any single ethnic group or coethnic family.

Transnationalism is both a cause and a consequence of in-marriage. Aided by networks of relations abroad, travel to Mexico fosters a strong Mexican American identity for those living in the United States. Transnational in-marriages are often driven by appreciation of one's ethnic heritage or hopes for conservative gender relations. Men who crave an idealized version of femininity and family unity that they associate with Mexican women especially desire to marry internationally. These wives, in turn, appreciate their husband's attraction to their Mexican homelands and willingness to sustain ties through regular travel. This international exposure yields bicultural children, more conservative gender relations, and expectations for the younger generation's marital endogamy. Although I had some male immigrants in my sample, their marriages were not as driven by the gender tropes about women presiding over the domestic hearth that inspire other men's international romantic desires.

With immigration and legal status as facts of everyday life for couples that included an immigrant, both partners became more race-cognizant and sensitive to laws and interactions tinged with racism. Their race cognizance led immigrants and their spouses to perceive membership in U.S. society as suspendable—revocable by racialized laws erected to preserve white privilege and question the legal status of Latinos.

Mixed-generation in-marriages involving the U.S.-born take multiple forms. First, later-generation Mexican Americans can "assimilate" their spouses who are closer to the immigration experience. By contrast, a pathway of high socioeconomic achievement can also accompany ethnic solidarity. Finally, feminist men feature prominently in cross-generational couples, who, in comparing the gender performances and expectations of two generations, become aware of the socially constructed quality of gender. This revelation about gender as a social construction is followed by the realization that gender norms, as they affect both marital relations and parent-child relations, are malleable.

Coethnic intramarriages are typically dismissed as uninteresting, yet one only needs to peek under the surface to see complex ripples of race, class, gender, and generation at work. Marital pairings are shaped by race, class, gender, and generation concerns in that all these factors figure into people's desire to fill voids or make cultural turns with the help of a partner. The paths that mixed-generation couples travel are not linear or uniform, yet patterns emerge in the consequences of their pairings. Mixed-generation couples are sites of intercultural exchange that can serve multiple functions, from rejuvenating cultural heritage through transnationalism to high-lighting legal issues, folding a newcomer into the mainstream, achieving upward mobility alongside ethnic solidarity, and actively reconstructing gender norms.

Chapter 7 | Intragenerational Marriages and Racial Strategies: Racial Erasing, Racial Easing, and Constrained Cultivation

"To COMMAND THE respect . . . I have to identify myself as white," said Braedon Toledo, a twenty-nine-year-old Californian who was one-quarter Cuban and one-quarter Mexican American (which he referred to as "Spanish") on his mother's side and one-quarter Mexican American and one-quarter Italian on his father's side. Braedon claimed a white racial identity in order to accrue the benefits of white privilege. This chapter on racial strategies details various ways in which Latinos use or conceal racial identity, and for what purpose, through two forms of social distancing: on the one hand, *erasing* their racial heritage by rejecting it outright, and on the other, *easing*, or loosening, their connection to their racial ancestry. Both strategies aim to gain socioeconomic mobility and avoid class- and race-based stereotypes.

My discussion of racial erasing is not meant to suggest that people can effectively erase their race; this is not possible in a world where race is not purely objective but susceptible to others' perceptions and projections.[1] But people do have the power to amplify or reduce attention to their race through cultural performances like speech, dress, and practices.[2] Economically vulnerable families use these social distancing maneuvers in conjunction with what I call "constrained cultivation": the deliberate attempts by working-class families to improve their children's lot in life by using scarce resources to mirror middle-class parenting. People who use social distancing tactics also use color-blind ideology, articulated as "humanity" or "individuality," as a way to rhetorically resist racial-ethnic, class, and gender stereotypes and achieve upward mobility. Although race is strategically elided this way

203

to evade racial issues on a personal level, this elision simultaneously denies the reality of race at a structural level, thereby incorrectly suggesting that society has transcended race.[3] Regional location helps explain the use of social distancing strategies: working-class families in California in areas with a heavy gang presence engaged in social distancing, whereas families in Kansas, having less of a gang problem, did not.

This chapter draws on couples who were not only intramarried (Latino-Latino pairings) but married intragenerationally—that is, they shared the same generation-since-immigration to the United States (second generation, third generation, and so on).[4] Featured are twenty-eight people (twenty adults and eight children) representing eleven families. Eight families were from California, and three families were from Kansas.

As seen in chapter 6, intramarriage is not a culturally static state, and in-marriage does *not* automatically lead to cultural retention or solidarity. Among the couples profiled in this chapter, in-marriage was the result of demographic opportunity (group size) combined with matching racial strategies. Region mattered in that those who lived in predominantly working-class Hispanic areas were most invested in racial erasing and easing strategies. Although both men and women engaged in social distancing strategies, Latino men retreated from race most vigorously in order to distance themselves from male gangs and the racialized and gendered "controlling image" associated with them.[5] My sample does not include any downwardly mobile people. Respondents had started in life as either poor or working-class—or, in a few cases, middle-class—and had increased in socioeconomic standing over time. Given most respondents' low socioeconomic and human capital starting points, they had experienced noticeable upward mobility in their lifetimes.[6] When I interviewed them, they were on surer financial footing than in prior years.

In-married parents who profess color-blindness erase or ease connection to their race as a means to achieve upward mobility, often through what I term "constrained cultivation," a modification of Annette Lareau's classic term "concerted cultivation."[7] "Constrained cultivation" highlights the racial and class constraints faced by parents who intentionally foster class advancement opportunities for their children. Doing so requires that parents diminish their racial ties, which they see as incompatible with nonwhite racial status. Constrained cultivation is aspirational in that it aims for future class advancement and is accompanied by a "humanity" or "individuality" narrative that conceals racial distinctions.

Many of the intragenerational in-marriages in California were the result of demographic opportunity. Among these Latinos who strategized to distance themselves, the preference was not for racial or ethnic connection, as seen in chapters 5 and 6, but rather for loosened ties to heritage. With the large number of Latinos in Los Angeles County (47.7 percent of the 9.8 million population, or over 4.6 million people, in 2010), possibilities abound for coethnic relationships between two people who are weakly ethnically identified.[8] Endogamous marriages are thus not necessarily synonymous with strong racial or ethnic identification. Indeed, in this study the vast majority of the intragenerational intramarriages included people who engaged in social distancing.[9] Although racial erasing—rejecting Latino identity and favoring whiteness—can promote out-marriage (see Rowena Cooper in chapter 2), it can also occur within Latino intramarriages, as this chapter shows. Less drastic than erasing, easing loosens but does not destroy the connection to a racial heritage in the pursuit of socioeconomic advantage. One key difference between erasing and easing is that those using the former strategy do not see positive group associations as compatible with their racial category, whereas those using the latter strategy have some allegiance to their group and do not disavow their race. Showcasing an intergenerational angle, this chapter demonstrates that parents struggle to endow their children with racial and class advantage through the use of constrained cultivation and that children's identity and attitudes are shaped by their parents.

SOCIAL DISTANCING STRATEGIES: AVOIDING LOW-CLASS AND GANG STEREOTYPES

Racial Erasing: Dichotomy and Denial

Respondents who were working-class or poor in their youth viewed being Latino, and specifically Mexican, as detrimental in a dichotomous framework in which brownness was the opposite of whiteness and threatened to hamper their upward mobility. The context of urban Los Angeles is especially relevant here: proximity to gangs and underclass minority ghettos constituted the backdrop against which the California Latinos viewed themselves. According to the Los Angeles Police Department, the County and City of Los Angeles are the "gang capital" of the nation, with over 450 active gangs in the city. Some of the gangs have been in existence for over fifty years, and the combined membership totals over 45,000 individuals.[10] In a local context where "Mexican ethnicity [was] tied tightly to gangs and poor school performance," suggesting that to be a Mexican youth was synonymous with being a gang member, "more pro-school enactments of Mexicanness" were crowded out.[11] In an effort to reject delinquency and socioeconomic stagnation, many interviewees from California who were not yet middle-class shied away from their Latino heritage because they saw it as conjoined with danger, downward mobility, and death.[12]

Audrey Figueroa and her son Braedon Toledo strategically erased their heritage to distance themselves from low-class and gang stereotypes and affiliate themselves with the racial and class privilege associated with whiteness. Their mother-and-son narrative was laced with color-blind ideology: both spoke in terms of individuality as a way to deny race, class, and gender stereotypes. Nevertheless, erasing is based on the very existence of race, class, and gender stereotypes that do not simply disappear when they are denied.

Fifty-year-old Audrey Figueroa's trajectory of erasing began with the teachings of her mother, a Mexican American who claimed to be "Spanish." Audrey's mother chose not to perpetuate Hispanic traditions, including not teaching her children Spanish, in order to dissociate her children from negative cultural stereotypes:

> AUDREY: [My mom] tells us we're just Caucasian. . . . She just told me, "You're white." . . . "Mexican" really wasn't said. Grandma's grandparents came from Spain. So we always talked about . . . being Spaniard.
>
> AUTHOR: [You said] they came from Spain through Chihuahua, Mexico, and then to Texas?
>
> AUDREY: Right.

Racial erasing began here not with identity claims (Audrey did say she was Hispanic), but with the omission of Mexican national origins as a way to manage stigma. Mexico was skipped over in the family tree in favor of the more distant tie to Spain. The association of Spain with Europe, light skin, and a conquering nation (rather than a conquered one) made it an appropriate origin story in this family's quest to climb racial, class, and national-origin ladders.

Just as her mother taught her, Audrey resisted being constrained by labels, group mentalities, or others' opinion of her. In junior high and high school, she resisted being racially categorized and was punished through violence. Audrey described her Pico Rivera, California, high school as segregated, complete with expectations for each racial group:

> If you were Mexican, you were supposed to be a chola in the seventies. If you were white, you were surfer. If you were black, you were black. If you were Asian, you were the nerds. And I didn't identify with any of the groups because I was white-colored—I didn't look Hispanic—but yet I had long black hair down to my butt. I wouldn't wear the makeup—in [those] days

that was chola, all the extra makeup. My mother would never allow that. It was deal with the peers or deal with my mother. So I chose to deal with the peers and not my mother.

Her ambiguous phenotype (light skin and black hair) and Hispanic surname placed Audrey at odds with all constituents who had a stake in her racial claims. No available category suited her. She recounted being physically assaulted in retaliation for her racial nonconformity:

> I got to high school and hated it! They made me have to fit in — the groups of people I was going to school with. I was jumped by Hispanics because I was trying to be white and I should look more like them. The whites thought I was trying to be Hispanic. I didn't dress either way. . . . Whatever my mother bought me was what I wore. . . . So I got jumped by both sides. After the third time, I said, "Mom, I'm not going to school no more." I was done. . . . In the seventies, there was no harassment [law]. . . . It was basically because of me that we moved out.

Her high school peers envisioned bounded racial groups and resorted to violence to shore up those boundaries. Audrey viewed her Hispanic (or "Spanish") identity as *compatible* with whiteness. Her Hispanic-and-white stance has been legitimized in recent U.S. censuses: since 1980, "white" has been listed as a racial option and "Hispanic" as an ethnicity option, allowing respondents to identify themselves as both racially white and ethnically Hispanic.[13]

In the Figueroa-Toledo family, we see the effective intergenerational transmission of ideology — a belief system about comportment that positions family members for racial advantage. Even more than his mother, twenty-nine-year-old Braedon was conscientious about the privilege he hoped to attain through his claim to whiteness. He was a tall, large-framed man with jet-black hair, dark eyes, and light-tan skin. He claimed to pass for white periodically, but his story of struggling to claim a white identity showed that people's perceptions of him (including my own) did not always align with his racial projections.

The first moment Braedon comprehended race was when he was perceived as Mexican at age ten:

> One of the kids identified me as being Mexican, where[as] I never really had identified myself [that way]. I was just like, "Well, what are you talking about . . . ?" And he goes, "Well, your last name's Toledo." . . . That was probably my first time [being told] . . . there's that differentiation, that boundary: "I'm white, you're Mexican."

By high school, Braedon was resolute in his claim to whiteness. He invested enormous effort in proclaiming and defending his whiteness, believing that respectability and money were at stake. As George Lipsitz argues, white Americans "invest" in their whiteness in order to achieve assets, resources, power, and opportunity.[14] For a racial eraser like Braedon, this meant defending himself and his racial claims. Like his mother a generation before, he too was drawn into physical fights with Latino and white peers in his Ontario, California, high school:

> In high school is where I really started to try to differentiate myself. . . . I don't really identify with any of these [Mexican] guys. . . . So then I started . . . hanging out with . . . the white guys and . . . I identified with them. . . . But my complexion . . . hair color, eye [color] . . . I'm not white to them. . . . I was always the outsider . . . looking in. . . . I had problems in school because it was like, "Well you're trying to be white." And I'm like, "Well, I am." And it's like, "Well, no, you're Hispanic." And I'm like, "No, I'm not." I actually got into a lot of fights about it. . . . It goes back to my last name. Because my last name's Toledo: "You're Mexican."

Physical fighting has been described as a masculine gender performance.[15] Fights on school grounds over racial classification also mimic earlier eras of racial violence such as the lynching, beating, and shooting of blacks and Latinos who were seen as treading too closely to whites' property (literally) or status position (figuratively).[16] Viewed as a racial trespasser for resisting Latino categorization and allying himself with whites, Braedon was beaten up by Latinos, whites, and blacks. These racial constituencies were all playing out society's distaste for racial ambiguity and using violence as a form of social control.

Braedon sought two practical advantages in his assertion of whiteness: respect and job acquisition. A claim of whiteness went far in testifying to his non-affiliation with a gang, which was a basis for respect.[17] Masculinity is relevant here in that young men are considered public threats as "bad boys."[18] Braedon was friends with Hispanic neighborhood gang members, although he shunned that identification and was derided for "acting like a white boy." Despite this heckling, Braedon preferred to be maligned by his peers than to be maligned by society. He embraced whiteness as a strategy to distance himself from gang affiliation and a stymied future:

> I don't want to be affiliated . . . at all. . . . [When] I was kind of into that I . . . saw the way people treated me was different. . . . People started to treat me like I was a gang member, like I was somebody that was not respectable or somebody . . . [who] isn't worth anything. . . . So therefore you get no respect from everybody else, but you do from everybody in the gang.

As Phillipe Bourgois argues in his ethnographic work on male Puerto Rican drug dealers, "Street culture and the underground economy provided them with an alternative forum for redefining their sense of masculine dignity." Although "promiscuity, conspicuous violence, and ecstatic substance abuse" are self-destructive behaviors, the operating logic is that if you cannot win by the rules of the dominant society, change the rules in your subculture so that you can earn respect through alternative means.[19] For Braedon, erasing his race and "investing" in whiteness sidestepped racial and class oppression and earned him dignity within mainstream society.[20]

The second practical advantage that white privilege carries is the assumption of having the skills and competence that aid job acquisition and promotion. Despite federal regulations aimed at eradicating racial inequalities in the labor market, employers continue to discriminate based on perceived race.[21] Racialization hinders Latinos in the labor market in that employers (even those who espouse color-blindness) routinely use race as a proxy for worker quality.[22]

The United States has a racialized labor hierarchy wherein the most powerful and highest-paying jobs are held by whites and less prestigious and menial jobs are occupied disproportionately by minorities.[23] There are occupational and income-generating consequences to perceived racial status. Observing this reality, Braedon understood that identification as white had labor market advantages in hiring, placement, pay, and promotions. He was so opposed to being categorized as Hispanic for fear of incurring a racial penalty that he once abruptly walked out of a job interview when the interviewer questioned his race. The question may have been asked for diversity outreach purposes, but Braedon opted out of the categorization and prematurely ended the interview because he was concerned about being negatively typecast. Regardless, however, of what he thought, said, or did to erase his race, others still imposed racialized categories on him.

Internalized racism was the underbelly of Braedon's reasons for identifying as white, his logic stemming from dichotomous thinking about whites as superior and minorities as inferior. As Karen Pyke and Tran Dang note, "By accepting and internalizing mainstream racist values and rationales . . . subordinates, often without a conscious awareness of doing so, justify the oppression of their group with a belief in their own inferiority."[24] Acting out internalized racism, Braedon changed his racial identity in order to be racially allied with the white bosses rather than the exploited class of brown workers. He even quit a job out of frustration: "Because [my boss] didn't identify me as white, [I] was always constantly proving myself." He entered his new job identifying himself as a capable white worker, features that he assumed went hand in hand. Braedon explained his performance of whiteness at his new job:

> I went in and tried to prove myself and who I am, right off the bat. . . . If I hadn't identified myself early enough . . . I would still be [wondering], "Should I [give this presentation] because it's not . . . expected of me . . . because of my race?" If you don't have that [winning] mind-set . . . you won't go anywhere. . . . Luckily, I self-identify with that [whiteness], so it's a lot easier for me. But somebody else who . . . identifies [as] Hispanic . . . or black might be more hesitant to . . . [perform well], because it's not expected of them.

Stereotype threat is defined as "being at risk of confirming, as self-characteristic, a negative stereotype about one's group."[25] Being at risk of endorsing a negative stereotype may cause stress that leads to under-performance. Braedon tried to evade stereotype threat by disidentifying as Hispanic and identifying as white. For Braedon, white racial performance was about commanding respect and creating positive assumptions about his character and abilities. In an age of federal laws prohibiting racial discrimination in the workplace, a turn toward "soft skills" such as motivation and customer-service abilities are racially coded ways to disadvantage minorities.[26] Middle-class, white cultural capital, including speech patterns, accents, and demeanor, become litmus tests for being hirable and promotable.[27]

Braedon recognized the racialized labor hierarchy and *tried to fit in it,* rather than alter the situation or change employers' views of minority workers.[28] He did not resist the notion implicit in the racialized labor hierarchy that to be professionally successful is to be white. He could have rejected this assumption and succeeded as a Hispanic, but he did not. An astute observer of how race structures social life, Braedon made strategic decisions to erase his race for the purpose of upward mobility. However, in so doing, he helped himself without touching the larger issue of structural inequality. Racial erasing also disqualified him from being a role model or mentor for Latinos. Insomuch as "internalized racism reveals dynamics by which oppression is reproduced," we see here how one man's striving for upward mobility perpetuated the status quo of structural advantages for whites and disadvantages for minorities.[29]

Racial strategies are also connected to how people select a life partner. Seventy-year-old U.S.-born Merle Andrade was the son of two U.S.-born Hispanics who lived in a Spanish-speaking Hispanic community in Albuquerque until his father's retirement from the Santa Fe Railroad in the mid-1940s. Merle's family then moved to South Los Angeles, which was "all white at the time," as opposed to East Los Angeles, "where all the Hispanics were." Owing to this relocation, Merle remarked, "my family sort of got away from following our ethnicity." Merle's parents engineered his white environment, which led him to marry someone who was similarly disaffiliated from her Latino background. Merle dated primarily white women in his young adulthood, although he fell in love with and married his Mexican American wife. He described her as "perfect" for him, but he was referring to her personality traits, he said; their compatibility had "nothing to do with background." Merle's wife was similarly disinterested in racial matters.[30] In this case, racial strategies were a source of attraction, as each partner was able to consolidate a racial trajectory with a like-minded spouse.

Merle explained the environment in which he raised his children as "mostly white, middle-class, not so much Hispanic." The following question-and-answer exchange reveals the extent to which Merle's orientation was decisive, resolute, and unchanged by in-marriage:

AUTHOR: Do you feel accepted in that environment—the white middle class?

MERLE: Oh sure.

AUTHOR: Are you at all active in terms of any Mexican American issues?

MERLE: No.

AUTHOR: Has your affiliation to your Hispanic background changed since you married [your wife]?

MERLE: No. . . . Pretty much the same. . . . [She was] brought up the same way. . . . So we were not really attached to our ethnic community.

Moving into a white community, sending his children to private school, and being removed from Mexican American issues were all ways in which Merle strove for racial privilege and upward mobility. Merle was not explicit about the racial or class reasons for his behavior, but his avoidance of participation in racial-ethnic organizations or causes was telling. Using the color-blind tactic of not referring to race, Merle insisted on a nonracial vision of himself and others: "I never thought of myself in any kind of racial [way]. . . . I never said to myself, 'I'm Hispanic, I'm Mexican American.' I just consider myself a person. And I always associate with all nationalities. . . . Race is never something that I even look at. . . . And I don't think I'm any less because of my race." Merle minimized his attention to race in the hopes that by deflecting race he would similarly be viewed without racial trappings.[31] Merle was aware of racial difference but refused to classify others based on race, hoping that others would share his color-blind view and demur from categorizing him. Yet it was clear that he was aware of racial power relations and used racial denial as a safeguard against feeling oppressed ("I don't think I'm any less because of my race"); thus, his color-blindness was an emotional defense mechanism. Used in this way by Latinos, color-blind discourse is a strategy for inclusion in American society.[32] The intragenerational intramarriage of two racial erasers enables them to continue on their disaffiliation pathway uninterrupted and, by employing color-blind discourse, strive for social integration unencumbered by negative racial connotations.

Not all of the intramarried Latino couples held fast to their natal culture. By using social distancing techniques, these couples (and families, more generally) believed that they could avoid the harsher side of life experienced by the nearby lower-class Latino community: gang warfare, economic insecurity, and family instability. These racial-erasing families seemed to be avoiding threats to their livelihoods, though proximity to under-class communities may have presented a pull toward delinquency.[33] For Latinos who hail from violent or already disaffiliated contexts, selecting a marital partner who agrees with social distancing as a safeguard against harm is important. Racial strategies can be an important component of marital decisions.

Racial Easing: Acknowledgment and Loosened Connection

In contrast to racial erasing, which is based on repudiation, racial easing is a more nuanced approach that is complicated by one's acknowledgment of a racial heritage and struggle against a racialized social system. For racial easers Cindy and John Ortega of California, their identical orientation to their Mexican American heritage was a point of attraction. The Ortegas were a blended family with five children: Cindy, age thirty-nine, brought three daughters from her first marriage, and John, age forty-nine, brought one son whose mother, John's first wife, had died; the couple also had a son together. The pair claimed to be "American" first and "Mexican" a distant second. The reasons undergirding their staunch claim of "American" identity were birthright and a desire not to be seen as distinct. Like all who engage in social distancing strategies, Cindy and John understood

"Latinos," "Mexicans," or "Mexican Americans" as equating with downward mobility and dim futures.

I conducted the interviews in the Ortegas' home in Whittier, a suburb twelve miles southeast of Los Angeles with a median income of $48,000 and a 61 percent Hispanic (of any race) population.[34] When I arrived, John was planting in the garden and dripping with sweat in the eighty-degree summer heat. In need of updating and a fresh coat of paint, the house was home to Cindy and John, two of their five children, and an elderly great-aunt. Inside the house, the printouts above the washer and dryer urging water and energy conservation (NO LAUNDRY 5–8 PM OR ON THURSDAYS) were indicative of their less-than-affluent status. Suggestive of the collective efforts required to run a dual-career family that had multiple dependents and lacked the discretionary funds to install a dishwasher, another sign over the sink read: CLEAN UP AFTER YOURSELF.

Cindy learned from her first marriage about the qualities to avoid for a healthier second marriage. She summarized her marriage to her first husband, a Mexican American who was a jobless gang member: "I was young, I was stupid, I wanted the bad boy type, I guess." She described the relationship as "a mess, [with] no trust, no honesty." After her divorce, Cindy looked for someone more stable and noticed that John "was very mature. He had a job. I saw him more as a protector, a provider." Having learned in her first marriage to avoid gang-involved, unemployed men, Cindy now favored men who could be role models and financial contributors:

> My first husband . . . did nothing for me. . . . He had gangbanger friends and . . . he would take off. . . . I knew I didn't want my children growing up around that because they'd be too close to the drugs and the violence. . . . And with John, my husband now, it's like night and day. . . . He can relate to what I went through as far as the gangbangers, because where he lived in the projects, he had friends that were cholos . . . and crazy and stuff. . . . He ultimately wants the same thing I want for the kids, which is to stay away from gangs and drugs and get their education, [whereas] my first husband . . . didn't care.

Cindy's desire to disassociate from a gang environment and achieve economic stability matched John's goals. In this marriage, corresponding racial strategies were a source of attraction, a way to verify that both partners possessed the same life goals.

Cindy and John Ortega met at work, their romance beginning with a lunch date. John's account was a reminder of how central attraction is to dating and marriage. He answered my question about what he found attractive in the women he dated by saying simply: "That they're beautiful [*laughs a lot*]." John described Cindy: "What intrigue, what. . . . She's got smarts . . . so that attracted me." Calling Cindy smart and beautiful, John concluded, "Yeah, I'd be nuts not to stick with her." Cindy fit the bill, not to mention that their orientations as racial easers matched. Racial endogamy mattered, since John stated that he was "not attracted to black [women]." Cindy also exhibited antiblack prejudice, remarking: "I think because my family members do, um, say . . . racial [racist] comments sometimes, that [I] probably would be afraid to bring another race home, like, for example, a black guy." While Cindy did not mention white men, John vacillated in his stance toward white women: if he had "come across a white woman," he would have been generally open to the experience, suggesting that white women were not in his immediate social circle in diverse Los Angeles. But John tempered this agreeability by hinting at a feeling that white women were "off-limits," as other Latino men expressed after being dismissed by white women or warded off by their families.[35]

Awareness of the local Los Angeles racial hierarchy pervaded John's logic regarding who was datable. The lessons he had learned about racial status began early. Having grown up in the predominantly Hispanic East L.A. projects—a poverty-ridden neighborhood and "main gang area" teeming with drugs and violence—John had seen friends and neighbors die in drive-by shootings. Leery of being another "human cost [of] gang activity," he was scared to walk home at night and hid in shadows as cars slowly crept by looking for an enemy gang member to be their next target.[36] John and his eleven siblings were eventually able to move out of the projects. With this background, however, John considered "Latino" and "lower-class gang life" to be equivalent. In response, he practiced racial easing, dissociating himself from the Latino category with the aim of leaving a grim life path behind him.

Coming from this poverty-ridden, segregated neighborhood that he now called a "ghetto," John had deduced that emphasizing his American identity might aid him:

> I am Mexican American, but I feel that I'm American too. . . . [It] really is like they say: that if you're a Mexican . . . you don't get too many of the benefits . . . you feel like you're one step below the white people, you know. So I just felt that there was a lower status there. . . . You do come across a lot of racism . . . but I just . . . [try] to make the best out of it.

Acknowledging racism, John's racial strategy was to stress his American status and back away from his Mexican heritage, which was "lower status" and did not accrue "benefits." When I asked how he and Cindy were raising their five children, he enacted racial easing by emphasizing their

Americanness: "We . . . have the same values, to bring up our kids [and promote] education. . . . I would say we just try to live as Americans."[37]

Trying to draw out the link between Mexican heritage and downward mobility—and between (non-Mexican) Americanness and brighter prospects—that inspired John's racial easing, I asked him whether the poverty and gangs in his background had anything to do with his desire to deemphasize his Mexican background in his family. John responded affirmatively: "Hmm . . . you know what? I thought about that a few times. . . . Yeah, like to say . . . why would you want to have that part of that life in your life? Yeah, yeah. . . . 'Cuz it seems like we get labeled after a while." Labeling theory, often researched in school settings, suggests that there is a strong correlation between one's outcomes and outsiders' expectations.[38] To avoid labeling and the stereotypes attached to those labels, John claimed "Americanness" and eschewed "Mexicanness" (seeing the two as discrete and polar opposites) for himself and his children. As a parent, he insulated his children from gang life, saying, "The gangbanger . . . you don't have to have hatred to them . . . but you . . . just keep your distance. . . . You just don't want to start anything where . . . you get them upset and then they're going to do something foolish and . . . shoot you up. . . . That's their lifestyle, this is our lifestyle. . . . We want to better ourselves." By increasing the social distance between "us" (marginally middle-class, not gang-affiliated) and "them," John aimed to "make it better" and have a chance at improved life prospects. He bought into the stereotype of dangerous Mexican masculinity and lower-class status. Believing he faced a binary choice, he opted for racial easing, a defense against becoming the stereotype that he believed to be true.

Their limited exposure to a diverse set of Mexican-origin or Latino populations had not challenged the lower-class Mexican stereotype from which the Ortegas recoiled. John had a high school education and Cindy dropped out of community college when she got pregnant at eighteen. Neither through education nor occupation had the Ortegas had a chance to become familiar with minority professionals; he was an electrician and she was a secretary working for white attorneys. Lacking exposure to professional, middle- or upper-income Latinos that would have expanded their notions about the Mexican American community, the Ortegas believed that they faced a bipolar choice between race and upward mobility. They chose to retreat from their race.

Gabby, Cindy's sixteen-year-old daughter from her first marriage, illustrated the cross-generational transmission of racial easing as a tactic to access an improved life path. She had been exposed to violence and drugs in her youth through her biological father, who was a gang member. Gabby would steer clear of her home when she was a child, spending a lot of time with her "nana," her maternal great-grandmother who was her "escape button." Gabby described her youth:

> My dad was . . . in a gang. According to him and his friends, once you're in a gang you can never get out. . . . He ended up getting shot in his back, so he got . . . paralyzed from the waist down. . . . When I grew up I never saw . . . him walking. . . . My dad was always doing drugs, and he just wasn't like a nice environment to grow your kids around. So my mom . . . got fed up and she left. . . . [We] stayed with her mom, so my grandma.

Gabby's negative childhood experiences surrounding her father's gang life countermanded the idea that his version of Mexican culture was worth preserving. Her father can be heard looming large in her early life experience in the phrase "*he . . . wasn't . . . a nice environment*." Gabby's gang-entrapped father catalyzed her social distancing.

Calling herself "more Americanized," Gabby focused on her education because of a bargain that she and her mother struck:

> [I didn't have] a stable home. . . . But . . . I had an escape button, my nana and my great-aunt. . . . They're sisters [who lived together]. My mom like, "If you do good . . . in school, like if you behaved all day . . . [you get a sticker]. . . . And if you get a sticker every day of the week . . . you can spend a weekend with Nana." And I was like, "Yes!" Like finally I'm away from this hell family life. . . . I know it sounds really sad, but . . . there was so much chaos in my family life. . . . [Going] to Nana's house . . . was an escape from reality. . . . I think that was my escape button, and I think that maybe helped me focus more on school. . . . I had a motivation, I wanted to be free.

Gabby concentrated on school to escape a home life that had introduced her to "things [she] shouldn't have known," such as the different colors of ecstasy pills, cocaine, and her parents' sexual infidelities. By striking the bargain with her mother that let her push the "escape button" that was her grandmother's house, Gabby tried her best to keep out of an environment where, in her poignant words, her "innocence was killed."

Calling her education and college plans her "first priority," Gabby played out the lesson that her mother instilled: academic success would be the way out of a harsh home life. Even as her home life had become more stable with her mother and stepfather, they both continued to transmit the message that racial easing can act as a shield against downward mobility. Like other racial erasers and easers, Gabby drew on a narrative of individualism to justify her social distancing strategy. Background does not proscribe behavior, as Gabby observed: "Personally, it's like, yeah, I'm Mexican, so what? [*laughs*] Why does it matter? . . . I know some people are like, "Oh 'cuz you're Mexican, you have to like beans," or something stupid like that. I really don't care. [*laughs*] I'm my own [individual] first." By delinking heritage from action, Gabby had created a space in which to pursue upward mobility.

Social distancing techniques are not required to access upward mobility.[39] Nevertheless, those who hail from more socioeconomically deprived backgrounds, like the Ortegas, associate their heritage with gang membership and use a racial easing strategy to avoid deleterious life circumstances and improve their prospects.

CONSTRAINED CULTIVATION

In her classic book *Unequal Childhoods,* Annette Lareau examines how a family's socioeconomic status shapes children's life experience. Lareau argues that different "cultural logics of child-rearing," rooted in class status, lead to the transmission of differential advantages to children, and that with middle-class parents, both white and black, this transmission takes the form of "concerted cultivation." Middle-class parents actively "develop" their children ("discussions between parents and children are a hallmark of middle class child-rearing"), and this training creates in children a sense of entitlement to question adults and relate to them as peers.[40] Working-class parents, by contrast, regardless of race, practice "accomplishment of natural growth," a child-rearing practice that maintains a clear boundary between adults and children, with adults using directives rather than persuasion and children having more control over their leisure activities.[41] Arguing that class status is preeminent in parenting practices, Lareau underdevelops the interaction of racial inequality with class inequality. In this dichotomous setup, there is little room for intermediary logics of child-rearing—for example, blended tactics or mismatched strategies in which parental class status does not correspond to parenting style.[42]

Parenting strategies are not inextricably tied to class status but are open to revision, adaptation, or appropriation. Here I modify Lareau's term "concerted cultivation" by elaborating the new term "constrained cultivation" in order to highlight the class and racial constraints faced by working-class Latino parents who nonetheless foster class advancement opportunities for their children. In constrained cultivation, working-class parents' paramount concern is class advancement, which they ardently try to attain despite their limited socioeconomic capacity. Parents who engage in constrained cultivation use a humanity or individuality narrative that conceals their racial and class position in order to rhetorically support their claim to class advancement through extracurricular investments in their children. Scholars of color-blind rhetoric argue that color-blind talk is insidious for its denial of how race structures society.[43] For minorities to participate in the elision of race suggests internalized racial oppression whereby they are upholding white privilege and instantiating their own subordination.[44] These negative appraisals of minorities' articulation of color-blindness may be true, but it may also be true that they are trying to take race out of the equation in order to gain distance from constricting visions of themselves and their destinies.

Vincent Venegas and Raven Salazar, both thirty-six, were Mexican-origin: he was a Mexican national and a resident alien in the United States, and she was born in the United States to a Mexican-born preteen mother. This couple was intent on providing their sons with a more stable home life and more opportunities for advancement than they had as children of working-class single mothers, even if costly extracurricular activities stretched their budget. They identified as Latino but did not emphasize that identity. Instead, they talked about humanity as a whole and, showing the aspirational nature of constrained cultivation, strove to provide their sons with enrichment activities that stretched their finances in the hopes of securing upward mobility.

Vincent, born in Mexico, migrated to California at age seven with his mother. He grew up in a neighborhood that was predominantly African American and Mexican-origin. His mother did not pass on cultural traditions to him because she was a Jehovah's Witness, a religious group that shuns celebrations. Vincent's mother worked long hours, and his father was absent from his life. ("I don't have a dad. I don't have a family.") He was thus left to be socialized by the street, neighborhood youth filling in the gaps of time and authority in his life.[45] Vincent's gang affiliation began when he associated with the older brothers of classmates, yet he struggled with issues of values, danger, and morality: "[At] thirteen or fourteen, I [ran] into gang members [and] I realized these guys are really up to no good. . . . I'd try to stay away from drugs. . . . I thought, 'My mom wouldn't approve. God wouldn't approve.' " Already ditching school with other neighborhood youth, however, he was peer-pressured into joining the gang:

> Some of the kids said, "Hey, do you want to join our gang?" I'm like, "Nah, I'm all right." They're like, "How come? You're kickin' it with us. . . . Let's just jump you in." I was like, "Nah." "Oh, what? You don't want to be with us?" I said, "All right, let's do it." So I got jumped in, got beat up by five kids. I think I wound up with a black eye that time. Still knowing that what I just did was wrong, still knowing that there is the risk of having to do things that I don't agree with. But . . . they are my friends. If I would get into a fight, they would back me up. So I thought I'm okay as long as I still have values.

In resisting gang violence, Vincent sacrificed his education in order to preserve his moral integrity:

> It created a lot of tension, because they constantly wanted to do things that weren't right. The way I got out of it was ditching school. . . . I wouldn't be convinced or coaxed to . . . grabbing a gun and going to another school and shooting somebody up. So what I started doing was falling behind on my grades. . . . I started ditching one class, writing myself my excuse notes. . . . I started ditching other classes and falling behind. *That's how I stayed true to myself: by, I guess, sacrificing my education.* [emphasis added]

At nineteen, Vincent was jumped out of the gang (disaffiliated): "By the time I was nineteen, I was getting fed up with seeing my friends die, go to jail, being on drugs."

Vincent became involved in a local antigang task force that worked with elementary and junior high school students. Becoming a gang and drug counselor is a chief way in which former gang members seek to "gain legitimacy for being reformed."[46] During this period of transition, working a part-time minimum-wage job, Vincent met Raven. On the job visiting a Venice high school, Vincent was counseling the graduating class about the emptiness of gang life and was later invited to a house party that Raven attended.

Raven Salazar was the daughter of a young Mexican immigrant and a white teenager whom she had never known (he was not told of her existence). Her mother (a victim of sexual assault, though the circumstances of her pregnancy are unclear) was twelve when she gave birth to her. Raven's Mexican immigrant grandmother conspired to pass the baby off as her own daughter. Under this arrangement, Raven's mother grew up with her aunts and uncles as if they were siblings. Raven summarized how "by default" she was raised by her maternal grandparents: "I was basically raised by my grandparents and led to believe that my grandparents were my parents and that my aunts and uncles were my brothers and sisters, including my mom." This deceit continued until she was seven years old and her mother "demanded that my grandmother tell me the truth . . . [because she] wanted her position as my mother."

With eight (faux) brothers and sisters, Raven received little (grand)parental supervision. Her youth corresponded to Lareau's concept of "accomplishment of natural growth." Raven's recollections accentuated the dangerous aspects of this parenting strategy:

> I remember being five years old and walking to kindergarten by myself. . . . It [was] . . . a far . . . stretch and . . . I was small for a five-year-old, and [I knew] that somebody could just grab me and throw me in their truck. . . . I had to

be responsible for myself. . . . There was no real supervision. Sure, there was a roof over my head. There was food in the kitchen. . . . But there was really no raising of me. Adults hardly spoke to me. Everybody was close to my age.

Remarking that she was "raised by society," Raven credited nonfamilial adults, such as older coworkers and bosses who took her "under their wings," for her personal growth. She attended five different high schools and dropped out to work full-time at age sixteen and became what she described as a "party girl" of the neighborhood gang in Santa Monica.[47] Raven observed that friendships and dating opportunities arose from her local, economically stressed environment:

All of the boys [in the apartment complex] became gang members. So most of my generation [of] . . . boys [were] killed, in jail, or just drugs, just bad stuff. . . . Where I lived there [were] drive-by shootings. It was a hangout of gangs—the Santa Monica Gang. The girls somehow thought that that's what they wanted; you know, the bad guys. And we would go party with gang members.

Women are less likely to be consumed by gang life than men, perhaps owing to a difference in supervision (though not in Raven's case), attraction to deviance, or peer pressure.[48]

Raven and Vincent met at a gang party because they lived in a working-class Latino area with a gang presence and there was peer pressure on Raven to be a gang party girl. Vincent, in his work for the antigang organization, hung out with "at risk" youth as both a counselor and a friend. Much as in Vincent's narrative, Raven described the disconnect between her values and her social circumstances:

I knew that [partying with gang members] was wrong. [But] the peer pressure. And that's where I was. . . . I didn't have the alternative, so we went and partied with the gang members. The gang members were all Mexican, so we very much felt at home with them. So that's how I met Vince, at one of those house parties. . . . I wasn't a gang member, though. There [were] girls that partied with the gang members, but they were not the gang member girls.

The constraints of Raven's working-class gang environment were powerful (she "didn't have [an] alternative"). Her complicated and stressful home environment and lack of economic resources "deterred" her away from focusing on her education and into the company of neighborhood gang youth.[49] Because of her social environment, Raven ended up, "just by default," with men with ongoing or former gang affiliations. She succinctly described what happened when she met Vincent: "So I met Vincent, partied, and in three months I was pregnant. . . . I was eighteen when I met him, nineteen pregnant, twenty I had [our son]. . . . I wasn't exposed to anything else."

As parents in their midthirties to two boys, Raven and Vincent were intent on providing them with extracurricular opportunities that would enhance their education and personal growth. Supporting a family of four with a household income between $110,000 and $130,000 in an expensive area, Raven vacillated between saying that they "don't make a lot of money" and describing themselves as "middle-income." Objectively, the couple made a lot of money relative to their families of origin, the rest of the United States, and even their local environment: the median household income for 2006–2010 for Santa Monica was $68,842 (and for California, $60,883).[50]

Attentive to money, Vincent described his job history in terms of hourly wages, complete with the increases that had marked his climb in income. While he was working in an emergency room earning $14 an hour, he considered getting a nursing degree to increase his earnings; in the end, he decided that "I needed the money to pay for my kids' education and activities. So I couldn't do that." Now earning $22 an hour, he was in a trades program and preparing to make "twice as much as . . . before." Strategic about job transitions that would garner more money, Vincent aimed to provide for his children's "education and activities" and eliminated the option of nursing school for this reason, deferring his own education in favor of opportunities for his children.

In concert with her husband, Raven engaged in constrained cultivation. Prioritizing her children's development, she used class-advantaged white women as the model of motherhood to which she aspired: "The people that went to the pediatrics office [where I worked] are . . . [from] Hollywood . . . [white] people with a lot of money. So . . . I would hear about things they were doing with their kids. Then I was curious. . . . I thought, 'What are they doing? I want to do that for my kid.' " This reflection helps make sense of Raven's earlier class claims—those claims were *relative*, both to her family of origin (which she surpassed) and her wealthy role models (against whom she underachieved). Raven and her husband were "middle-income" and prosperous relative to their humble beginnings, yet compared to millionaires, they did not make "a lot of money." From her workplace that serviced the wealthy, Raven learned lessons in upper-class standards of parenting and mimicked them. This translated to costly summer camps and theater classes for her children. The *constrained* part of constrained cultivation becomes clear when Raven remarked on her financial limitations: "We've done all kinds of things and . . . vacations that I hear people [talk about]. . . . Although it's bit me in the behind because . . . the people that were doing these things had much more money than me. . . . Wow, now that I've introduced my kids to this, they want it. I can't afford it." Constraint here is relative to where she wanted to go economically. In contrast to her own youth where "the children were just children, almost like a second-class citizen in the household," Raven's project was to use any spare finances to enrich her children's lives.

In a context where whiteness is equated with success—despite Asians ascending as the benchmark population for high achievement in multi-racial urban environments—the tactics of racial easing and constrained cultivation are mutually reinforcing.[51] Critiqued by her natal family as "Miss Perfect" and a white wannabe, Raven destabilized the notion that being Mexican must entail disadvantage. She insisted:

> I don't want to be white. I'm a very strong Latina woman. . . . [Those who criticize] have self-hate. They are Mexican. And in this country you're taught to have self-hate being Mexican because you see all the bad stuff. So the good stuff is supposed to be the white people. . . . There's nothing that's just white or just Mexican.

Here Raven alluded to hegemonic notions of white superiority and Mexican inferiority, which have deep-seated historical antecedents such as the Mexican-American War and U.S. labor recruitment from Mexico (and then the expulsion of those same laborers in lean economic times).[52] While she showed the porousness between "Mexican" and "white," between disadvantage and advantage, her aspiration to advantage was also criticized by others as aspiring to whiteness. Vincent concurred with Raven: "It's a pet peeve of ours when people say . . . '[Your] family [wants] to be white. . . .' You're being narrowed-minded. You're enclosing yourself in this capsule of what a Latino should be. Who says who and what we should be? . . . We're not defined by tradition. We're defined by who we want to be." Blasé about cultural retention at home, this couple rejected a notion of "racial authenticity" that might have stifled them and instead supported their children's chances of educational and socioeconomic attainment by employing racial easing and constrained cultivation.[53]

Constrained cultivation does indeed cultivate children, but among non-affluent classes it also puts stress on finances, time, and family relationships. Vincent detailed how their practice of constrained cultivation had strained their marriage: "In raising our kids, we neglected each other. We're constantly doing for them. . . . She took on the role of being 'super mom,' which meant no time for dad . . . : kids, family, PTA, then dad. We came pretty close to calling it quits." Raven concurred with her husband's assessment of the marital tension that constrained cultivation had entailed: "[Vincent] has been jealous. I would admit that the kids took a priority over him. In retrospect, if I had to do it over again, I'd try to balance it a little bit more." Children are not immune to the "time bind" inherent in constrained cultivation.[54] Fifteen-year-old Pablo, Vincent and Raven's son, also dealt with a time crunch on a daily basis: he had a two-hour bus commute each way to attend his high school, which specialized in the arts. Raven detailed her son's weekday schedule: "Pablo [has] two-hour commutes each way on the bus. He gets up at five o'clock. He's on the bus by six to be at school by eight. . . . Eight to four, school. Four to six, home."

Belief in a common humanity that overshadows racial identity buttressed the Venegas-Salazar family's claim to advancement opportunities. Their rejection of lowered expectations based on race liberated them from narrow visions of Latinos, honored the diversity within the population, and justified their efforts to improve their lives. Vincent minimized racial divisions by advancing a "citizens of the world" philosophy: "Why can't we as humans just be citizens of the world? I think I've always treated everyone, or tried to treat everyone, as that. That's . . . what I've pushed onto the boys as well. We're all equal but different. . . . When it comes down to it, we're all human. . . . I've tried to erase any racial divide." Indicating their race-consciousness, Raven remarked, "We do stand up for what's unfair. We speak up in a civilized way." Likewise, Vincent advised his children to pay special attention to Latinos in need: "I do push that whenever you see a Latino, help regardless of where you are at or what you are doing. . . . Help, especially if they don't know the language. Help because it could have been your grandmother. It could have been your dad. . . . You do help Latinos get ahead, definitely." Many racial easers, even those who try to transcend race, mobilize around race on occasion, unlike racial erasers, who typically reject any such effort.

Vincent and Raven's racial easing and constrained cultivation were rooted in their own racialized and classed histories. Raven recognized that "definitely there were times where I needed a lot more supervision, a lot more stability." She attempted to compensate for the deficits of her upbringing through "intensive mothering" of her own children.[55] Vincent outlined his parenting philosophy, one of self-sacrifice and improvement from one generation to the next: "You don't live for yourself. You live for future generations. . . . Growing up, I didn't have as much as I would have wanted. Materialist[ically] and [in] family life. I want [my children] to be able to continue to do better and pass on more and more and more." The Venegas-Salazar family engaged in racial easing and constrained cultivation to distance themselves from their race- and class-disadvantaged positions.

Pablo benefited from his parents' strategy of constrained cultivation, which kept him out of gangs and college-bound. Pablo was a short, slim young man with a cherubic face, chestnut brown hair, and medium pale skin that, he told me, tanned well in the summer. Indicative of racial easing, Pablo described living in the state of a "happy medium": he and his brother "think of ourselves as Americans because we were born here. We are from Mexican descent, but essentially we are from this land and this is the only land we know." He described the interpenetration of American and Mexican customs and said he was not always able to distinguish one from the other: "We're not very celebratory on many of the Mexican traditions. But I might not know because we do celebrate and it doesn't seem out of place." He placed himself at a "four or five" on a scale of one to ten regarding his attention to Mexican traditions. Pablo's family, like many families engaged in constrained cultivation, left culture on the back burner and focused their efforts instead on making gains in a racially stratified society by mimicking white middle-class parenting strategies.[56]

The emphasis on fundamental human equality in a discourse of humanity can legitimize racial minorities' reach for advancement. Taking up his father's "citizens of the world" idea, Pablo spoke philosophically about fostering a "human instinct":

PABLO: Instead of an animal instinct—science shows how we are very similar to animals and we protect our land, we are very defensive when someone approaches us—I would like to create this human instinct. . . . A *human* instinct where people protect other people . . . ; people who don't judge before they know . . . ; [a] human instinct to love thy neighbor. . . .

AUTHOR: Is that mission . . . related at all to race-ethnicity?

PABLO: I believe if people have that human instinct, we won't have to look at . . . race. . . . I'm not trying to raise one race over the other, I'm trying to bring them together.

The intergenerational transmission of a humanitarian worldview is evident in Pablo's articulation of a "human instinct" that triumphs over a defensive "animal instinct." Enacting his goal of defusing racial tensions, Pablo worked as a peer mediator at his school, creating dialogue and mending arguments between factions. This illuminates another difference between social distancing strategies: racial erasing views a Latino background singularly as a detriment, whereas racial easing sees it as a reality that must be reckoned with in a more sophisticated way than simple renunciation.

Parents engaged in constrained cultivation scrimp on themselves in order to provide their children with extracurricular activities, camps, travel, and study abroad programs. Forty-one-year-old Mexican American Corrina Nuñes (whose annual household income was between $100,000 and $150,000) spoke ardently about the constrained cultivation efforts in which she and her husband Lamar engaged: "We live in an apartment. We drive a Saturn. We drive a beat-up truck so our kids have no limits. . . . We do the best that we can. . . . We were responsible parents. . . . We just propel our kids to do whatever we want to do." They sent their daughter to study abroad in England, and their eighteen-year-old son Chad, whom I interviewed, had just been accepted to Princeton University and would be attending the next fall. The family's cultivation of Chad's prospects was constrained relative to affluent nearby populations, which had inspired his parents to take cost-saving measures to springboard their children into an upwardly mobile future.

Chad, who had almond-toned skin, black hair, dark brown eyes, and a slim body, grew up in Covina, a suburb of Los Angeles, and had "very limited encounters with racial issues." He emphasized his American identity, saying, "I'm . . . American, but then [I say] I hail from . . . Mexican heritage." He noted the generational and social distance between himself and newcomers: "[I'm] unlike . . . [those] who . . . are bilingual and who visit Mexico regularly. . . . There's definitely a difference." Unusual for a minority youth, Chad was politically conservative.[57] Since his family was not wealthy, Chad's Republican leanings were not based on fiscal policies that protect the elite. Much like Mexican Americans who check "white" on the U.S. census (as opposed to "racial other") because they view whiteness as American and nonwhiteness as separatist, Chad saw Republican conservatism as more American than Democratic liberalism.[58] He discussed the May 2006 immigrant rights demonstrations that occurred when he was in eighth grade: "My opinions are usually more conservative. . . . I'm not a big [advocate of] displaying my culture and heritage on a poster. . . . I didn't really approve of it [social activism in 2006], especially being a student with high aspirations." As a racial easer like his parents, Chad perceived racial solidarity as counterproductive to "high aspirations."

Chad viewed race-based cohesion as a threat to his upward trajectory. When he attended a high school camp for high achievers, he met several Advanced Placement (AP) students from inner-city Los Angeles whom he described as "fenced in" by their families:

Some [Los Angeles Unified School District students] were fenced in despite their academic achievement and potential. They came from homes that wanted them to stay close. So even though they were 4.4 [grade point average] students, their parents wanted them to go to Cal State L.A.... I was grateful that I was in a home that encouraged me to break out and ... follow what was best for me and didn't try to influence my decisions based on geographic ... boundaries.

What Chad was overlooking was the very presence of high-achieving minority students at the camp. Because they unfairly homogenized the Latino community, Chad and his parents engaged in racial easing and concerted cultivation as the only route, despite evidence to the contrary, to achievement. The family's race-based coding of success reinforced a racialized dichotomy of well-heeled white achievement and less affluent brown confinement.

In summary, racial erasing is based on denial, whereas racial easing loosens but does not eschew racial connection. Racial easing is often accompanied by constrained cultivation: using limited financial resources in ways that mirror whites' use of economic capital to create advantages for children. The rhetoric of humanity and race-blind equality that often accompanies constrained cultivation serves to justify striving to achieve improved opportunities and outcomes. Although it is a fallacy that all Latinos are working-class or poor (or that all whites are middle-class or wealthy), those who engage in racial erasing act on this generalization, whereas those who deploy racial easing retain their racial identity and may resist derisive stereotypes.

REGIONAL VARIATION

As of the 2010 census, California and Texas ranked second for the greatest percentage of Hispanics (37.6 percent), second only to New Mexico (46.3 percent), yet California boasted greater absolute numbers of Hispanics at over 14 million (with Texas at 9 million and New Mexico approaching 1 million).[59] The Hispanic population in Kansas, as of 2010, stood at 10.5 percent (nearly 300,000 of the state's 2.8 million residents).[60] In this study, Latino respondents from California were more invested than those from Kansas in social distancing strategies as a way to detach from stereotypes around poverty and delinquency. Population demographics and poverty rates shed light on the reasons for this pattern. From 2007 to 2011, the poverty rate for Hispanics in the city of Los Angeles was 26.4 percent (second only to 27.8 percent in New York City), as compared to the 12.7 percent poverty rate for non-Hispanic whites in the state of California.[61] Further, the gang population in Los Angeles is pronounced: in 2000 there were 152,000 documented gang members in Los Angeles County, topping the charts for all U.S. cities.[62]

In contrast to California, Douglas and Shawnee Counties, the two counties in Kansas in which I conducted the majority of the interviews, host much smaller populations of Hispanics—5.5 percent and 11.3 percent, respectively. The poverty rates in the Kansas field sites are also lower than in the California field site, the two counties averaging a poverty rate for all races (not Hispanics alone) of 18 percent.[63] These population and poverty numbers describe the contexts in which Latinos find themselves. In California the high poverty and gang membership rates inspired social distancing for a large share of the intragenerationally intramarried, who associated Mexican ancestry with underclass status, gangs, and violence, whereas in Kansas the pressure for interviewees to distinguish themselves from poor and delinquent coethnics was not severe.

Lisa Garcia Bedolla, who studied political activism in Los Angeles, has noted that not only do "gangs increase the social stigma attached to group members," but "the existence of gangs affects how people see [racial group members]." Her Latino respondents engaged in social distancing and "directed their anger at members of their own groups instead of at people of other races who were acting on stereotypes."[64] Relative to this social problem of stigma, my own Latino respondents in Los Angeles controlled what they could. Since they could not exert control over out-groups' stereotypes of them, they engaged in "impression management," exercising agency to distinguish themselves from a subset of their group that tarnishes their status.[65] Kansan Latinos, shielded from the negative connotations so readily applied to Californian Latinos by their state's white majority and lower poverty rates, were therefore not nearly as likely to deploy the social distancing strategies favored by their Californian counterparts.

Eight of the eleven intragenerationally in-married families (including two "neighboring generation" couples) used racial erasing (two families) or racial easing (six families) strategies.[66] All six couples from California noted that class, education, and gang concerns initiated their social distancing. The two intramarried Mexican American couples from Kansas cited different reasons for social distancing: one husband cited his experience in the U.S. military as a reason to care more about his American identity, and another couple pointed not to gang issues but to their intention to achieve class mobility.

Residing in Los Angeles, California, was associated with social distancing because in a dense Latino population with high poverty fates, race was cognitively linked to negative life outcomes such as unemployment, crime, violence, incarceration, and death. Moreover, the media have disseminated overly simplistic imagery of downtrodden and disaffected Latinos that has been codified as the "Latino threat narrative."[67] Such stereotyping compelled some in-married Latino Californians and their children to retreat from their heritage in hopes of avoiding negative associations and gaining a firm, unstigmatized foothold in society.

In Kansas, states away from Los Angeles—which has been dubbed the "epicenter of the American gang problem"—geographic distance from concentrated poverty and gangs buffered Latinos from negative stereotypes.[68] With geography attenuating the links between minority status, poverty, and delinquency, Kansan Latinos did not utilize social distancing strategies to break away from negative connotations. This is not to imply that racial discrimination was absent in Kansas, only to say that discrimination as a social problem was less obvious and less often the cause of a retaliatory racial strategy. The difference was that Kansans perceived discrimination largely as an *interpersonal* problem (though a few perceived institutional racism) that did not threaten downward leveling. For example, forty-five-year-old Orlando Puente reported driving to a gas station in his low-rider car and encountering a white woman who switched her purse to her opposite side upon seeing him. Orlando pinpointed the reason for her behavior as not his race but his presentation of self: "I have tattoos all over my arms . . . [and] earrings and everything. . . . I don't know if she just thought I was a threat because I was a rough-looking guy with tattoos." Orlando's attribution of the white woman's apparent fear not to his race but to his earrings, physical size, and tattoos was a logic unlikely to be used in California.

Besides racial meanings, another regional difference between California and Kansas is the accessibility of cultural resources that support Latino identity. In California both "unmediated resources" (direct relationships and interactions with Latinos) and "mediated resources" (consumption of television programming or retail products that does not require direct interaction with Latinos) are plentiful.[69] With these same Latino populations and products not as easily obtainable in Kansas, Latino Kansans referred to their proximate Latino family as a stronghold for their identity.

The Cota family illustrated the cultural centrality of family in the lives of Kansas Latinos. In the midst of our interview, Oscar received calls from both his mother and his daughter asking about scheduling a family dinner that night. They were arranging to meet at Oscar's mother's house, where she was going to cook a Mexican feast. Oscar's wife, Lorena, affirmed the importance of extended family and cultural activities to Hispanic identity in Kansas when she said: "I try to remind my kids of their heritage as far as just talking about the history of the families . . . and the . . . ethnic foods that we have. . . . We'll be making tamales at my parents' house next week, so I'll bring them to . . . help. . . . I want to give them more than what they have, but it's hard to do in the Midwest." She made an explicit comparison with other states: "It might have been different if we grew up in California or a state that had more . . . Latinos around." Absent a large Hispanic community offering plentiful resources, the Cotas, who were not churchgoers, relied on family members to sustain their Hispanic culture.

Lorena mused: "It would be nice to have my kids in a community that has the same background. Then I think, is it? Is it good? I don't know. I'm sure there are different issues wherever you are." Lorena hit on a central point revealed by this regional comparison: racial meanings vary by place. In Kansas, Lorena was not faced with the choice around racial erasing or racial easing that Californian interviewees wrangled with. Living in Kansas, where Latinos have more latitude in how they are defined, treated, and perceived because their scarce numbers have deflected negative attention, Lorena could wonder about what life in another locale might offer. But, as she rightly observed, different places have "different issues." Being in Kansas enabled Lorena to imagine the rewards of a Latino-dense community without having to suffer the drawbacks and decisions regularly encountered by her counterparts in California.

The important regional difference between diverse Los Angeles County and predominantly white northeastern Kansas turns on local narratives about the meaning of Latino identity that are shaped by proximity to the border, local demographics, and racial connotations. Being Latino in Kansas carries less threat of dire consequences than it does in dense underclass minority areas in California and therefore requires less fervent and frequent impression management through the use of social distancing techniques.

CONCLUSION

This chapter has profiled intragenerationally intramarried Latinos and their children, focusing on social distancing strategies. Most respondents who used social distancing strategies were in California, where they felt that a nonwhite background blocked their social mobility. The principal way for Latinos who shared generational status and were intramarried to counteract pervasive negative stereotypes was to retreat from the debased category.[70]

Racial erasing and racial easing rest on the notion that disaffiliation from Latino identity will facilitate escape from negative stereotypes such as low-class status and gang membership. Moving from disavowal to deemphasis of Latino heritage—racial erasing and racial easing, respectively—people strategically deploy these tactics to avoid negative attributions and increase their chances of upward mobility. Especially in the greater Los Angeles environment, where "Latino" conjures up images of underprivileged inner-city neighborhoods and violence, disassociating from a Latino heritage is an effort to exit from a self-defeatingly "reactive subculture."[71] The logic of racial erasing, especially, is based on and perpetuates a dichotomy: when people use the term "*Mexican* or *Latino* in opposition to *white,* [they are] explicitly categorizing them as non-white, with all the negative baggage that that implies in Anglo-American mainstream culture."[72] Given this destructive implication of labeling, erasers are trying to (at least) avoid a Latino "brown tax" and (at most) garner white privilege. While men and women in the study used social distancing strategies equally, the men were more concerned than the women with their racial group's associations with violence, criminality, and gang membership, their concern revealing how gendered treatment influences individuals' reasons for pursuing racial strategies.

Racial erasing rests on denial of a racial background, whereas racial easing is a less complete repudiation of nonwhiteness. The chief division between the two social distancing strategies lies in people's interpretation of what it means to be Latino and their ability to tolerate or resist apparent contradictions. Racial erasing is often a simplistic overreaction—a rejection of one's heritage for the sake of accruing racial and class advantage. Easing, by contrast, is more often a careful negotiation of racial heritage in the struggle for middle- or upper-middle-class achievement and freedom from damning stereotypes. Although both strategies are tools to overcome racial disadvantages, easing grants Latino identity neutral or even positive value and allows for small expressions of solidarity. Both techniques of social distancing are accompanied by a language of universal humanity that implies a future when racial difference will not be a basis of stratification. The nefarious downside of using a humanity rhetoric in a racially stratified society, however, is the temptation it raises to overlook racial disparities rather than acknowledge how they continue to shape life outcomes, including marital partnerships and identity politics.[73] The notable regional variation was that intragenerationally in-married Latino couples in California more ardently clung to erasing and easing strategies, their context compelling them to debunk any apparent linkage between race, class, and fate observed in inner-city neighborhoods and media.[74]

"Constrained cultivation," a stratagem for spending time and money on children's activities, is an aspirational component of easing. Based on the perception of a nexus between whiteness and middle-class achievement, constrained cultivation highlights the class and racial constraints that working-class Latino parents face as they foster advancement opportunities for their children. Following the model of "concerted cultivation" among middle-class whites noted by Lareau, working-class or marginally middle-class Latinos stretch their budgets to mimic the parenting behavior of the upper classes in the hopes of accruing class and racial advantage for their children.[75] There are three noteworthy meanings of "constrained":

First, parents believe that their financial resources are limited relative to the real or imagined wealth of white families and feel this monetary restriction despite their increase in socioeconomic stature since their childhood. Second, "constrained" describes the racial disadvantage that parents aim to resolve through their financial outlays to develop their children. Third, the term "constrained" recognizes that it takes skillful maneuvering to convert economic capital into social and cultural capital.[76]

Given how widely used these social distancing tactics are, it is clear that intramarriage (even among those who share a generational status) does *not* automatically lead to cultural retention. Instead, a shared racial strategy can be a source of attraction and foundational for a marital partnership. When people see their chosen racial strategy used by another, they see their own choice for survival—avoidance of poverty, escape from gangs, and skirting assumptions of incompetence—validated. Racial strategies also provide roadmaps for the next generation.

This chapter adds to our understanding of how endogamous Latino partnerships composed of people in the same generation-since-immigration are formed and the racial strategies they initiate and promote to the next generation. Demographic opportunity always plays a role in mate selection, but the story does not end there.[77] Racial strategies, tailored to position individuals to pursue their life goals free from stereotypes, can be a source of attraction and a factor in negotiated desire for couples. Lifetime partnerships are not simply a consequence of demographic chance but result from and can perpetuate racial strategies aimed at improving life trajectories.

Chapter 8 | Unpacking Marriage: Divorce, Repartnering, Ambivalence, and the Search for Love

NOT ALL MARRIAGES are created equal. Some are happy, and some are troubled. Some are long-lasting, and some ultimately end in divorce. Although this book began with questions about why people make their marriage choices and the ramifications of those choices for their cultural practices and racial consciousness, focusing on married couples, I realized, in looking at the patterns in the life histories that accumulated, that I could tell a larger story than the one I set out to tell: I could dig into the dynamics of partnering, separating, and repartnering.

As discussed in chapter 1, people do not simply search for "mythic love," as portrayed in the movies, but rather have compelling personal and practical reasons for searching out a specific type of partner. Their intersectional concerns are grounded in their natal family system and prior experience and play out in a local environment that offers different racial groups as potential dates. As Ann Swidler's study of contemporary love and marriage informs us, people utilize multiple framings to understand their relationships.[1] In juxtaposition to mythic love is an alternative frame of "prosaic realism" in which love is ambiguous, gradual, uncertain, and mundane, requiring effort and forbearance. People employ prosaic realism to discuss the day-to-day life of their marriage and the work they invest in maintaining their relationship. These framing devices for contemporary marriage are not mutually exclusive—people draw on mythic love to explain why they married, and on prosaic love to explain how they manage their love relationships—and examining them shed light on the complexity of love and marriage.

232

In Swidler's study, people drawing on the language of prosaic love "insist that love grows slowly or requires hard work."[2] This concept of prosaic realism can be extended beyond sustaining actions *within* marriage to the realistic concerns that underpin marriage preferences even *before* a marriage begins. When people permit love to include a measure of ambiguity, ambivalence, and everydayness, they challenge the dominant discourse of butterflies-in-the-stomach romance. Their awareness of their premarital practical concerns reveals that their attraction to a particular mate was not automatic and was driven by more than a winning smile.

The intersectional concerns deriving from familial and extrafamilial experiences that are documented throughout this book—such as color-coding, class calculations, and gendered and racialized stereotypes—are not just prosaic concerns but important concerns that drive spouse selection. By paying attention to the intersectional concerns that grow from the experience of inequality, we witness how personal experiences convert into preferences. Desires and needs may shift over the life course, and in a "culture of divorce" such shifts may lead to partnership dissolution, possibly succeeded by a new relationship.[3]

The United States boasts one of the highest levels of both marriage and divorce of any Western nation.[4] The divorce rate rose sharply during the 1960s and 1970s before leveling off and eventually declining. After 1960 the share of currently divorced or separated people in this country nearly tripled, rising from 5 percent in 1960 to 14 percent in 2008.[5] Most U.S. states passed liberal divorce laws in the 1970s, a decade marked by the distinction that "divorce overtook death as the primary means of marital dissolution."[6] By the 1980s, most states had some form of no-fault divorce.[7] All of these trends have eroded the notion that marriages last forever. These cycles of marriage and divorce demand attention.

Risk factors for divorce include:

> marrying as a teenager, being poor, experiencing unemployment, having a low level of education, living with one's future spouse or another partner prior to marriage, having a premarital birth, bringing children from a previous union into a new marriage . . . marrying someone of a different race, being in a second- or higher-order marriage, and growing up in a household without two continuously married parents.[8]

These variables may predict divorce, but it is unclear whether they *cause* divorce. This chapter is less concerned with the causes of marriage dissolution than with unpacking how people think about and experience union formation, separation, and repartnership. Moreover, not all unhappy marriages end. Some couples endure despite problems and experience ambivalence around marriage, while others successfully resolve marital conflict. "Marital ambivalence" characterizes a union that "simultaneously contain[s] both positive and negative aspects."[9] Ambivalence acknowledges that marital quality is rarely uniformly positive or negative and that both aspects instead "co-occur within close relationships"; the middle ground of ambivalence may be "a more accurate representation of marital processes."[10]

With the decline of "marriage culture"—the beliefs, symbols, and practices that reinforce marriage—and the introduction of "divorce culture"— the "symbols, beliefs, and practices that anticipate and reinforce divorce and, in the process, redefine marriage"—couples now recognize divorce as a possibility.[11] The next two sections delve into the process of divorce and then of remarriage. The third section empirically examines those who persist in a marriage despite conflict and ambivalence. The last section profiles a couple who found their love match in a first marriage as a result of specifying their intersectional needs and desires at the outset. The couples discussed in this chapter illustrate that love is a learning process in which people make an effort to know themselves, vet their romantic partners, strategize to dissolve relationships, or do the work of maintaining or improving their relationships.

DIVORCE TO ESCAPE DOMINATION

Sharon Cheng, a sixty-six-year-old Mexican American woman married to Russ, a Chinese American, was on her second marriage. Sharon—who said that she was often mistaken for Filipina—had dark eyes, a full face, dark-tan skin, and gray hair with flecks of black. She had married a Mexican American man at age nineteen to escape her authoritarian father. What Sharon did not count on, however, was the possibility of leaping from the frying pan into the fire—her husband turned out to be as domineering as her father. She intended her first marriage to be "satisficing": she "accept[ed] the first alternative that [was] 'good enough' to meet [her] needs or desires."[12] Except that it wasn't. After divorcing her first husband, Sharon spent over a decade as a single mother before marrying Russ.

A variation on the Latina women in chapter 2 who color-coded their childhood experience with a domineering Latino father, Sharon did not acquire an aversion to Latino men until *after* she was unhappily married to one. Only after suffering suffocating relationships with her father and her first husband did Sharon turn away from Latino men and direct her attention to non-Latino men. As an adult divorcée working in diverse Los Angeles, and possessing greater autonomy than she had at nineteen,

Sharon dated people from numerous racial groups. In her second marriage, Sharon achieved what she did not in the first: freedom to live her life outside of the gender norm restrictions that she associated with her Mexican heritage.

Sharon grew up in Chavez Ravine, a Mexican neighborhood whose residents were forcibly relocated in the 1950s for the development of Dodger Stadium. She lived there until she was ten years old, when "they came and evicted us. . . . They gave everybody money to move out." The family of nine moved into a Jewish area of town. Aside from nostalgic recollections about homemade Mexican food, Sharon painted a picture of her family as concerned with upward mobility, Americanness, and her strict father:

> My father was very strict . . . very, very protective of all of us. He wanted us
> to go to school, but the money wasn't there. . . . He was looking for upward
> mobility. . . . I don't feel a lot of association with the Mexican people that
> much, because he pulled us away a little bit. . . . There were a lot of white
> people, Jewish people [in the neighborhood]. . . . We weren't in East L.A. [a
> Latino-dense area]. We were . . . close to Chinatown.

The family's forced relocation due to the razing of Chavez Ravine to construct Dodger Stadium became conflated for Sharon with her memory of her father's quest for upward mobility, which the family coded as living close to Jewish and Chinese people.

The family's association of class ascension with whites and Chinese reveals the racial hierarchy of Los Angeles during her youth. Sharon called herself "American": "I'm an American first. . . . I see other people . . . really entrenched in the Mexican traditions . . . and I don't think we were raised that way. . . . I think it was . . . upward mobility, trying to assimilate into the mainstream." Drawing a generational distinction between herself and immigrants, as we saw with Bianca Stroeh in chapters 2 and 3, Sharon associated whites and Chinese with the "mainstream," with Mexicans outside the mainstream. This kind of logic is the basis for the racial erasing and racial easing strategies discussed in chapter 7.

Add this local racial hierarchy in which whites and Chinese represented upward mobility to Sharon's repressive Mexican-origin father and the result was her penchant for non-Mexican men. Sharon's authoritarian Mexican-origin father preferred that she marry a Mexican-origin man, with his preapproval; in his mind, living next door to whites and marrying them were two different propositions. Family has long served as a way to meet partners, and in this case Sharon met her first husband, Gael, through coethnic social networks: their parents belonged to the same social club.[13] I asked Sharon what type of qualities she had wanted in the people she dated, and she responded by discussing her father's tight grip on her social life:

> SHARON: My father was very strict, very Mexican, very strict. So dating wasn't really a thought in my mind.
>
> AUTHOR: Okay. And so then how did you come to be engaged and married to your first husband?
>
> SHARON: Initially . . . we were getting together as families. And then he started asking me to go out with him and his sister. . . . So it was chaperoned going-out initially. And then we started going out . . . to the drive-in, which was family-oriented . . . very simple things. . . . He asked me to marry him, and I was actually shocked. I hadn't ever thought about marriage until he asked me. I was just like shocked that he would ask me to marry him. 'Cuz it wasn't . . . coming up in my thoughts. . . . So yeah, so we got engaged.

It was probably a bad sign that Sharon was "shocked" at Gael's marriage proposal, apparently not having felt the love and passion that we typically think of as predating marriage. As a historical reminder, romance, emotional connection, and personal fulfillment are specific to modern-day marriage and may also be class- and race-specific as well.[14] Unlike Rosalinda Ornales, who declined a marriage proposal from someone she considered a friend and was not attracted to (chapter 6), Sharon accepted the proposal.

It was important to Sharon's father, but not to her, that she marry a Mexican-origin man. Families, especially parents, can exert a tremendous amount of influence on who their kin marry. Confrontations with racism, anxieties over cultural clashes, and antiblack racism can all contribute to the narrowing of options down to a same-race or same-ethnicity dating pool.[15] Sharon's father strongly favored a Mexican-origin mate for his daughter: "To my father, it was very important. My mother would go along with anything my father said. He ruled the household." Her father policed racial lines ("you just don't mix") to the point of discouraging her cross-racial friendships with boys, in which he worried that she "must be doing something [sexually] loose."

Accepting the meanings that her father attached to different racial groups, Sharon believed for a while that in-group romance was the only acceptable option: "I never thought of going out outside of my race." Then, having acted in accordance with the racial endogamy imperative enforced in her family of origin, Sharon moved from her father's home to her husband's home—from living under her father's authority to living under her husband's authority. The couple pushed up the wedding date from a year to six months—after a two-week breakup—because of Sharon's father: "We rushed it . . . because . . . my father was feeling like [he was] losing control of his daughter." The truncated dating period, chaperoned family dates, and speeded-up timeline to the wedding combined to prevent Sharon from uncovering how similar Gael and her father were: like her father, Gael was an alcoholic who had a hard time holding down a job. The similarities between her husband and her father ultimately led to her divorce.

Having traded a domineering father for a domineering husband, Sharon began to feel "something storming" inside herself in those oppressive environments—an emotional torrent that needed release. She explained that the release valve for domination in her youthful home had been marriage and in her married home it had been divorce:

SHARON: I was very quiet, reserved. There was something storming in me. . . . I went to see a psychologist, and he said that I was always running away from home. . . .

AUTHOR: So what was storming in you?

SHARON: Uh, being able to be without bindings, I guess. Being able to do things. [With] . . . the very strict father . . . I always felt like I had not gone through the different levels that you go through to being a woman, to being ready to be married. I was leaving home, escaping home, into marriage, which was now a different way of . . . being held in.

AUTHOR: . . . You go from your father's home to your husband's home. In either one, there were probably some rules about how to behave and be.

SHARON: Right. Yeah. . . . When I divorced . . . I broke all the rules and went out and danced and did a lot of things that I shouldn't have: drank and . . . a lot of things. [*laughs*] Broke the bonds. [I] felt like I was breaking the bonds. I felt like I wanted to try something, everything—everything that I could think of, I wanted to do it.

Describing her relationships with her father and first husband as "bindings," Sharon did not feel that she could mature and become independent when under the authority of a Latino man.

Fathers serve as either "models" or "anti-models" — that is, a man's children judge whether his behaviors should be replicated or compensated for.[16] This idea about repeating or repudiating a father's way of being has been applied to how new fathers parent their own children, but it can be extended to masculinity and family relationships generally.[17] Without conscious effort, people may seek out the familiar. As for Sharon, she married her first husband because his oppressive ways were comfortably uncomfortable: "When I first married, I felt like I was looking for my father's image with my husband." After accumulating some experiential knowledge, however, divorcées are better equipped to make more informed decisions in their next round of dating and remarriage. Unsatisfactory family-of-origin experiences can be a major impetus for people as they make the decisions that will chart their life trajectory.[18]

The model/antimodel framework can also be extended to major life choices such as marriage, divorce, and remarriage. While Latino interviewees viewed their domineering fathers as anti-models, their mothers were not let off the hook. Latino men got the lion's share of criticism, but their wives played a part in submitting to or tolerating their authoritarian behavior. The complement to Sharon's father's dominance was her mother's submission. As Sharon put it, "That bothered me a lot about my mother — that she felt like anything that my father said was right, whether it was or not. It was just supposed to be tolerated. That bothered me a lot." Children even blamed mothers who unsuccessfully resisted male domination through verbal or physical fights for putting up with an abusive situation. The core issue was a gender battle over control of one's life, as Sharon stated:

> My mother . . . was subservient. She went by what my father said, no matter what, whether he was right or wrong. . . . And when I got a divorce from my husband, I was possibly leaving my father, breaking away from everything. . . . I became . . . my own person. I see myself being stronger than I ever was as a young kid growing up. . . . I needed to rebel for those many years and find me.

For Sharon, part of "breaking away" was detaching herself from the models of both her father and her mother in order to develop as an individual and "find" herself. Families are starting points and agents of socialization, and yet they are not destiny: people can in fact resist and reject the socialization of their youths.

With both her father and mother as anti-models, Sharon learned through the unfolding of her love life who she wanted to *be* and who she wanted to *be with*. These lessons learned over the course of her life were the foundation for Sharon's negotiated desire: she wanted to be someone different from her mother, and she wanted to be with someone different from her father. As she learned these lessons, Sharon sharpened her needs and desires for a particular type of partner as a result of her first marriage. With the storm brewing, Sharon asserted herself through divorce, broke bonds, learned about herself, and ultimately entered into a second marriage that was very different from her first. Reflection on one's natal family system and a willingness to temper one's behaviors or demand different styles of relationships demonstrate that culture, including gender ideals, is not static but changes over family generations.[19] People can make mistakes, but they can later make different choices through breaking up unsatisfactory relationships, living solo, or repartnering.

As a divorced mother of two children, Sharon began to think that she needed to "settle down." As we will see with Audrey Figueroa, Sharon wanted the practical help that comes with a supportive marriage: "I was raising two children on my own, so I needed a shoulder to rely on, and it wasn't there, so it was hard." And yet Sharon was leery of introducing another man into her children's lives: "I had been divorced for a long time. I didn't feel comfortable having a man in my life with my children. I didn't want anybody to tell them what to do; so I had this aversion to having anyone come in and try to harm my children." Out of an instinct to protect her children, Sharon negotiated her way *out* of desire for heterosexual intimacy for a while. It had taken time and effort to break free from the "bindings" of two dominant men, and the stress of that experience had made her cautious.

Through the story of Sharon's experience of divorcing her first husband, being a single mother for over a decade, and then remarrying when her children were adults (ages twenty-five and thirty), we can see the progress of her life.[20] Her retrospective life story revealed the learning, development, and change she had undergone over time. Post-divorce, she learned about herself and about what she needed in a marital partner, and that helped her find Russ, to whom she had been married for sixteen years.

I asked Sharon about the type of man she thought she might marry the second time around. She replied that she had been categorically against marrying a Latino or Mexican: "It didn't . . . feel . . . like something I wanted to do. [To] marry someone who was Mexican . . . meant that someone was strict." Remembering that Gael was an alcoholic and struggled with job stability, Sharon learned from her first marriage that she "needed someone that was more upwardly mobile. . . . Someone who would say something and follow through." This lesson learned in her first marriage sharpened her desire for the traits she required in a second marriage. Sharon honed the list of qualities she desired and those she would not tolerate: "I was looking for something different the second time. . . . I had stopped drink-ing, so I didn't want to be with someone who was drinking. . . . Russ doesn't drink at all, so I thought that was great. [*laughs*] . . . I wanted someone more reliable." Russ also offered the upward mobility Sharon craved. He had been a government employee for decades and was financially supportive to her children, willing to provide money for college.

Sharon and Russ met through a mutual friend when they attended a vet-erans' organization social event. As with her first husband, social networks aided the introduction, but by this time her father had died and no longer had a vice grip on her life. When Sharon met Russ, "the idea of marriage wasn't really in my mind," but his positive attributes changed her mind. She explained: "I thought I needed to settle down. . . . And he wanted to travel, and that was so exciting to me. . . . And he was such a nice guy, so easygoing, and he has his work ethic . . . always working." In Russ she got an employed man whom she liked, who did not drink, and who offered her the stability she wanted.

Sharon and Russ's cross-racial minority intermarriage was aided by their local context. Russ was Chinese American, and the diversity of Los Angeles naturalized cross-racial friendships and romance; Sharon commented that she "had been raised to like all different kinds of people." Unlike in her youth, racial difference was no longer a barrier to romance when Sharon was an adult, a life stage when people have moved away from the sphere of parental influence and have more social power than they did in their youth.[21] Speaking to the wider racial climate, she pondered how the influ-ence of greater tolerance for intermarriage in the late twentieth century affected her confidence to engage in a mixed-race relationship:

> A long time ago it wasn't normal to go outside of your race. . . . I feel like I'm . . . the norm nowadays: the lady down the street [is] white and married to a Japanese man. . . . Now it's normal, before it wasn't. . . . At the time that I first married, I think [it] would have been a different time and I wouldn't have been able to handle it. Like I said, I was expected to marry a Mexican, because that's where my roots were—there wasn't a thought of . . . looking anywhere else. And my father was right there, so I definitely wouldn't have considered [marrying] . . . outside of my race.

Two factors had precluded Sharon's marrying a non-Latino as a late teen in the early 1960s: a historical milieu prior to the civil rights movement that was intolerant of intermarriage, and a father who personally oversaw her coethnic dating options.

As Sharon and I wrapped up our interview, she drove home the idea that love, like life, is a learning process. Life experience is required to make more knowledgeable, refined choices around love and marriage. Sharon concluded by speaking for herself and her husband (who was on his third marriage):

SHARON: My husband and I always felt that if we had met each other at a different time, we would never have married.

AUTHOR: Really? How come?

SHARON: We think we had to go through things before we got to the point where we married when we did. We were looking for different things in our life.

"We had to go through things" highlights how the sum of one's life experiences, from the natal family system to experiences beyond the family, sharpens the desire for a particular kind of person. Love and marriage are not spontaneously generated in a vacuum, but rather informed by life and situated in history, family dynamics, social circles, institutions, and local racial hierarchies. As Sharon's life progressed she acquired knowledge about herself and others and attempted to make more informed choices. A dance analogy for negotiated desire is applicable here: negotiating desire in the hope that one's choices will be pleasing requires as much attention and nimbleness as executing dance steps on the dance floor.

Although Sharon did not mention any difficulties between her and her husband, her notion that in earlier years they had been "looking for different things" opened up the possibility that her life—and her life with Russ—would continue to change. Some marriages last for decades of course, but the lived reality for many Americans is the "marriage-go-round" of partnering and repartnering.[22] Even though when she spoke with me Sharon was happy in her second marriage, her vision of love might continue to evolve.

Father figures loomed large for those Latina women who suffered under their domination. They either sought out similarly oppressive Latino husbands because their masculinity was familiar or outright rejected all Latino men. Few took the moderate approach of filtering out undesirable characteristics, though we will see an example of this in the Dominguez couple later in the chapter. In their first marriages, especially those entered into in the late teen years or early twenties, parental influence was strong in overseeing young people's dating and shaping their ideas about what type of partner was appropriate. As these Latina women respondents gained self-awareness and social power as they aged, they recognized their discomfort and took steps to dissolve those first relationships. In so doing, they rejected the socialization of their youth and crafted new desires that did not simply replicate natal family relationships that they had not appreciated in the first place. Insofar as repartnering or remarriage offers a second chance (or a higher-order chance) at love, these Latina women show us how both life and love proceed and how, with some self-awareness, we become better equipped to make more informed decisions that can improve our love lives.[23] Indeed, most people who marry at older ages report better-quality marriages.[24]

While Latino fathers cast a long shadow in the minds of their Latina daughters as they negotiated their dating and marital lives, Latina mothers did not have the same strong influence on their Latino sons. This gender difference in parental influence arose from the different gender norms for men and women: in general, respondents experienced their fathers as oppressive and their mothers as nurturing. The distaste of daughters and sons for their father's dominance directed the women's choice of marital partner (through either color-coding rejection or unwitting replication) and the men's development of masculinity (see chapter 6).[25] Mothers were overwhelmingly lauded as loving caretakers for the family and did not raise the same ire in their children as the fathers did. Daughters varied, however, in whether to take their mothers as models or anti-models: some were comfortable mirroring their mother's approach to femininity, whereas others updated what they considered female subservience. Sons appreciated their mothers' care for their families, criticized them less than did daughters, and did not report that their mothers influenced their vision of the women they might date in the future.

THE PRACTICALITIES OF STRESS, CONFLICT, AND REMARRIAGE

Audrey Figueroa, mother of Braedon Toledo (profiled in chapter 7), and Flor de Soto, mother of Jazmin Romo de Soto (profiled in chapter 6), reveal how conflicts around gender expectations and problematic extended family relationships give rise to divorce. Both Latina women, now single and in their fifties, were married and divorced twice to Mexican-descent men. These women exposed the common reasons I heard to account for divorce: stress around gender and conflictual relationships with a spouse's natal family.

For both Audrey and Flor, conflicts with their husbands about the responsibilities of husbands and wives led to divorce.[26] Both women were twice divorced for this reason. Flexibility in gender norms is key to stable relationships. Gender-flexible heterosexual couples in which men widen their conception of masculinity and perform household chores report greater marital satisfaction than those committed to a traditional breadwinner-homemaker divide.[27] Broadly defining "feminine" and "masculine" in ways that untie gender from specific duties is an adaptive response to stress that can preserve marriage. Since disagreements over the household division of labor reduce marital satisfaction, flexing definitions of gender and gender roles can rebalance gender inequality and help forge happier, more long-lasting heterosexual partnerships.

Audrey did not have a preference to marry another Latino, but in Los Angeles she had plenty of opportunity to fall in love with a Latino. She married her first husband, who was mixed Mexican and Italian, at age eighteen, right after high school. Her position as the oldest child in her natal home had readied her for domestic care work and shaped her goals:

> At a very young age . . . I did the cooking, the cleaning, the caring, the loving of the younger siblings all of my life. . . . We got up every morning and we cleaned. . . . It was what was expected. . . . [When] I was the eldest [child] in the house . . . I took care of the younger kids, cooked dinner . . . while my mother worked. . . . So that part of me was ready. And my goal in life at that point in time was to grow up, get married, and be a mom because I'm so good at it.

Audrey and her husband had their first child three years after they wed. Unexpectedly, "the whole [relationship] dynamics changed with the child." Audrey's husband left her when the children were ages one and three and, as the breadwinner, took his financial resources with him; her standard of living immediately plummeted.[28] She attributed his flight from the marriage to his being "overwhelmed" and "too young" at age twenty-four for the "responsibility of a wife and two children." Here Audrey tapped into the idea of an "expressive divorce," which derives from the American notion of "expressive individualism": "emphasiz[ing] the development of one's sense of self, the pursuit of emotional satisfaction, and the expression of one's feelings."[29] She remarked, "I think he was trying to find himself." Marrying at a young age, being overwhelmed by responsibility, and yearning to discover himself apart from a family all contributed to the departure of Audrey's first husband from the family.

How did Audrey's experience with her first husband inform her marriage decision the second time? What did she learn? Since her husband's unpreparedness was presumably due to his youth, Audrey remedied the age issue by selecting a man thirteen years her senior, "thinking older was better." She directly applied a lesson learned from her first marriage to her selection of a second spouse. Her error in judgment, however, was in overemphasizing age as a factor contributing to the breakup of her first marriage. She correctly identified gender relations, however, as another source of marital conflict. She also learned in her first marriage to avoid someone who ducked out of domestic responsibilities.

But how could Audrey, or anyone, be assured of what life will look like after saying, "I do"? She did the best she could: she had frank discussions with her second husband, Benny, before they married. Using prior experience as a guide, Audrey tried to protect herself from marital conflict over gender expectations by being forthright about the household division of labor she wanted:

> I knew that his family was kind of traditional. But we'd had that conversation in advance. I was very up front. . . . I don't cower down. I'm very vocal. I tell him exactly what I wanted, what I was looking for. So we had that conversation. . . . I'm more than willing to do my fair share, but I'm not doing it all.

Gender flexibility was critical to Audrey, and she communicated this to Benny. She used hindsight about her first marriage to negotiate her desires in her second marriage. Identifying age difference and clashing gender norms as factors contributing to the unraveling of her first marriage, Audrey selected an older man and conveyed her stance on gender. Despite her self-awareness and clear communication, however, gender again became a point of contention. Audrey related the conflict around gender she faced with Benny:

> The turning point . . . [was] the day he told me he didn't have any underwear in his drawer. I got so angry. I just saw like black. And all I said to him at that point was, "I suggest you turn the ones you have on inside out. I've got to go to work." And I left. And I left him standing there trying to figure out what he was going to do. . . . Take full responsibility. . . . I mean, he's thirteen years older than I am. . . . You cannot hold me accountable because you opened your drawer and there was no underwear in there. Am I supposed to go check too? . . . That was the [last] straw.

In an American context where "the ideology of gender quality has increasingly contested the reigning ideology of male dominance in marriage," former spouses complained that "conflict over roles" was a principal cause for marriage dissolution.[30] Despite the fact that "from that point on he washed his own clothes," the tension in Audrey's marriage around gendered responsibilities never diminished. In marriage, each partner's definitions of reality are repeatedly cross-checked against the other's, and difficulty ensues if the result is a mismatch or a lack of validation. Given this discrepancy in their "definitions of reality," it is no surprise that the marriage broke up.[31] Audrey left the house three years after the underwear drawer argument.

Benny's family of origin also influenced their marriage: his mother enforced a narrow definition of masculinity and femininity that was incompatible with Audrey's spoken desires. Audrey's mother-in-law interfered with their formation of an agreeable home life. Given Audrey's blunt discussion with Benny before marriage, his retreat into a "traditional" gender strategy was an unwelcome surprise.[32] Audrey summarized her second husband's natal family culture around gender, separating herself from this version of a "Hispanic family":

> All the women took care of the men. Thanksgivings, all the men were served first and the women ate second. To me, that's more of a . . . Hispanic family. That's more their culture. I say "their" because . . . I was foreign to it. . . . [The women] did everything, and the men did sit around and do nothing. Absolutely zero . . . but work and bring home the paycheck. And then they deserved to do whatever they wanted to do.

Audrey retreated from the Hispanic group label, saying, "[Hispanic is] my ethnic background [but] I'm not up on culture."

To Audrey's dismay, her mother-in-law attempted to enforce her gendered vision of family dynamics. Audrey was very clear about what type of woman she was, stressing that Benny "didn't marry a woman like that—[very subservient]. He knew that." As the marriage carried on, Audrey's mother-in-law wielded her influence: "In the very beginning, [my way] was accepted. The longer we were married . . . the less he became the man that I thought I had married. [His] mother started saying, 'Well, aren't you going to serve him?'" Audrey was insistent: "I said, 'I'm sorry, the last time I checked you had two arms and two legs.' I'm not serving him." According to Audrey's mother-in-law, she was failing at being a proper wife: "His mother was very influential in what he should be expecting and . . . receiving. . . . His mother would bring it up." Feeling criticized, Audrey recoiled from her husband's family of origin, yet he continued to be swayed by them: "The more I didn't like the family, the more I wanted to pull back. . . . He kept going [to see them], and then he'd bring it back to home." The conflict devolved into angry verbal arguments, with one fight nearly ending in a physical confrontation: "That day I started packing." Disagreements over how husbands and wives should treat each other and the household tasks they should perform, intensified by extended family, led to Audrey's second divorce. Her relationship with her mother-in-law only exacerbated the existing tension around gender flexibility.

All relationships go through changes, but love requires nurturance. As Audrey pondered the evolution and demise of her second marriage, she charted the changes from courtship to marriage. She philosophized that if one person refuses to nourish the love, then it will die:

> He promised me the world. The home, the father-figure for my kids. Blah, blah, blah, blah. . . . He courted me, love notes at my car, trinkets at my door, flowers being sent. . . . I've never been materialistic. I'm about love. Love is so inexpensive. And you just have to give it and receive it. But you've got to give and nurture. . . . If you're not nurturing, things start to wither away and die. . . . That's . . . the analogy that I gave him. . . . In the end he was a sponge and sucked the life out of me.

Here Audrey expressed that relationships can be tenuous, uneven, and changeable. She went to counseling to try to save her second marriage, but to no avail because her husband had checked out of the marriage, despite still sharing a home. She was disappointed at the prospect of another divorce, especially since she had tried to be smarter in selecting her second husband:

> I really thought I was going to change this. I tried counseling. Two marriages failed. See, I'm looking at myself: two marriages and I'm failing again. And I can't fail. . . . I was just getting to accept the fact that my first marriage had really ended, and I remarried thinking this was a whole lot different, this was going to be better. . . . And I tried so much harder with my second marriage than I did with my first.

Stressing her own action in phrases like "I tried so much harder" and "I'm failing again," Audrey was overlooking for the moment the fact that she was not alone in the marriage and that there was also an external influence (his mother) working contrary to her interests. One argument of this book is that natal family systems exert a powerful influence on what both partners want in a marriage. I was not able to interview Audrey's first or second husband, but it is no stretch to say that Benny's family of origin shaped his desire for a particular kind of wife and persisted in reinforcing this idea of a wife even when he married someone who told him she did not fit that description. Audrey and Benny were a typical couple headed for divorce in that a husband's refusal to accept influence from his wife is a key factor predicting divorce.[33]

Like Audrey, Flor married and divorced two Latino men, in part owing to the interference of an overbearing mother-in-law. But unlike Audrey in California, Flor, who moved between Kansas and Mexico, sought out Mexican-origin men because she perceived them as more respectful than white American men. I met Flor de Soto at her daughter Jazmin's store in downtown Lawrence, Kansas, where she sat knitting a hat when not working the cash register. Flor was born in Mexico City, her father's hometown, and then moved to her Mexican American mother's hometown of LeCompton, Kansas, when she was five years old.

Family and church are chief ways in which Latinos in Kansas connect to their heritage. Flor's two intragroup marriages did not happen by accident but were the result of her preference for sharing Mexican culture. She was firm about her cultural tastes: "I love my Latin music. I love my food. I like the idea of being with family; not just on holidays." Flor marked a distinction between herself and American men: "I love American men. [But] they're not for me. They're good people, but their ways I don't feel like I could live with. I just couldn't." When I asked her to elaborate, she pointed to child-rearing practices that she disagreed with: "Some . . . American [friends] tell me, 'Oh, I can't wait until my son turns eighteen so he can get out of the house.' . . . They're trying to kick their kids out already. We're not like that. We never kick our kids out until they're ready to go." Flor dismissed American men as culturally incompatible with her owing to their relative lack of family orientation. Although Latino families have been linked to the notion of familism—"a form of family values in which the needs of the family as a group are more important than the needs of any individual family member"—in truth, " 'family values' are important in all cultures."[34] Flor may have been generalizing about Americans, but her prior experience with them had suggested to her that they did not place the same premium on family cohesion that she did.

Flor also disliked white men's approach to courtship and sex. She viewed sexual propriety as a virtue, remarking, "In Mexico, you do not have sex with [men] until it's time for a marriage. They give you your respect." She contrasted this sexual more with the permissiveness around sexuality she saw in the United States and reflected on her daughter's experience: "She dated a lot of American [meaning white] young men, and they believed that she was supposed to have sex with them!?! And because she didn't she was real different." Juxtaposing Mexican and American sexual practices, Flor perceived a cultural gulf between the two groups. By extolling her ethnic culture as principled, she asserted its superiority over a degraded mainstream U.S. culture.[35] Flor portrayed Latina women as sexually modest and dedicated to family, Latino men as desirous of these virtues, and white men as aggressive and disrespectful. This imagery had reinforced the decisions both she and her daughter had made to marry Latino men.

Flor did not say that she felt sexual pressure from white men herself, but pointed out instead their lack of respect and deference to women. She recalled being asked out by another man while already out on a date. That her date, a white man, was unperturbed "really, really bugged" her and sent a signal that she interpreted as disrespect. She imagined a Latino man reacting differently, saying, "Hey, have respect, she's with me," a retort that "would make you feel like a real woman." Although Flor was racializing these men's (real and imagined) reactions, her experience matched up with other Latinas' tales of white men who tokenized, sexualized (see chapter 5), or disrespected them. In reaction, Flor rejected white men. Not feeling properly valued was foundational to her decision to exclude white men, a decision she made as a result of real-life experience. By investigating why people judge others not to be proper fits and observing how they turn their attention to other categories of people in response, we learn how dating "failures" or "mismatches" inform future decisions.

In Flor's case, her natal family's endorsement of Latino intramarriage and her predilection for shared culture, male deference, and control of her sexuality set the stage for her endogamous marriage. Her father counseled her: "It's hard to . . . live with somebody for the rest of your life. But it's even harder if you guys don't even understand [each other's] culture. . . . He never told me, 'No, no black. No white.' . . . [But] I feel like that's what his message was. [I did not marry another Latino] because I . . . followed his way of thinking. It was because I could *feel it*." Her firsthand experience with romantic failures with white men, combined with encouragement from her family of origin toward in-group romance, persuaded Flor to refine her desires toward Latino men.

In addition to cultural favoritism, Flor selected her first husband, a Chicano from Texas who became the father of her daughter Jazmin, by relying on contacts to introduce her to coethnics. Flor depended on social networks to facilitate her in-group dating in a Midwestern context where the Latino population was 8.7 percent in 1980 (which was around the time she was in search of a Latino husband), as compared to the Latino population in the West, which was 42.7 percent.[36] Flor's father, a small business owner, was the first to meet Flor's husband-to-be, who had just returned from military service. "He went to Vietnam. . . . He had become a friend of my dad's. My dad was running the bar. . . . That's how we met: there at the bar." In Kansas, social networks are more vital to the facilitation of in-group romance than in California, where opportunities to meet other Latinos abound. Family-based social networks were crucial for both Flor and Flor's daughter Jazmin in meeting their husbands. In both cases, the parent met the future spouse first, approved of him for the daughter, and then facilitated an introduction . . . at the very same family-owned restaurant-bar.

Married for twelve years, Flor and her husband "weren't getting along [and] were separated for quite a few years" before he died. "It wasn't working out very well," yet Flor liked the practical support she received when the marriage functioned smoothly. After her first husband passed away, Flor went to Mexico and met her second husband, who was a Mexican national with a postgraduate degree. Family networks again figured prominently in the relationship: Mauricio was a family friend living with her parents and working at their restaurant. Flor let me in on the logic that led to their marriage:

> FLOR: He was like my backup. The truth is, I didn't really love him at first. I felt like, "Oh my God. What am I going to do now?" I thought, "Well, I'll be okay. I'll be okay." But he was always backing me up and backing me up and we got married. The truth is, he was very good to me.
>
> AUTHOR: Did you grow to love him?
>
> FLOR: Yes, a lot. A lot.

Flor was practical about her second husband: he was a preapproved family friend, and after the death of her first husband left her a single mother, she wanted someone who would "back her up." She wanted a supportive adult in the home, even if she did not amorously love him in the beginning. When I asked if her marriage was driven by desire to add a second income to the household, she responded:

> Oh, no, no. . . . I made good money. It wasn't so much that. . . . I think when you have a child, you need somebody to be hugging on you and tell you it's going to be okay. . . . It's something I had never needed in my life, but I did at that moment. He was there, and he did a really good job of it. So, okay, I'll take advantage of it. When he asked me to, let's get married, I go, "Oh, but I don't even love you. I like you a lot." He goes, "You'll love me because I'll be good to you. I'll do anything for you." "Okay, let's get married." I was like that. Well, let's get married then.

When their marriage ends, women are less likely than men to say that they want to get married again.[37] Hedging on making a legal commitment, Flor suggested to Mauricio that they cohabitate instead—a trend that has gained in prevalence and that most view as a step toward marriage.[38] Mauricio retorted that he wanted to marry her to give her "respect . . . the place that a woman should have." Considering living together outside of marriage dishonorable, Mauricio pushed for marriage even when he knew that Flor did not (yet) love him. In light of Flor's preference for respect, it is no wonder that she was won over by Mauricio's offer of a "marriage of respect" that included practical support.[39]

Although contemporary marriages are commonly thought of as founded on love, stories like Flor and Mauricio's remind us that love waxes and wanes and does not always predate a wedding. Flor and Jazmin moved to Mexico to live with Mauricio, but as with Audrey, the influence of an overbearing mother-in-law contributed to their breakup after thirteen years. Flor had sought someone who was devoted to family, but the problem was that Mauricio's allegiance was cast too far in the direction of his mother. She recounted her impressions of her mother-in-law:

> I don't think his mom ever accepted [that he married] me. . . . [She was] very jealous. He was . . . her baby, you know. She was hoping that since he had a good education . . . that he would . . . stay home and give her more. He didn't. . . . So she didn't get all that rich [stuff] that she wanted from him. . . . She was hoping, "As soon as my son is done, he's going to get a great job and he's going to get me [luxuries]." . . . It wasn't like that.

The fact that Mauricio directed most of his financial resources to his marital family, not his mother, sowed seeds of resentment with his mother. Flor's troubled relationship with her mother-in-law centered on allocations of time, mental energy, and dollars. A battle ensued over whether she, as Mauricio's wife, or Mauricio's mother would have greater influence in his life.

Calling her relationship with her mother-in-law "pretty bad" once her husband was earning a high income, Flor described his mother as jealous:

> She was so unhappy. She liked saying, "Oh my God. He's making all this money and giving [his wife] a new car, new house." She was jealous. He bought her a lot of stuff, though. But it was like, "Why do you have to buy your mom all this when we need this, we need that? We're just getting started." . . . He wouldn't even tell me he gave [money] to her, but I could see in the checkbook the big checks he kept on giving his mom.

Mauricio's financial contributions to his mother's household economy raised Flor's ire because, as a young couple, they were working to establish their home together. Living in the same town, Flor began to decline invitations to socialize with her mother-in-law to avoid confrontation: "I didn't want to argue with her. She would act like she's very nice when [my husband] was around, but when he was not there she was really wicked. She was really mean." In the end Flor relented and left Mauricio, telling him: "You can have lots of wives, but you can only have one mother. So keep your mom. . . . I'm not fighting with her over you." With the help of her father, Flor moved out when Mauricio was on a business trip and lived with her father temporarily during the divorce process. She and Mauricio conversed a year later. Flor confided: "We went for dinner and we talked about what happened. . . . He wanted me to come back to him. . . . I told him I couldn't. It was really very mean of me, but I told him, 'As long as your mom's alive, I could never be around you.' "

Promising Flor the world during their courtship, Mauricio did not moderate his relationship with his mother or intercede when tension mounted. Flor's adversarial relationship with her mother-in-law provoked her to leave her husband. Ironically, Flor had prized Mauricio's family orientation, especially as a newly single mother to a toddler, but it was this virtue that fomented the demise of their marriage. This personal experience inflected the marriage advice Flor gave her daughter Jazmin:

> You have to love your in-laws because they're a part of him. If you don't get along with them, you're not going to have a good life, especially being a Latina. You know, the family thing. . . . These [Latin] guys are close to their families. . . . So if you don't get along with them—the brothers and sisters and the mom and the dad—then you're in trouble because you're not going to have a very good life with them.

Just as personal experience shapes one's decision about who to marry, so too does it contour one's marriage advice for the next generation.

These narratives about Audrey's and Flor's marriages and divorces remind us that in the modern age Americans elect to marry, divorce, and repartner at high rates.[40] Gender norm incongruities can foment marital tension and, when severe, prompt divorce. Natal family bonds can interfere with happy marriages, especially when meddlesome parents-in-law impose ill-fitting gender relations on the couple. Examining the process of remarriage suggests that life is a learning curve: people are inclined to learn from past relationships as they revise their needs for successive relationships.

LIVING THROUGH MARITAL TROUBLES AND AMBIVALENCE

Marriages can have rocky patches. In times of difficulty, conflict, or uncertainty, couples face a fork in the road: Will they stay together, despite their ambivalence, or will they part ways? This section profiles couples who lived through tough times; some continued to be plagued by unresolved tension and doubt about their marriage, and others resolved their conflicts.

The story of Celeste Collins, featured in chapters 2 and 3, illustrates that even getting the type of man one wants has unforeseen consequences that need to be reckoned with. In color-coding her experiences with her domineering father, Celeste rejected Latino men and favored white men. She married Doug, a nice, peaceful white man. Years into their marriage, Celeste grew resentful because she felt that she was carrying more of the load of the relationship, including earning more money than her husband. Celeste and Doug went to marriage counseling to vent and try to fix their problems. Her husband was nurturing like her mother, not dominant like her father. In counseling, she realized that if she had selected a more dominant mate, she would have suffered in more serious ways. I asked Celeste, "How have your expectations of individual freedom worked out since marrying somebody not like your father?" She replied:

> A couple of years ago, we had some problems in our marriage and . . . went to marriage counseling. After a lot of analysis, the counselor and I decided that one of the things . . . that was causing us problems was Doug's lack of being a strong male person. That had been my experience: that the male would be very much setting the path. . . . I was more taking on that role of saying, "Okay, the kids need this. . . . " I made the decision, really. We consulted, obviously, but I recognized that there was a problem, that changes needed to be made. . . . I just felt like, here I am, working a very demanding job and having to make some of these big decisions. . . . I sort of resented that, and thought, "Wouldn't it be nice to have the male, you know, *do* that for me so I wouldn't have to do that." . . . I had that expectation, and Doug wasn't fulfilling that. My counselor helped me understand that if I *had chosen* a person like my dad, I probably wouldn't be where I am. Because he would expect things from me that I didn't want to give him. So I couldn't really have it both ways. . . . I'm at peace with that now. I do have somebody that's more like my mother and less like my father. And so we're in a much better place. . . . I understand that now, and I appreciate the things that he does, and I understand that we . . . have worked out our roles. . . . So it seems to be working.

The marital discontent that Celeste reported was a case of "you get what you wish for," followed by a realization about the drawbacks of wishes fulfilled. Celeste picked a marital partner who did not replicate her dad's authoritarianism and then begrudged her husband's lack of the qualities associated with hegemonic masculinity, such as self-assurance, control, and decision-making acuity. In her natal family system, she had been socialized to expect that the man "set the path," and yet she recoiled against that model and deliberately pursued an alternative model in which *she* would be more in charge of "setting the path." She could not have it both ways. The counselor put the couple's marital troubles in perspective, showing Celeste that her disaffection resulted from her negotiated desire—her proactive choice to avoid her father's domineering traits.

Celeste's story also illustrates prosaic love: the everyday efforts invested in a relationship—or the "marital work," which "involves the ongoing reflexive and relational work necessary to create, sustain, and reproduce a gratifying marriage."[41] Seeking professional help to gain insight into her life choices was a form of marital work that reminded Celeste of how she had negotiated her desire before marriage. Like any deal, some negotiated desires incur costs in order to achieve one's priorities. Once Celeste recalled that her union was based on her own version of negotiated desire— a uniquely crafted set of aspirations for a partner and a relationship that still held true—she made peace with her uneasiness and transitioned to a "much better place" in her marriage.

Vincent Venegas and Raven Salazar, highlighted in chapter 7, argued about their personality styles, how they spent time, and sex. Vincent was introverted, quiet, and a homebody who wanted to spend a lot of time with his wife. Raven, on the other hand, was extroverted, vivacious, and involved in community leadership in addition to her full-time job. Married for nearly two decades, since they were teenagers, the couple negotiated their varying needs for companionship and physical affection. Raven explained their personality differences: "He just wants to be with me. That's great that he loves me that much. But I'm an extrovert. I need other people. It doesn't mean that because I need other people I love him less, but that's how he feels. So I've tried to reassure him but sometimes . . . we clash. Those have been the arguments." Their need for each other's physical presence was in conflict with their need to be more socially active. Raven's reassurances were not enough, and this rift had been a long-running source of marital discord.

Perhaps in reaction to what Vincent perceived as a lack of attention from his wife, he was flirtatious with other women. Both Raven and Vincent identified his sexual playfulness bordering on infidelity as dangerous for their marriage. Raven expanded:

He's had an issue with flirting with women. . . . I'm like, "That's not cool. Don't disrespect me and . . . hurt my feelings. I've never done that to you with another man." He will [do things] in front of me . . . like . . . massaging other women. I'm just like, "That's not appropriate." . . . We've had our issues about that. He downloaded one of my friend's pictures onto his phone in a bikini. I've had to say, "Why are you doing these things?" . . . I'd say, "Let's look into this and see why it's happening so that we can try to stop it before you end up in a bad divorce and before you end up losing me."

In citing divorce as an option if Vincent's flirtation with other women did not cease, Raven was positioning their marriage as "contingent," as conditional on mutual respect. As a counterpoint to "marriage as forever," contingent marriages, Karla Hackstaff notes, work to the advantage of women who are seeking greater equality: "Paradoxically, a sense of contingency can enable wives to elicit values such as commitment, responsibility, care-taking, and equality. In short, it provides a powerful lever to set the terms of marriage. . . . Contingent marriage may be crucial for redefining marriage in an egalitarian direction."[42] In patriarchal societies, men are rewarded with unearned advantage inside and outside the home and women are left to contend with the expectation of male authority. By marking their marriage as contingent and based on mutual agreement that can be rescinded, Raven countered Vincent's disregard for their union by threatening to topple it.

Reporting that they had gone around and around with the issue of sexuality unhinged from the marriage more than three times over the years, Raven recounted:

> Each time we've dived into why. Many times he felt neglected. I thought okay, when I was PTA [Parent-Teacher Association] president . . . I did so much. Sure, something had to be sacrificed, and that was my marriage, because he never spoke up. . . . No, instead I would be emailing at two o'clock in the morning. He'd be standing naked with his penis in my [face] . . . wanting attention. I'd be like, "C'mon. Let me just finish." He'd be like, "Are you serious?" I'd want him to wait for me. Just wait. . . . Two years took a toll. At the end of [the two years of being PTA president], it was really bad.

Vincent felt that any extra time Raven had available should be spent with him, not doing community service. The tension mounted and played out in their sex life. In this vivid scene, Raven was composing an email late one night when Vincent graphically suggested sex. Their priorities clashing, Vincent felt neglected. But absent Vincent expressing his feelings, Raven was left to guess at them, contend with his flirtation with other women, and determine how to respond to his naked plea for sexual attention.

Raven and Vincent's communication breakdown (a top reason for divorce) allowed Vincent's feeling of neglect to fester and transmogrify into salacious behavior outside of the marriage.[43] Two months after the downloaded bikini picture incident, the "icing on the cake" occurred when a neighbor informed Raven that on two occasions Vincent had fondled another neighbor when she was not home. She angrily confronted her husband about the accusation: "I said to my husband, 'You better tell me. Shit is about to hit the fan like never before.' So then he said, 'Well, I didn't do anything with her, but I did flirt heavily.'" Hearing two versions of the story—one that involved sexual touching and another that did not—Raven concluded, "I'll never know what really happened." In the course of the heated conversation, it became clear that the woman had been inside their house when Raven was at a PTA meeting. This realization put into stark relief the couple's struggle over Raven's priorities: was she caring for the community or for her husband?

Moreover, the couple had divergent expectations about how to spend leisure time. Vincent vented his frustration with his wife's use of care and time by engaging in illicit conduct when she was occupied in the activity that stoked his jealousy. Raven detailed her reaction, noting with hurt that her husband had disrespected their marriage when she was trying to improve the community while working full-time and doing the "second shift" at home:[44] "There I was busting my ass for the community. . . . I had to work full-time. I was PTA president. I would come home and have to still [clean] the house. . . . And they had to be fed. So I said, 'Wow. You know, there I was. And there you were doing that.' " Declaring that "men don't think," Raven recognized that unresolved marital problems might tempt a partner to retaliate through promiscuous behavior outside the marriage.

Vincent confirmed Raven's account: "I had a big problem flirting. . . . I wouldn't do it [to] her face. . . . It has caused problems, the flirting. It wasn't 'just flirting' once and . . . that's it. . . . What I tell her is, 'I wasn't looking to replace you. I wasn't looking to have an affair. I was just flirting and trying to get a reaction out of somebody.' " Feeling underappreciated by his wife, Vincent was titillated by sexual attention he received elsewhere. He chose to "get a reaction out of somebody," which, in turn, got a reaction out of his wife and stirred up problems at home. During this difficult period, his flirtation "escalated" to an online space where he reconnected with a flame from high school:

> I got in big trouble . . . because I had a crush on a high school sweetheart. She emailed me like, "Is that you?" She got me all excited. . . . I basically told her how I felt about her back in high school and that I couldn't come to tell her [then] and that I was hoping that we would meet each other again. Raven found the email, and I'm sure you can speculate on that. At that point . . . [my wife's priorities were] kids, family, PTA, then me. . . . She definitely hadn't realized that. She was oblivious to it happening till it manifested itself in that email.

Whether "it" referred to his feeling of neglect, being last on Raven's list of priorities, or his flirtation with other women is almost inconsequential because all of these possibilities were connected. Vincent's lascivious behavior had conjured up extramarital female attention, but it could also be read as a plea for attention from his wife—which, when he got it, was now directed toward him negatively.

Couples can improve a faltering relationship. Upon encountering problems, pairs can renegotiate desire. I asked Vincent, "Did you [two] adjust things as a result?" He confirmed, "Yeah, definitely. She's tried to spend more time with me. We go for walks, go get coffee. What she still doesn't get, though, is that the walks are for her. The coffee is for her. It's not my activity." In this negotiation, though there was room to include some of Vincent's chosen activities in their time together, Vincent's concession was to join Raven in activities she enjoyed for the sake of companionship. Examples like this highlight not only the imperfections in relationships but also their adaptability.

Saying that Vincent was "not good at communication . . . he feels neglected," Raven noted that she had "been compassionate towards him and loved him." Compassion and love had helped them move beyond their marital problems, if not solve them. For Vincent's part, when he and his wife had a conflict, Raven reported, "he would take it super hard, like he really f——ed up." This display of guilt and sorrow was an expression of Vincent's concern for his family, which he did not want to lose, despite engaging in behavior that might warrant it. In speaking to the ambivalence embedded in imperfect marriages, Raven revealed that the decision to stay or go could be a nightly decision:

> He wasn't the best dad when we were younger. Many times when I would go to bed I would think, "I have to leave him." . . . He wanted . . . to be . . . really strict. He didn't have as much compassion for the boys. I think he was jealous almost. He wanted to be just with me. He wanted me to himself. . . . He had unrealistic expectations of kids. I was like, "They're just kids." At times, what he would do . . . well, I felt it was abuse. It wasn't physical abuse, but it was definitely emotional abuse. He would grab them from the neck from behind and just . . . the child would then just be subservient. I was like, "You break their spirit like that." So yeah . . . I've had to say to him, "That's not okay." . . . Throughout, though, always, he's been open to working on things. . . . It wasn't that he was being a bad guy. . . . It was beyond his control—tunnel-vision anger.

The everyday quality of these decisions to stay in or leave a marriage shows the "prosaicness" of prosaic love. And even prosaic love has limits and can come with demands for modified behavior. As teen parents, Raven and Vincent grew up together as they learned how to be in a marriage and how to parent.

Both Raven and Vincent crafted their parenting strategies as a reaction to how they were parented by their own mother and father (although Vincent mirrored his father's undesirable behavior before he course-corrected):[45]

Vincent would get so upset at the kids dropping something. I'm like, "It's okay. What's the big deal? Let's just pick it up." He was raised with . . . the . . . [perspective that the] kid is just crying 'cuz kids whine . . . they're not really crying for some real reason. [Then the father says,] "Now . . . I'm going to hit you so you can really cry." Really stupid stuff like that. It comes from our own childhood. I would say to him, "You know, you need to question that." . . . I just knew instinctively. I would say to him, ". . . Just be nice." . . . They're little humans. . . . In our families [of origin], basically the children were never spoken to. The children were just children; almost like a second-class citizen in the household. We weren't abused but . . . we weren't developed. We weren't enriched. . . . [Our parents were] adults that don't realize what they are doing is affecting the next generation. The more conscious you are of that, the more you are going to be able to effect the change. I've always told Vincent since the beginning, "I want to change this cycle." And it's not been an easy cycle to change.

As seen in the "constrained cultivation" section of chapter 7, this couple aspired to provide more financial and emotional resources for their children than they had as children. They were criticized by those who coded middle-class provisions as white, an insult that challenged the family's racial identity. Raven sidestepped these racialized insults by asserting that she too "wants to do the good stuff" and refusing to view the provision of resources for children as the province of any one racial group.

Struggles in marriage range from interpersonal issues to doubts about whether one's partner was the right choice, to intimacy, to how to raise children. These conflicts produce mixed feelings. By taking an honest look at the inner workings of intimate relationships, we honor the messiness of marriage and see how people navigate muddy marital waters. This view of how and why marriages persist with ambivalence tarnishes mythic love with a dash of reality, adding a dimension to the notion of prosaic love. The couples in this section remained together; whether they will do so for the rest of their lives remains to be seen, but meanwhile, they show us that people stay in ambivalent marriages when they observe promising change or when their engagement in marital work has given them reason for optimism.

QUALITY-CODING AND GETTING IT RIGHT: SEARCHING FOR AND FINDING "THE ONE"

Heidi and Sal Dominguez, both Mexican-origin, were attentive to qualities they wanted in a spouse, and each was concerned about actually finding such a person; thus, once they found each other, they held on tight. At fifty-nine and sixty-six years old respectively, Heidi and Sal were thirty-four years into a happy marriage. This couple was worthy of an in-depth examination for a few reasons. First, like most couples in the United States, they married someone belonging to their same racial group and at their same education level. Second, they each learned from their natal families and social experiences about what they did and did not want in a partner, and they stuck with those priorities until they found someone who fit the bill. Finally, the Dominguezes illustrate the happiness that people can achieve in marriage when they have found their match.

Heidi was born in Denver but soon moved with her family to South Central Los Angeles (which was a Caucasian neighborhood before transitioning to predominantly black) because of her father's asthma. She was an attractive older woman with dark hair, pale skin, and blue eyes, her unwrinkled skin lending her a youthful appearance. With deep roots in Colorado, she referred to herself a "fifth-generation Hispanic" who grew up in a way that she called "pretty sheltered." Heidi's family moved from South Central L.A., where her family had become the numerical minority as "the only nonblack family," to Pico Rivera when she was ten years old. Before the family relocated, Heidi learned about the local racial hierarchy through notions of hair beauty:

> I had long curly hair, and every Sunday my mom made sausage curls [that] came down [my shoulders]. And all my girlfriends were black and . . . on Saturday morning . . . they would be in the kitchen pulling their hair with a hot comb. . . . Nobody actually said, "Oh, I like your hair better," but they always wanted to touch [it]. By Monday morning my hair was handled all the time.

Living among African Americans in South Central L.A. "really shaped" Heidi and strengthened her belief in equality between Latinos and blacks. Heidi's experience reveals a black-brown solidarity due to similar positions of racial subordination, as seen in the couples in chapter 4 who experienced a shared marginalization.[46] Heidi pondered the impact of growing up in South Central L.A. on her:

> I went through all those years with the riots and people hating black people and not understanding black people—they were my friends, they were my neighbors, they were like "auntie," they were family. My dad rescued a black woman from a burning house. . . . I never thought that being black was "less than." I went through the era when it was, and according to my dad, we were "less than" too, to most of society.

Growing up in South Central Los Angeles as it transitioned from white to black, Heidi learned about racial difference through conceptions of hair beauty as well as her experience of cross-racial friendship bonds that challenged a rigid racial hierarchy.

Heidi described her father as a "real negative person" who had "a lot of problems," including alcoholism. To what extent racism was a precipitating factor for these issues no one could say for sure, but Heidi recalled that her father endured racialized punishment as a child. This unearned punishment compelled him to quit school in the third grade:

> His teachers used to hit him with a ruler on the hand. Every day he got it. . . . He had a terrible experience. . . . He decided when we was very young . . . [that he would] never teach his children Spanish because of his negative experiences. So he was self-taught, [a] very intelligent man, but he never made it past third grade. He . . . told us there were barbershop signs that said: No MEXICANS OR DOGS.

Institutional discrimination, in the form of teachers wielding rulers and storefront signs that reduced Mexicans to animals, led to the premature exit from school of Heidi's father. These experiences in the public sphere soured Heidi's father, whereas Heidi's mother, to whom "being Hispanic was all about family," may have been shielded from the discrimination her husband encountered by her orientation toward the domestic realm.

Heidi's dating process complicated the sort of color-coding explored in chapter 2. She did not reject an entire category of men but instead "quality-coded": she rejected personality qualities reminiscent of her difficult father. For Heidi, as for her husband Sal, personality traits were a priority. They both preferred a mate with higher education, and marrying another Latino was a second-order preference. They both were skeptical about their ability to secure an educated Latino as a spouse because the time was marked by institutional discrimination that capped Latino graduation rates. Nevertheless, in the Dominguezes' love story, selecting on personality and educational achievement was of paramount importance. Color-coding and quality-coding are both strategies of negotiated desire, but quality-coding adds nuance to knee-jerk color-coding that does not specify avoidable characteristics but instead eliminates an entire racial group from romantic consideration.

Heidi answered my question about the type of person she was looking for:

> Well, I wanted someone the opposite of my dad. [*laughs*] And that's understandable. Someone who's patient. My dad had . . . problems with anxiety. My husband and the people that I dated, I noticed that right away—if they were anxious, I wasn't interested. . . . If they . . . weren't independent, because . . . I saw how dependent my dad was on my mom and . . . she was an

> independent person, but he hated that about her. . . . He was so jealous, and
> I didn't want . . . anybody who's jealous. And I think I found him.

With her dad as her anti-model, against whom she measured potential dates, Heidi did not color-code an entire category of men but instead quality-coded—she identified specific personality characteristics as undesirable and did not associate them with a particular racial group.

Beyond temperament, other traits were also important to Heidi: "[Sal] had a similar background. There was . . . a lot of stuff I didn't need to explain. We just had similar . . . backgrounds. He didn't have the best father either—we knew that we didn't want that in the relationship." "Background" refers here both to cultural heritage (not needing to be a cultural translator) as well as personal experience (having fathers who were not "the best"). Heidi mentioned a white ex-boyfriend to underscore the importance of being raised in a similar environment: "I . . . spent . . . a couple years with [a white man] who . . . was tall, blond, blue-eyed. But he was raised in South Central L.A., and he had a similar background." Sal was ultimately a better fit for Heidi. While sharing experiences of marginalization can be a source of bonding, as seen in chapter 4, Heidi and Sal extended that idea to include marginalization not based on race but subordination as a youth within a natal family system. She also proclaimed that "educational level was real important." Among seventy-six cousins, Heidi was the only one to earn a bachelor's degree. Her exceptional achievement—in contrast to the low expectations for Latinos that fed into bleak graduation rates in the late 1960s and early 1970s—was a testament to her determination and explains why educational attainment was an important quality for her in a would-be partner.[47]

As Heidi described her authoritarian and sexist father who saw little value in girls, the question became: what distinguished Heidi from other Latina women who color-coded these experiences and out-married? By discounting her father's misogyny as a personal problem, she could minimize it and more easily handle his impact on her life. Heidi used her experiences to inform her romantic decisions in ways that differed from Latinas who color-coded (rather than quality-coded) men in their search for romance.

Providing more background that illuminates her life course transition from dependent young daughter to quality-coding independent woman, Heidi discussed her father's gendered racism and her "stubbornness" as a protective attribute:

HEIDI: My dad didn't think very highly of women. He thought they
        should be pregnant and barefoot. He always gave me rewards
        for being quiet. I was his favorite, he told me, because I knew

how to be quiet. And when I went to school, the teachers would ask me, "Why are you so quiet?" Well, I was being good, I was doing the right thing. . . . He told me actually that my brains were wasted on me because I was a woman. He really did have problems with women.

AUTHOR: That's hard. So how did you end up getting an education?

HEIDI: I was just real stubborn. [*laughs*] I found out how to get there.

Heidi's father would reward her brothers for earning A's in school, but not her. "School was of no value" when it came to his daughter.

Without her father's backing, and in fact going against his wishes, Heidi learned computer programming and went to college. To punish her, he took away her car, thus terminating his material support: "I think because he did that, that motivated me even more. . . . I just saved and saved for about a year and a half. I found out how to get to [the community college], and I walked in and said, 'Okay, what do I do now?' And . . . they helped me. It was not a problem." When Heidi's father began charging her one-third of her monthly income ($100 out of $300) to live at home, she decided it would be cheaper to share an apartment with a friend. When Heidi moved out, her father disowned her. Her grit helped her not to feel beaten down:

It was okay, because . . . he put obstacles in front of me all the way, and I think it just made me stronger. He didn't let me sit down and do homework if there was a dish. I used to have to make dinner, iron clothes, do all the things. . . . It was not hard for me to move [out], because I already knew how to do everything. His stubbornness—he tried to keep me from college—just made it more desirable because I wasn't going to be stuck with a man like him. I was going to do everything I could to learn everything I could and make a good salary and live on my own if I needed to. I wasn't going to be like my mom, living with someone that negative. So I . . . went to college and lived on my own.

Oppression can either extinguish ambition or, as it did for Heidi, kindle initiative. With fortitude, Heidi converted obstacles into strength; rather than wilt, she rebounded. Grit—pursuing long-term goals with perseverance and passion—is a predictor of successful achievement of objectives.[48] Heidi's mother, whom she called a "good mom," endured her husband's "negativity" and did not countermand him. Heidi placed the bulk of the blame for her family's dysfunction on her father; even as a child, she had prayed that her parents would divorce, calculating that her prospects would be better if their marriage dissolved.[49] Heidi wanted to live outside the walls of her intolerable family dynamics. With "all the confidence in the world" because she "knew how to do everything" and "did well at school," Heidi moved away from her father's misogyny and learned that most people were "very supportive" of her.

Sal offered Heidi many qualities she sought, including calm, safety, and support. Choosing to settle down with a spouse who satisfies one's list of desired qualities sometimes requires gently reminding oneself about why that person is a good match, as seen with Celeste Collins earlier. For Heidi, pondering her relationship with her husband reaffirmed her choice. She drew on prosaic love and quality-coding to explain the enduring nature of their happy marriage:

> I think that this is in every marriage. Some of the things that you look for and you get irritate you. And then you have to be reminded, well, that's exactly why you wanted somebody stable, somebody calm. And when you want a little excitement, you go, "You're boring or whatever [*laughs a bit*] but actually, it's a good thing." So, you know, he's very even-keeled. I tend to be a little more anxious—I anticipate things and I'm shy. He's not shy at all, as you can tell [*referring to our three-hour-plus interview*]. I think we have a good match.

Heidi had married the man she wished for and searched for. In extolling her husband's virtues, such as his patience and calm, Heidi recognized the flip side to these qualities, such as a lack of "excitement." Nevertheless, she concluded, they had "a good match." Heidi had learned through experience in her natal family that she needed an "even-keeled" man like her husband to make her feel safe, even if that quality in him that she loved could border on boring.

In prosaic love, she pointed out, a spouse's character traits can be a source of attraction and the glue to a happy union. The trivial and the mundane are foundational to love, especially when a spouse's persona is favorably contrasted with that of an anti-model father. Heidi explained:

> I knew from the very beginning [that we would be a good match]. One time [when] we were dating, [Sal] made a wrong turn. . . . That would have set my dad off. Oh my gosh, we would have heard about it the whole trip—it would have ruined the trip. And [Sal] said, "So what? That's why they have U-turns." . . . Just his attitude towards things. . . . There's no obstacle that he can't get around. . . . He's just very calm about it all . . . and supportive.

Even though she occasionally needed to remind herself that she had wanted a calm man, she knew she had married the man she desired. Heidi's intersectional concerns shaped and sustained her desire for Sal.

Like Heidi, Sal's experience laid the groundwork for his romantic desire for his spouse. Sal said that he "lucked out" with Heidi, because he had wanted a Latina partner with an education. He also had grown into adulthood during a time—in his case, the late 1950s and early 1960s—characterized by institutional and interpersonal discrimination against Latinos that undermined their educational attainment.[50] So also like Heidi, Sal had become pessimistic about the possibility of having an educated spouse. With Latino men and women graduating from high school and college at depressed rates relative to whites—40 percent of native-born teenage Hispanics completed high school in 1970 compared to 65 percent of whites their age—it is no wonder that Sal was cynical about his prospects.[51]

While luck may have been on his side, saying that he "lucked out" did not give himself enough credit for knowing not only himself but what he needed in a spouse. Sal did not blindly date but instead considered the type of person who would suit him. He prioritized race and education when he was dating, doing his part to select on qualities he cared about. As we saw, Heidi was equally thoughtful, and their mutual mindfulness had contributed to their long-lasting marriage and happiness.

Sal grew up in downtown Los Angeles in a lower-class, racially diverse area:

> Although it was a poor neighborhood—sort of a port of entry for . . . people from different states—I think it was a benefit to us because of the fact that it wasn't an all-Latino [neighborhood]. If you went three blocks in one direction, there was . . . Little Tokyo. . . . If you went . . . in the opposite direction, there was the fringe of the black community. And then if you went in another direction, there was a lot of Chinese American families. And so we were exposed to all of those [communities], we had friends from all ethnicities.

That his family was "open-minded" regarding race is no surprise given the racial heterogeneity of the area. Unlike interviewees who lived in Latino-dense neighborhoods that naturalized endogamy, Sal was poised for diverse dating opportunities, given his heterogeneous local context.[52] College offers people expanded dating pools, and true to form, Sal thought he would marry a Japanese American because a lot of his friends in college were Japanese American. Yet Sal left his "options open" when it came to race and secretly hoped to find an educated Latina.

Graduation rates for Latinas cast doubt, however, on Sal's chances of finding a college-educated Latina:

> I knew I wanted to marry someone who had college, because I just appreciated it so much, that I wanted to marry someone who had that same

experience, you know? Now, the reality was, how many Latinos were there in college during the time that I went? There weren't too many. So, even if I was leaning toward someone who was Latina, I thought, "God, you know, the odds were against me."

"Very focused" on his college education, Sal "didn't want to get serious about anybody." After college graduation, Sal got drafted to serve in the Vietnam War.

Transitioning back to civilian life at age twenty-seven, Sal felt "very out of place" because he "never really held on to high school friends" and his college friends had dispersed. Most of his college friends had married, but military service had held that phase of Sal's life in abeyance, since he had not married prior to being drafted. He described his social discomfiture: "I found myself at a very odd place, in terms of . . . just normal relationships."

Sal's mother became acquainted with Heidi before he did because Heidi and his cousin would "pal around together" on the weekends at his mother's house. In contrast to mothers who were meddlesome and caused friction in relationships, as seen earlier in the chapter, Sal's mother played matchmaker:

My cousin . . . started bringing . . . my now wife, Heidi, to my mother's house when I was away in the service. So my mother got to know [her] before I did. And the more she came to the house, my mom would tell Heidi, "You should meet my son." "Well, where is he?" "Well, he's in Vietnam right now." "Well, did he go to school?" "Oh yeah, he went to college." . . . My mom would tease her, "You got to meet my son."

When Heidi asked Sal's mother for a picture of him, she procured a recent picture of him in Vietnam in which, owing to the heat and rations, he had lost thirty pounds, and he was also "very dark because it's like a hundred, a hundred and ten degrees." Sal reported that Heidi said, "Well, thanks but no thanks." In the meantime, Heidi began dating a cousin of Sal's. This relationship was doomed, however, because, as Sal explained, his cousin had the fatal flaw of commanding authority: "They'd go out to eat and he'd order for her, that kind of thing." This show of dominance was the death knell for the pair.

Sal met Heidi at his mother's house when she dropped by with his cousin. He laughed that, upon his return from Vietnam, he "had no car . . . had no money to speak of, no job." But as we heard from Heidi, he had a personality that suited her. As for Sal, his interest in her was piqued upon seeing her: "I was all excited. I thought, 'Here's my little cousin . . . and look at her friend. Wow, this girl is really cute!' " His physical attraction to her was immediately clear. He also saw some of his ambition in her, a feature that he admired:

> When I met Heidi, I was impressed with her because she was only just turning nineteen, she was working part-time, and going to college. . . . I almost saw myself in her . . . seven years prior. . . . And she was fun-loving, she had a sense of humor about her, she was up on life . . . life hadn't beaten her up yet, you know? And I thought, this is the kind of person I want to be around. . . . I saw Heidi as having that hopeful spirit and wanting college pretty bad, and working.

After his service in Vietnam, Sal wanted to be around "happy people." He saw both levity and drive in Heidi. Above and beyond race, Sal sought a "good person": "I wasn't looking for a Latina to marry, I was just looking for a good person to marry. And I think I found it in Heidi, see." Because of the premium he placed on education, Sal was open to racial exogamy: "I used to think, what's the [chance] of me meeting a Latina with a college education? Very slim. So I'll probably end up meeting some Japanese American girl or some white girl . . . from a nice family who was able to send 'em to college. . . . I think Heidi was a very lucky find." Despite his skepticism about finding an educated Latina to marry, family networks put him in contact with his future wife. Sal's assessment of racial groups' aggregate educational achievement led to his suspicion that he might marry a Japanese American or white woman. Calling Heidi a "lucky find" because she fulfilled his romantic wish list, Sal appreciated that they had both struggled against financial hardship, combated their respective fathers' lack of understanding, and beaten the odds to earn a college degree.

This couple's similar natal family structure and culture led to a bond. Sal remarked, "Her father was like my father. He was a reformed alcoholic, he didn't believe women should go to college. He was doing nothing to help her. . . . So she was going to have to do it on her own." Heidi's sexist father was an anti-model to be avoided in a romantic partnership, whereas Sal bolstered her value system. As a man who believed in Heidi's pursuits, Sal was a very different man than her father; Sal said of himself:

> I was her encouragement. I said, "Stick to it." . . . Things were tough with her dad because he wanted to ignore she was going to college. . . . He said, "You come home from work, you cook dinner, you clean house." She was nineteen! I said, "No, you don't have to do that." "So what do I do?" I said, "You move. I'll help you find an apartment. I'll move you." We loaded up the car, we put the bed in there, and we got her an apartment. . . . She did it on her own. . . .

I let her study during the week and I'd take her out on the weekends. . . . [By] then I had a job. . . . I just admired the fact that she wanted it [college] as much as I did.

Sal's narrative adds detail to Heidi's claim that he was "supportive" of her. That support encompassed emotional care, admiration, and practical help. By using life experience to refine what they wanted in a spouse, Sal and Heidi found their match in each other: an educated person with a similar background who was happy and encouraging. Sal offered his views on finding marital happiness by honing romantic desires in thoughtful reaction to life experience: "As you get older, you get down to just the basic things, you know—what makes you happy."

Rather than duplicate their natal family cultures, Heidi and Sal rejected their prior socialization and opted for change. And rather than color-code their experiences with difficult Latino fathers, they quality-coded instead, eschewing problematic characteristics and zeroing in on desired compensatory traits. Heidi and Sal did not simply react to their early experiences; each added desired specific attributes to the criteria for a good partner, such as education and calm temperament. Their knowledge of their own needs and desires and willingness to search for—and if need be, wait for—the right person paid off, resulting in a decades-long happy union.

CONCLUSION

This chapter has provided an in-depth examination of couples who experienced differing levels of marital satisfaction, moving from respondents who told tales of divorce to those who lived through marital difficulty, to others who were happily married. Those couples who divorced offered a few rationales for the dissolution of their marriages that illustrated the role of gender, extended family, and cultural values. Their stories confirm that conflicting gender ideologies hasten the process of falling out of love. Women struggle under the patriarchal expectations that materialize as tension around gendered household responsibilities arises, and if the tension cannot be resolved, they feel justified in divorcing their husbands. Lack of emotional nurturance also leads to the demise of some marriages. Extended families, especially parents-in-law, play a large role in either bolstering or undermining couples' marital lives.

Not all difficult marriages end in divorce. Some couples muddle through ambivalently, whereas others remedy their problems. Some spouses wrangle with the same issues over and over again, their conflicts manifesting in infidelity and assertions of marital fragility and contingency. Still other people become frustrated with the underbelly of the attributes in their spouse they once valued and need to remind themselves of the "fit" they do have with their spouse but have begun to take for granted.

Some marriages are happy and last a lifetime. These marriages are founded on an awareness of personal needs and desires stemming from early family life and romantic experiences. By honing in on specific companionable traits, couples correct for harmful experiences and aim for an appropriate match. Effective quality-coding is predicated upon people knowing themselves, identifying damaging attributes, and accurately appraising potential spouses. When effectually executed, the payoff is a happy marriage in which love and mutual support reign supreme and conflicts are managed with mutual conviction.

Chapter 9 | Conclusion: Negotiated Desire

THIS BOOK HAS examined how people make sense of their choice of marriage partner and the consequences of those choices. Natal family systems, social experiences outside the family, and the local context (demographics, hierarchies, and meanings) all contribute to the construction of romantic preferences. Early family life experiences, be they of poverty or patriarchy, shape adult yearnings for particular kinds of partnerships, ones that avoid or compensate for earlier aggrieved experiences. Beyond natal family dynamics, other social experiences, from confrontations with racism to encounters with stereotypes in dating, sharpen preferences for partners whom respondents view as safer bets for filling their needs. These two experiential points amount to intersectional concerns revolving around race, gender, and class that build desires for certain types of people as mates. Negotiated desire is the process by which these matters of experience convert into matters of preference and then play out in an environment with a particular racial-ethnic population and racial hierarchy. Desire is not innate or immutable but constructed in reaction to life experience and animated in a local dating scene.

By extending racial formation theory, which was developed to explain group dynamics at the nation-state level to the personal realm, we observe how processes leading to intimacy are inflected with racial representations and significations.[1] Far from being untouched by society and history, intimacy can be a "racial project": racial group statuses, cultures, and meanings can influence a predilection for differently racialized partners. The value of applying racial formation theory to family is in unearthing the ways in which public processes like racial representations and meanings inform hearts and minds and ultimately structure private lives.

Marriage Vows and Racial Choices has attended to both sides of two-party relationships, examining bidirectional cultural and racial consciousness shifts. A corrective to earlier immigration and intermarriage literature, this

268

book does not presume that only minorities change as a result of marriage but empirically assesses both partners. This book has revealed family as a site of race, class, and gender achievement, status guarding, and social change. As history reminds us, families are political institutions, a way to preserve or accrue privilege and temper oppression.[2] People do not love and marry indiscriminately. Instead, desire is constructed in response to life experience with eyes wide open to perceive advantage, disadvantage, and points of connection.

PEEKING INSIDE MARRIAGE: DECISION-MAKING, RATIONALES, AND CONSEQUENCES

Decision-Making and Relationship-Building

People try—often very self-consciously—to improve their lives through their marriage decisions. Love was certainly present in the relationships considered here, but interviewees, rather than telling only tales of being swept away by emotion, spoke of how their prior experiences informed the type of love they wanted and who they were most likely to fall in love with. Such self-knowledge need not take the excitement out of love and relationships: it simply enlightens people about where their emotions spring from. As humans with histories and the ability to think, reflect, emote, and act, it is really no wonder that people bring their backgrounds and lessons learned into their personal lives. Whether race, gender, class, or other concerns were foremost in their minds, interviewees utilized prior experiences to try to achieve their goals.

People make marriage decisions in complex situations, with incomplete information, and must forecast an imagined future. How do they sort out their requirements? How do they imagine their future? People reflect on their personal histories and make observations about society to determine what is essential to them in a mate and to envision a future with that person. This book has documented the invisible mechanisms of this decision-making. In concert with literature that views humans as goal-seekers, the life stories in this book unravel the mysteries of subjective decision-making: people engage their pasts and knowledge about the world as they try to accomplish their goals and feel fulfilled through rejecting or selecting someone to enter into a long-term romantic relationship with.[3] As people consider their options for the future, matters of experience convert into matters of preference.

Love is shaped by needs, desires, and notions of acceptability. Personal histories matter as people react to their pasts by trying to replicate or change the patterns of the interpersonal family dynamics they witnessed. The consensus for both the men and women in this study was to avoid oppression and seek liberation. This translated into some Latinas seeking mates with a different racial or national-origin background from their oppressive father, class-oppressed people seeking financial stability in a partner, and Latino men altering their expression of masculinity. But the pursuit of liberation is not the entire story, for some men wanted to retain dominance in their personal relationship.

Marriages are functional and long-lasting to the extent that people's needs match up: some marriages considered here broke up owing to misaligned needs and desires, while others muddled through the conflicts. The married couples who reported the greatest levels of marital happiness were those who had quality-coded potential mates in their love search: they had thoughtfully identified the personality qualities (not simply group-based characteristics) that they required in a mate as well as the traits they rejected. Personal experiences shape the requirements of love.

Once in a relationship, people are tasked with building a common culture, or "nomos-building"—constructing the social codes, habits, and customs around which their life together will be organized. Couples construct a shared culture as part of the marriage process. Making sense of racial, class, and national similarity or difference, as well as religious roots and gender ideologies, is crucial to relationship-building. We have seen that marriage "is a *dramatic* act": people act out their past and their present as they form (and unform, and re-form) their unions.[4] Charged with redefining themselves in a union, people strip their personal histories down to the bare essentials and jointly create a culture that values certain codes of conduct, cultural elements, and perspectives as fundamental while dismissing others. This relationship- and nomos-building exercise is a redefinition process that highlights one's chosen families as fundamental building blocks of social life and identity consolidation.

Marriage Rationales: Intersectional Concerns, Negotiated Desire, Preferences, and Opportunities

Marriage decisions are not only critical junctures in the life course but intersectional critical junctures: intersectional concerns spring from racial, gender, and class inequality and are played out in—and indeed, drive—major life-changing choices. Racial, gender, and class experiences within families of origin and while dating in early adulthood shape desires for particular kinds of long-term romantic partnerships. Intimacy is a product of complex intersectional desires that reflect forms of inequality and reveal people's agency to try to remedy them. People *negotiate* their romantic desire, first within their own heads and hearts and then within the context of an amorous duo. Moreover, people must negotiate desire within a local environment that offers a delimited supply of people as possible mates. Given these intervening personal, interpersonal, and structural factors, romance is not as private as we often assume.

Personal, cultural, and structural influences bear on partnership formation. For example, many Latina women with domineering fathers color-code this experience and seek non-Latino men as partners as a reaction to their prior aggrieved experience.[5] Other Latinas observe a racialized labor hierarchy and set their sights on white men, hoping to achieve both racial and class privilege.[6] Both Latino and white men desire Latina women as stereotypically "good wives." Latino men are drawn to Latinas owing to cultural similarity, whereas white men view Latina women as sexually alluring. Choices are inevitably constrained (and facilitated) by local demographics, which make certain types of partnerships more numerically probable than others. Yet within local environments, people are attuned to race, gender, and class issues. As goal-seeking decision-makers, people rely on their intersectional concerns to construct their romantic desires: people seek to *achieve* their desires as well as *escape* problems through their marriage choices.

Family is best viewed as a movie rather than a snapshot.[7] From this perspective, romantic desires for a same-race or cross-racial partner are not spontaneously generated but are linked to prior life experience. People can replicate their natal family models, either consciously or unwittingly. People can also react against their prior socialization and change patterns of oppression in their lives. Those who express the greatest marital satisfaction are those who are cognizant of their own deepest needs and desires. For some, color-coding is a successful strategy, but for most, a measure of quality-coding—prioritizing certain character traits—is a key ingredient for happiness. Divorcées are especially aware of problems in their prior marriage(s) and attempt to avoid those issues by selecting new partners without the same problematic traits. By this logic, people who are on the "marriage-go-round"—the American pattern of partnering, breaking up, and repartnering—appear to become aware of and fulfill their needs over successive relationships.[8]

Pulling back the curtain on marriages shows that people seek to satisfy their intersectional needs, which they bundle into romantic desires, through dating and marriage. The *cultural* element to this equation includes understandings of race, gender, class, and nationality that direct people toward some groups and away from others. The *structural* element to who marries whom lies in the opportunity structure of local demographics: certain types of people are available to engage in romance, while others who are not living or working nearby are not a possibility. The local racial hierarchy is another looming structural component that must be negotiated: people are aware of their prospects possessing racialized bodies, perspectives, and statuses, and this knowledge can brighten or dim their ideas about a romantic future.

Referring to culture, *preference creates opportunity*. People seek out what they desire, which they perceive to be embodied by people with particular racialized experiences, gender ideologies, class standings, and national origins. Referring to structure or demographics, *opportunity shapes preference*. People view the field of possibilities before them and tailor their preferences given the options they see. Thus, the preferences versus opportunities debate is based on a false dichotomy. Preferences (culture) and opportunities (structure) do not impinge on marriage choices as competing factors but instead reciprocally shape those choices. Individuals must strike a balance between their preferences and opportunities, and this amounts to negotiated desire: the process of identifying, acting on, and adjusting one's preferences within a local environment.

Marriage Consequences: Culture and Racial Consciousness

The life stories told here present several telling patterns with regard to shifts in cultural practice and racial consciousness. First, this analysis of these narratives expands what we know about intermarriage, filling a void in assimilation theory. Moving away from the assumption of white superiority and dictating one-way cultural change, assimilation theory now acknowledges that change occurs "in groups on both sides of the boundary."[9] And yet, a "black box" that can show us how cultural change happens, who is involved, and the myriad possible outcomes remains. This book has examined exactly this: how multidirectional transformation unfolds, who participates, and the cultural and cognitive results of Latino exogamous and endogamous unions.

Contrary to assimilation literature, *Marriage Vows and Racial Choices* views marriage as a starting point for investigation rather than declaring it a successful endpoint. Marriage may represent a high watermark for a relationship—and the beginning of a new stage in that relationship—but it is *also* a new stage of cultural practice, cultural blending, and racial awareness. This holds true for both racial intermarriage and intramarriage. Racial intermarriage, excitedly theorized as an exception because of its low incidence nationally, is not an end unto itself but the starting gate for various forms of biculturalism, newfound understandings of race, and shared marginalization. Upending existing theory, intermarried whites raise their consciousness around race through intimate life with a Latino who is differently racialized, less privileged, and subject to racist slights. An unanticipated effect of intermarriage is that white men's racial cognizance increases after marriage to Latinas—who are "double" or "triple" minorities by virtue of their racial, gender, and possibly class status.[10] By stepping into a loved one's shoes, a privileged person apprehends the power of social distinctions in newfound, poignant ways. Although life course literature acknowledges marriage as a major event in adulthood, this book shows the decisive influence of marriage and family on spouses' racial consciousness, emotional sympathies, and cultural practices.[11]

Second, racial intermarriage does not necessitate the racial minority partner's removal from his or her ethnic community or culture but instead can usher a white partner into nonwhite terrain. Intermarried white women migrate into the cultural realm of their husbands, becoming "affiliative ethnics" by adopting and passing on their husbands' Latino culture.[12] White women's active engagement in Latino culture is an unforeseen consequence of intermarriage that runs contrary to assimilation theory. Feeling that their own white ethnic heritage is difficult to identify with because it lacks specificity or a nearby community, these white women creatively twist their sense of gendered responsibility for home life and represent a culture that was relatively unfamiliar to them until marriage.

Third, Latino–non-Latino minority intermarriages are a wellspring of creative interconnections. These dual-minority intermarriages are founded upon experiences of *racialized affinity* and *shared marginalization* that enable minorities hailing from different nonwhite racial backgrounds to find empathy and solace in one another. Racial marginalization and the joint understanding that stems from this position binds these relationships. These couples' mutually marginalized life perspective leads to a critique of race relations in the United States.

Fourth, investigating Latino intramarriage, which tends to be cast aside as uninteresting because it is commonplace, reveals the complexity within this modal marital category. Endogamous marriages are the norm, and this book uncovers and unpacks their internal diversity. Rather than being emblematic of cultural entrenchment, Latino in-group marriage reveals dynamism around generational differences, transnationalism, feminism, and panethnicity. Within-group marriage does not predict adherence to any single vision of Latino culture—a category that is already heterogeneous.[13] Instead, type of partnership (cross-national, intergenerational, intragenerational) and region influence consequences: cross-national spouses teach and learn about another culture, intergenerational unions embrace a wide variety of outcomes from adaptation to mainstream whiteness to racial solidarity, and intragenerational marriages in California (but not Kansas) distance themselves from deleterious racial stereotypes in hopes of upward mobility. Latinos and their families are not a monolithic category: the variation seen within intramarriages testifies to the effect of race, nation, generation in the United States, and regional location on families. By theorizing Latino intermarriage and intramarriage simultaneously, we see the steps people take as they learn, grow, and act in different racial and cultural directions because of family life.

Fifth, parental instruction and advice influence but do not automatically determine children's orientations to their racial background. With age and generation-specific experiences, children hear but do not always heed their elders' instruction. Parents set examples for their children, and while many follow this lead, departures tend toward liberalism, including progressive attitudes about interracial romance. In contrast with their parents who witnessed greater levels of overt racism, children tout American values of diversity in that they express strong approval of cross-racial platonic and romantic love.

Finally, these findings have policy implications for immigration and racial diversity. With respect to immigration, since love can cross borders—and indeed, some people crossed international borders in order to find love or crossed borders for work and found love—immigration policy should permit families to live together as citizens with greater ease. Although family reunification is a "cornerstone" of U.S. immigration policy—nearly 70 percent of all visas for legal immigration are currently reserved for that purpose—a streamlined pathway to citizenship would facilitate the reunion and incorporation of more families.[14] Allowances for family reunification and the state's assumption of some responsibility for integration (as it does with refugees) would ease the conflict many immigrants face between desires for economic livelihood and for family unity.[15]

Required educational programs that teach about America's racial histories, with specific attention to marginalized groups, would open up space for conversations about multiculturalism and intersectional oppressions. Moving into the workplace, cultural sensitivity trainings may also foster positive relationships across racial lines. More inventively, given the importance of residential segregation in delimiting marriage markets, implementing residential policies that aim to integrate racially homogeneous areas would increase interracial contact and the opportunities for friendships and romantic relationships. Short of enacting state policies that incentivize marriage and child-rearing with fiscal rewards, as in Singapore, governments could deploy diversity policies in community development, education, and occupations that foster interracial contact and might have a ripple effect in family creation.[16]

FLEXING THE RACIAL HIERARCHY

Choices around family formation and family dynamics have an impact on the racial hierarchy. Given rising—but still quite slim—intermarriage rates among Latinos and whites, is that racial boundary blurring? Even while Latino–non-Latino minority pairings are rare, what do the dynamics that draw those couples together and occur within them say about race in America today? And what are the implications for contemporary race relations of the fact that most Latinos intramarry with other Latinos?

Based on the findings I report here, the racial boundary between Latinos and whites, at least among the intermarried, *is* blurring as these intermarried spouses borrow a differently racialized perspective from each other, broadening their understandings of race. Remembering that not all Latinos and whites are equally likely to marry each other—education, class status, and geographic placement influence the likelihood of partnership—those who intermarry shift cultural behaviors and engage in one of several forms of biculturalism.[17] Significantly, whites become aware of race and racism as a result of intermarriage. Although there is cause for optimism around changing race relations, the racist social practices of parents, peers, and the community effectively prevent many interracial relationships from coming to fruition, tempering claims about the porousness of boundaries.[18]

Regarding Latino–non-Latino minority couples, the social forces that make those in these pairs attractive to one another and the dynamics within these relationships speak to the racial climate in the United States. Racial subordination is fundamental to these partnerships: with race such an inescapable feature in these minorities' lives, they feel that only another nonwhite person could fully comprehend them. Race is so crucial to their lives that these couples seek each other out on the basis of marginality, believing whites to be ill fitting and having ruled out their own racial group either for personal reasons or because it is not well represented in their dating pool. An awareness of shared marginalization that keeps discussions of race alive in daily life provides comfort and understanding to these nonwhite cross-racial couples. These interracial coalitions forge creative alliances that not only provide support but also leverage their criticism of racist policies and practices, both historical and contemporary. A ground-up understanding of privilege and oppression based on people's perceptions of commonalities and disjunctures can redraw boundaries, sometimes in contradistinction to contemporary racial categories.[19] Perhaps inching toward reformulating racial categories, nonwhite cross-racial marriages founded on marginality are bedrocks of solace, solidarity, and social critique.

What implication does Latino intramarriage have for race relations? While Latino respondents were all quite aware of their "socially nonwhite" social location, their racial status did not predict their racial ideology.[20] Racial strategies ran the gamut: from avid social distancing and refusal of the label "Latino/Hispanic" to cross-cultural exchange to allegiance to one's racial community. Contrary to notions of same-race relations equaling a cultural status quo, endogamous Latino partnerships include people who are revising gender norms, hoping to achieve class advantage, engaging in transnationalism, or creating panethnic home lives.

The movement within this "racial middle" of the racial hierarchy indicates that the racial hierarchy is in flux.[21] Irrespective of marital partner, social distancing strategies pay off for some Latinos and help them achieve status as "honorary whites," while others retain strong cultural ties and still others—the darker-skinned—are reminded of their racial status by others, making their movement out of the category implausible.[22] Prevalent antiblack prejudice among Latinos contributes to a durable racial barrier as some Latinos attempt to secure a modicum of racial privilege over African Americans, especially in contexts marked "by symbolic, if not actual, socioeconomic competition."[23] However, antiblack prejudice is not uniform among Latinos; some form lifelong bonds with African Americans, a cross-racial linkage founded on a racialized affinity that highlights the meaningfulness of a broad nonwhite category within the racial hierarchy.

Place shapes the contours of the racial hierarchy. The regional comparison between California and Kansas yields insight into racial demographic realities, racial attitudes, ease of access to Latino identity resources, and local racial hierarchies that imbues racial categories with meaning. California's non-Hispanic white population (40.1 percent) is well below the national average (63 percent), whereas this subpopulation in Kansas is substantially above (78.2 percent) that watermark. California's Hispanic population (of any race), at 38.2 percent, is over double the national average (16.9 percent), whereas in Kansas it is considerably lower (11 percent). Germane here is the size of the racial groups among which possible mates are available. The dating pool in California is replete with racially and ethnically heterogeneous options as compared to Kansas, where whites are the majority. Kansas, a majority-white state with a small Latino population, offers a dearth of in-marriage partners for Latinos and is a setting that supports numerous demographically "convenient" out-marriages.[24] Racial group populations also affect racial attitudes. The white community was less tolerant of whites dating Latinos in Kansas because there was an abundant supply of other whites to date. On the flip side, Latinos in Kansas perceived intermarriage with whites to be reasonable and likely, an attitude reflecting the bounty of whites plus the social value of whiteness. In contrast, respondents in California, the state that leads the country in levels of multiracial reporting, expressed much greater tolerance for interracial intimacy.[25]

In addition to marriage markets, local context offers differential access to Latino resources. In California, plentiful resources, from relatives and friendship networks to retailers that offer specialized goods, cuisine, and ethnic music, refurbish Latino identity.[26] In Kansas, where these resources are less readily available, local Latino family members and the Catholic Church are more important to Latino identity. Geographic proximity to Mexico and other Latin American countries also matters; families in California are more likely to live transnationally or to be the result of an international love-match search.

The degree of flexibility in racial hierarchies may depend on region. In California, a traditional immigration gateway, Latinos and their non-Latino partners not only perceived cross-racial marriage to be common-place but viewed themselves as part of the vanguard of a more racially mixed and tolerant racial future. The intermarried in California saw their intimate lives as a reflection of their heterogeneous environment. (Racial diversity notwithstanding, some intramarried couples in California spoke of residential segregation delimiting their romantic choices.)[27] The close proximity of diverse racial groups may lead to racial conflict, but it may also foster cooperation and a sense of shared positionality.[28] In contrast, in Kansas, a newer immigrant destination, interviewees' perspective on intermarriage depended on their race. Latinos considered intermarriage with whites more desirable than did whites: while some white family members espoused multiculturalism, others encouraged racial endogamy to preserve white privilege.[29] This comparative evidence points to the greater ease with which traditional immigration gateways with long histories of interracial contact give rise to multiracial families.

Racial hierarchies and racial connotations also differ by locale. While some symbols, meanings, and metaphors are salient across the nation, in some local contexts specific racial connotations are exaggerated or attenuated.[30] Revealing an intersection between race, gender, and class, Latino men in California with poor backgrounds who were working-class or marginally middle-class as adults were attuned to negative stereotypes that would cramp their upward mobility and reacted by deploying social distancing techniques. These disassociation moves were not prevalent among those in Kansas because, while race and racism exist there, negative stereotypes are applied less stringently and less pervasively than in Latino-dense California. Because of a shifting racial hierarchy due to high interracial contact, Latino and non-Latino Californians alike considered mixed marriages or multiracial people harbingers of a multiracial future, a sentiment not present in Kansas. By contrast, intermarried whites in Kansas were more likely to experience a heightened salience of race as a consequence of their intermarriage, having encountered a racialized perspective through their spouse that had been less available to them in this largely white place. Since racial demographics, cultural resources, and racial hierarchies are always ensconced in a local context, future research testing the regional effects of attitudes and practices will shed light on the importance of region as an axis of difference that shapes lived experience.

Latino marriage patterns flex portions of the racial hierarchy, with some racial boundaries being more porous than others: the Latino-white color line is more regularly traversed in both directions, whereas the Latino-black color line is more rigidly upheld by antiblack prejudice, though some partnerships of this variety show the gaps in this color line. Among intermarriages, similar class status and spatial proximity lead to interracial romance. Intermarriage notwithstanding, racist pressures are exerted *down* the racial hierarchy—from whites against Latinos and from Latinos against blacks.[31] Thus, racial discrimination stands in the way of complete boundary erosion. Although this is a cross-sectional study and does not speak to change over time, the generational data suggest that white antagonism toward Latinos and Latinos' bias against blacks abate over generations—that is, parents more rigorously police the racial boundary than their children do.[32] The racial hierarchy may be structurally durable, owing to forces like residential segregation, but the ability of marriage to flex racial boundaries casts doubt on the immutability of the current racial hierarchy configuration.

Some say "love makes the world go round," but this book's findings suggest that "love changes the world as it goes round." Love is not a panacea for racial ills, but it does put people in close, caring contact that enables them to borrow perspectives and see the world from a different vantage point. This experience of "stepping into another person's shoes" jars people from their own perspective and opens the door to empathy, which may lead to changed attitudes or behavior and may be a source of comfort. The children in these families by and large feel included in society: one mixed-race teenager described her biculturalism as making her "more a part of things . . . in this giant river of things," while a teenage descendant of an intramarried couple remarked that she had "the opportunity to be whatever [she] want[s] to be," including remaining connected to her culture. Yet racial inequality persists, a reality that these youth learn to confront or sidestep, often with the coaching of their parents. Families and their strategies for navigating love, race, gender, and class are slowly reconfiguring the racial hierarchy as intimacy connects people and their sympathies in ways that, even as they sometimes entrench racial boundaries, can also transcend or even redraw those boundaries.

Appendix A | Methodology

To RECRUIT INTERVIEWEES, I worked with Latino organizations, high schools, Catholic churches, and preexisting professional networks (other professors across the nation with whom I am acquainted and students I taught or mentored who knew about my research study). I used purposive sampling, reasoning that I could locate Latinos and their families through these organizations. I also employed snowball sampling, asking respondents to recommend other people to interview. I recruited fourteen respondents through Latino organizations, nine through high schools, three through Catholic churches, twenty-four through preexisting professional networks, and fifty-nine through snowball sampling (friends, neighbors, or relatives of seventeen individuals who referred them). These fifty-nine respondents represented twenty-eight families of varying size. Because thirteen of the seventeen individuals who referred others who would qualify for the study successfully recommended only one family to me, my snowball sampling was not overly dependent on any one individual and thus avoided sample bias (the friendship networks of any given person varying in patterned ways from the wider population). I aimed to avoid skew in my sample by ensuring that my respondents were garnered through different institutional channels, friendship networks, and family circles. The one interviewee who successfully recommended four couples to me (eight total respondents) was probably this effective because not only was he well integrated into the Latino community but his outreach to these couples was the *second* notification they had received about the project. I had initiated the *first* point of contact through a church function, a university-sponsored event or club, or an email advertisement. I counted respondents gathered in this way (a "yes" after multiple contact attempts) in the snowball sampling category because the personal relationship was meaningful: despite other forms of contact, consent to an interview followed a personal referral. That said, my initial outreach laid the groundwork for their eventual participation. The individuals counted here were typically part of a marital pair, meaning that any one

279

referral usually yielded two respondents (a husband-and-wife pair) and sometimes four respondents (a husband-and-wife pair and two children).

By using these two sampling techniques and various sites to recruit participants, I connected with a broad swath of the Latino population in my two field sites. Respondents did not represent a single network of people but were dispersed across professional and friendship systems. I restricted my sample such that at least *one* Latino in the partnership was U.S.-born or 1.5-generation (those born in a Latin American country who immigrated to the United States with their parents prior to their twelfth birthday).[1] This sample design excluded partnerships wherein both Latinos in an intramarriage immigrated to the United States in adulthood. My work is not centered on the immigration experience yet came to include immigrants by two means: by including some from the 1.5 generation and by not restricting by nativity the second Latino partner in intramarriages. I limited my study in this way because of my greater interest in integration than immigration experiences. Yet foreign-born 1.5-generation Latino youth and foreign-born adult migrants who married U.S.-born or 1.5-generation Latinos were eligible for participation. This book therefore speaks to the experience not only of later-generation Latinos and their spouses but that of more recent arrivals.

I used a life history approach in the semistructured interviews, inquiring about respondents' racial-ethnic background, identity claims, natal family, marital family, child-rearing strategies, and cultural practices. Life history analysis permits the examination of the "interplay between social constraints, psychological motivation, and the developing actor . . . [and can trace] people's paths as they age, face critical choice points, and make consequential decisions."[2] In-depth life history interviews allow access to the personal histories, emotions, and cognition that influence people's decision-making. I honed the interview schedule through "focusing" — that is, sharpening the questions and question order as I conducted interviews.[3] Questions I asked later interviewees included how their parents reacted to news of their engagement and marital advice they gave their children, if they were parents. Using interviews to tackle the questions of rationales for and consequences of marriage allowed an in-depth examination of partnerships that other methods cannot offer.

My goal in the interviews was to procure information concerning how the adult generation accounted for their in- or out-marriage and how intramarriage or intermarriage had influenced the racial-ethnic identity and cultural attachments of the marital partners and their children. Rather than parsing out a singular "marriage effect," my life history narrative approach foregrounded meaning-making, relationships, and cultural practices within families. I used a family analytical lens that not only was concerned with "magnified moments," like marriage choices, but emphasized how subjectivity emerges from everyday life, practices, emotions, and relationships.[4] Following the lead of Kathleen Gerson, who urges us to think of family as a movie rather than a snapshot, I showed how preferences for partnerships unfold from a web of experiences.[5]

By taking a life history approach in the interviews with married couples, I could address the complex issue of *why* marriage partners make the decisions they do. Interview-based research relies heavily on respondents' honesty, self-awareness (for example, their knowledge about why they do what they do), and recollection of past events. However, it is the researcher's job to make connections that may not be apparent to the individual. As I linked a respondent's past to the present and phrased my budding theory as a question to get feedback, I often heard a version of: "I never quite put it together like that, but you are absolutely right!" As such, the interview process can be a vehicle of self-discovery.

I interviewed couples individually unless they preferred otherwise, which occurred in three cases. For those three couples, I prioritized the comfort level of the respondents by conducting the interviews with the two of them together. Stated reasons for these dual interviews included lack of time (interviews were often scheduled after work or on weekends), the shyness of a respondent, or an unspecified desire to do the interview in the company of the spouse. Whether the interview was conducted individually with each spouse or simultaneously with both spouses affected the kind and quality of the interview data. In individual interviews, respondents revealed more information about their dating histories prior to their current marriage, instances of sexual, physical, or verbal abuse (though none implicated their spouse), and details about hardships encountered with their spouse, such as mental health issues. When I interviewed couples together, sometimes I asked my questions directly to one spouse in an uninterrupted format (much as in an individual interview, but in the presence of a third party), but more often I asked one question and both spouses took turns answering. When I interviewed individuals in the company of their spouse, the discussion of their prior dating or marital experiences was somewhat abbreviated. Yet I still garnered valuable data: on many occasions, the observing spouse prompted the memory of the interviewee, filling in details or suggesting that the spouse tell me a particular story. This technique of dual interviews provided extensive data. During data analysis, I was especially mindful of not only who was telling a particular story but at whose suggestion the information was presented. There were both benefits and drawbacks to each kind of interview; my experience indicates that interviewing spouses alone and interviewing them together both render very useful narratives. As an interviewer, I operate by the informal rule that privileging a respondent's comfort is not only ethical but likely to foster their ease and willingness to reveal aspects of their internal world.

In a two-person marriage, not just one but *two* people's needs and preferences must be sufficiently satisfied to formalize the relationship.[6] In *The Future of Marriage*, Jessie Bernard famously observes the "his and hers" of heterosexual marriage, meaning that the husband and wife may have sincere but "different versions of the same events."[7] By interviewing husbands and wives, I captured multiple life history trajectories and desires that had led to marriage, as well as sometimes contrasting perceptions of the ramifications of the partnership. This holistic approach allowed for a more comprehensive understanding of how couples satisfy each other's needs and how they are changed by their union.

I do not believe that certain racial or national-origin groups were more likely to consent to be interviewed about marriage. There was likely a sampling bias toward those who were happily married, however, since those in rocky relationships would be less inclined to be forthcoming about their marriage. Since I included a small number of divorcées who were currently single as well as people who had divorced and were remarried, I was able to tap the process of marriage, divorce, and remarriage. In this way, as well as by asking about prior relationships that did not culminate in marriage, I uncovered sources of conflict. Even married respondents revealed to me points of contention in their marriage, providing a realistic view of marriage rather than an overly optimistic one. While interviewing mostly married couples presupposes a marriage outcome, this information pool also adds to our knowledge about families, race, and culture.

I tape-recorded and transcribed all interviews in order to utilize verbatim narratives in the coding and writing process and wrote field notes after each interview to document the personal affect that evaporates from written transcripts. I used an inductive, grounded theory approach to analyze the data.[8] Using a qualitative data analysis software program allowed me to code sections of interview material based on keywords and themes. Analytic memos written during and after the data collection period served as the basis for empirical chapters.

This interview-based book reveals that natal family systems, personal history, and social context all bear on family formation processes.

It is through asking people to narrate their lives, experiences, opinions, and perspectives that meanings and mechanisms that lead to choices are uncovered. Surveys document trends, yet qualitative studies like this one can get "inside" marriages to examine meanings, interpretations, and intricate connections that link past to present. As goal-seeking decision-makers, people transport their pasts—their life histories and lessons learned—into the present as they defy, change, or build from those pasts through their romantic relationships. Interviews are a road into people's heads and hearts, a vehicle to investigate their inner workings. It is through interviews that we gain insight into how people endeavor to endow lived experience with meaning as they digest and respond to their social experiences and make intimate life decisions.

Appendix B | Respondent Demographic Information: Aggregated

Table B.1   Respondent Demographic Information: Aggregated

Characteristic	Percentage	Number (N = 109)
Gender		
Women	53%	58
Men	47	51
State		
California	45	49
Kansas	55	60
Race		
Latino/a only	64	70
White only	14	15
Black only	0	0
Native American only	1	1
Asian only	3	3
Mixed-race: black, white	2	2
Mixed-race: Latino/a, Native American	3	3
Mixed-race: White, Latino/a[a]	14	15
Skin color code		
1 (racially white appearance)	30	33
2 (light tan)	27	29
3 (medium tan)	30	33
4 (dark tan)	12	13
5 (racially black appearance)	1	1
Age		
Fourteen to nineteen	16	17
Twenty to twenty-nine	11	12
Thirty to thirty-nine	16	17
Forty to forty-nine	31	34
Fifty to fifty-nine	13	14
Sixty to sixty-nine	9	10
Seventy to seventy-nine	5	5
Nativity		
U.S.-born	87	95
Foreign-born	13	14
Marital status (including children)		
Single/never married	18	20
Married	77	84
Divorced	5	5

(Table continues on p. 287.)

Table B.1   *Continued*

Characteristic	Percentage	Number (N = 109)
Education		
Less than high school	2	2
Current high school student	13	14
High school degree or GED	11	12
Current college student	4	4
Some college	25	27
College degree	21	23
Graduate degree	25	27
Occupation[b]		
Blue-collar jobs	9	10
Service or sales jobs	19	21
White-collar managerial or professional jobs	45	49
Students	18	20
Unemployed (including homemakers)	6	6
Retirees with undisclosed prior employment	3	3
Household income[c]		
Under $20,000	0	0
$20,001 to $50,000	11	12
$50,001 to $80,000	16	17
$80,001 to $100,000	22	24
$100,001 to $150,000	28	31
$150,001 to $200,000	10	11
$200,001 to $250,000	6	7
Not reported	6	7

Source: Author's compilation.
[a]All respondents in this category self-identified as Latino when prescreened for participation in the study.
[b]National Opinion Research Center (NORC) occupational classifications were used. See Colorado Adoption Project: Resources for Researchers, "NORC: Prestige Scores for All Detailed Categories in the 1980 Census Occupational Classification," available at: http://ibgwww.colorado.edu/~agross/NNSD/prestige%20scores.html (accessed December 15, 2016).
[c]Dependent children were coded as having the same household income as their parents reported.

Appendix C | Respondent Demographic Information: Individualized

Table C.1   Respondent Demographic Information: Individualized

Name (Pseudonym)	Relation Notes	Age	Sex	State (Number of Years in State)	U.S.-Born?	Marital Status (Number of Years Married)	Inter-married or Intra-married
Merle Andrade	Wife not interviewed	70	M	CA (62)	Yes	Married (46)	Intra
Valentina Arroyo		50	F	CA (14)	No	Married (14)	Intra
Ernesto Arroyo		63	M	CA (57)	No	Married (14)	Intra
Maya Assante	Adult child (to Martinezes)	40	F	CA (40)	Yes	Married (10)	Intra
Diego Assante		36	M	CA (36)	Yes	Married (10)	Intra
Ana Bermudez		28	F	CA (7)	Yes	Married (2)	Intra
Mario Bermudez		34	M	CA (34)	Yes	Married (2)	Intra
Martha Camacho		59	F	CA (59)	Yes	Married (not reported)	Intra
Terry Camacho		60	M	CA (60)	Yes	Married (not reported)	Intra
Glenda Carlisle		23	F	KS (1)	No	Married (2.5)	Inter
Ryan Carlisle		25	M	KS (1)	Yes	Married (2.5)	Inter
Russ Cheng		74	M	CA (74)	Yes	Married (16, second)	Inter
Sharon Cheng		66	F	CA (66)	Yes	Married (16, second)	Inter
Celeste Collins		43	F	KS (43)	Yes	Married (18)	Inter
Doug Collins		49	M	KS (49)	Yes	Married (18)	Inter

Own Race	Partner Race	Occupation	Education	Individual Income	Household Income	Skin Color Code (1–5)
Hispanic	Hispanic	Retired	High school/ GED	$40,001 to $50,000	$40,001 to $50,000	3
Latino	Colombian	Art designer	College degree	$40,001 to $50,000	$80,001 to $100,000	1
Mexican	Latino	Art collector	Master's	$100,001 to $150,000	$150,001 to $200,000	1
Hispanic	Hispanic	Law enforce-ment	Some college	$40,001 to $50,000	$80,001 to $100,000	3
Hispanic	Hispanic	Teacher	College degree	$60,001 to $70,000	$80,001 to $100,000	3
Mexican/ white	Mexican	Probation officer	Master's	$40,001 to $50,000	$100,001 to $150,000	2
Mexican American	Mexican/ white	Teacher	Master's	$60,001 to $70,000	$100,001 to $150,000	4
Mexican American/ white	Mexican American	Teacher	Master's	$70,001 to $80,000	$150,001 to $200,000	2
Mexican American	Mexican American/ Irish	Architect	Master's	$70,001 to $80,000	$150,001 to $200,000	1
Hispanic	White	Housewife	Some college	N/A	$15,001 to $20,000	2
White	Mexican	Student	Some college	$20,001 to $30,000	$30,001 to $40,000	1
Chinese American	Latino	Retired	Some college	$60,001 to $80,000	$80,001 to $100,000	2
Latino (Mexican American)	Chinese	Retired	Some college	$80,001 to $100,000	$80,001 to $100,000	2
Latina/ Native American	Caucasian	Lawyer	Master's/ profes-sional (JD)	$80,001 to $100,000	$150,000 to $200,000	3
White	Mexican/ Native American	Small busi-ness owner	Some college	$70,001 to $80,000	$150,000 to $200,000	1

(Table continues on p. 292.)

Table C.1   *Continued*

Name (Pseudonym)	Relation Notes	Age	Sex	State (Number of Years in State)	U.S.-Born?	Marital Status (Number of Years Married)	Intermarried or Intramarried
Rowena Cooper		62	F	CA (62)	Yes	Married (3)	Inter
Scott Cooper		57	M	CA (57)	Yes	Married (3)	Inter
Astrid Cota	Child	17	F	KS (17)	Yes	Single/ never married	N/A (child)
Lorena Cota		43	F	KS (43)	Yes	Married (20)	Intra
Oscar Cota		44	M	KS (n.r.)	Yes	Married (20)	Intra
Sarah Crosby	Ex-husband not interviewed	53	F	KS (3)	No	Divorced	Intra
Flor De Soto	Ex-husbands not interviewed; mother to Jazmin Romo de Soto	55	F	KS (40)	No	Divorced (twice)	Intra
Heidi Dominguez		59	F	CA (32)	Yes	Married (34)	Intra
Sal Dominguez		66	M	CA (66)	Yes	Married (34)	Intra
Liz Downing		28	F	KS (28)	Yes	Married (3)	Inter
Shawn Downing		31	M	KS (17)	Yes	Married (3)	Inter
Alicia Duarte	Husband not interviewed; sister-in-law to Lydia Duarte	42	F	CA (40)	No	Married (not reported)	Intra

Own Race	Partner Race	Occupation	Education	Individual Income	Household Income	Skin Color Code (1–5)
Spanish	Caucasian	Management	Some college	$50,001 to $60,000	$150,001 to $200,000	1
Caucasian	Spanish	Management	High school/ GED	$100,001 to $150,000	$150,001 to $200,000	1
Hispanic	N/A	Student	High school student	Not reported (student)	$40,001 to $50,000	2
Mexican	Mexican	Office manager	College degree	$20,001 to $30,000	$40,001 to $50,000	4
Hispanic	Hispanic	Civilian contractor	High school graduate	$30,001 to $40,000	$50,001 to $65,000	3
White/ Latina	Brazilian (ex-husband)	Higher education	Doctorate	$70,001 to $80,000	Same	1
Mexican	N/A	Restaurant owner	High school	$30,001 to $40,000	Not reported	4
Hispanic	Hispanic	Teacher	Master's	$70,001 to $80,000	$100,000 to $150,000	1
Mexican American	Latina	Retired	College degree	$80,001 to $100,000	$100,000 to $150,000	3
Hispanic/ white	White	Accountant	College degree	$30,001 to $40,000	$50,001 to $65,000	2
Caucasian	Latino	Accountant	Some college	$20,001 to $30,000	$65,000 to $80,000	1
Latino	Peruvian American	Student	Some college	Under $15,000	$65,001 to $80,000	2

(Table continues on p. 294.)

Table C.1   *Continued*

Name (Pseudo-nym)	Relation Notes	Age	Sex	State (Number of Years in State)	U.S.-Born?	Marital Status (Number of Years Married)	Inter-married or Intra-married
Lydia Duarte	Husband not inter-viewed; daughter to Solis couple; sister-in-law to Alicia Duarte	39	F	CA (39)	Yes	Married (10, second)	Intra
Arturo Esposito	Child	17	M	KS (14)	Yes	Single/ never married	N/A (child)
Rob Esposito	Wife not inter-viewed	52	M	KS (52)	Yes	Married (30)	Intra
Daria Fernandez	Husband not inter-viewed	61	F	CA (61)	Yes	Married (29)	Intra
Audrey Figueroa	Mother to Braedon Toledo	50	F	CA (50)	Yes	Divorced/ separated	Intra
Courtney Flores		46	F	KS (46)	Yes	Married (21)	Inter
Roland Flores		49	M	KS (49)	Yes	Married (21)	Inter
Shane Flores	Child	17	M	KS (17)	Yes	N/A	N/A (child)
Summer Flores		19	F	KS (19)	Yes	N/A	N/A (child)
Ava Gonzalez	Child	19	F	KS (10)	Yes	Single/ never married	N/A (child)
Deirdre Gonzalez		44	F	KS (10)	Yes	Married (21)	Inter
Ignacio Gonzalez		47	M	KS (10)	Yes	Married (21)	Inter
Adriana Guthrie		41	F	KS (41)	Yes	Married (21)	Inter

Own Race	Partner Race	Occupation	Education	Indi-vidual Income	House-hold Income	Skin Color Code (1–5)
American Mexican	American Costa Rican/ Peruvian	Banking	Some college	Not reported	$100,000 to $150,000	3
Latino	N/A	Student	High school student	N/A (depen-dent)	$80,001 to $100,000	4
Hispanic/ Native American	Hispanic (Mexican American)	Human resources	College degree	$50,001 to $60,000	$80,001 to $100,000	4
White/ Hispanic	White/ Hispanic	City employee	College degree	$100,001 to $150,000	$150,001 to $200,000	1
Spanish/ Cuban	N/A	Manager	High school/ GED	$100,001 to $150,000	Not reported	1
Caucasian	Mexican	Social worker	Master's	$30,001 to $40,000	$80,001 to $100,000	1
Latino	White	Medical research	Some college	$50,001 to $60,000	$80,001 to $100,000	3
Mexican American	N/A	Student	High school student	Under $15,000	Not reported	1
Mexican American	N/A	Student	College student	Under $15,000	$65,001 to $80,000	2
Mexican	N/A	Student	College student	Under $15,000	Not reported	3
White	Latino-Mexican American	Education administra-tion	Master's	$50,001 to $60,000	$100,000 to $150,000	1
Mexican American	White	Professor	Doctoral degree	$50,001 to $60,000	$80,001 to $100,000	3
Hispanic	White	Restaurant manager	High school	Not reported	$65,001 to $80,000	2

(Table continues on p. 296.)

Table C.1   *Continued*

Name (Pseudonym)	Relation Notes	Age	Sex	State (Number of Years in State)	U.S.-Born?	Marital Status (Number of Years Married)	Inter-married or Intra-married
Kaleigh Guthrie	Child	15	F	KS (15)	Yes	Single/ never married	N/A (child)
Kent Guthrie		41	M	KS (25)	Yes	Married (21)	Inter
Camille Herrera	Child	15	F	KS (15)	Yes	Single/ never married	N/A (child)
Julio Herrera		41	M	KS (41)	Yes	Married (16)	Inter
Susan Herrera		42	F	KS (42)	Yes	Married (16)	Inter
Cynthia Herrera-Redgrave	Husband: Mitch Redgrave	46	F	KS (46)	Yes	Married (22)	Inter
Cassie Hoffman		46	F	KS (46)	Yes	Married (6, second)	Inter
Sheldon Hoffman		54	M	KS (53)	Yes	Married (7, second)	Inter
Larissa Jaramillo	Husband: Miguel Moya	40	F	KS (5)	No (13 years in the United States)	Married (13)	Intra
Darnell Korteweg		37	M	CA (15)	Yes	Married (13)	Inter
Inez Korteweg		37	F	CA (27)	No	Married (13)	Inter
Blair Lucero	Adult child; parent to Haley	50	F	KS (50)	Yes	Married (25)	Inter

Own Race	Partner Race	Occupation	Education	Individual Income	Household Income	Skin Color Code (1–5)
Mexican/ white	N/A	Student	High school student	Not reported	Not reported	2
Caucasian	Hispanic	Medical services	College degree	$70,001 to $80,000	$65,001 to $80,000	1
Mexican American		Student	High school student			2
Mexican American/ Latino	White	Banker	Some college	$30,001 to $40,000	$65,001 to $80,000	3
Caucasian/ German	Mexican American	Nurse	College degree	$60,001 to $70,000	$100,001 to $150,000	1
Mexican	White	Housewife	College degree	Under $15,000	$100,001 to $150,000	2
Mexican American	White	Retail	High school	$30,001 to $40,000	$80,001 to $100,000	3
White	Mexican	Retail	College degree	$60,001 to $70,000	$80,001 to $100,000	1
Latina	Latino	Professor	Doctoral degree	$80,001 to $100,000	$150,001 to $200,000	4
Black/white	Latina	Education administration	Master's	$100,001 to $150,000	$100,001 to $150,000	5
Mexican	European, Native American, African American	Housewife	Some college	Under $15,000	$100,001 to $150,000	4
White	Mexican	Management	Some college	$100,001 to $150,000	$100,001 to $150,000	1

(Table continues on p. 298.)

Table C.1   *Continued*

Name (Pseudonym)	Relation Notes	Age	Sex	State (Number of Years in State)	U.S.-Born?	Marital Status (Number of Years Married)	Inter-married or Intra-married
Haley Lucero	Child	17	F	KS (17)	Yes	Single/never married	N/A (child)
Joaquin Lucero	Parent to Myra and Nathan; grandparent to Haley and Paloma	76	M	KS (76)	Yes	Married (54)	Intra
Magda Lucero	Parent to Myra and Nathan; grandparent to Haley and Paloma	73	F	KS (73)	Yes	Married (54)	Intra
Myra Lucero	Adult child; parent to Paloma	49	F	KS (49)	Yes	Divorced	Inter
Nathan Lucero	Adult child; parent to Haley	51	M	KS (51)	Yes	Married (25)	Inter
Paloma Lucero	Child	21	F	KS (21)	Yes	Single/never married	N/A (child)
Daniel Martinez	Parent to Maya Assante	75	M	CA (75)	Yes	Married (24, second)	Intra
Patty Martinez	Parent to Maya Assante	60	F	CA (60)	Yes	Married (24, second)	Intra
Miguel Moya	Wife: Larissa Jaramillo	40	M	KS (6)	No (25)	Married (14)	Intra
Drake Nakamura		46	M	CA (n.r.)	Yes	Married (4, second)	Inter
Luisa Nakamura		41	F	CA (41)	Yes	Married (4, second)	Inter

Own Race	Partner Race	Occupation	Education	Indi-vidual Income	House-hold Income	Skin Color Code (1–5)
Half Mexican, half white	N/A	Student	High school student	Not reported	Not reported	3
Mexican	Mexican	Retired	High school/ GED	$50,001 to $60,000	$100,001 to $150,000	3
Mexican	Mexican	Retired	High school/ GED	$50,001 to $60,000	$100,001 to $150,000	3
Mexican	White (ex-husband)	Public sector	College degree	$40,0001 to $50,000	$40,0001 to $50,000	4
Mexican American	White	Unemployed (banking)	College degree	$20,001 to $30,000	$100,001 to $150,000	4
Mexican	N/A	Student	Current student	Under $15,000	$40,0001 to $50,000	2
Mexican American	Mexican American	Urban planner	Doctoral degree	Over $150,000	$200,001 to $250,000	3
Hispanic	Hispanic	Retired	College degree	$100,001 to $150,000	$200,001 to $250,000	1
Mexican	Brazilian	Customer service	Some college	$50,001 to $60,000	$100,000 to $150,000	3
Asian/ Japanese American	Latina	Information technology	College degree	$80,001 to $100,000	$150,000 to $200,000	2
Ecuadorian/ South American	Japanese	Housewife	Some college	$15,001 to $20,000	$150,000 to $200,000	3

(Table continues on p. 300.)

Table C.1   *Continued*

Name (Pseudonym)	Relation Notes	Age	Sex	State (Number of Years in State)	U.S.-Born?	Marital Status (Number of Years Married)	Inter-married or Intra-married
Derek Nava-Kelly		44	M	KS (5)	Yes	Married (18)	Inter
Sylvia Nava-Kelly		43	F	KS (5)	Yes	Married (17)	Inter
Hyacinth Navarrez	Child	14	F	KS (14)	Yes	Single/ never married	Intra
Yvette Navarrez	Husband not interviewed	29	F	KS (8)	Yes	Married (15)	Intra
Chad Nuñes	Child	18	M	CA (18)	Yes	Single/ never married	N/A (child)
Corrina Nuñes		41	F	CA (41)	Yes	Married (21)	Intra
Lamar Nuñes		40	M	CA (40)	Yes	Married (21)	Intra
Gilbert Ornales		62	M	CA (62)	Yes	Married (21)	Intra
Rosalinda Ornales		53	F	CA (21)	No	Married (21)	Intra
Vanessa Ornales	Child	19	F	CA (19)	Yes	Single/ never married	N/A (child)
Cindy Ortega		39	F	CA (39)	Yes	Married (8)	Intra
Gabby Ortega	Child	16	F	CA (16)	Yes	Single/ never married	N/A (child)
John Ortega		49	M	CA (49)	Yes	Married (8)	Intra
Noelle Puente		41	F	KS (41)	Yes	Married (12)	Intra
Orlando Puente		45	M	KS (45)	Yes	Married (12)	Intra

Own Race	Partner Race	Occupation	Education	Indi-vidual Income	House-hold Income	Skin Color Code (1–5)
White	Cuban/Czech	Professor	Doctoral degree	$80,001 to $100,000	$100,001 to $150,000	1
Hispanic/white	White (Irish-Russian)	Lawyer	Master's (JD)	$40,001 to $50,000	$100,001 to $150,000	2
Mexican American	N/A	Student	High school student	N/A	$50,000 to $65,000	3
Mexican American	Mexican	Education	Less than high school	$30,001 to $40,000	$50,000 to $65,000	3
Mexican American	N/A	Student	High school student	Under $15,000	$100,001 to $150,000	2
Hispanic	Hispanic	Writer	Some college	$15,001 to $20,000	$100,001 to $150,000	2
Hispanic	Hispanic	Management	College degree	$100,001 to $150,000	$100,001 to $150,000	3
Latino	Mexican	Architect	Master's	$40,001 to $50,000	$40,001 to $50,000	1
Mexican	Latino	Housewife	Some college	Not reported ($0)	$40,001 to $50,000	3
Mexican American	N/A	Student	College student	Under $15,000	$40,001 to $50,000	3
Mexican American	Mexican American	Secretary	Some college	$40,001 to $50,000	$80,001 to $100,000	2
Mexican	N/A	Student	High school student	Under $15,000	$80,001 to $100,000	3
Mexican American	Mexican American	Technician	High school/GED	$40,001 to $50,000	$80,001 to $100,000	2
Hispanic	Hispanic	Public sector	College degree	$40,001 to $50,000	$80,001 to $100,000	3
Mexican	White/Mexican	Machinist	High school	$20,001 to $30,000	$50,001 to $65,000	3

(Table continues on p. 302.)

Table C.1   *Continued*

Name (Pseudonym)	Relation Notes	Age	Sex	State (Number of Years in State)	U.S.-Born?	Marital Status (Number of Years Married)	Inter-married or Intra-married
Lisandro Quiñonez	Wife: Julia Vega	38	M	CA (38)	Yes	Married (14)	Intra
Caleb Redgrave	Child to Cynthia Herrera-Redgrave and Mitch Redgrave	17	M	KS (17)	Yes	Single/ never married	N/A (child)
Mitch Redgrave	Wife: Cynthia Herrera-Redgrave	48	M	KS (22)	Yes	Married (22)	Inter
Tristan Redgrave	Child to Cynthia Herrera-Redgrave and Mitch Redgrave	15	M	KS (15)	Yes	Single/ never married	N/A (child)
Penelope Río	Husband: Travis Strong	46	F	KS (39)	Yes	Married (7)	Inter
José Romo	Husband to Jazmin Romo de Soto	24	M	KS (4)	No	Married (4)	Intra
Jazmin Romo de Soto	Adult child; daughter to Flor De Soto	28	F	KS (15)	Yes	Married (3)	Intra
Raven Salazar	Husband: Vincent Venegas	36	F	CA (36)	Yes	Married (17)	Intra
Claude Solis	Parent to Kyle Solis and Lydia Duarte	65	M	CA (65)	Yes	Married (14)	Intra
Kyle Solis	Adult child	36	M	CA (34)	Yes	Divorced (3)	Inter

Own Race	Partner Race	Occupation	Education	Individual Income	Household Income	Skin Color Code (1–5)
Chicano/ Latino	Chicano/ Latino	Artist	Master's	$70,001 to $80,000	$200,001 to $250,000	4
American, Mexican, Irish, Italian	N/A	Student	High school student	Not reported	Not reported	1
White	Mexican	Retail management	College degree	Over $150,000	$200,001 to $250,000	1
Hispanic, Irish, Italian	N/A	Student	High school student	Not reported	Not reported	3
Mexican American/ American Indian	American Indian	Education	Master's	$30,001 to $40,000	$50,001 to $65,000	4
Mexican	Mexican American	Self-employed (construction)	Some college	Under $15,000	$20,001 to $30,000	3
Mexican American	Mexican	Retail store owner	College degree	$15,001 to $20,000	$20,001 to $30,000	2
Latina	Mexican	Secretary	Some college	$60,001 to $70,000	$100,001 to $150,000	1
Latino	Latino	Retired	Some college	$50,001 to $60,000	$100,000 to $150,000	3
Mexican American	White (ex-wife)	City planner	College degree	$80,001 to $100,000	$80,001 to $100,000	3

(Table continues on p. 304.)

Table C.1 *Continued*

Name (Pseudonym)	Relation Notes	Age	Sex	State (Number of Years in State)	U.S.-Born?	Marital Status (Number of Years Married)	Inter-married or Intra-married
Regina Solis	Parent to Kyle Solis and Lydia Duarte	60	F	CA (60)	Yes	Married (14)	Intra
Bianca Stroeh		41	F	CA (41)	Yes	Married (15)	Inter
Chuck Stroeh		44	M	CA (44)	Yes	Married (15)	Inter
Tito Stroeh	Child	15	M	CA (15)	Yes	Single/ never married	N/A (child)
Travis Strong	Wife: Penelope Rio	47	M	KS (25)	Yes	Married (7)	Inter
Braedon Toledo	Son to Audrey Figueroa	29	M	CA (29)	Yes	Single/ never married	N/A (child)
Rodrigo Valencia		29	M	KS (29)	Yes	Married (7)	Inter
Trinity Valencia		29	F	KS (8)	Yes	Married (6)	Inter
Julia Vega	Husband: Lisandro Quiñonez	39	F	CA (34)	Yes	Married (14)	Intra
Enzo Velasco		38	M	KS (20)	No	Married (3)	Intra
Xochitl Velasco		39	F	KS (35)	Yes	Married (3)	Intra
Pablo Venegas	Child	15	M	CA (15)	Yes	Single/ never married	N/A (child)
Vincent Venegas	Wife: Raven Salazar	36	M	CA (29)	No	Married (17)	Intra

Own Race	Partner Race	Occupation	Education	Individual Income	Household Income	Skin Color Code (1–5)
Mexican	Mexican	Retired	Some college	$60,001 to $70,000	$100,000 to $150,000	2
Hispanic	Anglo	Office manager	Some college	$20,001 to $30,000	$80,001 to $100,000	3
Caucasian	Hispanic	Teacher	College degree	$70,001 to $80,000	$80,001 to $100,000	1
Hispanic/ Caucasian	N/A	Student	High school student	N/A	$80,001 to $100,000	1
Native American	Mexican/ Ojibwe	Janitorial services	Some college	$30,001 to $40,000	N/A	3
White	N/A	Retail	Some college	$30,001 to $40,000	$100,001 to $150,000	2
Hispanic	Biracial (half white, half black)	Educational counselor	Master's/ professional	$30,001 to $40,000	$50,001 to $65,000	4
Biracial (half white, half black)	Hispanic	Education administration	Master's/ professional	$30,001 to $40,000	$65,000 to $80,000	2
Mexican American	Mexican American	Information technology	College degree	$100,001 to $150,000	$100,001 to $150,000	1
Caucasian/ Hispanic	Hispanic	Software engineer	Master's	$60,001 to $70,000	$100,001 to $150,000	4
Caucasian/ Hispanic (Mexican American)	Caucasian/ Hispanic (Bolivian)	Writer	Master's	$40,001 to $50,000	$80,001 to $100,000	2
Latino	N/A	Student	High school student	Not reported	Not reported	2
Mexican/ Latino	Mexican American	Mechanic	High school/ GED	$50,001 to $60,000	$100,001 to $150,000	2

(Table continues on p. 306.)

Table C.1   *Continued*

Name (Pseudonym)	Relation Notes	Age	Sex	State (Number of Years in State)	U.S.-Born?	Marital Status (Number of Years Married)	Intermarried or Intramarried
Caroline Wu		31	F	KS (28)	Yes	Married (11)	Inter
Bryce Wu		35	M	KS (35)	Yes	Married (11)	Inter
Duncan Ybarra	Child	26	M	KS (24)	Yes	Single/never married	N/A (child)
Luke Ybarra		57	M	KS (54)	Yes	Married (30)	Inter
Trudy Ybarra		58	F	KS (39)	Yes	Married (30)	Inter
Helen Zelaya		37	F	CA (17)	No	Married (17)	Intra
Omar Zelaya		48	M	CA (48)	Yes	Married (17)	Intra
Stella Zelaya	Child	16	F	CA (16)	Yes	Single/never married	N/A (child)

Source: Author's compilation.

Own Race	Partner Race	Occupation	Education	Individual Income	Household Income	Skin Color Code (1–5)
Hispanic; half Ecuadorian	Asian American	Museum manager	Master's	$30,001 to $40,000	$80,001 to $100,000	1
Chinese American	Latin American	Education administration	Master's	$50,001 to $60,000	$80,001 to $100,000	1
White/ Hispanic	N/A	Machinist	Some college	$20,001 to $30,000	Not reported	1
Hispanic	Caucasian	Lawyer	Professional (JD)	$100,001 to $150,000	$100,001 to $150,000	3
Caucasian	Hispanic (Mexican American)	Teacher	College degree	Under $15,000	$100,001 to $150,000	1
Mexican American	Mexican	Housewife	Eleventh grade	$0	Not reported	2
Mexican American	Mexican	Education	Master's	$30,001 to $40,000	Not reported	2
Mexican American	N/A	Student	High school student	N/A	N/A	1

Notes |

CHAPTER 1: INTRODUCTION: CONSIDERING FAMILY FORMATION

1. Xochitl (whose name is pronounced *SO-chill*) was mixed-race Mexican American and Caucasian. Mixed-race Latinos may eventually "disappear" by electing not to identify as Latino (Alba and Islam 2009; Duncan and Trejo 2011), but Xochitl's identification as Latina, implying how she saw herself and how she was judged and treated by others (Cornell and Hartmann 1998; Rodriguez 2000), rendered her whiteness invisible. This choice fed into her racial identity claims and her desire to find a mate who had similar experiences with race.

   All names used in this book are pseudonyms that correspond to the Spanish and Anglophone first and last names of respondents to maintain the degree to which their actual names suggested Hispanic identity.
2. Cherlin 2009, 136.
3. Omi and Winant 1994, 55.
4. Swidler 2001.
5. Cherlin 2009; Coontz 2006.
6. Schwartz 2013, 452.
7. Landale, Oropesa, and Bradatan 2006; Rosenfeld 2009; Stevens and Swicegood 1987.
8. Alba and Nee 2003, 99; Alba, Jiménez, and Marrow 2014; Telles and Ortiz 2008.
9. Kalmijn 1998.
10. On marriage as marking the transition to adulthood, see Rosenfeld 2009; Thornton, Axinn, and Xie 2007. On marriage as a way to amass wealth, see Casas 2007; Coontz 2006. On marriages that transfer wealth or economic disadvantage intergenerationally, see Conley 1999; Oliver and Shapiro 1995.
11. Fry 2012; Klinenberg 2012; Schwartz 2013.
12. Edin and Kefalas 2007, 307.

13. Alba and Nee 2003.
14. Alba and Nee 2003; Bonilla-Silva 2004; Fox 2010; Jiménez 2010b; Kasinitz et al. 2008; Lee and Bean 2010; O'Brien 2008; Ochoa 2004; Portes and Rumbaut 2001; Santa Ana and González de Bustamante 2012; Vallejo 2012; Waters 1999.
15. For such accounts, see Novkov 2008; Pascoe 2009.
16. Alba 2009.
17. Kennedy 2003; Murguia 1982; Qian and Lichter 2007; Telles and Ortiz 2008.
18. On racial formation theory, see Omi and Winant 1994.
19. See Saperstein, Penner, and Light 2013, 369.
20. Nagel 2000, 111 (emphasis in original).
21. On Mexican and Anglo unions, see Pascoe 2009. On the prevalence of racial endogamy, see Fox and Guglielmo 2012.
22. Telles and Ortiz 2008, 77.
23. Alba and Nee 2003, 90. On the southern and eastern European immigrants of a century ago, see Alba 1990; Glazer and Moynihan 1963; Hansen 1938. On their white ethnic descendants, see Gans 1996; Waters 1990.
24. Gordon 1964, 80.
25. Ibid., 81.
26. Ibid., 80.
27. Feagin and Sikes 1994; Jiménez 2010b; Tuan 1998; Vasquez 2011.
28. Alba and Nee 2003, 26.
29. Gordon 1964, 115.
30. Shiao 2005, 6.
31. Golash-Boza 2015; Haney López 1996; Ngai 2004.
32. Spickard 1991, 7.
33. Gordon 1964, 262.
34. Alba and Nee 2003.
35. On the multiculturalism of the contemporary era, see Fischer and Hout 2006. On the "ascriptive or exclusivist norms" underlying American identity, see Schildkraut 2014, 447.
36. Gordon 1964; Rosenfeld 2002. Although I use the term "marriage," I do not intend to privilege heterosexual couples. I tried to interview same-sex couples by using the term "lifetime partners" in my recruitment efforts, but none agreed to an interview.
37. Hereafter I use "white" as shorthand for "non-Hispanic white," a stylistic choice that makes for easier reading. I use "Latino," "Latina," and "Hispanic" interchangeably. In this use of terminology, I am not claiming that Latinos or Hispanics are not racially white, but instead that they are dissimilar from non-Hispanic whites. Latinos are divided as to whether or not they identify as racially white: in the 2000 census, 42 percent of Hispanics categorized themselves as "some other race," while 48 percent selected white,

4 percent selected black, and 1 percent selected American Indian (Dowling 2014; Gómez 2007, 153).

38. Alba and Nee 2003, 11.
39. Ibid., 12.
40. Alba 1990, 164; Alba and Nee 2003, 12.
41. Alba and Nee 2003, 287.
42. Vasquez 2014c.
43. Alba and Nee 2003.
44. Roediger 2005, 198.
45. Omi and Winant 1994.
46. Alba and Nee 2003, 45; Ignatiev 1995; Roediger 1999.
47. Chavez 2008; Cornelius 2002; Flores and Benmayor 1997; Jiménez 2010b; Lee and Bean 2010; Marrow 2011; Ochoa 2004; Perlmann 2005; Vallejo 2012; Vasquez 2011.
48. Lee and Bean 2010. Mexico is the leading country of origin for both legal and undocumented immigration into the United States (Rytina 2006), accounting for more than one-quarter of the foreign-born population (Farley and Alba 2002, 681).
49. Murguia 1982, 105–6.
50. O'Brien 2008; Spickard 1991.
51. Jiménez 2010a.
52. To define endogamy and homogamy, I refer to Schwartz (2013, 453): "Endogamy and exogamy are . . . often used, respectively, for in- or out-group marriage (for example, by religion, race/ethnicity, or nativity), and homogamy and heterogamy for marriages between people with similar or dissimilar traits (for example, by years of schooling, income, or attractiveness)."
53. Gullickson and Fu 2010; Merton 1941; Robnett and Feliciano 2011; Scott 1965.
54. Gullickson and Fu 2010, 1; see also Kalmijn 1993.
55. Scott 1965.
56. Rosenfeld 2005; Spickard 1991.
57. Bean and Stevens 2003; Lee and Bean 2010. Internet daters also prefer racial endogamy: "Men and women from all racial backgrounds disproportionately initiate contact with other site users from the same racial background [although] . . . the size . . . of this preference decreases" when studying replies (Lewis 2013, 18815).
58. Lofquist et al. 2012, 17.
59. Rosenfeld 2008.
60. For an exception, see Vasquez 2015.
61. On the manufacturing of Latino similarity, see Mora 2014. On the dimensions of Latino heterogeneity, see Alba, Jiménez, and Marrow 2014; Zambrana 2011.
62. Altman 2001; Hodes 1997; Kennedy 2003; Ngai 2004.
63. Ngai 2004, 52.

312   Notes

64. Gordon 1964.
65. Alba, Jiménez, and Marrow 2014; Valdez 2011; Zambrana 2011.
66. Telles and Ortiz 2008, 27.
67. Waters 1999, 45.
68. Kalmijn 1998; Rosenfeld 2009.
69. Vasquez 2015.
70. On *Loving v. Virginia,* see Kennedy 2003.
71. Childs 2005, 10.
72. On interracial couples as "unnatural," see Pascoe 2009.
73. On companionate marriage, see Hirsch 2003; Smith 2006. On "mythic love," see Swidler 2001. On the "love match," see Coontz 2006. On the historical purposes of marriage, see Casas 2007; Cherlin 2009; Coontz 2006; Zelizer 1994, 2005.
74. On "talk of love," see Swidler 2001. On marriage as a political institution, see Altman 2001; Yamin 2012. On mobilizing to access marriage, see Whitehead 2012.
75. Edin and Kefalas 2007.
76. Haney López 1996; Heath 2012; Kennedy 2003; Randles 2013; Root 2001; Whitehead 2012; Yamin 2012.
77. On the history of marriage, see Coontz 2006.
78. Lichter et al. 2007; Qian and Lichter 2011.
79. Qian and Lichter 2011, 1081.
80. Alba and Nee 2003; Lieberson 1963; Rosenfeld 2008.
81. On the impact of coethnic residential patterns, see Kalmijn 1998. On marrying coethnics from the same country of origin, see Chavez 2008, 61.
82. Murguia 1982; Telles and Ortiz 2008.
83. Alba, Jiménez, and Marrow 2013, 11.
84. Alba, Jiménez, and Marrow 2014; Lichter et al. 2007; Okamoto 2007; Spickard 1991; Telles and Ortiz 2008.
85. Wright, Holloway, and Ellis 2013, 396.
86. Kalmijn 1998, 397.
87. On the importance of race over education or religion, see Feliciano, Robnett, and Komaie 2009, 45. On race as a forbidding line to cross, see Qian and Cobas 2004; Spickard 1991.
88. Schwartz 2013, 454.
89. Rytina et al. 1988.
90. Collins 1991, 225.
91. Rosaldo 1993, 209.
92. Collins 1991, 225.
93. On educational aspirations and achievement, see MacLeod 2004. On expressions of class status, see Bettie 2003. On parenting strategies, see Lareau 2003. On the production of gendered subjects, see Ferguson 2000; Salzinger 2003.

94. Lorde 1984, 190.
95. Dreby and Schmalzbauer 2013; Schmalzbauer 2014.
96. Omi and Winant 1994, 55.
97. Brown 2011; Gonzales 2011; McDermott 2006; Menjívar and Abrego 2012.
98. Ochoa 2013, 6.
99. King 1988; Segura 1986.
100. Gerson 1986, 36–37.
101. Ibid., 37.
102. Berger and Kellner 1964, 1.
103. Ibid.
104. Ibid., 2.
105. Ibid., 5.
106. Ibid., 4 (emphasis added).
107. Ibid.
108. Ibid., 5 (emphasis in original).
109. Smith et al., forthcoming.
110. Ibid.
111. Tallman and Gray 1990, 407.
112. 411.
113. Ibid., 422.
114. For details on how people make decisions in a transnationalized social space, see Smith et al., forthcoming.
115. Berger and Kellner 1964, 16.
116. Ibid., 9.
117. Beaver 2006.
118. Ennis, Ríos-Vargas, and Albert 2011.
119. On "circular" migrants, see Bean and Stevens 2003. The border has been increasingly militarized by state legislation such as Texas's Operation Hold the Line (1993) and California's Operation Gatekeeper (1994), which, in severely hampering workers' ability to return-migrate to their home countries, have inadvertently caused permanent settlement in the United States (Fernández-Kelly and Massey 2007; Massey, Durand, and Malone 2002). Under the Obama administration, deportations—with an emphasis on immigrants convicted of crimes—have continued to rise. "Congress appropriated $690 million" in 2011 for four programs that were focused on locating criminal aliens, the largest of which is the Criminal Alien Program (CAP), "up from $23 million in 2004. This funding led to an increase in annual arrests through these programs from 11,000 to 289,000 during that time" (Golash-Boza and Hondagneu-Sotelo 2013, 278).
120. Massey, Durand, and Malone 2002.
121. De Genova 2005; Gutiérrez 1995; Hondagneu-Sotelo 1997; Ngai 2004.

122. On the "structural" need built into the U.S. economy, see Cornelius 2002. On the vulnerable labor force, see Foley 1997.

123. De Genova 2005, 227.

124. Hondagneu-Sotelo 2014.

125. Kansas Historical Society, "Mexican Americans in Kansas," Kansapedia, August 2012, available at: http://www.kshs.org/kansapedia/mexican-americans-in-kansas/17874 (accessed September 12, 2014). On the Latino migrant labor force since the early 1900s, see Stull, Broadway, and Griffith 1995.

126. Glenn 2002, 151, 152.

127. Jiménez 2010b.

128. Almaguer 1994.

129. Ibid., 59; Casas 2007, 23.

130. Acuña 2011; Glenn 2002.

131. Blau, Blum, and Schwartz 1982; Davis 1941; Feliciano, Robnett, and Komaie 2009; Gullickson and Fu 2010; Merton 1941/2000.

132. Acuña 2011.

133. On migrant labor in meat-processing plants, see Stull, Broadway, and Griffith 1995. On how newcomers adapted to rural locales, see Cantú 1995; Millard and Chapa 2004; Williams, Alvarez and Hauk 2002. On intraracial relations, see Jiménez 2010b; Lopez 2000.

134. Lichter et al. 2007.

135. Anderson 1991.

136. Kansas generates approximately 15 percent of the nation's total wheat crop. Its largest crop is wheat, which accounts for 12 percent of the state's total agricultural production, followed by corn, soybeans, sorghum grain, and hay. See Kansas, "Kansas Economy," available at: http://www.netstate.com/economy/ks_economy.htm (accessed November 8, 2013).

137. California is on the forefront of immigration policy. For example, Texas (2001), California (2002), and New York (2002) were the first states to approve in-state tuition for undocumented high school graduates. Kansas followed in 2004 (Reich and Barth 2010).

138. Hondagneu-Sotelo 2014.

139. For more details on the study methodology, see appendix A. For more details on the study participants, see appendices B and C.

140. See *People en Español* at http://www.peopleenespanol.com/.

141. Fry 2012.

142. Taylor 2010.

143. U.S. Census Bureau, "Quick Facts: United States," available at: http://quickfacts.census.gov/qfd/states/20000.html (accessed July 4, 2013).

144. See appendix A for more detail on the methodology.

145. Omi and Winant 1994, 55.

146. Cornell and Hartmann 1998; Duster 2003; Fischer et al. 1996; Morning 2011; Obasogie 2009.
147. Obasogie 2014.
148. Cornell and Hartmann 2004, 25.
149. Omi and Winant 1994, 55. See also Bonilla-Silva 2004; Collins 1991; O'Brien 2008.
150. Chavez 2008; Golash-Boza and Hondagneu-Sotelo 2013; Gutiérrez 1995; Hondagneu-Sotelo 1999; Maldonado 2009; Menjívar and Abrego 2012; Romero, Ortiz, and Hondagneu-Sotelo 1997; Telles and Ortiz 2008.
151. Gómez 2007.
152. Lee and Bean 2004.
153. Flores-Gonzalez 1999; Golash-Boza 2006; Golash-Boza and Darity 2008; Telles and Ortiz 2008.
154. Omi and Winant 1994, 15.
155. Waters 1990, 16.
156. Cornell and Hartmann 1998, 17.
157. Vasquez 2014a.
158. Gerson 2010.

CHAPTER 2: LATINO AND WHITE INTERMARRIAGE: PREFERENCES AND CONVENIENCE

1. Omi and Winant 1994, 48.
2. On Latino/a out-marriage rates, see Lee and Bean 2010; Qian and Lichter 2001, 2011.
3. Root 2001, 156 (emphasis added).
4. Gray and Tallman 1987.
5. Chodorow 1978; Gerson 1986.
6. Gerson 1986, 32.
7. Ibid., 34 (emphasis added).
8. Tallman and Gray 1990.
9. Ibid., 416.
10. Kasinitz et al. 2008.
11. On homogenizing Latino masculinity, see Barajas and Ramirez 2007; Gutmann 2003. On the elimination of Latino men as dating partners, see Vasquez 2011.
12. Segura 1986.
13. Even the terms "farm owners" and "farmhands" are telling: white employers own farms aimed to produce profit, whereas Hispanic laborers "own" their hands, the tools of labor.
14. Goffman 1973.
15. Chong 2013, 196.

16. On homogamy, see Blackwell and Lichter 2004; Rosenfeld 2005; Spickard 1991.
17. Lee and Bean 2010, 96.
18. Bourdieu 1984.
19. Ibid., 1–2.
20. Ibid., 6 (emphasis added).
21. Ibid., 471.
22. Merton 1941; Robnett and Feliciano 2011.
23. Feliciano and Robnett 2014.
24. Conley 1999; Massey and Denton 1993; Oliver and Shapiro 1995.
25. Dreby 2010; Gerson 2015; Randles 2013; Sherman 2009b.
26. Casas 2007; Cherlin 2009; Coontz 2006.
27. Altman 2001, 2. This section draws from people who are not in this marital category.
28. Dalmage 2000; Vasquez 2015.
29. Blumer 1958, 5.
30. Blumer 1958.
31. Bobo and Tuan 2006; McDermott 2006.
32. Feliciano and Robnett 2014.
33. On "racial projects," see Omi and Winant 1994. On parents trying to influence their children's romantic outcomes, see Thornton, Axinn, and Xie 2007.
34. Lee and Bean 2010; Warren and Twine 1997.
35. Hordge-Freeman 2013, 1518.
36. Childs 2005; Yuval-Davis 1997.
37. Nagel 2003, 10.
38. Donovan 2003, 723.
39. On family pressure to form in-group liaisons, see Okamoto 2007. On anti-black prejudice, see Kasinitz et al. 2008; Marrow 2011. On the decreasing likelihood of an interracial relationship with age, see Joyner and Kao 2005.
40. Ocampo 2012.
41. Robinson 2015, 319.
42. Collins 1991, 2004; Nagel 2003; Spickard 1991.
43. Glenn 2002, 165.
44. Molina-Guzmán 2010, 14.
45. Such images of Latina women were also expressed by Latino men. These patterns demonstrate the power of gendered and racialized imagery in making certain categories attractive to others. In this case, men's preference for Latina women, based on stereotypes of sexuality, fealty, and domesticity, crosscuts race.
46. Molina-Guzmán 2010, 9.
47. Nagel 2000, 113.
48. This logic has been used to explain international migration; see Massey, Durand, and Malone 2002.

49. Root 2001.
50. Vasquez 2010a.
51. Gutiérrez 1995; Sanchez 1994.
52. Shiao 2005.
53. Ibid., 7.
54. Ibid., 8.
55. Fischer and Hout 2006.
56. Bell and Hartmann 2007; Bloemraad, Korteweg, and Yurdakul 2008.
57. Vasquez 2010b.
58. Monhollon 2004.
59. Schoem and Hurtado 2001.
60. Jiménez 2010b, 103.
61. On "ethnic sojourning," see Nagel 2003. On "affiliative ethnic identity," see Jiménez 2010a.
62. Frankenberg 1993; Hartigan 1997; Lipsitz 2006.
63. Glenn 1986; Nagel 2003; Sassen 1989.
64. Markus and Conner 2013; Perry 2002; Yancey 2007.
65. McDermott 2006, 8.
66. Burk and Espinoza 2012, 401; Butler and Wilson 1978.
67. Glenn 2009; Hunter 2002; Nagel 2003; Saraswati 2010.
68. Segal 1989.
69. Chambliss and Schutt 2012.
70. Kalmijn 2010, 282.
71. Qian and Lichter 2011, 1081.
72. Census 2000 figures from U.S. Census Bureau, "Quick Facts: United States," available at: http://quickfacts.census.gov/qfd/states/20/2038900.html (accessed June 16, 2014).
73. On marital homogamy, see Rosenfeld 2005; Spickard 1991.
74. Spickard 1991.
75. On Catholic Latinos in the Midwest, see Vega 2015.
76. For a "nucleus of community events," see ibid., 79; for a "de facto ethnic institution," see Ocampo 2015.
77. For a thorough consideration of how the Catholic Church serves as a refuge from neighborhood violence in South Los Angeles, see Martinez 2016.

CHAPTER 3: CONSEQUENCES OF LATINO AND WHITE INTERMARRIAGE: BICULTURALISM AND RACIAL CONSCIOUSNESS

1. Portions of this chapter were previously published in *Sociological Forum* (Vasquez 2014c) and *Du Bois Review* (Vasquez 2014b).
2. Rosenfeld and Kim 2005, 541, 547.

3. Lee and Bean 2010, 87–88. In contrast, 7.1 percent of non-Hispanic whites intermarry (ibid., 87).

4. Spickard 1991, 15.

5. For the sake of simplicity, when referring to culture or a mixed-sex group of people, I use "Latino(s)" instead of "Latino/a(s)." I do not intend to privilege males or masculinity in so doing, but find this style less visually distracting.

6. See Alba 1990.

7. Gordon 1964, 80.

8. Padilla 2006, 469.

9. Murguia 1982, 105–6.

10. O'Brien 2008, 165.

11. Gordon 1964; O'Brien 2008.

12. O'Brien 2008.

13. Bonilla-Silva 2003.

14. Chong 2013; Jiménez 2010a, 2010b.

15. Shiao and Tuan 2008.

16. Alba and Nee 2003, 286.

17. Nagel 2003, 15.

18. Jiménez 2010a, 1758.

19. Bean and Stevens 2003; Feliciano, Lee, and Robnett 2011; Lee and Bean 2010; Qian and Lichter 2007.

20. Two middle-aged respondents in the adult category were also children of older respondents in their seventies (the Lucero family), but I include them in the adult category because they were intermarried and parents to young adult children who were also interviewees.

21. Of the thirty adults, ten were Latina women, six were Latino men, five were white women, and nine were white men. Ten couples were Latina women married to white men; I interviewed both partners in all but one case in which the woman was divorced. Six couples comprised Latino men and white women; I interviewed both spouses except in the case of a divorced man, whose ex-spouse I did not interview.

22. The German sociologist Max Weber (1864–1920) coined the term "ideal type," which refers to abstract analytic concepts ("ideal" referring to ideas, not perfection). "Ideal types" or "pure types" are the basis for comparative study, as they allow for typologies of concepts (Coser 2003).

23. Race cognizance and color-blindness are emergent categories, and thus some people did not address them (or were not asked about them). As such, the numbers presented here probably underreport both phenomena.

24. Molina 2014; Ochoa 2013.

25. Dowling 2014; Gómez 2007; Sue 2013.

26. Rockquemore, Laszloffy, and Noveske 2006.

27. Joyner and Kao 2005, 577.

28. On the evolution of racial diversity and interracial romance in the United States, see Fischer and Hout 2006.
29. See also Chong 2013 on intermarried Asians.
30. Alba 2006, 293; Duncan and Trejo 2011.
31. Waters 1990.
32. Chavez 2008.
33. Feliciano, Robnett, and Komaie 2009, 41.
34. On supporting white superiority this way, see Feagin and Cobas 2008.
35. Spickard 1991, 8.
36. Gans 1979, 9.
37. Gans 1979.
38. Kasinitz et al. 2008, 83.
39. Gordon 1964; Park 1950.
40. Gerson 2015; Sherman 2009b, 161.
41. Vasquez 2014a.
42. On natal families, see Coltrane 1996; Daly 1993; Dienhart 1998; Snarey 1993; Vasquez 2014a.
43. Waters 1990, 25.
44. Jiménez 2010a.
45. Yuval-Davis 1997, 67. See DeVault 1991; Stack and Burton 1994; Vasquez 2010b.
46. Nagel 2003; Jiménez 2010a.
47. Yuval-Davis 1997, 46; Vasquez 2010b.
48. Frankenberg 1993.
49. Hurtado, Alvarado, and Guillermo-Wann 2015, 147.
50. Frankenberg 1993.
51. Cornell and Hartmann 1998; Dowling 2014; Rodriguez 2000.
52. See De Genova 2005; Gonzales 2011; Zhou et al. 2008.
53. Sue and Golash-Boza 2013, 1589.
54. Chavez 2008; De Genova 2005; Haney López 2006.
55. See chapter 1 for how I measured skin color in this study.
56. Apfelbaum et al. 2012, 205.
57. Bonilla-Silva 2003, 2.
58. Haney López 1996.
59. Frankenberg 1993.
60. Obasogie 2010, 585.
61. Bonilla-Silva 2003; Brown 2003; Collins 2004.
62. For some respondents, color-blindness preceded rather than followed their intermarriage; for example, some had been raised by racially tolerant or progressive parents.
63. Lee and Bean 2010; Root 2001.
64. Lewis 2003; Markus and Conner 2013; Perry 2002; Root 2001; Vasquez 2005; Yancey 2007.

65. Vasquez 2011.
66. This is not to suggest that racial inequalities do not exist in the private sphere. As this book and other scholarship show, families can harbor and perpetuate various forms of inequality along the lines of race, gender, class, and sexuality. Because these inequalities exist in the intimate and concealed space of the family, they are harder to recognize or resist.
67. On political correctness, see Childs 2005.
68. Bonilla-Silva 2003.
69. These teenagers had both intermarried and intramarried parents, yet parentage was far less important in how they related to their heritage than the force of regional context and the presence of nearby Latino kin.
70. Frankenberg 1993.
71. Macias 2006.
72. Gordon 1964, 77, 81.
73. On "key conduits of ethnic culture," see Chong 2013, 203.

CHAPTER 4: CROSS-RACIAL MINORITY PAIRINGS: LATINOS INTERMARRIED WITH NON-LATINO RACIAL MINORITIES

1. Portions of the interview data featured in this chapter were published in an edited collection on mixed-race families (see Vasquez-Tokos, forthcoming).
2. Romo 2011.
3. Arizona Senate Bill 1070 is one of the broadest and strictest anti-immigration measures in recent U.S. history. The law makes it a state misdemeanor for non-U.S. citizens who are temporary or permanent residents to be in Arizona without carrying the required documents. It also requires state law enforcement officers to try to determine an individual's immigration status during unrelated stops, detentions, and arrests. The law's constitutionality and compliance with civil rights laws was the basis of *Arizona v. United States*. In June 2012, the U.S. Supreme Court upheld the provision requiring immigration status checks during law enforcement stops but struck down three other provisions as violations of the Supremacy Clause of the U.S. Constitution.
4. Collins 1986.
5. Although the U.S. census considers Latinos an ethnic group, not a racial group, I defer to my respondents' understandings of their identities and refer to Latinos as a nonwhite racial group. I use the term "race" instead of "ethnicity" to suggest a more durable social dividing line. In terms of how Latinos self-identify, in the 1980, 1990, and 2000 U.S. censuses, there was a "decreasing tendency for Hispanics to identify themselves as white (from 58 percent in 1980 to 48 percent in 2000) and an increasing tendency to claim either some other race or more than one race (from 38 percent in 1980 to 49 percent in

2000)" (Deaux 2006, 96). Again revealing their self-conception as a nonwhite racial group, 97 percent of the people who used the category "some other race" when filling out the census forms were Latino (Deaux 2006; Gómez 2007; Lee and Bean 2004).

6. On black-white couples, see Childs 2005; Dalmage 2000; Moran 2001; Root 2001; Rosenfeld and Kim 2005; Sollors 2000; Spickard 1991. On Latino-white couples, see Jiménez 2004; Lee and Edmonston 2006; Murguia 1982; Qian and Cobas 2004; Vasquez 2011.
7. Childs 2005, 42.
8. Dowling 2014, 125.
9. Mumford 1997, xii.
10. Root 2001.
11. Holm, Pearson, and Chavis 2003.
12. Smith 2005.
13. Berger and Kellner 1964.
14. Frankenberg 1993.
15. Haraway 1988.
16. Collins 1986, S26.
17. Haney López 1996; Lipsitz 2006; Oliver and Shapiro 1995.
18. Berger and Kellner 1964, 11.
19. This sentiment of unity among Native Americans and Mexican Americans may be shaped by the Kansas context, where they live alongside each other amicably. This cross-racial coalitional perspective may be different in areas that have a large Native American population or substantial in-migration from Mexico and the two groups may thus be separated by group size or racial politics.
20. Ocampo 2014, 426.
21. Brown and Jones 2015.
22. Vasquez and Wetzel 2009.
23. Smith 2007.
24. On the damage done to Native American identity, see Child 2000; Lomawaima 1995. See also Smith 2007.
25. Ocampo 2014, 441 (emphasis added).
26. Oliver and Shapiro 1995.
27. Smith 2014, 522.
28. Jones and Bullock 2012.
29. Childs 2005; Hodes 1997; Omi and Winant 1994.
30. Harris 1993; Lipsitz 2006.
31. Childs 2005, 131.
32. On whites' "investment" in their position, see Lipsitz 2006.
33. Childs 2005; Vasquez 2015.
34. Duster 2003; Obasogie 2009.

35. Smith 2014, 520.
36. Almaguer 1994; Harris 1993; Ignatiev 1995; Lieberson 1980; Oliver and Shapiro 1995.
37. Chou, Lee, and Ho 2015, 313.
38. Four people preferred in-marriage or a minority, two preferred out-marriage, and two said race-ethnicity was unimportant. The one person who had a racially mixed background who preferred out-marriage from one half of her heritage and in-marriage to the other half of her heritage is counted as preferring a minority partner. Five females and three males expressed this sentiment.
39. Haney López 2006, 147.
40. Rodriguez 2000.
41. Anzaldúa 1987; Macias 2006; Ortiz and Telles 2012.
42. Jones 2012.
43. Among the Latino–non-Hispanic white couples, it was Latinos who usually raised racial issues for discussion.
44. Collins 1986.
45. Feagin 2000.
46. Haskell Indian Nations University, "School History," available at: http://www.haskell.edu/about/history.php (accessed December 15, 2016).
47. Collins 1986, S14.
48. Johnson O'Malley, "Mission," available at: http://johnsonomalley.com/default.html (accessed September 21, 2015).
49. Dawson 1994.
50. Benford and Snow 2000; Omi and Winant 1994.
51. Yuval-Davis 1997.
52. Vasquez 2011.
53. Smith 2007.
54. Dowling 2014.
55. Ethier and Deaux 1994, 249.
56. Collins 1991, S14.
57. Berger and Kellner 1964; Tallman and Gray 1990.

CHAPTER 5: CROSS-NATIONAL LATINO MARRIAGES: RACIAL AND GENDER HAVENS

1. On the rising Mexican American middle class, see Jiménez 2010b; Vallejo 2012; Vasquez 2011. On changing gender norms among Mexican Americans, see Vasquez 2014a.
2. This use of "cross-national" is also referred to by other scholars as "interethnic." I prefer "cross-national" over "interethnic" because the debate over whether "Latino" is a racial or ethnic category makes the latter term confusing. When I mention the "international" couples profiled in other chapters, I am

referring to those who have different nations of birth (for example, the United States and Mexico) but share the same ancestral heritage (Mexico).

3. Vasquez and Wetzel 2009.
4. Root 2001.
5. Brown 2011.
6. Hochschild 1979.
7. Cherlin 2009.
8. Vasquez 2015.
9. Cherlin 2009; Coontz 2006.
10. On social capital, see Hunter 2002.
11. Berger and Kellner 1964, 4.
12. Cornell and Hartmann 1998; Tuan 1998.
13. O'Brien 2008.
14. Xochitl was not alone in her resistance to a long-term relationship with a white man. Using a similar logic, Lydia Duarte excluded white men from her dating pool with the rationale that they were seeking a stereotype that she did not fit: "I've never, ever had a serious relationship with a white guy. Ever . . . I don't fit the bill. Some [white] men have said, 'Oh yeah, we love Mexican girls. You . . . are hot and spicy. . . .' I've probably got too big of a mouth for them. . . . I answer back too much, and I'm probably just too strong." Both women resisted being defined by white men's understandings of Latina womanhood. They felt that Latino men, who occupied the same position in the racial hierarchy and were unlikely to hold the same alienating stereotypes held by white men, would understand them best.
15. Bell and Hartmann 2007, 909.
16. Vasquez 2010a.
17. Fiske 2004, 398.
18. Jiménez 2010b.
19. When he referred to "Americans," he usually meant all U.S.-born people, but at times he used this term to refer specifically to non-Hispanic whites. He often conflated "American" and "white," making it difficult to decipher exactly to whom he referred.
20. DeVault 1991.
21. This issue of conflict over gender in a marriage is not limited to cross-national couples. Endogamous and exogamous couples deal with similar issues, the distinction being that nations set expectations for gender relations in ways that trickle down to the micro level.
22. Barajas and Ramirez 2007; Gutmann 2003.
23. Hondagneu-Sotelo 1994; Smith 2006.
24. Pew Research Center 2010.
25. Hirsch 2003.
26. Hochschild 1989.

27. On the "globalization of care work," see Ehrenreich and Hochschild 2003; Parrenas 2000; Romero 2011.
28. Menjívar and Abrego 2012, 1383.
29. Markus and Conner 2013, 129–30.
30. Coltrane 1996; Daly 1993; Snarey 1993.
31. Vasquez 2014a.
32. The positive effects of a "raceless" identity (as opposed to a minority racial-ethnic identity) on academic achievement have been overstated (Harris and Marsh 2010). Nonetheless, the "acting white" hypothesis—suggesting that minorities who achieve educationally trade in their minority identity and try to perform whiteness (Ogbu and Fordham 1986)—still carries weight in popular understandings of race-ethnicity and school outcomes.
33. On symbolic ethnicity, see Gans 1979.
34. DeVault 1991; Vasquez 2014c.
35. Twine 2010.
36. Lamphere 2007, 1137.
37. Okamoto and Mora 2014, 221.
38. O'Brien 2008; Twine 2010; Vasquez 2014c.
39. Itzigsohn 2009; Mora 2014; Okamoto and Mora 2014; Roth 2012.
40. Hordge-Freeman 2013; Telles 2004, 2014.
41. Roth 2012.
42. Hochschild 1989.
43. Vasquez 2014a.
44. People who did not value their heritage are discussed in chapter 7.
45. We may be seeing the effects of sample bias here, since those who were unhappy in their current marriage may have been less likely to participate in a study on marriage.
46. Okamoto and Mora 2014, 221.
47. DeVault 1991; Di Leonardo 1984.

CHAPTER 6: MIXED-GENERATION MEXICAN-ORIGIN MARRIAGES: FROM TRANSNATIONALISM TO FEMINISM

1. This is why intermarriage has historically been so troubling: it complicates the racial order, calling into the question the relative ranking of groups and the boundaries between them.
2. Flores 2013, 78.
3. Basch, Schiller, and Szanton Blanc 1994, 6.
4. Levitt 2001, 22.
5. On the influence of residence in the United States on gender ideologies, see Hondagneu-Sotelo 1994; Smith 2006. On the resistance of gender ideologies to dramatic change, see Dreby 2010.

6. Thai 2008.
7. Hirsch 2003.
8. Contratto 1987.
9. Hirsch 2003, 143.
10. Ibid.
11. Minorities also follow this logic of "preemptive discrimination," in Kevin Lewis's (2013, 18,817) term, in Internet dating: "Minority site users . . . do not express interest in individuals from a different racial background . . . because they anticipate—based on a lifetime of experiences with racism—that individuals from a different background will not be interested in them."
12. Barajas and Ramirez 2007.
13. Smith 2006.
14. On "legitimate" language, see Bourdieu 1991, 55.
15. Spickard 1991; Thornton, Axinn, and Xie 2007.
16. On college as a site for expanded dating opportunities, see Kibria 2002.
17. Colonia Designers is a pseudonym.
18. Brown 2003.
19. Logan and Stults 2011.
20. I draw from four in-married couples that included an immigrant in this section, but issues of legality, illegality, and citizenship extended beyond intra-marriages. See also chapter 3, especially the discussion of the Carlisle couple, and chapter 4's analysis of the Kortewegs.
21. Fischer and Hout 2006.
22. FitzGerald and Cook-Martín 2014, 8.
23. Bean, Brown, and Bachmeier 2015.
24. HoSang 2010. These legal propositions used metaphors to subtly but effectively promote racist thinking (Santa Ana 2002).
25. On the trend among Mexicans, see Massey and Pren 2012.
26. Ten people—not just immigrants and their spouses—spontaneously mentioned SB 1070 in their interviews. Concern over racist laws transcended immigration status, generation, and region. Of the ten interviewees, one was an immigrant, four were spouses of immigrants, and five were U.S. citizens married to other U.S. citizens. Seven were in California, and three in Kansas; eight were adults and two were teenage children.
27. SB 1070's constitutionality has been challenged, and the most controversial provisions blocked.
28. Amaya 2013, 3.
29. Ochoa 2004.
30. De Genova 2005; Haney López 1996; Jacobson 1998; Oliver and Shapiro 1995.
31. Anderson 1991; De Genova 2005; Haney López 1996; Ngai 2004.
32. Golash-Boza 2012, 110.
33. Ibid., 109, 138.

34. Menjivar 2006, 1004.
35. Golash-Boza 2015.
36. Bhabha 2004.
37. After our two interviews, Jazmin asked if I would write them a character reference ("since [you] now know [our] whole story") to be placed in José's citizenship file. She asked that I include a reference to their family-owned business in Kansas, which she owned and operated, to indicate the hardship that would be incurred by José's extended stay away in Mexico and to demonstrate their status as upright community citizens. I consented and wrote the letter, which, in my view, was not only a small token of reciprocity (they had given me permission to use their life stories for my professional career) but also a gesture in the effort to legalize a hardworking immigrant who was contributing to the economy and to keep a family unified.
38. I describe the mainstream as "white" because, even as demographic shifts—births, deaths, migration—keep the mainstream constantly changing, its power base continues to be coded as white (Bell and Hartmann 2007; Schildkraut 2014). Although some respondents, especially those in California, took care to explain that the presence of racial minorities, racial intermarriages, and multiracial individuals is changing mainstream society, the sentiment remains that the inclusion of these groups is conditional (based on class status, nation of birth, educational attainment, and occupational prestige).
39. Vasquez 2010a.
40. Alba and Nee 2003; Bean and Stevens 2003; Perlmann 2005; Telles and Ortiz 2008.
41. On white ethnics, see Alba 1985; Perlmann 2005; Waters 1990.
42. Frankenberg 1993.
43. Alba 2006; Alba and Nee 2003.
44. Lareau 2003. In thinking about the potential variants of Annette Lareau's concept of "concerted cultivation," I thank Amanda Lewis (2004, 841), who coined the term "constrained entitlement" to refer to the sense of entitlement that black middle-class children develop that acknowledges their confrontations with racism.
45. Gerson 2015; Sherman 2009a.
46. Vasquez 2011.
47. Vasquez 2014a; Kasinitz et al. 2008.
48. Non-Latino male respondents had another reason for wanting to change their expression of masculinity: they wanted closer relationships with their sons than they had with their fathers. A desire to change masculinity therefore was not exclusive to the Latino men in the study. Also, feminism among the Latino men extended beyond those in mixed-generation marriages (see, for example, Miguel in chapter 5).
49. Flores 2013; Smith 2006; Vigil 2002a.

50. Flores 2013.

51. Coltrane 1996; Dienhart 1998; Snarey 1993.

52. Dreby 2010.

53. Negrón-Muntaner 2014, 104.

54. On the media's power to "construct" our understanding of the world, see Chavez 2008, 5. On stereotypical depictions of Latinos, see Merskin 2011; Negrón-Muntaner 2014.

55. Merskin 2011, 172.

56. Ibid., 158.

57. Molina-Guzmán 2010, 9.

58. Ibid., 180.

59. Deutsch 2007.

60. The wives who inspired change in their spouse's masculinity were not limited to the mixed-generation, Mexican-origin marital pairings: Merle Andrade (chapter 7) similarly changed his ways out of a desire to maintain good relations with his wife and daughters.

61. Lewis 2003; Markus and Conner 2013; Perry 2002.

CHAPTER 7: INTRAGENERATIONAL MARRIAGES AND RACIAL STRATEGIES: RACIAL ERASING, RACIAL EASING, AND CONSTRAINED CULTIVATION

1. Cornell and Hartmann 1998; Rodriguez 2000; Roth 2012.

2. Both fiction and nonfiction have dealt with issues of racial-ethnic "passing" or change, from multiple viewpoints; see Baldwin 1952/2000; Ellison 1947/1995; Larsen 2001; Roth 2001.

3. Bonilla-Silva 2003.

4. I make two exceptions to this intragenerational organization. The two couples included in this chapter who were not married intragenerationally were in "neighboring" generations (for example, second generation and third generation). There was a logic to this decision. I included the Salazar-Venegas couple because the complicated experience of Raven Salazar (technically second generation) of being raised as her (teenage) mother's sister and by her grandparents was much like that of the immigrant generation. And I included the Ortegas, another "neighboring generations" couple (she was second generation, he was third generation), to make the analytical point that racial strategies can serve as points of attraction for couples.

5. Collins 1991; Vasquez-Tokos and Norton-Smith 2016.

6. Flores 2013; Zhou et al. 2008.

7. Lareau 2003.

8. U.S. Census Bureau, "Quick Facts: Los Angeles County, California," available at: http://www.census.gov/quickfacts/table/RHI705210/06037,00 (accessed March 18, 2016).

9. Of eleven couples who were Mexican-origin and had the same generational status, only three claimed their heritage without reserve. It was the preponderance of people engaged in the stratagems of racial erasing and racial easing that led me to devote a chapter to the subject.

10. Los Angeles Police Department, "Gangs," available at: http://www.lapd online.org/get_informed/content_basic_view/1396 (accessed January 14, 2016).

11. Smith 2014, 522.

12. Filipinos in Los Angeles similarly distance themselves from lower-class Latinos (but not middle-class Latinos) owing to their class status and criminalization (Ocampo 2015).

13. To a degree, the U.S. census categories "represent public consensus on how populations are viewed and counted" (Rodriguez 2000, xiii–xiv). Of note is the change in racial categories over time. In 1930, "Mexican" was considered a race, but never before or since. In 1993, Hispanics proposed making "Latino" a race (not an ethnic group), but this idea was eventually dropped. For 2020, the U.S. census is considering a combined race question that would list Hispanic/Latino as a racial category alongside white, black, Native American, and Asian/Pacific Islander (Dowling 2014; Mora 2014; Roth 2012).

14. Lipsitz 2006, vii.

15. Ferguson 2000.

16. Almaguer 1994; Collins 2004; Massey and Denton 1993; Montejano 1987.

17. Despite the existence of white gangs, most of the literature on gangs concentrates on racial minority gangs (Sánchez-Jankowski 1991; Smith 2006; Vigil 1988, 2002b).

18. Baldwin 1952/2000; Bourgois 2002; Ferguson 2000.

19. Bourgois 2002, 288.

20. Lipsitz 2006.

21. Bertrand and Mullainathan 2004; Pager 2007.

22. Maldonado 2009.

23. Feagin and O'Brien 2003. Some diversification in the power elite in terms of gender, race-ethnicity, and sexual orientation has occurred (Zweigenhaft and Domhoff 1998).

24. Pyke and Dang 2003, 150–51.

25. Steele and Aronson 1995, 797.

26. Moss and Tilly 1996.

27. Bourgois 2002.

28. A similar phenomenon happens concerning gender inequality in response to increased pressures at work. Arlie Hochschild (1997) argues in *The Time Bind* that the vast majority of workers respond to demands on their time by

regimenting their home life. While this does not strike at the structural cause of the social problem, it is a common response because it is what workers can actually control.

29. Pyke and Dang 2003, 151.
30. Merle's wife declined the interview request, claiming to be shy.
31. Bonilla-Silva 2003.
32. Dowling 2014.
33. Pattillo-McCoy 1999.
34. Whittier Area Chamber of Commerce, "Whittier Demographics," available at: https://www.whittierchamber.com/whittier-demographics/ (accessed December 15, 2016).
35. Vasquez 2015.
36. Garcia Bedolla 2005, 158.
37. Although the Ortegas held aspirations for their children, they were not engaging in constrained cultivation—that is, they were not using their limited means to buy extracurricular activities for their children in an attempt to mirror middle-class parenting practices.
38. Ferguson 2000; Ochoa 2013; Steele and Aronson 1995; Valenzuela 1999.
39. Jiménez 2010b; Valdez 2011; Vallejo 2012; Vasquez 2011.
40. Lareau 2003, 1.
41. Ibid., 3.
42. In a review of *Unequal Childhoods*, the race scholar Amanda Lewis (2004, 841) emphasized the racial differences between the families in Lareau's study and proposed: "Although both Black and White middle-class parents engage in strategies of concerted cultivation, there might well be differences in children's developing sense of their relationship to the world. For example, given the experiences with institutional or individual-level discrimination that some Black parents discuss, perhaps Black middle-class children are developing a sense of *constrained entitlement*—one in which confrontations with racism need to be taken into account in thinking about what to expect in the world around them." I build on this critique in developing the idea of *constrained cultivation*.
43. Bonilla-Silva 2003.
44. Feagin and Cobas 2008; Pyke 2010.
45. Sánchez-Jankowski 1991; Smith 2006; Vigil 2002a.
46. Flores 2013, 111.
47. Vincent explained the difference between a gang girl and a party girl: "There is gang girls and then there's . . . party girls; girls . . . like to go out every weekend with their friends and just happen to like that edgy gang life but never really got involved with it." In the parlance of Mary Pattillo-McCoy (1999), gang members are "consumed" with "ghetto behavior" (fully engaged, including violence), whereas party girls are "thrilled" by it (excited by ghetto language and styles, but not gang members themselves).

48. Pattillo-McCoy 1999, 143.
49. Zhou et al. 2008.
50. U.S. Census Bureau, "Quick Facts: United States," available at: http://quickfacts.census.gov/qfd/states/06/0670000.html (accessed April 17, 2015).
51. On the ascension of Asians, see Jiménez and Horowitz 2013; Lee and Zhou 2015.
52. De Genova 2005; Hondagneu-Sotelo 1997.
53. Vasquez and Wetzel 2009.
54. Hochschild 1997.
55. Hays 1996.
56. How parents' racial and class aspirations for their children are carried out (or not) in the next generation is an important question for race and family studies. Pablo encountered identity conflicts that were related to his parents' trajectory of racial easing coupled with financial stability. Raven told me, "He ended up having a huge identity crisis because he wasn't fitting in with the white kids because he's not white. And then he wasn't fitting in with his Mexican counterparts." Downward-leveling pressure demands conformity to the group, group members perceiving efforts to move beyond the group as a threat to solidarity and respect (Portes and Landolt 1996). Raven observed Pablo's Mexican American peers exert this type of negative influence: "Basically, [Pablo] was succeeding and they [his Mexican American peers] wanted to pull him down." A budding theatrical performer, Pablo endured harassment from his peers who did not have the same opportunities to attend enrichment programs. Add to this that theater is not a normatively masculine activity, and Pablo was opened up to masculinist and homophobic accusations of being gay (Pascoe 2007). Pablo was tempted to give up his acting passion, yet Raven counteracted the downward-leveling pressure by supporting her child's talents. Pablo's younger brother, who was too young to participate in the study, had an altogether different experience that approximated downward (segmented) assimilation with low-income African American youth. Raven described her dark-skinned youngest son: "He has said that he won't deny he's Mexican. He won't go that far. But he has said that he doesn't like his color. He doesn't want to be called [his Hispanic first name]. He has almost wanted to be black. . . . [He asked], 'Can you give me braids?' We did it. . . . He wanted to assimilate with blacks, maybe because he was darker-skinned. That's where he thought he could fit in." Two sons in the same family followed two different racial identity trajectories, influenced by skin color and participation in extracurricular activities.
57. Bejarano 2014, 8; Rogowski, Sandoval, and Cohen, n.d.
58. Dowling 2014, 40.
59. Ennis, Ríos-Vargas, and Albert 2011.
60. U.S. Census Bureau, "Quick Facts: Kansas," available at: http://www.census.gov/quickfacts/table/PST045215/20 (accessed March 18, 2016).
61. The poverty rate in the city of Los Angeles for the Mexican-origin population, as a subset of the Hispanic population, was even higher, at 27.9 percent (U.S.

Census Bureau, "Quick Facts: United States," available at: http://quickfacts.census.gov [accessed April 28, 2014]).

62. Flores 2013, 2.
63. U.S. Census Bureau, "Quick Facts: United States," available at: http://quickfacts.census.gov (accessed April 28, 2014).
64. Bedolla 2005, 158.
65. Goffman 1973.
66. Of the three (out of eleven) couples who expressed an assertive Latino identity and did not engage in social distancing tactics, the Californians were among the highest-income earners, at approximately $200,000 annual household income. Since this racial strategy was the exception rather than the norm, it is not discussed here. See chapter 6 for a discussion of racial solidarity.
67. Chavez 2008.
68. Flores 2013, 2.
69. Macias 2006.
70. The desire to retreat from a connection to Latinos is not exclusive to in-group members. Since Latinos in Los Angeles are not viewed as academically high-achieving, Filipinos weaken their association with Latinos if it appears likely to "compromise their middle-class standing or mobility" (Ocampo 2014, 439).
71. Portes and Zhou 1993.
72. Rumbaut and Portes 2001, 72.
73. Bonilla-Silva 2003.
74. Chavez 2008.
75. Lareau 2003.
76. Bourdieu 1986.
77. Alba and Nee 2003; Kalmijn 1998; Qian and Lichter 2011; Telles and Ortiz 2008.

CHAPTER 8: UNPACKING MARRIAGE: DIVORCE, REPARTNERING, AMBIVALENCE, AND THE SEARCH FOR LOVE

1. Swidler 2001.
2. Ibid., 117.
3. Hackstaff 1999.
4. Cherlin 2009, 4.
5. Taylor 2010, 19, 1.
6. Hackstaff 1999, 1.
7. Cherlin 2009.
8. Amato 2010, 651.
9. Birmingham et al. 2015, 743.
10. Ibid., 744.

11. Hackstaff 1999, 2.
12. Tallman and Gray 1990, 414.
13. Ansari and Klinenberg 2015; Rosenfeld and Thomas 2012.
14. On romance and modern marriage, see Amato 2009; Cherlin 2009; Coontz 2006. On class- and race-specific aspects of marriage, see Swidler 2001.
15. Vasquez 2015.
16. Snarey 1993.
17. Coltrane 1996; Dienhart 1998; Snarey 1993.
18. Dienhart 1998.
19. Vasquez 2014a.
20. Gerson 2010.
21. Eaton et al. 2009; Rosenfeld 2009.
22. Cherlin 2009.
23. The chance of divorce increases with each subsequent marriage: in the United States, 50 percent of first marriages, 67 percent of second marriages, and 73 percent of third marriages terminate in divorce. One explanation for the progressive increase in divorce rates is that people enter a subsequent marriage "on the rebound" and without taking sufficient time to "internalize the lessons of their past experience," making them "liable to repeat their mistakes" (Banschick 2012). While the future is never certain, the couples in this section devoted time and energy to learning from their prior marriage so that they could make a better selection in a subsequent formal relationship.
24. Amato 2009.
25. Vasquez 2014a.
26. Amato 2009; Hackstaff 1999.
27. Sherman 2009a, 599.
28. Weitzman 1985, 323.
29. Cherlin 2009, 29.
30. Hackstaff 1999, 2; Kitson and Holmes 1992.
31. Berger and Kellner 1964.
32. Hochschild 1989.
33. Gottman et al. 1998.
34. Zambrana 2011, 39.
35. Espiritu 2000, 416.
36. Despite the rise in the Internet as a "social intermediary" in dating (see Ansari and Klinenberg 2015; Rosenfeld and Thomas 2012), none of my interviewees reported meeting over the Internet. For Latino population figures, see Stepler and Brown 2016.
37. Taylor 2010, 36.
38. Fry and Cohn 2011.
39. Hirsch 2003; Smith 2006.
40. Cherlin 2009.

41. Hackstaff 1999, 21.
42. Ibid., 202–3.
43. Kitson and Holmes 1992.
44. Hochschild 1989.
45. Vasquez 2014a.
46. Jones 2012.
47. Suro 2005.
48. Duckworth et al. 2007.
49. Li 2010.
50. Grebler, Moore, and Guzman 1970; Montejano 1987.
51. Suro 2005, 16.
52. Vasquez 2015.

CHAPTER 9: CONCLUSION: NEGOTIATED DESIRE

1. Omi and Winant 1994.
2. Cherlin 2009; Coontz 2006. On families as political institutions, see Yamin 2012.
3. Tallman and Gray 1990.
4. Berger and Kellner 1964, 5 (emphasis in original).
5. Root 2001.
6. Maldonado 2009.
7. Gerson 2010.
8. Cherlin 2009.
9. Alba and Nee 2003, 11.
10. King 1988; Segura 1986.
11. Elder, Johnson, and Crosnoe 2003.
12. Jiménez 2010a.
13. Alba, Jiménez, and Marrow 2014; Jiménez, Fields, and Schachter 2015; Zambrana 2011; Zavella 1994.
14. Lee 2013, 2.
15. Abrego 2014; Dreby 2010; Golash-Boza 2015. On refugees, see Brown 2011; Garcia 1996.
16. On Singapore, see Teo 2011.
17. Alba, Jiménez, and Marrow 2014; Kalmijn 1998; Lichter, Carmalt, and Qian 2011; Qian and Lichter 2007; Rosenfeld 2008; Spickard 1991.
18. Vasquez 2015.
19. Ocampo 2014. On redrawing racial boundaries, see Brown and Jones 2015; Okamoto and Mora 2014.
20. Dowling 2014. On the "socially nonwhite" social location, see Gómez 2007.
21. O'Brien 2008.

22. Bonilla-Silva 2003; Flores-Gonzalez 1999; Golash-Boza 2006; Golash-Boza and Darity 2008.
23. Lee and Bean 2010; O'Brien 2008; Vasquez 2015; Marrow 2011, 127.
24. Kalmijn 1998; Lichter et al. 2007; Lichter et al. 2011; Qian and Lichter 2011.
25. Lee and Bean 2004.
26. Macias 2006.
27. Vasquez 2015.
28. Brown and Jones 2015; Jones 2012; Martinez and Rios 2011; Ocampo 2015.
29. Vasquez 2015.
30. Chavez 2008; Santa Ana 2002.
31. Vasquez 2015.
32. Taylor, Funk, and Craighill 2006.

APPENDIX A: METHODOLOGY

1. Portes and Rumbaut 2001.
2. Gerson 1986, 38.
3. Chambliss and Schutt 2012.
4. Hochschild 2003.
5. Gerson 2010.
6. This study does not include polyamorous families, an area that remains understudied.
7. Bernard 1982, 4.
8. Glaser and Strauss 1967; Strauss 1987.

References

Abrego, Leisy. 2014. *Sacrificing Families: Navigating Laws, Labor, and Love Across Borders.* Stanford, Calif.: Stanford University Press.

Acuña, Rodolfo. 2011. *Occupied America: A History of Chicanos.* New York: Longman.

Alba, Richard D. 1985. *Italian Americans: Into the Twilight of Ethnicity.* Englewood Cliffs, N.J.: Prentice-Hall.

———. 1990. *Ethnic Identity: The Transformation of White America.* New Haven, Conn.: Yale University Press.

———. 2006. "Mexican Americans and the American Dream." *Perspectives on Politics* 4(2): 289–96.

———. 2009. *Blurring the Color Line: The New Chance for a More Integrated America.* Cambridge, Mass.: Harvard University Press.

Alba, Richard, and Tariqul Islam. 2009. "The Case of the Disappearing Mexican Americans: An Ethnic-Identity Mystery." *Population Research and Policy Review* 28(2): 109–21.

Alba, Richard, Tomás R. Jiménez, and Helen B. Marrow. 2013. "Mexican Americans as a Paradigm for Contemporary Intra-Group Heterogeneity." *Ethnic and Racial Studies* 37(3): 446–66.

———. 2014. "Mexican Americans as a Paradigm for Contemporary Intragroup Heterogeneity." *Ethnic and Racial Studies* 37(3): 446–66.

Alba, Richard D., and Victor Nee. 2003. *Remaking the American Mainstream: Assimilation and Contemporary Immigration.* Cambridge, Mass.: Harvard University Press.

Almaguer, Tomas. 1994. *Racial Fault Lines: The Historical Origins of White Supremacy in California.* Berkeley: University of California Press.

Altman, Dennis. 2001. *Global Sex.* Chicago: University of Chicago Press.

Amato, Paul R. 2009. *Alone Together: How Marriage in America Is Changing.* Cambridge, Mass.: Harvard University Press.

———. 2010. "Research on Divorce: Continuing Trends and New Developments." *Journal of Marriage and Family* 72(3): 650–66.

Amaya, Hector. 2013. *Citizenship Excess: Latinas/os, Media, and the Nation.* New York: New York University Press.

Anderson, Benedict R. 1991. *Imagined Communities: Reflections on the Origin and Spread of Nationalism.* London: Verso.

Ansari, Aziz, and Eric Klinenberg. 2015. *Modern Romance: An Investigation.* New York: Penguin Press.

Anzaldúa, Gloria. 1987. *Borderlands/La Frontera: The New Mestiza.* San Francisco: Spinsters/Aunt Lute.

Apfelbaum, Evan P., Michael I. Norton, and Samuel R. Sommers. 2012. "Racial Color Blindness: Emergence of Practices and Implications." *Current Directions in Psychological Science* 21(3): 205–09.

Baldwin, James. 2000. *Go Tell It on the Mountain.* New York: Random House. (Originally published in 1952.)

Banschick, Mark. 2012. "The High Failure Rate of Second and Third Marriages: Why Are Second and Third Marriages More Likely to Fail?" *Psychology Today* (February 6).

Barajas, Manuel, and Elvia Ramirez. 2007. "Beyond Home-Host Dichotomies: A Comparative Examination of Gender Relations in a Transnational Mexican Community." *Sociological Perspectives* 50(3): 367–92.

Basch, Linda G., Nina Glick Schiller, and Cristina Szanton Blanc. 1994. *Nations Unbound: Transnational Projects, Postcolonial Predicaments, and Deterritorialized Nation-States.* Langhorne, Penn.: Gordon and Breach.

Bean, Frank D., Susan K. Brown, and James D. Bachmeier. 2015. *Parents Without Papers: The Progress and Pitfalls of Mexican-American Integration.* New York: Russell Sage Foundation.

Bean, Frank D., and Gillian Stevens. 2003. *America's Newcomers and the Dynamics of Diversity.* New York: Russell Sage Foundation.

Beaver, Janice Cheryl. 2006. "U.S. International Borders: Brief Facts." Washington: Library of Congress, Congressional Research Service.

Bejarano, Christina E. 2014. *The Latino Gender Gap in U.S. Politics.* New York: Taylor & Francis.

Bell, Joyce M., and Douglas Hartmann. 2007. "Diversity in Everyday Discourse: The Cultural Ambiguities and Consequences of 'Happy Talk.'" *American Sociological Review* 72(6): 895–914.

Benford, Robert D., and David A. Snow. 2000. "Framing Processes and Social Movements: An Overview and Assessment." *Annual Review of Sociology* 26: 611–39.

Berger, Peter, and Hansfried Kellner. 1964. "Marriage and the Construction of Reality: An Exercise in the Microsociology of Knowledge." *Diogenes* 12(46): 1–24.

Bernard, Jessie 1982. *The Future of Marriage.* New Haven, Conn.: Yale University Press.

Bertrand, Marianne, and Sendhil Mullainathan. 2004. "Are Emily and Greg More Employable Than Lakisha and Jamal? A Field Experiment on Labor Market Discrimination." *American Economic Review* 94(4): 991–1013.

Bettie, Julie. 2003. *Women Without Class: Girls, Race, and Identity*. Berkeley: University of California Press.

Bhabha, Jacqueline. 2004. "The 'Mere Fortuity' of Birth? Are Children Citizens?" *Differences* 15: 91–117.

Birmingham, Wendy C., Bert N. Uchino, Timothy W. Smith, Kathleen C. Light, and Jonathan Butner. 2015. "It's Complicated: Marital Ambivalence on Ambulatory Blood Pressure and Daily Interpersonal Functioning." *Annals of Behavioral Medicine* 49(5): 743–53.

Blackwell, Debra L., and Daniel T. Lichter. 2004. "Homogamy Among Dating, Cohabiting, and Married Couples." *Sociological Quarterly* 45(4): 719–37.

Blau, Peter M., Terry C. Blum, and Joseph Schwartz. 1982. "Heterogeneity and Intermarriage." *American Sociological Review* 47: 45–62.

Bloemraad, Irene, Anna Korteweg, and Gokce Yurdakul. 2008. "Citizenship and Immigration: Multiculturalism, Assimilation, and Challenges to the Nation-State." *Annual Review of Sociology* 34(1): 153–79.

Blumer, Herbert. 1958. "Race Prejudice as a Sense of Group Position." *Pacific Sociological Review* 1(1): 3–7.

Bobo, Lawrence D., and Mia Tuan. 2006. *Prejudice in Politics: Group Position, Public Opinion, and the Wisconsin Treaty Rights Dispute*. Cambridge, Mass.: Harvard University Press.

Bonilla-Silva, Eduardo. 2003. *Racism Without Racists: Color-Blind Racism and the Persistence of Racial Inequality in the United States*. Lanham, Md.: Rowman & Littlefield.

———. 2004. "From Bi-racial to Tri-racial: Towards a New System of Racial Stratification in the USA." *Ethnic and Racial Studies* 27(6): 931–50.

Bourdieu, Pierre. 1984. *Distinction*. Cambridge, Mass.: Harvard University Press.

———. 1986. "The Forms of Capital." In *Handbook of Theory and Research for the Sociology of Education*, edited by John E. Richardson. Westport, Conn.: Greenwood Press.

———. 1991. *Language and Symbolic Power*. Cambridge, Mass.: Harvard University Press.

Bourgois, Philippe. 2002. *In Search of Respect: Selling Crack in El Barrio*. New York: Cambridge University Press.

Brown, Hana E. 2011. "Refugees, Rights, and Race: How Legal Status Shapes Liberian Immigrants' Relationship with the State." *Social Problems* 58(1): 144–63.

Brown, Hana, and Jennifer A. Jones. 2015. "Rethinking Panethnicity and the Race-Immigration Divide: An Ethnoracialization Model of Group Formation." *Sociology of Race and Ethnicity* 1(1): 181–91.

Brown, Michael K. 2003. *Whitewashing Race: The Myth of a Color-Blind Society*. Berkeley: University of California Press.

Burk, James, and Evelyn Espinoza. 2012. "Race Relations Within the U.S. Military." *Annual Review of Sociology* 38: 401–22.

Butler, John Sibley, and Kenneth L. Wilson. 1978. "The American Soldier Revisited: Race Relations and the Military." *Social Science Quarterly* 59(3): 451–67.

Cantú, Lionel. 1995. "The Peripheralization of Rural America: A Case Study of Latino Migrants in America's Heartland." *Sociological Perspectives* 38(3): 399–414.

Casas, Maria Raquél. 2007. *Married to a Daughter of the Land: Spanish-Mexican Women and Interethnic Marriage in California, 1820–1880.* Reno: University of Nevada Press.

Chambliss, Daniel F., and Russell K. Schutt. 2012. *Making Sense of the Social World: Methods of Investigation.* Thousand Oaks, Calif.: Sage Publications.

Chavez, Leo R. 2008. *The Latino Threat: Constructing Immigrants, Citizens, and the Nation.* Stanford, Calif.: Stanford University Press.

Cherlin, Andrew J. 2009. *The Marriage-Go-Round: The State of Marriage and the Family in America Today.* New York: Vintage Books.

Child, Brenda J. 2000. *Boarding School Seasons: American Indian Families.* Lincoln: University of Nebraska Press.

Childs, Erica Chito. 2005. *Navigating Interracial Borders: Black-White Couples and Their Social Worlds.* New Brunswick, N.J.: Rutgers University Press.

Chodorow, Nancy J. 1978. *The Reproduction of Mothering: Psychoanalysis and the Sociology of Gender.* Berkeley: University of California Press.

Chong, Kelly H. 2013. "Relevance of Race: Children and the Shifting Engagement with Racial/Ethnic Identity Among Second-Generation Interracially Married Asian Americans." *Journal of Asian American Studies* 16(2): 189–221.

Chou, Rosalind, Kristen Lee, and Simon Ho. 2015. "Love Is (Color)blind: Asian Americans and White Institutional Space at the Elite University." *Sociology of Race and Ethnicity* 1(2): 302–16.

Collins, Patricia Hill. 1986. "Learning from the Outsider Within." *Social Problems* 33(6): 14–32.

———. 1991. *Black Feminist Thought.* New York: Routledge.

———. 2004. *Black Sexual Politics: African Americans, Gender, and the New Racism.* New York: Routledge.

Coltrane, Scott. 1996. *Family Man: Fatherhood, Housework, and Gender Equity.* New York: Oxford University Press.

Conley, Dalton. 1999. *Being Black, Living in the Red: Race, Wealth, and Social Policy in America.* Berkeley: University of California Press.

Contratto, Susan. 1987. "Father Presence in Women's Psychological Development." In *Advances in Psychoanalytic Sociology,* edited by Jerome Rabow, Gerald M. Platt, and Marion S. Goldman. Malabar, Fla.: Krieger.

Coontz, Stephanie. 2006. *Marriage, a History: How Love Conquered Marriage.* Penguin Group.

Cornelius, Wayne A. 2002. "Ambivalent Reception: Mass Public Responses to the 'New' Latino Immigration to the United States." In *Latinos: Remaking America,* edited by Marcelo Suárez-Orozco and Mariela Paez. Berkeley: University of California Press.

Cornell, Stephen E., and Douglass Hartmann. 1998. *Ethnicity and Race: Making Identities in a Changing World.* Thousand Oaks, Calif.: Pine Forge Press.

———. 2004. "Conceptual Confusions and Divides: Race, Ethnicity, and the Study of Immigration." In *Not Just Black and White: Historical and Contemporary Perspectives on Immigration, Race, and Ethnicity in the United States,* edited by Nancy Foner and George M. Fredrickson. New York: Russell Sage Foundation.

Coser, Lewis A. 2003. *Masters of Sociological Thought: Ideas in Historical and Social Context.* New York: Harcourt Brace Jovanovich.

Dalmage, Heather M. 2000. *Tripping on the Color Line: Black-White Multiracial Families in a Racially Divided World.* New Brunswick, N.J.: Rutgers University Press.

Daly, Kerry. 1993. "Reshaping Fatherhood: Finding the Models." *Journal of Family Issues* 14(4): 510–30.

Davis, Kingsley. 1941. "Intermarriage in Caste Societies." *American Anthropologist* 43: 376–95.

Dawson, Michael C. 1994. *Behind the Mule: Race and Class in African-American Politics.* Princeton, N.J.: Princeton University Press.

Deaux, Kay. 2006. *To Be an Immigrant.* New York: Russell Sage Foundation.

De Genova, Nicholas. 2005. *Working the Boundaries: Race, Space, and "Illegality" in Mexican Chicago.* Raleigh, N.C.: Duke University Press.

Deutsch, Francine M. 2007. "Undoing Gender." *Gender and Society* 21(1): 106–27.

DeVault, Marjorie L. 1991. *Feeding the Family: The Social Organization of Caring as Gendered Work.* Chicago: University of Chicago Press.

Dienhart, Anna. 1998. *Reshaping Fatherhood: The Social Construction of Shared Parenting.* Thousand Oaks, Calif.: Sage Publications.

Di Leonardo, Micaela. 1984. *The Varieties of Ethnic Experience: Kinship, Class, and Gender Among California Italian-Americans.* Ithaca, N.Y.: Cornell University Press.

Donovan, Brian. 2003. "The Sexual Basis of Racial Formation: Anti-Vice Activism and the Creation of the Twentieth-Century 'Color Line.'" *Ethnic and Racial Studies* 26(4): 707–27.

Dowling, Julie A. 2014. *Mexican Americans and the Question of Race.* Austin: University of Texas Press.

Dreby, Joana. 2010. *Divided by Borders: Mexican Migrants and Their Children.* Berkeley: University of California Press.

Dreby, Joanna, and Leah Schmalzbauer. 2013. "The Relational Contexts of Migration: Mexican Women in New Destination Sites." *Sociological Forum* 28(1): 1–26.

Duckworth, Angela L., Christopher Peterson, Michael D. Matthews, and Dennis R. Kelly. 2007. "Grit: Perseverance and Passion for Long-Term Goals." *Journal of Personality and Social Psychology* 92(6): 1087–1101.

Duncan, Brian, and Stephen J. Trejo. 2011. "Intermarriage and the Intergenerational Transmission of Ethnic Identity and Human Capital for Mexican Americans." *Journal of Labor Economics* 29(2): 195–227.

Duster, Troy. 2003. *Backdoor to Eugenics.* New York: Routledge.

Eaton, Asia A., Penny S. Visser, Jon A. Krosnick, and Sowmya Anand. 2009. "Social Power and Attitude Strength over the Life Course." *Personality and Social Psychology Bulletin* 35(12): 1646–60.

Edin, Kathryn, and Maria Kefalas. 2007. *Promises I Can Keep: Why Poor Women Put Motherhood Before Marriage.* Berkeley: University of California Press.

Ehrenreich, Barbara, and Arlie Russell Hochschild. 2003. *Global Woman: Nannies, Maids, and Sex Workers in the New Economy.* New York: Metropolitan Books.

Elder, Glen H., Jr., Monica Kirkpatrick Johnson, and Robert Crosnoe. 2003. "The Emergence and Development of Life Course Theory." In *Handbook of the Life Course,* edited by Jeylan T. Mortimer and Michael J. Shanahan. New York: Springer.

Ellison, Ralph. 1995. *Invisible Man.* New York: Random House. (Originally published in 1947.)

Ennis, Sharon R., Merarys Ríos-Vargas, and Nora G. Albert. 2011. "The Hispanic Population: 2010." Washington: U.S. Census Bureau.

Espiritu, Yen Le. 2000. "We Don't Sleep Around Like White Girls Do." *Signs* 26(2): 415–40.

Ethier, Kathleen A., and Kay Deaux. 1994. "Negotiating Social Identity When Contexts Change: Maintaining Identification and Responding to Threat." *Journal of Personality and Social Psychology* 67(2): 243–51.

Farley, Reynolds, and Richard Alba. 2002. "The New Second Generation in the United States." *International Migration Review* 36(3): 669–701.

Feagin, Joe R. 2000. *Racist America: Roots, Current Realities, and Future Reparations.* New York: Routledge.

Feagin, Joe R., and José Cobas. 2008. "Latinos/as and the White Racial Frame: The Procrustean Bed of Assimilation." *Sociological Inquiry* 78(1): 39–53.

Feagin, Joe R., and Eileen O'Brien. 2003. *White Men on Race: Power, Privilege, and the Shaping of Cultural Consciousness.* Boston: Beacon Press.

Feagin, Joe R., and Melvin P. Sikes. 1994. *Living with Racism: The Black Middle-Class Experience.* Boston: Beacon Press.

Feliciano, Cynthia, Rennie Lee, and Belinda Robnett. 2011. "Racial Boundaries Among Latinos: Evidence from Internet Daters' Racial Preferences." *Social Problems* 58(2): 189–212.

Feliciano, Cynthia, and Belinda Robnett. 2014. "How External Racial Classifications Shape Latino Dating Choices." *Du Bois Review* 11(2): 295–328.

Feliciano, Cynthia, Belinda Robnett, and Golnaz Komaie. 2009. "Gendered Racial Exclusion Among White Internet Daters." *Social Science Research* 38(1): 39–54.

Ferguson, Ann Arnett. 2000. *Bad Boys: Public Schools in the Making of Black Masculinity.* Ann Arbor: University of Michigan Press.

Fernández-Kelly, Patricia, and Douglas S. Massey. 2007. "Borders for Whom? The Role of NAFTA in Mexico-U.S. Migration." *Annals of the American Academy of Political and Social Science* 610(1): 98–118.

Fischer, Claude S., and Michael Hout. 2006. *Century of Difference: How America Changed in the Last One Hundred Years*. New York: Russell Sage Foundation.

Fischer, Claude, Michael Hout, Martín Sánchez-Jankowski, Samuel Lucas, Ann Swidler, and Kim Voss. 1996. *Inequality by Design: Cracking the Bell Curve Myth*. Princeton, N.J.: Princeton University Press.

Fiske, Susan T. 2004. *Social Beings: A Core Motives Approach to Social Psychology*. Hoboken, N.J.: Wiley.

FitzGerald, David, and David Cook-Martín. 2014. *Culling the Masses: The Democratic Origins of Racist Immigration Policy in the Americas*. Cambridge, Mass.: Harvard University Press.

Flores, Edward Orozco. 2013. *God's Gangs: Barrio Ministry, Masculinity, and Gang Recovery*. New York: New York University Press.

Flores, William Vincent, and Rina Benmayor. 1997. *Latino Cultural Citizenship: Claiming Identity, Space, and Rights*. Boston: Beacon Press.

Flores-Gonzalez, Nilda. 1999. "The Racialization of Latinos: The Meaning of Latino Identity for the Second Generation." *Latino Studies Journal* 10(3): 3–31.

Foley, Neil. 1997. *The White Scourge: Mexicans, Blacks, and Poor Whites in Texas Cotton Culture*. Berkeley: University of California Press.

Fox, Cybelle. 2010. "Three Worlds of Relief: Race, Immigration, and Public and Private Social Welfare Spending in American Cities, 1929." *American Journal of Sociology* 116(2): 453–502.

Fox, Cybelle, and Thomas A. Guglielmo. 2012. "Defining America's Racial Boundaries: Blacks, Mexicans, and European Immigrants, 1890–1945." *American Journal of Sociology* 118(2): 327–79.

Frankenberg, Ruth. 1993. *White Women, Race Matters: The Social Construction of Whiteness*. Minneapolis: University of Minnesota Press.

Fry, Richard. 2012. "No Reversal in Decline of Marriage." Washington, D.C.: Pew Research Center.

Fry, Richard, and D'Vera Cohn. 2011. "Living Together: The Economics of Cohabitation." Washington, D.C.: Pew Research Center.

Gans, Herbert J. 1979. "Symbolic Ethnicity: The Future of Ethnic Groups in America." *Ethnic and Racial Studies* 2(2): 1–20.

———. 1996. "Symbolic Ethnicity: The Future of Ethnic Groups and Cultures in America." In *Theories of Ethnicity: A Classical Reader*, edited by Werner Sollors. New York: New York University Press.

Garcia, Maria Cristina. 1996. *Havana USA: Cuban Exiles and Cuban Americans in South Florida, 1959–1994*. Berkeley: University of California Press.

Garcia Bedolla, Lisa. 2005. *Fluid Borders: Latino Power, Identity, and Politics in Los Angeles*. Berkeley: University of California Press.

Gerson, Kathleen. 1986. *Hard Choices: How Women Decide About Work, Career, and Motherhood*. Berkeley: University of California Press.

———. 2010. *The Unfinished Revolution: How a New Generation Is Reshaping Family, Work, and Gender in America.* Oxford: Oxford University Press.

———. 2015. "Falling Back on Plan B: The Children of the Gender Revolution Face Uncharted Territory." In *Families as They Really Are,* edited by Barbara J. Risman and Virginia E. Rutter. New York: W. W. Norton.

Glaser, Barney G., and Anselm L. Strauss. 1967. *The Discovery of Grounded Theory: Strategies for Qualitative Research.* Hawthorne, N.Y.: Aldine de Gruyter.

Glazer, Nathan, and Daniel P. Moynihan. 1963. *Beyond the Melting Pot: The Negroes, Puerto Ricans, Jews, Italians, and Irish of New York City.* Cambridge, Mass.: MIT Press.

Glenn, Evelyn Nakano. 1986. *Issei, Nisei, War Bride: Three Generations of Japanese American Women in Domestic Service.* Philadelphia: Temple University Press.

———. 2002. *Unequal Freedom: How Race and Gender Shaped American Citizenship and Labor.* Cambridge, Mass.: Harvard University Press.

———. 2009. *Shades of Difference: Why Skin Color Matters.* Stanford, Calif.: Stanford University Press.

Goffman, Erving. 1973. *The Presentation of Self in Everyday Life.* Woodstock, N.Y.: Overlook Press.

Golash-Boza, Tanya. 2006. "Dropping the Hyphen? Becoming Latino(a)-American Through Racialized Assimilation." *Social Forces* 85(1): 27–56.

———. 2012. *Immigration Nation: Raids, Detentions, and Deportations in Post-9/11 America.* Boulder, Colo.: Paradigm Publishers.

———. 2015. *Deported: Policing Immigrants, Disposable Labor, and Global Capitalism.* New York: New York University Press.

Golash-Boza, Tanya, and William Darity Jr. 2008. "Latino Racial Choices: The Effects of Skin Colour and Discrimination on Latinos' and Latinas' Racial Self-identifications." *Ethnic and Racial Studies* 31(5): 899–934.

Golash-Boza, Tanya Maria, and Pierrette Hondagneu-Sotelo. 2013. "Latino Immigrant Men and the Deportation Crisis: A Gendered Racial Removal Program." *Latino Studies* 11(3): 271–92.

Gómez, Laura E. 2007. *Manifest Destinies: The Making of the Mexican American Race.* New York: New York University Press.

Gonzales, Roberto G. 2011. "Learning to Be Illegal: Undocumented Youth and Shifting Legal Contexts in the Transition to Adulthood." *American Sociological Review* 76(4): 602–19.

Gordon, Milton Myron. 1964. *Assimilation in American Life: The Role of Race, Religion, and National Origins.* New York: Oxford University Press.

Gottman, John M., James Coan, Sybil Carrere, and Catherine Swanson. 1998. "Predicting Marital Happiness and Stability from Newlywed Interactions." *Journal of Marriage and the Family* 60(1): 5–22.

Gray, Louis N., and Irving Tallman. 1987. "Theories of Choice: Contingent Reward and Punishment Applications." *Social Psychological Quarterly* 50: 16–23.

Grebler, Leo, Joan W. Moore, and Ralph C. Guzman. 1970. *The Mexican-American People: The Nation's Second Largest Minority.* New York: Free Press.

Gullickson, Aaron, and Vincent Kang Fu. 2010. "Comment: An Endorsement of Exchange Theory in Mate Selection." *American Journal of Sociology* 115(4): 1243–51.

Gutiérrez, David. 1995. *Walls and Mirrors: Mexican Americans, Mexican Immigrants, and the Politics of Ethnicity.* Berkeley: University of California Press.

Gutmann, Matthew C. 2003. "Introduction: Discarding Manly Dichotomies in Latin America." In *Changing Men and Masculinities in Latin America,* edited by Matthew C. Gutmann. Durham, N.C.: Duke University Press.

Hackstaff, Karla B. 1999. *Marriage in a Culture of Divorce.* Philadelphia: Temple University Press.

Haney López, Ian. 1996. *White by Law: The Legal Construction of Race.* New York: New York University Press.

———. 2006. *White by Law: The Legal Construction of Race,* revised and updated tenth anniversary edition. New York: New York University Press.

Hansen, Marcus. 1938. *The Problem of the Third Generation Immigrant.* Rock Island, Ill.: Augustana Historical Society.

Haraway, Donna. 1988. "Situated Knowledges: The Science Question in Feminism and the Privilege of Partial Perspective." *Feminist Studies* 14(3): 575–99.

Harris, Angel L., and Kris Marsh. 2010. "Is a Raceless Identity an Effective Strategy for Academic Success Among Blacks?" *Social Science Quarterly* 91(5): 1242–63.

Harris, Cheryl I. 1993. "Whiteness as Property." *Harvard Law Review* 106(8): 1707–91.

Hartigan, John, Jr. 1997. "Establishing the Fact of Whiteness." *American Anthropologist* 99(3): 495–505.

Hays, Sharon. 1996. *The Cultural Contradictions of Motherhood.* New Haven, Conn.: Yale University Press.

Heath, Melanie. 2012. *One Marriage Under God: The Campaign to Promote Marriage in America.* New York: New York University Press.

Hirsch, Jennifer S. 2003. *A Courtship After Marriage: Sexuality and Love in Mexican Transnational Families.* Berkeley: University of California Press.

Hochschild, Arlie Russell. 1979. "Emotion Work, Feeling Rules, and Social Structure." *American Journal of Sociology* 85(3): 551–75.

———. 1989. *The Second Shift: Working Parents and the Revolution at Home.* New York: Viking.

———. 1997. *The Time Bind: When Work Becomes Home and Home Becomes Work.* New York: Metropolitan Books.

———. 2003. *The Commercialization of Intimate Life: Notes from Home and Work.* Berkeley: University of California Press.

Hodes, Martha Elizabeth. 1997. *White Women, Black Men: Illicit Sex in the Nineteenth-Century South.* New Haven, Conn.: Yale University Press.

Holm, Tom, J. Diane Pearson, and Ben Chavis. 2003. "Peoplehood: A Model for the Extension of Sovereignty in American Indian Studies." *Wicazo Sa Review* 18(1): 7–24.

Hondagneu-Sotelo, Pierrette. 1994. *Gendered Transitions: Mexican Experiences of Immigration*. Berkeley: University of California Press.

———. 1997. "The History of Mexican Undocumented Settlement in the United States." In *Challenging Fronteras: Structuring Latina and Latino Lives in the U.S.*, edited by Mary Romero, Vilma Ortiz, and Pierrette Hondagneu-Sotelo. New York: Taylor & Francis.

———. ed. 1999. *Gender and U.S. Immigration: Contemporary Trends*. Berkeley: University of California Press.

———. 2014. *Paradise Transplanted: Migration and the Making of California Gardens*. Berkeley: University of California Press.

Hordge-Freeman, Elizabeth. 2013. "What's Love Got to Do with It? Racial Features, Stigma, and Socialization in Afro-Brazilian Families." *Ethnic and Racial Studies* 36(10): 1507–23.

HoSang, Daniel. 2010. *Racial Propositions: Ballot Initiatives and the Making of Postwar California*. Berkeley: University of California Press.

Hunter, Margaret. 2002. " 'If You're Light You're Alright': Light Skin Color as Social Capital for Women of Color." *Gender and Society* 16(2): 175–93.

Hurtado, Sylvia, Adriana Ruiz Alvarado, and Chelsea Guillermo-Wann. 2015. "Thinking About Race: The Salience of Racial Identity at Two- and Four-Year Colleges and the Climate for Diversity." *Journal of Higher Education* 86(1): 127–55.

Ignatiev, Noel. 1995. *How the Irish Became White*. New York: Routledge.

Itzigsohn, José. 2009. *Encountering American Faultlines: Race, Class, and the Dominican Experience in Providence*. New York: Russell Sage Foundation.

Jacobson, Matthew Frye 1998. *Whiteness of a Different Color: European Immigrants and the Alchemy of Race*. Cambridge, Mass.: Harvard University Press.

Jiménez, Tomás R. 2004. "Negotiating Ethnic Boundaries." *Ethnicities* 4(1): 75–97.

———. 2010a. "Affiliative Ethnic Identity: A More Elastic Link Between Ethnic Ancestry and Culture." *Ethnic and Racial Studies* 33(10): 1756–75.

———. 2010b. *Replenished Ethnicity: Mexican Americans, Immigration, and Identity*. Berkeley: University of California Press.

Jiménez, Tomás R., Corey D. Fields, and Ariela Schachter. 2015. "How Ethnoraciality Matters: Looking Inside Ethnoracial 'Groups.' " *Social Currents* 2(2): 107–15.

Jiménez, Tomás R., and Adam L. Horowitz. 2013. "When White Is Just Alright: How Immigrants Redefine Achievement and Reconfigure the Ethnoracial Hierarchy." *American Sociological Review* 78(5): 849–71.

Jones, Jennifer A. 2012. "Blacks May Be Second Class, but They Can't Make Them Leave: Mexican Racial Formation and Immigrant Status in Winston-Salem." *Latino Studies* 10(1-2): 60–80.

Jones, Nicholas A., and Jungmiwha Bullock. 2012. "The Two or More Races Population: 2010." U.S. Census Briefs C2010BR-13. Washington: U.S. Department of Commerce, U.S. Census Bureau (September).

Joyner, Kara, and Grace Kao. 2005. "Interracial Relationships and the Transition to Adulthood." *American Sociological Review* 70(4): 563–82.

Kalmijn, Matthijs. 1993. "Trends in Black/White Intermarriage." *Social Forces* 72(1): 119–46.

———. 1998. "Intermarriage and Homogamy: Causes, Patterns, Trends." *Annual Review of Sociology* 24: 395–421.

———. 2010. "Consequences of Racial Intermarriage for Children's Social Integration." *Sociological Perspectives* 53(2): 271–86.

Kasinitz, Philip, John H. Mollenkopf, Mary C. Waters, and Jennifer Holdaway. 2008. *Inheriting the City: The Children of Immigrants Come of Age*. New York: Russell Sage Foundation.

Kennedy, Randall. 2003. *Interracial Intimacies: Sex, Marriage, Identity, and Adoption*. New York: Pantheon.

Kibria, Nazli. 2002. *Becoming Asian American: Second-Generation Chinese and Korean American Identities*. Baltimore, Md.: Johns Hopkins University Press.

King, Deborah. 1988. "Multiple Jeopardy, Multiple Consciousness." *Signs: Journal of Women in Culture and Society* 14(1): 42–72.

Kitson, Gay C., and William Holmes. 1992. *Portrait of Divorce: Adjustment to Marital Breakdown*. New York: Guilford Press.

Klinenberg, Eric. 2012. *Going Solo: The Extraordinary Rise and Surprising Appeal of Living Alone*. New York: Penguin.

Lamphere, Louise. 2007. "Migration, Assimilation, and the Cultural Construction of Identity: Navajo Perspectives." *Ethnic and Racial Studies* 30(6): 1132–51.

Landale, Nancy S., R. Salvador Oropesa, and Cristina Bradatan. 2006. "Hispanic Families in the United States: Family Structure and Process in an Era of Family Change." In *Hispanics and the Future of America*, edited by Marta Tienda and Faith Mitchell. Washington, D.C.: National Academies Press.

Lareau, Annette. 2003. *Unequal Childhoods: Class, Race, and Family Life*. Berkeley: University of California Press.

Larsen, Nella. 2001. *Quicksand and Passing*. London: Serpent's Tail.

Lee, Catherine. 2013. *Fictive Kinship: Family Reunification and the Meaning of Race and Nation in American Immigration*. New York: Russell Sage Foundation.

Lee, Jennifer, and Frank D. Bean. 2004. "America's Changing Color Lines: Immigration, Race/Ethnicity, and Multiracial Identification." *Annual Review of Sociology* 30: 221–42.

———. 2010. *The Diversity Paradox: Immigration and the Color Line in Twenty-First Century America*. New York: Russell Sage Foundation.

Lee, Jennifer, and Min Zhou. 2015. *The Asian American Achievement Paradox*. New York: Russell Sage Foundation.

Lee, Sharon, and Barry Edmonston. 2006. "Hispanic Intermarriage, Identification, and U.S. Latino Population Change." *Social Science Quarterly* 87(5): 1263–79.

Levitt, Peggy. 2001. *The Transnational Villagers*. Berkeley: University of California Press.

Lewis, Amanda E. 2003. *Race in the Schoolyard: Negotiating the Color Line in Classrooms and Communities*. New Brunswick, N.J.: Rutgers University Press.

———. 2004. "Book review of *Unequal Childhoods: Class, Race, and Family Life* by Annette Lareau." *Journal of Marriage and Family* 66(3): 840–41.

Lewis, Kevin. 2013. "The Limits of Racial Prejudice." *Proceedings of the National Academy of Sciences* 110(47): 18814–19.

Li, Jui-Chung Allen. 2010. "Briefing Paper: The Impact of Divorce on Children's Behavior Problems." In *Families as They Really Are,* edited by Barbara J. Risman. New York: W. W. Norton.

Lichter, Daniel T., J. Brian Brown, Qian Zhenchao, and Julie Carmalt. 2007. "Marital Assimilation Among Hispanics: Evidence of Declining Cultural and Economic Incorporation?" *Social Science Quarterly* 88(3): 745–65.

Lichter, Daniel T., Julie H. Carmalt, and Zhenchao Qian. 2011. "Immigration and Intermarriage Among Hispanics: Crossing Racial and Generational Boundaries." *Sociological Forum* 26(2): 241–64.

Lieberson, Stanley. 1963. *Ethnic Patterns in American Cities*. New York: Free Press of Glencoe.

———. 1980. *A Piece of the Pie: Blacks and White Immigrants Since 1880*. Berkeley: University of California Press.

Lipsitz, George. 2006. *The Possessive Investment in Whiteness: How White People Profit from Identity Politics*. Philadelphia: Temple University Press.

Lofquist, Daphne, Terry Lugaila, Martin O'Connell, and Sarah Feliz. 2012. "Households and Families: 2010." *2010 Census Briefs*. Washington: U.S. Census Bureau.

Logan, John R., and Brian J. Stults. 2011. "The Persistence of Segregation in the Metropolis: New Findings from the 2010 Census." Census brief prepared for Project US2010. New York: Russell Sage Foundation and American Communities Project (March 24).

Lomawaima, K. Tsianina. 1995. *They Called It Prairie Light: The Story of Chilocco Indian School*. Lincoln: University of Nebraska Press.

Lopez, D. A. 2000. "Attitudes of Selected Latino Oldtimers Toward Newcomers: A Photo Elicitation Study." *Great Plains Research* 10(2): 253–74.

Lorde, Audre. 1984. *Sister Outsider: Essays and Speeches*. Trumansburg, N.Y.: Crossing Press.

Macias, Thomas. 2006. *Mestizo in America: Generations of Mexican Ethnicity in the Suburban Southwest*. Tucson: University of Arizona Press.

MacLeod, Jay. 2004. *Ain't No Makin' It: Aspirations and Attainment in a Low-Income Neighborhood*. Boulder, Colo.: Westview.

Maldonado, Marta Maria. 2009. "'It Is Their Nature to Do Menial Labour': The Racialization of 'Latino/a Workers' by Agricultural Employers." *Ethnic and Racial Studies* 32(6): 1017–36.

Markus, Hazel Rose, and Alana Conner. 2013. *Clash! 8 Cultural Conflicts That Make Us Who We Are*. New York: Hudson Street Press.

Marrow, Helen B. 2011. *New Destination Dreaming: Immigration, Race, and Legal Status in the Rural American South.* Stanford, Calif.: Stanford University Press.

Martinez, Cid. 2016. *The Neighborhood Has Its Own Rules: Latinos and African Americans in South Los Angeles.* New York: New York University Press.

Martinez, Cid, and Victor M. Rios. 2011. "Conflict, Cooperation, and Avoidance." In *Just Neighbors? Research on African American and Latino Relations in the United States,* edited by Edward Telles, Mark Sawyer, and Gaspar Rivera-Salgado. New York: Russell Sage Foundation.

Massey, Douglas S., and Nancy A. Denton. 1993. *American Apartheid: Segregation and the Making of the Underclass.* Cambridge, Mass.: Harvard University Press.

Massey, Douglas S., Jorge Durand, and Nolan J. Malone. 2002. *Beyond Smoke and Mirrors: Mexican Immigration in an Era of Free Trade.* New York: Russell Sage Foundation.

Massey, Douglas S., and Karen A. Pren. 2012. "Unintended Consequences of U.S. Immigration Policy: Explaining the Post-1965 Surge from Latin America." *Population and Development Review* 38(1): 1–29.

McDermott, Monica. 2006. *Working-Class White: The Making and Unmaking of Race Relations.* Berkeley: University of California Press.

Menjivar, Cecilia. 2006. "Liminal Legality: Salvadoran and Guatemalan Immigrants' Lives in the United States." *American Journal of Sociology* 111(4): 999–1037.

Menjívar, Cecilia, and Leisy J. Abrego. 2012. "Legal Violence: Immigration Law and the Lives of Central American Immigrants." *American Journal of Sociology* 117(5): 1380–1421.

Merskin, Debra L. 2011. *Media, Minorities, and Meaning: A Critical Introduction.* New York: Peter Lang.

Merton, Robert K. 1941. "Intermarriage and the Social Structure: Fact and Theory." *Psychiatry* 4: 361–74.

———. 2000. "Intermarriage and the Social Structure: Fact and Theory" (1941). In *Interracialism: Black-White Intermarriage in American History, Literature, and Law,* edited by Werner Sollors. New York: Oxford University Press.

Millard, Ann V., and Jorge Chapa. 2004. *Apple Pie and Enchiladas: Latino Newcomers in the Rural Midwest.* Austin: University of Texas Press.

Molina, Natalia. 2014. *How Race Is Made in America: Immigration, Citizenship, and the Historical Power of Racial Scripts.* Berkeley: University of California Press.

Molina-Guzmán, Isabel. 2010. *Dangerous Curves: Latina Bodies in the Media.* New York: New York University Press.

Monhollon, Rusty L. 2004. *This Is America? The Sixties in Lawrence, Kansas.* New York: Palgrave Macmillan.

Montejano, David. 1987. *Anglos and Mexicans in the Making of Texas, 1836–1986.* Austin: University of Texas Press.

Mora, G. Cristina. 2014. *Making Hispanics: How Activists, Bureaucrats, and Media Constructed a New American.* Chicago: University Of Chicago Press.

Moran, Rachel F. 2001. *Interracial Intimacy: The Regulation of Race and Romance.* Chicago: University of Chicago Press.

Morning, Ann Juanita. 2011. *The Nature of Race: How Scientists Think and Teach About Human Difference.* Berkeley: University of California Press.

Moss, Philip, and Chris Tilly. 1996. " 'Soft' Skills and Race: An Investigation of Black Men's Employment Problems." *Work and Occupations* 23(3): 252–76.

Mumford, Kevin J. 1997. *Interzones: Black/White Sex Districts in Chicago and New York in the Early Twentieth Century.* New York: Columbia University Press.

Murguia, Edward. 1982. *Chicano Intermarriage: A Theoretical and Empirical Study.* San Antonio: Trinity University Press.

Nagel, Joane. 2000. "Ethnicity and Sexuality." *Annual Review of Sociology* 26: 107–33.

———. 2003. *Race, Ethnicity, and Sexuality: Intimate Intersections, Forbidden Frontiers.* New York: Oxford University Press.

Negrón-Muntaner, Frances. 2014. "The Gang's Not All Here: The State of Latinos in Contemporary U.S. Media." In *Contemporary Latina/o Media: Production, Circulation, Politics,* edited by Arlene Dávila and Yeidy M. Rivero. New York: New York University Press.

Nemoto, Kumiko. 2009. *Racing Romance: Love, Power, and Desire Among Asian American/ White Couples.* New Brunswick, N.J.: Rutgers University Press.

Ngai, Mae M. 2004. *Impossible Subjects: Illegal Aliens and the Making of Modern America.* Princeton, N.J.: Princeton University Press.

Novkov, Julie Lavonne. 2008. *Racial Union: Law, Intimacy, and the White State in Alabama, 1865–1954.* Ann Arbor: University of Michigan Press.

Obasogie, Osagie. 2009. "Playing the Gene Card? A Report on Race and Human Biotechnology." Oakland, Calif.: Center for Genetics and Society.

———. 2010. "Do Blind People See Race? Social, Legal, and Theoretical Considerations." *Law and Society Review* 44(3-4): 585–616.

Obasogie, Osagie K. 2014. *Blinded by Sight: Seeing Race Through the Eyes of the Blind.* Stanford: Stanford University Press.

O'Brien, Eileen. 2008. *The Racial Middle: Latinos and Asian Americans Living Beyond the Racial Divide.* New York: New York University Press.

Ocampo, Anthony C. 2012. "Making Masculinity: Negotiations of Gender Presentation Among Latino Gay Men." *Latino Studies* 10(4): 448–72.

———. 2014. "Are Second-Generation Filipinos 'Becoming' Asian American or Latino? Historical Colonialism, Culture, and Panethnicity." *Ethnic and Racial Studies* 37(3): 425–45.

———. 2015. *The Latinos of Asia: How Filipinos Break the Rules of Race.* Stanford, Calif.: Stanford University Press.

Ochoa, Gilda. 2004. *Becoming Neighbors in a Mexican American Community: Power, Conflict, and Solidarity.* Austin: University of Texas Press.

———. 2013. *Academic Profiling: Latinos, Asian Americans, and the Achievement Gap.* Minneapolis: University of Minnesota Press.

Ogbu, John U., and Signithia Fordham. 1986. "Black Students' School Success: Coping with the 'Burden of Acting White.'" *Urban Review* 18(3): 176–206.

Okamoto, Dina. 2007. "Marrying Out: A Boundary Approach to Understanding the Marital Integration of Asian Americans." *Social Science Research* 36(4): 1391–1414.

Okamoto, Dina G., and G. Cristina Mora. 2014. "Panethnicity." *Annual Review of Sociology* 40(1): 219–39.

Oliver, Melvin L., and Thomas M. Shapiro. 1995. *Black Wealth/White Wealth: A New Perspective on Racial Inequality*. New York: Routledge.

Omi, Michael, and Howard Winant. 1994. *Racial Formation in the United States: From the 1960s to the 1990s*. New York: Routledge.

Ortiz, Vilma, and Edward Telles. 2012. "Racial Identity and Racial Treatment of Mexican Americans." *Race and Social Problems* 4(1): 41–56.

Padilla, Amado M. 2006. "Bicultural Social Development." *Hispanic Journal of Behavioral Sciences* 28(4): 467–97.

Pager, Devah. 2007. *Marked: Race, Crime, and Finding Work in an Era of Mass Incarceration*. Chicago: University of Chicago Press.

Park, Robert Ezra. 1950. *Race and Culture*. Glencoe, Ill.: Free Press.

Parrenas, Rhacel Salazar. 2000. "Migrant Filipina Domestic Workers and the International Division of Reproductive Labor." *Gender and Society* 14(4): 560–80.

Pascoe, C. J. 2007. *Dude, You're a Fag: Masculinity and Sexuality in High School*. Berkeley: University of California Press.

Pascoe, Peggy. 2009. *What Comes Naturally: Miscegenation Law and the Making of Race in America*. New York: Oxford University Press.

Pattillo-McCoy, Mary. 1999. *Black Picket Fences: Privilege and Peril Among the Black Middle Class*. Chicago: University of Chicago Press.

Perlmann, Joel. 2005. *Italians Then, Mexicans Now: Immigrant Origins and Second-Generation Progress, 1890 to 2000*. New York: Russell Sage Foundation.

Perry, Pamela. 2002. *Shades of White*. Durham, N.C.: Duke University Press.

Pew Research Center. 2010. "Gender Equality Universally Embraced, but Inequalities Acknowledged." Washington, D.C.: Pew Research Center.

Portes, Alejandro, and Patricia Landolt. 1996. "The Downside of Social Capital." *The American Prospect* (May–June): 18–22.

Portes, Alejandro, and Rubén G. Rumbaut. 2001. *Legacies: The Story of the Immigrant Second Generation*. Berkeley: University of California Press.

Portes, Alejandro, and Min Zhou. 1993. "The New Second Generation: Segmented Assimilation and Its Variants." *Annals of the American Academy of Political and Social Science* (530): 74–96.

Pyke, Karen D. 2010. "What Is Internalized Racial Oppression and Why Don't We Study It? Acknowledging Racism's Hidden Injuries." *Sociological Perspectives* 53(4): 551–72.

Pyke, Karen, and Tran Dang. 2003. "'FOB' and 'Whitewashed': Identity and Internalized Racism Among Second Generation Asian Americans." *Qualitative Sociology* 26(2): 147–72.

Qian, Zhenchao, and José A. Cobas. 2004. "Latinos' Mate Selection: National Origin, Racial, and Nativity Differences." *Social Science Research* 33(2): 225–47.

Qian, Zhenchao, and Daniel T. Lichter. 2001. "Measuring Marital Assimilation: Intermarriage among Natives and Immigrants." *Social Science Research* 30(2): 289–312.

———. 2007. "Social Boundaries and Marital Assimilation: Interpreting Trends in Racial and Ethnic Intermarriage." *American Sociological Review* 72(1): 68–94.

———. 2011. "Changing Patterns of Interracial Marriage in a Multiracial Society." *Journal of Marriage and Family* 73(5): 1065–84.

Randles, Jennifer M. 2013. "Repackaging the 'Package Deal': Promoting Marriage for Low-Income Families by Targeting Paternal Identity and Reframing Marital Masculinity." *Gender and Society* 27(6): 864–88.

Reich, Gary, and Jay Barth. 2010. "Educating Citizens or Defying Federal Authority? A Comparative Study of In-State Tuition for Undocumented Students." *Policy Studies Journal* 38(3): 419–45.

Robinson, Brandon Andrew. 2015. "'Personal Preference' as the New Racism: Gay Desire and Racial Cleansing in Cyberspace." *Sociology of Race and Ethnicity* 1(2): 317–30.

Robnett, Belinda, and Cynthia Feliciano. 2011. "Patterns of Racial-Ethnic Exclusion by Internet Daters." *Social Forces* 89(3): 807–28.

Rockquemore, Kerry Ann, Tracey Laszloffy, and Julia Noveske. 2006. "It All Starts at Home: Racial Socialization in Multiracial Families." In *Mixed Messages: Multiracial Identities in the "Color-blind" Era*, edited by David L. Brunsma. Boulder, Colo.: Lynne Rienner Publishers.

Rodriguez, Clara E. 2000. *Changing Race: Latinos, the Census, and the History of Ethnicity in the United States.* New York: New York University Press.

Roediger, David R. 1999. *The Wages of Whiteness: Race and the Making of the American Working Class.* London: Verso.

———. 2005. *Working Toward Whiteness: How America's Immigrants Become White.* New York: Basic Books.

Rogowski, Jon C., Claudia Sandoval, and Cathy J. Cohen. N.d. "Understanding the Latino Youth Vote in 2012." *Democracy Remixed: Black Youth and the Future of American Politics.* Chicago: Black Youth Project.

Romero, Mary. 2011. *The Maid's Daughter: Living Inside and Outside the American Dream.* New York: New York University Press.

Romero, Mary, Vilma Ortiz, and Pierrette Hondagneu-Sotelo, eds. 1997. *Challenging Fronteras: Structuring Latina and Latino Lives in the U.S.* New York: Taylor & Francis.

Romo, Rebecca. 2011. "Between Black and Brown: Blaxican (Black-Mexican) Multiracial Identity in California." *Journal of Black Studies* 42(3): 402–26.

Root, Maria P. P. 2001. *Love's Revolution: Interracial Marriage.* Philadelphia: Temple University Press.

Rosaldo, Renato. 1993. *Culture and Truth: The Remaking of Social Analysis.* Boston: Beacon Press.

Rosenfeld, Michael. 2002. "Measures of Assimilation in the Marriage Market: Mexican Americans 1970–1990." *Journal of Marriage and the Family* 64(1): 152–62.

———. 2005. "A Critique of Exchange Theory in Mate Selection." *American Journal of Sociology* 110(5): 1284–1325.

———. 2008. "Racial, Educational, and Religious Endogamy in the United States: A Comparative Historical Perspective." *Social Forces* 87(1): 1–31.

———. 2009. *The Age of Independence: Interracial Unions, Same-Sex Unions, and the Changing American Family.* Cambridge, Mass.: Harvard University Press.

Rosenfeld, Michael J., and Byung-Soo Kim. 2005. "The Independence of Young Adults and the Rise of Interracial and Same-Sex Unions." *American Sociological Review* 70(4): 541–62.

Rosenfeld, Michael J., and Reuben J. Thomas. 2012. "Searching for a Mate: The Rise of the Internet as a Social Intermediary." *American Sociological Review* 77(4): 523–47.

Roth, Philip. 2001. *The Human Stain.* New York: Knopf.

Roth, Wendy D. 2012. *Race Migrations: Latinos and the Cultural Transformation of Race.* Stanford, Calif.: Stanford University Press.

Rumbaut, Rubén G., and Alejandro Portes. 2001. *Ethnicities: Children of Immigrants in America.* Berkeley: University of California Press.

Rytina, Nancy F. 2006. "Estimates of the Legal Permanent Resident Population and Population Eligible to Naturalize in 2004." Washington: U.S. Department of Homeland Security, Office of Immigration Statistics.

Rytina, Steven, Peter M. Blau, Terry Blum, and Joseph Schwartz. 1988. "Inequality and Intermarriage: A Paradox of Motive and Constraint." *Social Forces* 66(3): 645–75.

Salzinger, Leslie. 2003. *Genders in Production: Making Workers in Mexico's Global Factories.* Berkeley: University of California Press.

Sanchez, George J. 1994. "'Go After the Women': Americanization and the Mexican Immigrant Woman, 1915–1929." In *Unequal Sisters: A Multicultural Reader in U.S. Women's History,* edited by Vicki Ruiz and Ellen DuBois. New York: Routledge.

Sánchez-Jankowski, Martín. 1991. *Islands in the Street: Gangs and American Urban Society.* Berkeley: University of California Press.

Santa Ana, Otto. 2002. *Brown Tide Rising: Metaphors of Latinos in Contemporary American Public Discourse.* Austin: University of Texas Press.

Santa Ana, Otto, and Celeste González de Bustamante. 2012. *Arizona Firestorm: Global Immigration Realities, National Media, and Provincial Politics.* Lanham, Md.: Rowman & Littlefield.

Saperstein, Aliya, Andrew M. Penner, and Ryan Light. 2013. "Racial Formation in Perspective: Connecting Individuals, Institutions, and Power Relations." *Annual Review of Sociology* 39: 359–78.

Saraswati, L. Ayu. 2010. "Cosmopolitan Whiteness: The Effects and Affects of Skin-Whitening Advertisements in a Transnational Women's Magazine in Indonesia." *Meridians: Feminism, Race, Transnationalism* 10(2): 15–41.

Sassen, Saskia. 1989. "America's Immigration 'Problem.'" *World Policy Journal* 6(4): 811–32.

Schildkraut, Deborah J. 2014. "Boundaries of American Identity: Evolving Understandings of 'Us.'" *Annual Review of Political Science* 17(1): 441–60.

Schmalzbauer, Leah. 2014. *The Last Best Place: Gender, Family, and Migration in the New West.* Stanford, Calif.: Stanford University Press.

Schoem, David, and Sylvia Hurtado, eds. 2001. *Intergroup Dialogue.* Ann Arbor: University of Michigan Press.

Schwartz, Christine R. 2013. "Trends and Variation in Assortative Mating: Causes and Consequences." *Annual Review of Sociology* 39: 451–70.

Scott, John Finley. 1965. "The American College Sorority: Its Role in Class and Ethnic Endogamy." *American Sociological Review* 60(4): 514–27.

Segal, David R. 1989. *Recruiting for Uncle Sam: Citizenship and Military Manpower Policy.* Lawrence: University Press of Kansas.

Segura, Denise. 1986. "Chicanas and Triple Oppression in the Labor Market." In *Chicana Voices: Intersections of Class, Race, and Gender.* Austin: University of Texas, Center for Mexican American Studies.

Sherman, Jennifer. 2009a. "Bend to Avoid Breaking: Job Loss, Gender Norms, and Family Stability in Rural America." *Social Problems* 56(4): 599–620.

———. 2009b. *Those Who Work, Those Who Don't: Poverty, Morality, and Family in Rural America.* Minneapolis: University of Minnesota Press.

Shiao, Jiannbin Lee. 2005. *Identifying Talent, Institutionalizing Diversity: Race and Philanthropy in Post–Civil Rights America.* Durham, N.C.: Duke University Press.

Shiao, Jiannbin Lee, and Mia H. Tuan. 2008. "Korean Adoptees and the Social Context of Ethnic Exploration." *American Journal of Sociology* 113(4): 1023–66.

Smith, Andrea. 2005. "Native American Feminism, Sovereignty, and Social Change." *Feminist Studies* 31(1): 116–32.

———. 2007. "Soul Wound: The Legacy of Native American Schools." *Amnesty International* (March 26): 1–5.

Smith, Robert C. 2006. *Mexican New York: The Transnational Lives of New Immigrants.* Berkeley: University of California Press.

———. 2014. "Black Mexicans, Conjunctural Ethnicity, and Operating Identities: Long-Term Ethnographic Analysis." *American Sociological Review* 79(3): 517–48.

Smith, Robert C., Don Waisanen, Manuel Castro, Aracelis Lucero, and Guillermo Yrizar Barbosa. Forthcoming. *Lessons from the Seguro Popular Project: How We Should Communicate with Immigrants.* Basingstoke, U.K.: Palgrave.

Snarey, John. 1993. *How Fathers Care for the Next Generation: A Four-Decade Study.* Cambridge, Mass.: Harvard University Press.

Sollors, Werner. 2000. *Interracialism: Black-White Intermarriage in American History, Literature, and Law.* Oxford: Oxford University Press.

Spickard, Paul R. 1991. *Mixed Blood: Intermarriage and Ethnic Identity in Twentieth-Century America.* Madison: University of Wisconsin Press.

Stack, Carol B., and Linda Burton. 1994. "Kinscripts: Reflections on Family, Generation, and Culture." In *Mothering: Ideology, Experience, and Agency,* edited by Evelyn Nakano Glenn, Grace Chang, and Linda Rennie Forcey. New York: Routledge.

Steele, Claude M., and Joshua Aronson. 1995. "Stereotype Threat and the Intellectual Test Performance of African Americans." *Journal of Personality and Social Psychology* 69(5): 797–811.

Stepler, Renee, and Anna Brown. 2016. "Statistical Portrait of Hispanics in the United States." Washington, D.C.: Pew Research Center (April 19). Available at: http://www.pewhispanic.org/2015/05/12/statistical-portrait-of-hispanics-in-the-united-states-1980-2013-trends (accessed September 3, 2015).

Stevens, Gillian, and Gray Swicegood. 1987. "The Linguistic Context of Ethnic Endogamy." *American Sociological Review* 52(1): 73–82.

Strauss, Anselm L. 1987. *Qualitative Analysis for Social Scientists.* Cambridge: Cambridge University Press.

Stull, Donald D., Michael J. Broadway, and David Griffith, eds. 1995. *Any Way You Cut It: Meat Processing and Small-Town America.* Lawrence: University of Kansas.

Suárez-Orozco, Carola, Hirokazu Yoshikawa, Robert T. Teranishi, and Marcelo Suárez-Orozco. 2011. "Growing Up in the Shadows: The Developmental Implications of Unauthorized Status." *Harvard Educational Review* 81(3): 438–72.

Sue, Christina A. 2013. *Land of the Cosmic Race: Race Mixture, Racism, and Blackness in Mexico.* New York: Oxford University Press.

Sue, Christina A., and Tanya Golash-Boza. 2013. "'It Was Only a Joke': How Racial Humour Fuels Colour-Blind Ideologies in Mexico and Peru." *Ethnic and Racial Studies* 36(10): 1582–98.

Suro, Robert. 2005. "Hispanics: A People in Motion." Washington, D.C.: Pew Hispanic Center.

Swidler, Ann. 2001. *Talk of Love: How Culture Matters.* Chicago: University of Chicago Press.

Tallman, Irving, and Louis N. Gray. 1990. "Choices, Decisions, and Problem-Solving." *Annual Review of Sociology* 16: 405–33.

Taylor, Paul. 2010. "The Decline of Marriage and Rise of New Families." Washington, D.C.: Pew Research Center.

Taylor, Paul, Cary Funk, and Peyton Craighill. 2006. "Guess Who's Coming to Dinner: 22% of Americans Have a Relative in a Mixed-Race Marriage." Washington, D.C.: Pew Research Center.

Telles, Edward Eric. 2004. *Race in Another America: The Significance of Skin Color in Brazil.* Princeton, N.J.: Princeton University Press.

———. 2014. *Pigmentocracies: Ethnicity, Race, and Color in Latin America.* Chapel Hill: University of North Carolina Press.

Telles, Edward, and Vilma Ortiz. 2008. *Generations of Exclusion: Mexican Americans, Assimilation, and Race.* New York: Russell Sage Foundation.

Teo, Youyenn. 2011. *Neoliberal Morality in Singapore: How Family Policies Make State and Society.* New York: Routledge.

Thai, Hung Cam. 2008. *For Better or for Worse: Vietnamese International Marriages in the New Global Economy.* New Brunswick, N.J.: Rutgers University Press.

Thornton, Arland, William G. Axinn, and Yu Xie. 2007. *Marriage and Cohabitation.* Chicago: University of Chicago Press.

Tuan, Mia. 1998. *Forever Foreigners or Honorary Whites? The Asian Ethnic Experience Today.* New Brunswick, N.J.: Rutgers University Press.

Twine, France Winddance. 2010. *A White Side of Black Britain: Interracial Intimacy and Racial Literacy.* Durham, N.C.: Duke University Press.

Valdez, Zulema. 2011. *The New Entrepreneurs: How Race, Class, and Gender Shape American Enterprise.* Stanford, Calif.: Stanford University Press.

Valenzuela, Angela. 1999. *Subtractive Schooling: U.S.-Mexican Youth and the Politics of Caring.* Albany: State University of New York Press.

Vallejo, Jody Agius. 2012. *Barrios to Burbs: The Making of the Mexican American Middle Class.* Stanford, Calif.: Stanford University Press.

Vasquez, Jessica M. 2005. "Ethnic Identity and Chicano Literature: How Ethnicity Affects Reading and Reading Affects Ethnic Consciousness." *Ethnic and Racial Studies* 28(5): 903–24.

———. 2010a. "Blurred Borders for Some but Not 'Others': Racialization, 'Flexible Ethnicity,' Gender, and Third Generation Mexican American Identity." *Sociological Perspectives* 53(1): 45–71.

———. 2010b. "Chicana Mothering in the Twenty-First Century: Challenging Stereotypes and Transmitting Culture." In *Twenty-First-Century Motherhood: Experience, Identity, Policy, Agency,* edited by Andrea O'Reilly. New York: Columbia University Press.

———. 2011. *Mexican Americans Across Generations: Immigrant Families, Racial Realities.* New York: New York University Press.

———. 2014a. "Gender Across Family Generations: Change in Mexican American Masculinities and Femininities." *Identities: Global Studies in Culture and Power* 21(5): 532–50.

———. 2014b. "Race Cognizance and Colorblindness: Effects of Latino/Non-Hispanic White Intermarriage." *Du Bois Review: Social Science and Research on Race* 11(2): 273–93.

———. 2014c. "The Whitening Hypothesis Challenged: Biculturalism in Latino and non-Hispanic White Intermarriage." *Sociological Forum* 29(2): 386–407.

———. 2015. "Disciplined Preferences: Explaining the (Re)Production of Latino Endogamy." *Social Problems* 62(3): 455–75.

————. Forthcoming. "Cross-Racial Minority Intermarriage: Mutual Marginalization and Critique." In *Red and Yellow, Black and Brown: Decentering Whiteness in Mixed Race Studies*, edited by Paul R. Spickard, Joanne L. Rondilla, and Rudy Guevarra. New Brunswick, N.J.: Rutgers University Press.

Vasquez-Tokos, Jessica, and Kathryn Norton-Smith. 2016. "Talking Back to Controlling Images: Latinos' Changing Responses to Racism over the Life Course." *Ethnic and Racial Studies* (June 30): 1–19.

Vasquez, Jessica M., and Christopher Wetzel. 2009. "Tradition and the Invention of Racial Selves: Symbolic Boundaries, Collective Authenticity, and Contemporary Struggles for Racial Equality." *Ethnic and Racial Studies* 32(9): 1557–75.

Vega, Sujey. 2015. *Latino Heartland: Of Borders and Belonging in the Midwest*. New York: New York University Press.

Vigil, James Diego. 1988. *Barrio Gangs: Street Life and Identity in Southern California*. Austin: University of Texas Press.

————. 2002a. "Community Dynamics and the Rise of Street Gangs." In *Latinos: Remaking America*, edited by Marcelo M. Suárez-Orozco and Mariela Paez. Berkeley: University of California Press.

————. 2002b. *A Rainbow of Gangs: Street Cultures in the Mega-City*. Austin: University of Texas Press.

Warren, Jonathan W., and France Winddance Twine. 1997. "White Americans, the New Minority? Non-Blacks and the Ever-Expanding Boundaries of Whiteness." *Journal of Black Studies* 28(2): 200–218.

Waters, Mary C. 1990. *Ethnic Options: Choosing Identities in America*. Berkeley: University of California Press.

————. 1999. *Black Identities: West Indian Immigrant Dreams and American Realities*. New York: Russell Sage Foundation.

Weitzman, Lenore J. 1985. *The Divorce Revolution: The Unexpected Social and Economic Consequences for Women and Children in America*. New York: Collier Macmillan.

Whitehead, Jay Cee. 2012. *The Nuptial Deal: Same-Sex Marriage and Neo-Liberal Governance*. Chicago: University of Chicago Press.

Williams, L. Susan, Sandra Alvarez, and Kevin Hauk. 2002. "My Name Is Not Maria: Young Latinas Seeking Home in the Heartland." *Social Problems* 49(4): 563–84.

Wright, Richard, Steven R. Holloway, and Mark Ellis. 2013. "Gender and the Neighborhood Location of Mixed-Race Couples." *Demography* 50: 393–420.

Yamin, Priscilla. 2012. *American Marriage: A Political Institution*. Philadelphia: University of Pennsylvania Press.

Yancey, George A. 2007. *Interracial Contact and Social Change*. Boulder, Colo.: Lynne Rienner.

Yoshikawa, Hirokazu. 2011. *Immigrants Raising Citizens: Undocumented Parents and Their Young Children*. New York: Russell Sage Foundation.

Yuval-Davis, Nira. 1997. *Gender and Nation*. Thousand Oaks, Calif.: Sage Publications.

Zambrana, Ruth Enid. 2011. *Latinos in American Society: Families and Communities in Transition*. Ithaca, N.Y.: Cornell University Press.

Zavella, Patricia. 1994. "Reflections on Diversity Among Chicanas." In *Race*, edited by Steven Gregory and Roger Sanjek. New Brunswick, N.J.: Rutgers University Press.

Zelizer, Viviana A. Rotman. 1994. *Pricing the Priceless Child: The Changing Social Value of Children*. Princeton, N.J.: Princeton University Press.

———. 2005. *The Purchase of Intimacy*. Princeton, N.J.: Princeton University Press.

Zhou, Min, Jennifer Lee, Jody Agius Vallejo, Rosaura Tafoya-Estrada, and Yang Sao Xiong. 2008. "Success Attained, Deterred, and Denied: Divergent Pathways to Social Mobility in Los Angeles's New Second Generation." *Annals of the American Academy of Political and Social Science* 620(1): 37–61.

Zweigenhaft, Richard L., and G. William Domhoff. 1998. *Diversity in the Power Elite: Have Women and Minorities Reached the Top?* New Haven, Conn.: Yale University Press.

Index |

357

love and purpose of marriage, 2, 4–5, 15–16. *See also* search for love

Lucero, Blair, 96–97

Lucero, Haley, 75–76

Lucero, Joaquin, 75

Lucero, Magda, 75

Lucero, Myra, 63, 74–75

Lucero, Nathan, 49, 61, 63–64, 74

Lucero, Paloma, 62–63, 66, 75

machismo, impact and opposition to. *See* patriarchy

marginalization. *See* shared marginalization

marital ambivalence, 234, 251–57, 266–67

marriage: as bidirectional conduit for cultural transmission, 6; comfort issue in coethnic choice, 109, 116; decline of marriage culture, 234; as dramatic act, 270; framing devices for, 232–33; intersectionality, 3, 8, 17–19, 42, 270–72; as nomos-building exercise, 20–21, 107, 131, 270; as self-definition, 20; socioeconomic motivations for, 4; as well-established social contract, 15. *See also* intermarriage; intramarriage

masculinity: deployment of to improve upon father's, 164–65; gang affiliation as demonstration of masculine dignity, 209; men's feminist transformation of, 169–70, 192, 195–200, 323n48; transnational in-marriage and support for, 172, 174. *See also* patriarchy

McDermott, Monica, 57

meaning making in romantic partner choice, 20–21, 107, 131

media stereotyping of Latinos, 197–98

melting pot theory, 10, 162–63

men: awareness of national context for gender expectations, 153–55; deploy-ment of masculinity to improve upon father's, 164–65; feminism of, 169–70, 192, 195–200, 323n48; gang affiliation as demonstration of masculine dignity, 209; marriage's influence on attitude toward family, 200; masculinity support through transnational in-marriage, 172, 174; preference for "traditional" submissive Latina, 35, 52–53, 139–40, 313n45, 320n14; style of carrying culture, 126–27; whites' lack of respect for women according to Latinas, 247–48; women's stereotyping of Mexican-origin, 36–40, 80–82. *See also* gender ideologies and strategies

methodology, 24–28, 73, 279–83, 285–86, 288–305

Mexican Americans: Anglo versus Mexican cultural mores, 247; in cross-national couples, 140; emigration to solve gender inequality for family, 153–54; influence of culture in cross-national partnerships, 155–56, 158–60; as largest group of Latinos, 308n48; Latinas' stereotyping of, 36–40, 80–82; machismo tradition, 132, 146, 149; Native American affinity with, 110–11; reluctance to claim heritage without reserve, 325n9. *See also* intragenerational marriages and racial strategies; mixed-generation coethnic marriages

military experience, influence on intermarriage acceptance and multiculturalism, 57–60

miscegenation. *See* intermarriage

mixed-generation coethnic marriages, 168–202; adaptation to white mainstream, 185–89; feminist men in, 192, 195–200; immigrant political-legal